Diarmaid Ó Muirithe
A DICTIONARY OF ANGLO-IRISH

A Dictionary of

ANGLO-IRISH

WORDS AND PHRASES FROM GAELIC
IN THE ENGLISH OF IRELAND

Diarmaid Ó Muirithe

FOUR COURTS PRESS

Set in 8.5 on 9 point Ehrhardt by
Verbatim Typesetting & Design for
FOUR COURTS PRESS
7 Malpas Street, Dublin 8, Ireland
www.fourcourtspress.ie
and in North America for
FOUR COURTS PRESS
c/o ISBS, 920 N.E. 58th Avenue, Portland, OR 97213.

First published 2000
Reprinted 2013

A catalogue record for this title
is available from the British Library.

ISBN 978-1-85182-445-8

Printed in Dublin
by SPRINT-Print, Dublin

For Mary Gallagher

... wel I woot that folk han here-beforn
... ropen, and lad away the corn;
And I am come after, glenynge here and here,
An am ful glad if I may fynde an ere
Of any goodly word that they han left.

Chaucer

Contents

Preface

Apart from those contributors mentioned in the list of abbreviations, I must thank sincerely those many friends and colleagues who have assisted me: Séamus Ó Murchú, first and foremost, for saving me from more errors than I care to remember; Dr Brigitte van Ryckeghem; Professors Bö Almqvist, Séamas Ó Catháin, and Dr Dáithí Ó hOgáin of the Department of Irish Folklore, University College, Dublin; Marion Gunn, MA, Archivist, Department of Irish in the same college; Críostóir and Seán Ó Gallchóir; Professor J.F. Killeen; Dr Séamas Ó Maoláin; Professor P.L. Henry; Seán Mac Connchradha; Caoimhín Ó Flannagáin. My thank, too, to Stiofán Ó hAnnracháin, MA, former Registrar of St Patrick's College of Education, Drumcondra, Dublin, and to Professor Richard Wall of the University of Calgary, for allowing me to pillage their printed works, and to Pádraig Ó Mathúna, Seán Ó Donnagáin and Diarmuid Breathnach. If I have inadvertently omitted other helpers in this wide and difficult field, I hope they will forgive me.

It would be a poor thanks to all my friends if I failed to make it clear that the deficiencies in this book are my responsibility alone.

Introduction

In a memorable talk given on RTÉ Radio's Thomas Davis Lectures series in the winter of 1973, Professor P.L. Henry of University College, Galway, spoke of the three major strands that are woven together in the English of Ireland:

> Firstly, a characteristically rural variety compounded of Irish and English or Irish and Scots. This developed chiefly in the last century and a half and is properly called Anglo-Irish. The second is a more urban, regional and standard variety tending towards international or so-called Standard English. This derives ultimately from British settlers in Ireland and its germinal period was the 17th century. It is properly called Hiberno-English. The third strand is Ulster Scots from the same period.

I readily concede that the term 'Anglo-Irish' does not please everybody, but the fitness of names need not concern us here. Let us instead consider the origin of this rural English. I quote Professor Henry at length:

> The outcome of war in Ireland in the 17th century was the split society of the eighteenth, in which the winner proceeded to take all. The winner was the English Protestant colonist, the loser the Irish Catholic native. It became a rule of privilege versus deprivation and disability. English became the language of politics, of public service, of commerce and of education. Irish clung to the countryside remote from where the action was. If you give a people who are not particularly dull one century to learn the lesson, you may expect that they will put it into practice when the day comes. It was not yet clear that the day would come, but the nineteenth century made it crystal clear that acquiring the language of privilege could be a key to survival in a land apparently forsaken by Providence.
>
> The policy of replacing the Irish language by English, a policy frequently reiterated by Dublin statesmen from the 14th century on, got under way with the national schools under their clerical managers from 1831. Prior to the founding of Maynooth in 1795 Irish clergy had to be trained on the continent in a surreptitious manner. There

was nothing there to weaken their grip on their own particular way of life and world view which a language characteristically represents and preserves. On the contrary, the encounter with continental languages would serve to inculcate a conscious sense of what their own Irish language stood for. The founding of Maynooth to train Catholic clergy weakened a link which had lasted one thousand years. It left the Irish-speaking community isolated on the edge of the English-speaking block and depending on it for their education. What they learned from it was, naturally, that they and all they represented were inferior, unfashionable, and gross; moreover they were impoverished. Were they to improve, they must copy their urban brethren who spoke English. In time they would acquire their prejudices, embedded in the language.

The replacement of Irish by English could not have happened without the favouring circumstances of the dreadful disasters of the 19th century. There are examples on record of the tentative efforts of those who survived the mid-century Famine to speak the foreign language. Professor Henry gives the example of a County Clare boy who grumbles about how little milk he was given at table; his father replies impatiently, 'Drink what's that in your noggin, you bacach, and you'll get more while ago when you'll drink what's that.' Here we have a parent who would speak Irish to his wife but not to his children, on the grounds that they would need English for survival. He clearly doesn't understand the phrase *a while ago*, and his use of *what's that* shows that he is uncertain about how to handle English demonstratives. He would use much of his Irish vocabulary in his conversations with his children. Professor Henry goes on:

One of the reasons why sentences such as the above are recorded and rehearsed is that they were found amusing later by people who had made progress in learning English. However, from a linguistic point of view they are vastly more interesting than the ordinary conventional kind which is learned or acquired by imitation; because they show the creative spirit at work forging an instrument for personal use, rather than adopting it ready-made from others. What I am suggesting in fact is that creating Anglo-Irish is a different thing from learning English. Or to put the matter differently, what the Irish people set out to do was to learn English; what they managed by 1900 was to create Anglo-Irish, which Hyde, Yeats, Synge, Lady Gregory and others found to be a vastly more stimulating and worthwhile achievement. It may be added that these writers, working by intuition, were the only group in the country to grasp that the mind of the people working for decades on new material had forged a new language which could develop a literature in its own right. This understanding is what underlies the literary work of Synge. A normal development would have been to adopt the new language at the appropriate level for all other spheres of activity inside Ireland. This is what occurred in 13th and 14th-century England when the native language had been displaced by French: the newcomers were absorbed and the people hammered out and adopted the new French-English. But circumstances favoured this, and favoured the growth of an independent English spirit. Whereas in 19th-century Ireland the colonist stock held the reins, the tie with England was close, and there was no scope for the rise of Anglo-Irish as a national speech norm fashioned by the people and therefore adapted to their own needs, educational, social and political. The situation is symbolised by an education machine which could not understand the *creation* but only the *imitation* and *learning* of language.

This compilation of Irish words and phrases is not being presented solely for its linguistic interest, but as an indication of the extent to which the Gaelic lexis has continued to enrich daily speech in rural Ireland, thus continuing to fulfil a social function. There are, between the covers of this book, thousands of Irish words that were collected during my lifetime in places where Irish had long since died. I can personally vouch for the fact that some of the people from whom words were collected thought that they were Standard English, and had no idea that they were in fact Irish.

The late John Braidwood of Queen's University, Belfast, often spoke and wrote about the richness of Irish rural speech. He found that the most striking parallel between Elizabethan English and Anglo-Irish is the sheer delight in language for its own sake. The Elizabethan period, linguistically the most uninhibited in the history of the English language, gave us a Shakespeare thanks to 'his stimulating collaborator, the Elizabethan speaker and listener', to use another scholar's phrase. 'To-day', wrote Braidwood, 'probably only the Irishman, especially the southern Irishman, and some Welshmen, work in the Elizabethan linguistic, mastering the language, where the rest of us, with pusillanimous notions of correctness and good taste hammered into us at school, let the language master us.'

The standardisation of speech and writing, is, I suppose, inevitable in the Ireland of to-day, given the influence of the educational system, television and radio, the newspapers and the advertising copy-writers. The late Alan Bliss drew the fire of many teachers of English when he remarked that provided he does not try to ape the speech of others, the Irishman has at his command a form of language which distinguishes him from all others, and which accurately reflects the social history of his country. Bliss, like Braidwood, was worried at how little Anglo-Irish is used by modern Irish writers, a matter that the Tyrone novelist, my friend Benedict Kiely, also remarked upon: 'In a world so tied up in a tight bundle, language must renew itself from such a variety of sources as was never before available: it must renew itself or die in clichés. But in the long run it is only an inborn taste, afterwards cultivated more by talkative company than by the rules of academies, that will find the living phrase and record it in writing.'

I thank the talkative company who gave me this collection of words and phrases that have filtered from Irish into the English of Ireland. It would give me immense pleasure if many of them filtered into the English literature written by the Irishmen and Irishwomen of to-day.

Let us remember John Synge who, casting his mind back to the Elizabethans, said: 'In a good play, every speech should be as fully flavoured as a nut or apple, and such speeches cannot be written by anyone who works among people who have shut their lips on poetry.'

THE ANGLO-IRISH FORMS OF IRISH WORDS

I have given all of the Irish headwords in their orthodox Irish spelling. Many of those people who contributed words, their own or other people's, gave them in this form, allowing me no choice but to print them as I received them, even though I know full well that the pronunciation of the Anglo-Irish may differ slightly from the Irish. (See the note on Pronunciation of Anglo-Irish words, below.)

In those cases where correspondents, or writers of books etc., used a quasi-phonetic form, I have given it also, even though the visual image of those words often looks eccentric or even downright absurd. A glance at the words used by 19th-century novelists in the dictionary will show what I mean. The reader will have no difficulty with words such as *shebeen* or *banshee*, whose Anglo-Irish spelling has long been established; but forms such as *joolyuck*, instead of Irish *diúlach*; *koorjeek* instead of *cuardaíocht*; *clootough* instead of *cliútach*, illustrate the difficulty of a rapprochement between English orthography and Irish phonetic structure.

The English glosses, it should be noted, are not mine. They are valuable both as a guide to the meaning of the words in the districts they come from and as an illustration of the Anglo-Irish syntax of those districts.

THE PRONUNCIATION OF IRISH WORDS IN ANGLO-IRISH

When Irish people first adopted English they spoke it with their native Irish sounds and sound patterns. For example, they used the Irish broad *f*-sound (a bilabial fricative) for the English *wh*-sound what, why, etc. And they put /ʃ/ in place of /s/ in words like stick, west, etc., because in Irish only /ʃ/ could precede an alveolar stop.

Some of these Irish sound-features were maintained in Anglo-Irish for several generations. For example, the pronunciation of *st* with /ʃ/ is still common in Munster and Connaught, even in areas where Irish has long ceased to be spoken. But many of the Irish features were soon lost or modified. Perhaps the only Irish-based feature still widespread is the use of dental stops /t, d/ for the dental fricatives /θ, ð/ in thin, there, etc. Even this feature seems to be losing ground today as the fricatives are becoming more common. In the towns and cities alveolar stops are commonly heard in this case: this would seem to be an old feature, perhaps unrelated to Irish.

Anglo-Irish accents are still easily recognized as such. But their characteristics do not generally derive from Irish, except in rural areas of the South and West.

The first generation of Anglo-Irish speakers, who were largely bilingual, pronounced Irish words in English exactly as in Irish. But as soon as Irish ceased to be spoken Irish words underwent the same process of adaptation as English words.

At an early stage distinctively Irish sounds were replaced by the nearest English sounds. For example, the Irish *ch*-sound /x/ (a velar fricative) was commonly replaced by a *k*-sound; e.g. *asachán* /asə'xaːn/ 'gibe' became Anglo-Irish /asə'kaːn/ (Cork). In Northern and Western counties /x/ was often replaced by /h/; e.g. *buachalán* /'buəxəlaːn/ 'rag-weed' became /'buːhəlaːn/ (Galway). This example also shows the usual substitution of /uː/ for the Irish diphthong /uə/.

Broad and slender quality in consonants was modified, and came to depend on the vowels preceding and following. So, *bóithrín* /boː'rʹiːnʹ/ 'country lane' became Anglo-Irish /boː'riːn/ (southern counties). The slender *r* was replaced by the neutral Anglo-Irish *r* (similar to the Irish broad *r*). But the initial *b* retained its broad quality, more or less, because of the following back vowel. Similarly the final *n* retained some of its slender quality because of the preceding front vowel.

Broad and slender *l* (dark and clear respectively) were retained in some areas, e.g. West Cork, Kerry. But generally a clear or neutral *l* came to be used for both. So, *lán a mhála* /laːn ə'vaːlə/ 'full and plenty' becomes Anglo-Irish /laːn ə waːlə/ with neutral alveolar *l* in both cases. A distinction between dental and aveolar stops (*t, d*) was widely retained in Munster.

Dental *t* is found for example in *taoscán* /teːsˈgɑːn/ 'a little drop'; dental *d* is found in the very common word *amadán* /aməˈdɑːn/ 'fool'. In Leinster, where Irish died out earlier, alveolar *t* and *d* may occur in these and similar words.

Some words may change in unpredictable ways. This is not surprising, considering that these words were in most cases never written, and often had an unusual structure (when compared with English words). A few examples:

builín bán /bilʹiːnʹˈbɑːn/ 'white loaf' becomes *bully bawn* (Wexford).

teaspach /tʹisˈbɑx/ 'high spirits' becomes regularly Anglo-Irish /təsˈbɑk/ but also appears as *taspy* (perhaps from the genetive form *teaspaigh*) (Cork).

mí-adh /mʹiːˈɑː/ 'misfortune' is usually pronounced in English as in Irish, but is occasionally changed into /miːˈɑu/ (perhaps in imitation of the word for a cat's cry) (Cork).

Despite the assimilation of Irish words to English phonology, some Irish dialect features are still evident.

The most obvious of these features is the position of word-stress. In Munster Irish the stress usually falls on the second syllable if this contains a long vowel: *caipín* 'cap' is pronounced /kɑˈpʹiːnʹ/, rather than /ˈkɑpʹiːnʹ/ as in Connacht and Ulster. This southern stress-pattern is found in many words in Anglo-Irish e.g. *bastún* 'lout', *camán* 'hurley stick', *ciotóg* 'lefthanded person', *plámás* 'flattery'. It also applied to the diminutive ending *-ín* when this is added to English words; e.g. *biteen*, *houseen* /hauˈʃiːn/ (the attenuation of the *s* follows an Irish rule), *Jackeen*. These pronunciations are typical of Munster and South Leinster, and they would hardly occur north of a line from Dublin to Galway.

Also in Munster Irish the stress may fall on the third syllable if its vowel is long and the two preceding vowels are short. So *amadán* is stressed on the third syllable in Munster in English as well as in Irish. However some words of this structure are stressed on the first syllable even in Munster; e.g. *cruiteachán* /ˈkritʹəxɑːn/ 'hunchback'.

Another Munster feature is the stressing of *ach* in words of two syllables if the vowel of the first syllable is short; e.g. *bacach* /bəˈkɑx/ 'cripple (or 'beggar man'). In Connacht this word is pronounced /ˈbɑkəx/, in Ulster /ˈbɑkɑx/.

Some minor dialect features may be found in particular areas. For example, Irish slender *nn*, originally palatal *n* (/Nʹ/) falls together with slender *n* /nʹ/ in Kerry: *bainne* 'milk' is pronounced /banʹe/. In most of Cork and Waterford slender *nn* becomes a velar (ng): /baŋʹə/. The variation between /nʹ/ and /ŋʹ/ emerges in a few words in Anglo-Irish; e.g. *ainnis* 'wrecthed' is usually pronounced /anʹiʃ/ in Kerry, /aŋʹiʃ/ in Cork.

Another minor feature is the development of /rʹh/ into /ʃ/ in Kilkenny and Wexford, so that *bóthrín* is pronounced /boːˈʃiːn/ in those counties.

Abbreviations

Cross-references are to the Bibliography.

AG (s. Tipperary)	Ann (Lee) Gallagher, Glen of Aherlow. Words courtesy of her son, Críostóir Ó Gallchóir, New Inn.
AK (Kildare)	Anne Kent, Naas.
AM (Leitrim)	Augustine Martin, Ballinamore.
An Cho (w. Mayo)	See *An Choinneal*.
AOL (mid-Waterford)	Annraoi Ó Liatháin.
BASJ (Cavan and Leitrim)	See *Breifny Antiquarian Society's Journal*.
BC (s. Wexford)	See Colfer, B.
BMacM (n. Kerry)	Bryan MacMahon, Ballyheigue.
BOD (w. Cork)	Bruno O'Donoghue. See *Bandon Historical Journal*.
By (s.e. Wexford)	Peter Byrne, Tomhaggard.
C (e. Limerick)	Patrick MacCarthy, Drumkeen.
CBD (n. Kerry)	See Ó hAnnracháin, Stiofán, *Caint an Bhaile Dhuibh*.
CBE 34 S (Galway)	Séamas Ó Dubhda, N.T., Loughrea, 1937-38. In Schools Collection, Department of Irish Folklore Archives, University College, Dublin.
CBE 47 S (Galway)	Micheál Ó Tuathaigh, N.T., Kiltartan, 1937-39. In Schools Collection, Department of Irish Folklore, University College, Dublin.
CBE 104 (Leitrim)	Tadhg Ó Rabharthaigh. In Main Collection, Department of Irish Folklore Archive, University College, Dublin. From the Arigna mining district.
CBE 266 (n. Tipperary)	Eamonn O Duibhir, Goold's Cross. Department of Irish Folklore Archives, University College, Dublin, main collection.
COG (s. Tipperary)	Críostóir Ó Gallchóir. Words from the Glen of Aherlow.
Con (Louth, Meath)	Margaret Conway. See *Ríocht na Midhe* and *County Louth Archaeological Journal*.
Cor (Cavan)	Pádraig Ó Corbaidh. See *The Heart of Breifne*.
CW (e. Wicklow)	Cecil Walby, Greystones.
D (s.e. Wexford)	Jack Devereux, Kilmore Quay.
D Kildare	Rita Dempsey, Rathangan.
DA (e. Cork)	Darina Allen, Ballymaloe.
DC (Galway)	Detta Collins, Galway city.
Dee (w. Waterford)	Thomas Dee, Ardmore district.
Del (Antrim)	Séamas Delargy.

DG (Sligo)	Dermot Gallagher, Sligo town.
Dinn	See Dinneen, P.S.
DM (w. Cork)	Jer Murray, Milleens, parish of Ballyvourney.
DOC (e. Limerick)	Dáithí Ó Cantúil, Croom.
DOH (e. Limerick)	Dáithí Ó hÓgáin, Bruff.
EASI	See Joyce, P.W., *English as We Speak It in Ireland*.
ED (Tipperary)	Eamonn Dalton, Golden.
EDD	See *English Dialect Dictionary*.
ER (Louth)	Etienne Rynne. See *Journal of the County Louth Archaeological and Historical Society*.
FF (Monaghan, Cavan)	Fred Fitzsimons, Drumbracken, Kingscourt.
Fin (Mayo)	Thomas Finnegan, Bohola district.
F (Mayo)	John Flanagan, Carrowmore district.
F (e. Limerick)	Peter Franklin, Drumkeen.
FM (s.e. Wexford)	Frank Murray, New Ross.
G (n.w. Donegal)	John Gallagher, Dunlewey.
G (s. Kilkenny)	Thomas Greene, Moulerstown, parish of Glenmore.
GC (Laois)	See *The Gaelic Churchman*.
H (Clare)	Patrick Henchy, Corofin. See *North Munster Antiquarian Journal*.
H (Donegal)	H.C. Hart. MSS sources. See also *Notes on Ulster Dialect, Chiefly Donegal*. Extensive use of his MSS in Traynor, *The English Dialect of Donegal*.
Ham (e. Clare)	Monsignor Michael Hamilton. See *North Munster Antiquarian Journal*.
HG (n.w. Donegal)	Hugh Gallagher, Mín na gCapóg, parish of Cloughaneely.
IG	See *Gaelic Journal*.
J (s.e. Wexford)	Elizabeth Jeffries, Kilmore.
JB (Armagh, Louth)	J. Bradley. See *Ulster Folk Life*.
JC (w. Cork)	Julia Crowley, Clohina, Kilnamartyra parish.
JCHAS	See *Journal of the Cork Historical and Archaeological Society*.
JF (n. Wexford)	James Furlong, Gorey.
JG (Westmeath)	John Geoghegan, Mullingar.
JH (e. Limerick)	Joseph Hayes, Cloverfield, Drumkeen.
JH (w. Waterford)	James Hourigan, Old Parish.
JJH (w. Waterford)	John Joe Hourigan, Old Parish.
JK (Kildare)	Jane King, Naas.
JKAS	*Journal of the Kildare Archaeological Society*.
JL (w. Cork)	Jer O'Leary, Cúm an Liabáin, parish of Kilnamartyra, Macroom.
JM (s. Kilkenny)	Jim Mackey, The Rower.
JM (w. Cork)	Jerry Murray, Clohina, parish of Kilnamartyra, Macroom.

JON (Armagh)	John O'Neill, Lurgan.
JPL (w. Cork)	John Patrick Lehane, Rath, Kilnamartyra parish, Macroom.
JS (e. Limerick, w. and e. Kerry)	Jerry O'Sullivan, Pallasgreen.
Ju (Sligo)	Michael Judge.
JV (e. Wicklow)	John Vines, Kilpedder.
JVD (Cavan)	John V. Doherty, Virginia.
KB (e. Limerick)	Kathleen Breathnach. See *Ballyguiltenane Rural Journal*.
LB (s.w. Dublin)	Liam Ó Broin.
LOS (w. Clare)	Liam Ó Sé, Kilrush.
Lys (n. Kerry)	Patrick Lysaght, Listowel district. See *North Munster Antiquarian Journal*.
M Nic M (Derry)	Máire Nic Mhaoláin.
Mac C (Monaghan)	Canon M. Mac Carville. MS loaned. Most words published in *Clogher Record*, q.v.
Mas (Tipperary)	T. Mason, Thurles district.
MC (Cavan)	Matt Cooke.
MC (e. Mayo)	Rev. Michael Comer, Beckan.
MC (w. Clare)	Máirín, Bean Mhic Cárthaigh.
McK (Leitrim)	M. J. McKenna, National Teacher, Gortletteragh. Words courtesy of Aiden Kelleher, Errew, Lough Rinn, Mohill.
MF (Westmeath)	Eamonn Mhac an Fhailigh. See *Éigse*.
MG (Kilkenny)	Mary Grace, Kilkenny city.
MG (n.w. Donegal)	Mary Gallagher, Dunlewey.
MH (Tyrone)	Marie Heaney, Arboe.
MJD (w. Cork)	Mike Jack O'Donoghue, Rath, Kilnamartyra parish, Macroom.
MJM (Cavan)	Michael J. Murphy, folklore collector.
MKN (s. Wexford)	Mary Kate Nolan, New Ross.
MM (e. Wicklow)	Michael Magee, Delgany.
MP (mid-Tipperary)	Maggie Purcell. Words courtesy of her son, Diarmuid Breathnach, Bray, Co. Wicklow.
MS (e. Limerick)	Mainchín Seoighe, Tankardstown.
MW (s. Wexford)	Margaret Whitty, Horeswood, Campile.
N&Q	See *Notes and Queries*.
NB (n. w. Donegal)	Neil O'Boyle, Dungloe.
NB (w. Limerick)	Nioclás Breathnach. See *Eigse*.
NM (w. Cork)	Neilius Murphy, Doire Finín, parish of Kilnamartyra.
O'K (Tyrone)	William O'Kane, Dungannon.
OC (Monaghan)	Peadar Ó Casaide, Dromainn, Carrickmacross.
OCn (Laois)	D. Ó Conchubhair. See *Eigse*.
OD (n. Clare)	Edward O'Dwyer, Gortaclare district.

PB (s. Tipperary)	Pádraig Breathnach. Words courtesy of his son, Diarmuid Breathnach, Bray, Co. Wicklow.
PB (s.e. Wexford)	Pete Bates, Kilmore.
PBB (w. Kerry)	Paddy Bán Brosnan, Dingle.
PC (n. Clare)	Pádraic Collins, Fanore.
PC (n. Wexford)	Paddy Cullen, Kilquade, Co. Wicklow. Words from his native Gorey district.
PD (s. Carlow)	Paddy Doyle, St Mullins.
Pe (Wexford)	See *The People*.
PF (w. Limerick)	Paddy Foley, Ballyguiltenane.
PJG (mid-Donegal)	Patrick Joseph MacGill, Glenties district.
PLH	See Henry, P.L.
PON (n. Co. Dublin)	P. O'Neill. Words sent in typescript by Paddy Weston, Lusk. See also *Béaloideas*.
Poole (s.e. Wexford)	See Poole, Jacob.
R (s. Galway)	Raymond Roland, Loughrea district.
RBB (s. Kilkenny and Waterford, mainly w. Waterford)	Risteard B. Breatnach, Slieverue, Co Kilkenny.
RIA Dictionary	See *Dictionary of the Irish Language*.
RS (Antrim)	Robert Sharpe, Glenariffe.
S (e. Kerry)	Joan O'Sullivan, Kilgarvan.
S (n.w. Donegal)	Mary Sweeney, Meenbanad, Dungloe.
S (s. Wexford)	John Sutton, Ballynaboola.
SF (s. Wexford)	Séamus Furlong, New Ross.
S Ua G (s. Tipperary)	Seán Ua Gruagáin, Glen of Aherlow, Co. Tipperary.
Smy (n. Clare)	Jimmy Smyth, Ruane.
SOB (s. Tipperary)	Seán Ó Briain, Clonmel.
SOM (e. Kerry, w. Cork)	Seán Ó Mathúna, Rathmore.
Su (s.e. Wexford)	Bridie Sutton, Forth.
Sy (Monaghan)	Anne Shirley, Carrickmacross.
T McC (Westmeath)	Tom Mc Clennan.
TB (Cavan)	Thomas Baxter, Carrigallen.
TdeB (Galway)	An tOllamh Tomás de Bhaldraithe.
TM (w. Cork)	Tom Murray, Ráth, parish of Kilnamartyra.
TOM (Tipperary)	Archbishop Thomas Morris of Cashel and Emly. Words from Killenaule.
Tr (Donegal)	See Traynor, Michael.
UJA	See *Ulster Journal of Archaeology*.

A

A babún interj. As a **baboon**. 'Said with a shudder of horror at the thought of having to go through some terrible experience' MF (Westmeath).

A bhean chóir voc. phr. As **a ban chohr** in Wm. Carleton, *The Lianhan Shee* 1, 78 (Tyrone). Dear lady. 'A bhean chóir, you are talking nonsense' JL (w. Cork).

A bhuachaill dheas voc. phr. As **a bouchal dhas**. My nice boy, in Wm. Carleton, *The Poor Scholar* 2, 276 (Tyrone).

A chait as sin voc. phr. As **catshin**. Cat, out of there! *IG* (Kilkenny).

A chara voc. phr. Also as **ahorra, achora**. My friend. The usual way of addressing somebody in a letter. James Joyce, *Ulysses* 294: 'Never better, a chara, says he'; Wm. Carleton, *Phelim O'Toole's Courtship* 2, 220: 'achora' (Tyrone); 'Ahorra' TOM (s. Tipperary).

A cheana voc. phr. My love. 'Said to a child' *CBD* (n. Kerry).

A chroí voc. phr. As **a cree, achree**. Term of affection: my heart. Anon., *Sir John Oldcastle*: 'Ahone, ahone, ahone a cree'; Richard Head, *Hic et Ubique*: 'O yea, between me and God achree ...'; William Carleton, *Fardorougha the Miser* 6: '"Conor, achree", said his mother' (Tyrone).

A chuid voc. phr. As **a hudg, achudth**. Diminutive, **a hudgeen**. My store, my all. Term of endearment. Michael Banim, *Crohoor of the Billhook* 1, 268 (Kilkenny): 'a hudg'; ibid. 1, 268: 'a hudgeen-ma-chree' (*lit.* store, treasure of my heart); Somerville and Ross, *A Misdeal* 108: 'don't be unaisy, achudth; he's doing grand' (w. Cork).

A chuisle voc. phr. As **a cushla, acushla**. My pulse. A term of endearment. Mrs S. C.

Hall, *Irish Life and Character* 225: 'I'll tell you what, Peggy a cushla' (s. Leinster); James Joyce, *Ulysses* 527: 'remove him, acushla'. In phrase **a chuisle mo chroí**, my heart's pulse, in form **cushla ma chree** in Wm. Carleton, *The Geography of an Irish Oath* 2, 11: 'What language has a phrase equal in beauty and tenderness to cushla ma chree – pulse of my heart?' (Tyrone).

A ghile mo chroí voc. phr. As **a guilla macree**, brightness of my heart, in John Banim, *John Doe* 338 (Kilkenny).

A ghrá voc. phr. As **a gra, agra**. Thomas Dekker, *The Honest Whore* Part 2: 'A mawhisdeer [see *máistir*] a gra, fare de well ...'; George Farquhar, *The Twin Rivals*: '... but foo shall bail poor Teague agra'; Gerald Griffin, *The Collegians* 115: 'Heaven help us, agra' (Limerick); Mrs S. C. Hall, *Irish Life and Character* 223: 'Have ye got anything striking handsome under thim dirty seaweeds and dawny shrimpeens, agra?' (s. Leinster).

A iníon voc. phr. As **nhien, inien**. My daughter. Wm. Carleton, *Tubber Derg* 2, 409: 'Alley, nhien macree ...' (Tyrone); ibid., *Fardorougha the Miser* 264: 'Why don't you cry, inien machree?'

A lao voc. phr. My calf. Term of endearment. 'How are you, a lao?' JL (w. Cork); RBB (Waterford). As **elaygil** (my bright calf) in George Fitzmaurice, *The Pie-Dish*: 'Elaygil, Margaret, when the heart is set on doing a thing, 'tisn't far to go to find an excuse for it' (Kerry).

A leanbh voc. phr. As **alanna, alanah, alannah**. My child. Charles James Lever, *The Confessions of Harry Lorrequer*: 'Miss Betty, alanah' (Munster); ibid., *Charles O'Malley*: 'Whose then, alannah'; M.J. Mulloy, *The King of Friday's Men* 21: 'Maura, alannah, is that yourself?' (Galway).

Phrase, **a leanbh chumhra**, in form **alan-nah coora**, my fragrant child (voc.) MKN (Wexford). **A leanbh mo chroí**, child of my heart (voc.), in form **a-lanna-ma-chree** in Michael Banim, *Crohoor of the Billhook* 1, 137: 'Musha, what miau is cum over you, Cauth, a-lanna-ma-chree?' (Kilkenny). **A leanbh dheas**, my pretty child, in form **alanna dhas**, in Wm. Carleton, *Geography of an Irish Oath* 15 (Tyrone).

A mhaoineach voc. phr. *al.* **a mhaoinigh**; **aweinach**. My darling. 'Well, a mhaoineach, what can I do for you?' JM (w. Cork; Gen. Munster); 'Safe home, a mhaoinigh' JL (w. Cork); George Fitzmaurice, *The Pie-Dish*: 'aweinach' (Kerry).

A mhic voc. phr. Also as **avic, a vig**. Diminutive, **avikeen**. Vocative case of **mac**, son. Seumus MacManus, *Bold Blades of Donegal* 341: 'Ay, sleepin', a mhic dhílis (darling son)'; Seumus MacManus, *In Chimney Corners* 196: 'Come in avic an ye're welcome'; ibid. 168: 'Aisy, aisy, master, sez Donal, aisy avic' (Donegal); James Stephens, *The Crock of Gold* 27: 'A vig, vig o. A cailin vig o'; James Joyce, *Finnegans Wake* 565: 'avikeen'. Phrase, **a mhic mo chroí**, son of my heart, in form **a vich ma-chree** in Michael Banim, *Crohoor of the Billhook* 1, 24 (Kilkenny); Wm. Carleton, *The Geography of an Irish Oath* 2, 12: '... vick macree, wuil thu marra wo'um?, son of my heart art thou dead from me?' (Tyrone). Phrase, **a mhic ó**, my dear son, in Gerald Griffin, *The Collegians* 81, in form **a vich-o** (Limerick). Phrase **a mhic na hOighe**, O son of the Virgin, in form **vich na hoiah** in William Carleton, *Phelim O'Toole's Courtship* 2, 211: 'Vick na hoiah, Phelim; do you tell me so?' (Tyrone).

A mhilis voc. phr. As **a villish**. My sweet. Wm. Carleton, *The Geography of an Irish Oath* 56: 'When I rise in the mornin', a villish, where'll be your smile ...?' (Tyrone).

A Mhuire interj. As **wisha, wirra, musha**. Mary! (Gen.)

A mhúirnín voc. phr. As **a-vourneen, avourneen**. Also as possessive: **mavourneen**. Michael Banim, *Crohoor of the Billhook* 1, 158: 'Pierce, a-vourneen, wait, a doochy-bit' (Kilkenny); Wm. Carleton, *Going To Maynooth* 2, 102: 'But, Dinny, avourneen ...' (Tyrone). Mrs S. C. Hall, *Irish Life and Character* 174: 'Oh, blessed be the day ... when I saw ye first, mavourneen!'; ibid. 224: 'I've the world and all of shawls, Peggy, avourneen' (s. Leinster); Gerald Griffin, *The Collegians* 81: 'Ma vourneen' (Limerick).

A rún voc. phr. As **aroon, aroun**. My darling. 'Sleep well, aroon' AM (Leitrim; Gen.); James Joyce, *Finnegans Wake* 11: '... who goes cute goes siocur and shoos aroun ...' (Here Joyce is punning on the line of a song, *My Mary of the Curling Hair*, a line of which is *siúl go socair agus siúl a rún*, meaning walk easily, and walk, my darling.)

A sholais mo chroí voc. phr. As **a sollish machree**. Light of my heart. Wm. Carleton, *Fardorougha the Miser* 250 (Tyrone).

A stór voc. phr. Also as **asthore**, diminutive **astoreen**. Term of endearment: my treasure. Seumus MacManus, *A Lad of the O'Friels* 173: 'God grant your wish, Dinny, a stor' (Donegal); Gerald Griffin, *The Collegians* 48: 'Mr Daly, asthore, I ask your pardon' (Limerick); Somerville and Ross, *A Misdeal* 107: 'ye're desthroyed entirely asthore!' (w. Cork); James Joyce, *Finnegans Wake* 528: 'astoreen'.

A thaisce voc. phr. Also as **a haskey**. My treasure. Seumus MacManus, *In Chimney Corners* 247: 'Why, Jack, a thaisce, said his mother, it's a dangersome task' (Donegal; Gen.); 'A drop for the road, the bang of the latch, ahaskey' PC (Wexford).

A théagair voc. phr. As **ahagur**. My dear. Wm. Carleton, *The Geography of an Irish Oath* 2, 72: 'Ahagur, that wasn't the way their hard-workin' father an' mother made the money' (Tyrone); PON (n. Co. Dublin); ER (Louth).

A thiarcais voc. phr. Euphemistic form of **a thiarna**, O Lord! 'A thiarcais, did you ever hear the like of that for a story!' JL (w. Cork); NB (w. Limerick).

A thiarna voc. phr. As **cheerna**. Lord! (vocative). Wm. Carleton, *Fardorougha the Miser* 195: 'Cheerna dheelish' (dear Lord) (Tyrone).

Abhac n. Also as **amach, ammache, owk.** Diminutive, **abhacán,** in form **owkan.** 1. A dwarf. 'You wouldn't get much for that abhac of a calf' JM (w. Cork); PB (s. Tipperary); 'That abhacán will never make the grade' JL (w. Cork); PC (n. Clare); 'A little owk of a man' PD (s. Carlow); 'He's fierce strong, for such a little owkan' G (s. Kilkenny). 2. *CBE* 266 (mid-Tipperary): 'Abhacán applied here only to a worn spade or shovel.'

Abhac na rátha n. phr. As **outnarawka.** The dwarf of the fairy fort. 'An ungainly, badly-built man' DOC (Limerick).

Ábhar n. 1. 'A boil, an ulcer' *IG* (Leinster). 2. In phrase, **on his/her/its ábhar** – independently. 'The boat was going on her own ábhar: drifting' PC (n. Clare). Translation of Irish, *ar a hábhar féin.*

Abhó interj. As **avoch.** Alas! *IG* (Leinster); John and Michael Banim *Father Connell* 191: 'Avoch, I don't know whose child I am' (Kilkenny).

Ablach n. 1. A carcass. 'The flu nearly killed him. He's gone into an ablach altogether' JM (w. Cork). 2. 'A dirty, slovenly person' MG (n.w. Donegal). 3. 'An ungainly person' G (s. Kilkenny). 4. 'A gluttonous person' RBB (s. Kilkenny). 5. 'Depradation, such as that done by cows in a field of wheat' *CBD* (n. Kerry).

Abú interj. Also as **aboo.** In phrase, 'O'Donnell Abú!' (song); slogans such as 'Dev. abú!'; James Joyce, *Finnegans Wake* 500: 'Crum abu!' (the slogan of the Limerick FitzGeralds); ibid. 464: 'A leal of the O'Looniys, a Brazel aboo!' [< dialect English, *aboo,* above.]

Achasán n. A slur. 'He was always throwing achasáns' *CBD* (n. Kerry); **asachán** JL (w. Cork).

Adag n. 'A small stack of corn. When the stooks of corn are fairly dry, they make them into adags' FF (Monaghan); TB (Cavan).

Ádh n. Good luck. 'He never had a day's ádh since he married her' JL (w. Cork; Gen.). See *Mí-ádh.*

Adharcachán n. 'A cross-eyed person' PC (n. Clare).

Adhascaid n. 1. Nausea. 'I can't suffer him. The very look of him puts adhascaid on me' JL (w. Cork). 2. Specifically, morning sickness. 'It's natural in her condition, the adhscaid' JC (w. Cork).

Adhastar n. A halter. 'She has him on adhastar – she has control over him' JM (w. Cork). Hence **adhastaring.** 'Poking one's way out: "I was adhastaring along by the dyke"' NB (w. Limerick).

Aerach adj. Also as **airy.** 1. Light-hearted, buoyant, gleeful. 'It is used especially of someone who is unexpectedly so: a widow, an elderly person. It has undertones of fresh air and light summery clothing. "Isn't it you that's aerach in your light shirt (dress) on a cold evening like this!" But these are mere external trappings: being aerach belongs essentially to the spirit and to the heart' *An Cho* (w. Mayo); Eric Cross, *The Tailor and Ansty* 91: '"Those were the airy times. It was worth being alive in those days"' (w. Cork); 'He's an airy man; he couldn't care less where the night might fall on him' JL (w. Cork). 2. Believed to be haunted by fairies. William Allingham, *The Fairies*: 'Up the airy mountain' (Fermanagh, Donegal); George Russell: 'Upon an Airy Upland'; 'They said it was an aerach place, that the fairies were seen there' RBB (mid-Waterford).

Ag bualadh vb. n. As **booleyin,** moving briskly. 'He was booleyin down the road' D (s.e. Wexford).

Ag cur uilinn ar phr. As **crivling.** Putting an angle on. 'Building a turf rick in such a fashion as that the sides are slanted, like a pyramid' MG (n.w. Donegal).

Ag déanamh amach phr. In translated form **making out.** Standard English equivalent, starting for home. M.J. Mulloy, *The King of Friday's Men* 79: 'We'll be making out, girl' (Galway).

Ag déanamh orm phr. In translated form **making for me.** Standard English equivalent, coming towards me. 'I saw the bull making for me' JL (w. Cork. Gen.)

Ag fáil bháis phr. In translated form **getting death**. Dying. J.M. Synge, *The Well of the Saints* 68: 'I'll be getting my death now, I'm thinking, sitting alone in the cold air ...'; 'You'll get your death, going out on a night like this without a coat' FM (Wexford; Gen.).

Ag gearán vb. n. As **gerning**. Complaining. 'He never stops gerning about everything, from the weather to his corns' FF (Cavan).

Ag prep. **1.** **At.** In phrases *at me, at you, at him* etc., possessed by me, etc.; belonging to; that I, etc. had. Peadar O'Donnell, *Adrigoole* 147: 'A fine place at him'; ibid. 202: 'She was on a string at Mickey' (Donegal). **2.** **By.** 'The family is nearly all reared at him' ibid. 111; Dermot O'Byrne, *Children of the Hills* 135: 'Sure we're destroyed at him' (Donegal). **3.** **With.** Peadar O'Donnell, op. cit. 143: 'You'd think it was a burden-rope I was lavin' back at him' (Gen.). [1-3 < **agam**, **agat**, **aige**, etc., prepositional pronouns, in phrase *tá ... agam*, I have. Literally, there is ... at me.]

Aghaidh fidil n. As **eye fiddle**. 'A mask worn by children at Hallow E'en and such festivals' MS (e. Limerick); LOS (w. Clare); *CBD* (n. Kerry); PB (s. Tipperary).

Aguisín n. Also as **ogisheen**. **1.** A little extra. 'He always gives the right amount, but never an aguisín' MS (e. Limerick); PB (s. Tipperary). **2.** A tailpiece, an appendix. 'I'm afraid there's another aguisín on to that: that there's more to the matter than what has been said' *CBD* (n. Kerry); 'Don't be putting any of your aguisíns to it' *CBE* 266 (mid-Tipperary); 'She had so many ogisheens to the rosary that it went on for hours' PD (s. Carlow).

Aililiú interj. Also as **alilu**. 'An exclamation of surprise or sorrow' *CBD* (n. Kerry); JL (w. Cork); Gerald Griffin, *The Collegians* 37: 'Alilu! such a message for the world' (Limerick).

Áilleán n. *al.* **áilleagán**. **1.** A lovely young woman; a darling, doll, plaything. 'I wouldn't mind a tear out of that little áilleán' JL (w. Cork). **2.** Often used ironically. 'He's the áilleán who ruined us on Sunday when

he left in the goal' PD (s. Carlow); *Pe* (Wexford); Ju (Sligo); PB (s. Tipperary); MP (mid-Tipperary); 'He married an áilleagán from Kenmare direction' JM (w. Cork); *JKAS* (Kildare).

Ailp n. Also as **alp**, **yolp**. A bite, mouthful. 'He ate the cake in one ailp' RBB (s. Kilkenny); NB (w. Limerick); 'It refers especially to a mouthful which has been taken from something and shows a gap remaining. One could also describe something as having an alp gone out of it – such as an apple, a stocking, or even a mountain' *An Cho* (w. Mayo). Hence **yolpin**: 'The pigs were yolpin' their food' *CBE* 266 (mid-Tipperary).

Ailpín n. As **alpeen**. 'A heavy ashplant or blackthorn stick; a shillelagh' *IG* (Leinster). In compound, **cleith ailpín**, knobbed stick, alpenstock, used in faction fighting. 'I remember well men going to the fair with a cleith ailpín, just looking for fight' JL (w. Cork); Michael and John Banim, *John Doe* 4: '... every alpeen was at work in senseless clatter and unimaginable hostility' (Kilkenny).

Aimpléis n., v. As **amplish**, **amplush**. Trouble, complication; a disadvantage, a state of unreadiness. 'I didn't expect to see him, so I was at a bit of an amplish' PJG (Donegal); Wm. Carleton, *The Battle of the Factions* 1, 141: 'He was driven at last to such an amplush that he had no other shift for employment' (Tyrone); Samuel Lover, *Legends and Stories of Ireland:* 'There was no sitch thing as getting him at an amplush' (Connacht); John Boyce, *Shandy Maguire* 177: '... prayin' to us this minit ... to help ye in in the amplish that yer in' (Donegal); TOM (s. Tipperary); MG (n.w. Donegal); Samuel Lover, *Legends and Stories of Ireland*: 'He'd have amplushed me long ago' (Connacht). [Represents *non-plus EDD*.]

Aimseach n. As **amsha**. Bad luck, misfortune, an accident. 'He had an amsha. Too much to drink and he went freewheeling down the brae right into the lake' MG (n.w. Donegal). [From *aimseach*, adj., accidental, unfortunate.]

Aingceal n. As **anckle**. 'A boor. A cantankerous person' RS (Antrim).

Ainimh n. A blemish, disfigurement. In phrase, **agus ainimh air**, and a blemish on it. '"That's a tradesman agus ainimh air" would be said of a botch tradesman; also of a badly executed piece of work' *IG* (Leinster).

Ainle n. As **annleh**. 'A crying child' MC (e. Mayo).

Ainnis adv., adj. Also as **angish**. 1. Miserable, poorly, sickly, in bad health. (Gen.). 'I'm sorry to tell you, my father is only angish' PD (s. Carlow). [< Old French *anguisse;* Middle English *anguisse.*]

Ainniseoir n. Also as **angashore**. 1. 'A miserable, sickly person' *CBD* (n. Kerry); 'A foolish, wretched person' PLH (n Roscommon); MP (mid-Tipperary); JM (w. Cork); RBB (s. Kilkenny); Patk. Kennedy, *Legendary Fictions of the Irish Celts* 87 (Wexford); and George Fitzmaurice, *The Pie-Dish* (Kerry): 'angashore'. 2. A mean person. 'That angashore wouldn't spend Christmas' Smy (n. Clare).

Ainscian n. As **ounskane**. 'A wild character' FF (Monaghan); *IG* (Meath, Cavan).

Airceach n. Also as **arkagh**. Greedy; eager. 'He's not very airceach for work, that boyeen' PC (n. Clare); 'Arkagh: eager' *Poole* (s.e. Wexford); 'He's as arkagh as a banbh on a sow's tit' PD (s. Carlow).

Aird n. As **airt, art, ait**. Direction, place, point of compass. 'What art of the country are you from?' O'K (Tyrone); LB (s.w. Dublin); 'They were there from all airts' MH (Tyrone); 'From all aits' D (s.e. Wexford).

Aireatúil adj. '(Of a person) careful; fastidious' H (n. Clare).

Airgead n. As **argott, airighad**. Money. Beaumont and Fletcher, *The Coxcomb*: 'By my trot I will give dye worship two shillings in good argott, to buy dy worship pippines'; Wm. Carleton, *The Poor Scholar* 2, 288: 'airighad' (Tyrone). [Latin, *argentum*, silver]

Airgead bán n. phr. As **araguth bawn**. White money. Silver. Michael Banim, *Crohoor of the Billhook* 1, 154: 'Is there any araguth bawn where the gould came frum?' (Kilkenny).

Airgead lámha n. phr. As **hand money**. In that directly translated form, ready cash, cash on the nail. 'It's always hand money; no credit given there' Smy (n. Clare).

Airgead luachra n. phr. Literally, silver of rushes. Meadow-sweet, *Spirea ulmaria*: MG (n.w. Donegal).

Airgead síos n. phr. Also as **araguth chise**. 'Airgead síos: money down; hard cash' *CBD* (n. Kerry); Michael Banim, *Crohoor of the Billhook* 1,139: 'A love for araguth chise ...' (Kilkenny).

Áirneál n. *al.* **áirneán**. 1. A friendly night visit. Patrick Gallagher, *My Story* 35: '"What is an airneal?" said Jane. I said that it was a gathering of all the people of the townland into one house for dancing, singing and storytelling'; ibid: 84: 'In Cleendra most of the kitchens were big, eighteen to twenty feet long by fourteen. All the neighbours gathered into one of the houses each night for an airneal, old men and women, young boys and girls. After the youngsters would have some dancing the storytelling would commence' (Donegal); 'Airneán: a chat beside the fire late at night' *CBD* (n. Kerry). Hence, **áirneáning, arnauneen**. 'Staying talking by the fire late at night. "They were áirneáning beside the fire"' *CBD* (n. Kerry); 'Arnauneen: working late at night' *Poole* (s.e. Wexford). 2. Work done at night. 'A day's work is enough for a body without airneán after it' C (e. Limerick); 'She kills herself airneáning to feed the children' C (e. Limerick); NB (w. Limerick).

Áirseoir n. The Devil. 'He's a right little áirseoir' PC (n. Clare). [< Latin *adversarius*]

Áirsiúil adj. 'Careful, handy, crafty. "He won't go far astray: he's as áirsiúil as be damned"' *CBE* 266 (mid-Tipperary).

Aistear n. As **asater**. A journey. 'You have a long asater before you' FF (Cavan).

Aiteann n. 'Furze' JL (w. Cork). **Aiteann Gaelach**, literally, Irish furze, *ulex galii*. 'A species of small furze' *CBD* (n. Kerry);

Sguab (w. Cork) **Aiteann Gallda**, literally, English furze, coarse furze, *ulex europaeus*: CBD (n. Kerry); *Sguab* (w. Cork).

Ál n. 'A clutch of chickens, etc.' JL (w. Cork); R (s. Galway): 'How well the hen knows that that chicken doesn't belong to her ál.'

Alabhog adj. Lukewarm. 'There was a lovely allabhog light as the sun went down' JL (w. Cork); 'The reception we got was what you could describe as allabhog' RBB (mid-Waterford); NB (w. Limerick).

Álainn adj. Also as **awling**. 1. Lovely. 'Isn't she álainn!' JM (w. Cork). 2. Splendid. 'Christy Ring. God but he was an álainn hurler' PC (n. Clare). 3. Happy-go-lucky, fond of pleasure. Michael Banim, *Crohoor of the Billhook* 1, 252: '... went by the title or surname of "Andy Awling", or airy Andrew' (Kilkenny).

Alamais n. As **alamash, alomes**. 'Alamash: presents, such as nuts, apples and sweets given to children on Hallow E'en' AOL (mid-Waterford). [Perhaps from English *Hallow Mass*, or from *almous*, in general dialect use in Scotland, Ireland and n. England. *Poole* (Wexford): 'alomes.' 'Money or food bestowed in charity, gifts offered to a child on its first round of visiting' EDD Related to *alms*]

Albanach n. As **allibans**. 1. A species of puffin, *fratercula artica* H (n. Donegal). 2. 'An albanach to us is a Scotsman, or a Presbyterian' MG (n.w. Donegal).

Alfraits n. 1. 'A rough-spoken man or woman' JM (w. Cork). 2. 'A scoundrel' S (e. Kerry). ['Apparently from dialect English *fratch*, a testy person, ol' *fratch* becoming *alfraits*' Dinn.]

Allagaistí n. pl. As **allagashtees**. 'Geegaws; flashy, shoddy items of clothing. "Wisha, don't let anyone see them ould allagashtees on you"' CBE 266 (mid-Tipperary). [Irish?]

Allaibhre n. Partial deafness. 'Let ye shut up! You'd give anyone allaibhre' JL (w. Cork).

Alpachán n. 'A voracious eater' PC (n. Clare).

Alpais n. 'A person who eats ravenously or has a great appetite' IG (Leinster).

Alt n. Also in form **ailt**. A cliff, glen-side; a gully. Seumus MacManus, *A Lad of the O'Friels*, 86: 'Mickey's comin' down the alt above' (Donegal); 'The Blessed Virgin was supposed to appear down at the ailt' MG (n.w. Donegal).

Altán n. A hillock. 'The cows are up at the altán' G (n.w. Donegal).

Amach adv. In phrase **amach go brách leo**, out forever with them, or, away they went. As **magh go bragh with them** in Patk. Kennedy, *Legendary Fictions of the Irish Celts* 46. Glossed, erroneously, as 'the field for ever'; *mach* being confused with *macha*, a plain (Wexford).

Amach díreach adv. phr. Out straight, directly. 'I told it to him amach díreach' CBD (n. Kerry).

Amadán n. Also as **omadhaun, omadhawn, omadaun**. A fool. Samuel Lover, *Paddy at Sea* 24: '"And did you take me for your mother, you omadhaun?", says he'; *Lays and Legends of the North of Ireland* 10: 'The ghost av Fannet ... made omadhauns of the three'; A. Hume, *Irish Dialects* 22: 'We shall specially avoid an omadaun' (Antrim and Down); Jane Barlow, *Irish Idylls* 64: 'Just wait, ye big omadhawn, standin' there stargazin' like a stuck pig' (n. Ireland); Seumus MacManus, *In Chimney Corners* 218: 'Why, ye amadan, didn't ye come back and say ye wanted it?' (Donegal); James Joyce, *Grace* 181: 'It is supposed – they say, you know – to take place in the depot where they get these thundering big country fellows, omadhauns, you know, to drill'; Somerville and Ross, *Poisson d'Avril* 202: 'Well, and can't ye put the palliase on the floor under it, ye omadhawn?' (w. Cork).

Amail n. 1. 'An untidy, inefficient person' JL (w. Cork). 2. 'A job untidily done, a mess' RBB (mid-Waterford). 3. A misfortune. 'There's some amail on you' PD (s. Carlow); IG (Kilkenny).

Amalach adj. As **amaluck**. Awkward, clumsy. 'He's an amaluck craythur' S (s. Wexford)

Amalán n. 'A half-wit' PB (s. Tipperary).

Amalóg n. 1. 'A foolish woman' JM (w. Cork). 2. 'A clumsy woman' Dee (w. Waterford).

Amalóir n. 1. 'A foolish man. A bit of a gamal' (q. v.) JM (w. Cork). 2. 'An awkward workman' JL (w. Cork); RBB (w. Waterford).

Ambaiste interj. *al.* **ambasa; ambaist; ambaic.** (Gen. Munster). Also as **am bostha, amostha.** An inocuous expletive. Indeed! Really! Eric Cross, *The Tailor and Ansty* 184: 'Am bostha! You wouldn't expect him to live for ever, I suppose!' (w. Cork); George Fitzmaurice, *The Pie-Dish*: 'amostha' (Kerry).

Amhantar n. Chance, fortune. 'That's a grand suit you have. What amhantar came by you?' JL (w. Cork).

Amharc interj. As **awirck.** Wm. Carleton, *The Lianhan Shee* 1, 78: 'awirck, awirck! look! look!' (Tyrone).

Amhas n. 'A wild man, a hooligan' FF (Monaghan).

Amhastrach n. Barking. 'You'd hear the amhastrach of her a mile away' JL (w. Cork).

Amhrán n. Wild carrot. Variant of **feabhrán,** *heraclium sphondylium.* 'It was thought that they (amhráns) blistered the feet of scythesmen' CBD (n. Kerry).

Amparán n. 'A useless person; a fool; an awkward person' CBD (n. Kerry).

Amplais n. 'A fat, slovenly person' CBD (n. Kerry).

Amscaí adj. Untidy, unkempt, careless. 'That's an amscaí way of doing your homework' MG (n.w. Donegal).

Amú adv. Astray. 'He's gone amú' RBB (mid-Waterford).

An def. art. Often used in Irish English as it would be in Irish: M. J. Mulloy, *The King of Friday's Men* 27: 'Is Cormac giving in to the death at last?' (Galway). [Irish equivalent: *an bás.*]

An airíonn tú leat phr. As **nor-i-een-thou lath.** Do you hear? Michael Banim, *Crohoor of the Billhook* 1, 316: 'Nor-i-een thou-lath, but you're a great fellow iv a boccoch' (Kilkenny).

An ea inter. phr. As **inagh, inyadh, inyah.** Is it? Gerald Griffin, *The Collegians* 98: 'My husband, inagh?' (Limerick). Also an ironic interjection of disbelief. Wm. Carleton, *The Geography of an Irish Oath* 69: 'Lend me your ears, inagh!'; Glossed by Carleton as 'forsooth.' (Tyrone); Patk. Kennedy, *Legends of Mount Leinster* 95: '... what a purty squire and estated gentleman we are, inyadh?' (Wexford); James Joyce, *Ulysses* 424: 'High angle fire, inyah!'

An Fear Thuas phr. As **The Man Above.** God. *EASI* 291: 'They use this term, The Man Above, all through the South: "as cunning as he is he can't hide his knavery from The Man Above".'

An gcluin tú mé? phr. As **glun ta mee, gluntho ma.** Do you hear me? Misused in Richard Head, *Hic et Ubique*: 'I will tell dee tale if thou wilt glun ta mee', when he meant 'listen to me'; Wm. Carleton, *Tubber Derg* 2, 392: 'gluntho ma?' (Tyrone).

Anam n. Soul, life. In following forms. As interjection, **m'anam!,** my soul! Also in phrase **to make my soul** – to go to confession; translation of *m'anam a dhéanamh.* John Boyce, *Shandy Maguire* 49: 'It's fitter ye'd be makin' yer sowl' (Donegal); Patk. Kennedy, *The Banks of the Boro* 209: 'Maybe it would be bebther for me to think of mekin me sowl. It's ten years since I was at a priest's knee' (Wexford). In phrase **m'anam ye** < *m'anam thú,* meaning, 'you are my soul, i.e. you are as dear as life to me' Tr (Donegal). Phrase, **th'anam 'on diabhal,** your soul to the devil, as **Hanim an dioul,** in Wm. Carleton, *Phelim O'Toole's Courtship* 2, 217 (Tyrone; Gen. in Munster).

Anchuma n. Bad, unnatural appearance. 'You put an anchuma on it – you have spoiled it' *IG* (Leinster).

Angaire n. 'A salmon after spawning' *CBE* 98 (Kilkenny) [Cf. *angarais*, a misshapen person or animal *Dinn.*]

Angalálaí n. An argumentative, boorish person. 'A miserable angalálaí, always raising a row' PC (n. Clare).

Anglais n. As **anglish**. 1. 'Milk and water mixed' *IG* (Leinster). 2. Diluted spirits. 'It's not whiskey he sells, but anglish' PD (s. Carlow).

Ann adv. In form **in it**. Alive. James Joyce, *The Sisters* 14: 'We wouldn't see him want anything while he was in it.'

Anois adv. Now. As **anish** in Wm. Carleton, *Phil Purcel, the Pig-Driver* 1, 419 (Tyrone).

Anois tú interj. Also in translated form **now you!** An asseveration. 'You'd say either "anois tú" or "now you" when you wanted to show a person that you were agreement with something he said, or amazed by it' JL (w. Cork).

Anró n. 'Worry caused by trouble, a death, an accident, a public disgrace, and the worry of having to make decisions while so distressed. And you don't say a person has anró: no, the anró *is on* him. Sarcastically one asks: "What anró is on you now?"' *An Cho* (w. Mayo).

Ar a choimeád phr. In translated form **on his keeping**. On the run. James Joyce, *Finnegans Wake* 191: '... one remove from an unwashed savage, on his keeping and in yours ...'.

Ar ball adv. phr. Also as **arraball**. After a while; presently. 'He keeps putting things on the long finger. Everything is "ar ball" with him' JL (w. Cork); Richard Head, *Hic et Ubique*: '... my shelf will run away. Arraball'.

Ar éigin phr. As **horeigin, hush éigin**. Scarcely, hardly. 'The cow gave the full of the can of milk horeigin', i.e. she scarcely filled it' Tr (Donegal); '"Hush éigin", said by a person who has narrowly won a card trick' *CBE* 98 (Kilkenny).

Ar gor phr. As **on gur, on the gur**. Literally, hatching. 1. 'Mitching from school' SF (Dublin city). 2. 'Staying away from home for a few days until trouble blows over' PON (n. Co. Dublin).

Ar seisean phr. Also as **ershishin**. Said he. '"Go home quietly now" ar seisean to the tinker, and be damn but he went' JL (w. Cork); in Wm. Carleton, *The Brothers*, 227: 'ershishin' (Tyrone).

Ara interj. Also as **aru, airiú, arrah, arra, arah, yerra, eroo, rhoo, yerrou**. Ah! Indeed! 'Ara, give him the money. It's his due' G (s. Kilkenny; Gen.); 'Arú, stop the fooling' JS (w. Kerry); 'I don't know, airiú' JM (w. Cork); John Michelburne, *Ireland Preserved*: 'Arrah joy, cozen Teigue...'; Richard Head, *Hic et Ubique*: 'Arra moistare...' [see *máistir*]; ibid., 'rhoo fuate de deole ale thee'; Anon., *A Dialogue Between Teague and Dermot:* 'Yerrou but how came that about?'; George Farquhar, *The Twin Rivals:* 'Arah, you fool, ish it not the saam ting'; Gerald Griffin, *The Collegians:* 'Do you know Myles, aroo?'; ibid, 'Stop her Lowry eroo.' (Limerick); James Joyce, *Ivy Day in the Committee Room* 142: 'Yerra, sure the little hop-o'- my thumb has forgotten all about it'; Joyce, *Finnegans Wake* 7: 'Arrah sure we all love little Anna Rayiny ...'; Joyce, *Ulysses* 294: 'Arrah, give over your bloody codding, Joe, says I.'

Arán n. As **arran**. Bread. Wm. Carleton, *Phelim O'Toole's Courtship* 2, 199: 'Oh, mudher, mudher, gi' me a piece o' arran' (Tyrone).

Arán seagail n. As **rawnsha, reansha**. Rye bread. 'My mother used to make the nicest rawnsha, rye bread, don't you know' J (s.e. Wexford). *EASI:* **reansha**, brown bread (Wexford).

Áras n. In phrase **Áras an Uachtaráin** – the President's official residence. [*Uachtarán*, President. *Áras*, residence.]

Arc n. Also as (diminutive) **arcán** JM (w. Cork); **orcán** RBB (w. Waterford); **aeracaun** D (s.e. Wexford); **acaran** ER (Louth); 'The smallest banbh (q.v.) in the litter' RBB (w. Waterford).

Arc luachra n. As **art-loochra, arc-loochra, wark luhar**. 'A lizard' MS (e. Limerick). Irish English forms in *EASI* 212, other than 'wark luhar' *CBE* 98 (Kilkenny). [*Arc*, lizard; *luachra* genitive of *luachair*, rushes.]

Ard adj. High, tall. In phrase **tall English**, translation of *ard-Bhéarla*. Wm. Carleton, *Shane Fadh's Wedding* 2, 68 (footnote): 'the peasantry are often extremely fond of hard and long words, which they call tall English' (Tyrone).

Ardchíos n. High rent. Authority, domination. 'You'd think he had ardchíos on the people: said about a person who is magisterial, authoritative' *CBD* (n. Kerry).

Arís adv., interj. *al.* aríst. As '**Hureesh** = encore' PON (n. Co. Dublin).

Arsa mise phr. As **ersi misha**. Say I. 'Go home now, arsa mise' *CBE* 266 (mid-Tipperary). Wm. Carleton, *The Three Tasks* 1, 47: 'ersi misha' (Tyrone).

As éadan phr. In translated form **out of face**. *Patterson:* 'To do a thing out of face is to do it right through from first to last without stopping' (Down and Antrim); *EASI* 43: 'Do that out of face i.e. begin at the beginning and finish it out and out'; 'Out of face: incessantly, straight through without stopping' *EDD* (Ulster); 'To do, take, work out of face – to do it methodically, in an orderly manner' Tr (Donegal); M.J. Mulloy, *The King of Friday's Men* 60: 'We'll fight ... and beat them out of face at last' (Galway).

As go brách phr. In phrase 'as go brách with him' – away he went *IG* (Kilkenny); PD (s. Carlow); PC (n. Clare); JL (w. Cork).

As meon phr. Beyond measure, exceeding. 'He was as meon as a scholar: he was outstanding' S Ua G (s. Tipperary).

Asal n.; interj. 1. An ass. 'What sort of a divil's asal are you?' JL (w. Cork). 2. 'A word of encouragement to an ass' *CBD* (n. Kerry).

Asclán n. 'A bundle or parcel carried under the arm' AOL (w. Waterford).

Athbhall n. 'Cultivated ground that was lea last year' Mac C (Monaghan). See *athbhán*.

Athbhán n. 'Former lea (in second tillage)' FF (Cavan). See *athbhall*.

Athchaladh n. *al.* athchalaithe. As **aholl-ah**. 'The second cutting from a bog. I was standing on the ahollah"' LOS (w. Clare).

B

B'fhéidir sin phr. Also as **baithershin**. That could be. 'I could believe that, aye. B'fhéidir sin, all right' G (n.w. Donegal); G (s. Kilkenny); Gerald Griffin, *The Collegians* 39: 'Baithershin: the name of a dog' (Limerick).

Bá n. Affection. 'He had an old bá for you' MP (mid-Tipperary).

Báb n. 'A small baby, a doll' JL (w. Cork). diminutive **báibín** JM (w. Cork); DC (Galway); **bábóg** PD (s. Carlow); S (n.w. Donegal); **bábóigín** *CBD* (n. Kerry).

Bábhún n. As **bawn**. 1. A walled enclosure for cattle. Spenser, *State of Ireland:*'These round hills and square bawnes which ye see so strongly trenched and thrown up'; Jane Barlow, *Strangers at Lisconnel*: 'He built some superior sheds in the bawn to the bettering of his cattle's condition' (Connacht); Patk. Kennedy, *The Banks of the Boro*: 'Six of the twelve ... entered in the afternoon the bawn of Father James Murphy' (Wexford); Aubrey de Vere, *Innisfail*: 'I trailed a rose tree our grey bawn o'er' (Leinster); W.B. Yeats, *Fairy and Folk Tales of the Irish Peasantry*: 'The woman was on the bawn ditch' (Connacht). 2. The fortified yard or enclosure built around a castle of a country house as a defence for cattle against marauders. Charles James Lever, *Davenport Dunn*: 'Holding "in capite" from the king, with the condition that he builds a strong castle and a bawn' (Connacht).

Bac n. As **bock**. 1. 'The hob of a fire' G (n.w. Donegal). 2. 'A beam supporting the roof of a house. Common in old houses' Mac C (Monaghan).

Bac v. In form **bock**. To balk or hinder. 'He bocked me all the way' PON (n. Co. Dublin); 'Nothing would bock him' *BASJ* (Cavan).

Bacach adj. 1. Lame. 'He's bacach since the accident' JL (w. Cork); (Gen.). 2. Out of kilter. 'A bacach door is one that won't open or shut properly' H (n. Clare).

Bacach n. Also as **bocky**; **baccagh**. 1. 'A lame person' H (n. Clare); JL (w. Cork); RBB (Waterford); 'A lame person is called a bocky' PON (n. Dublin). 2. 'A tramp or other decrepit person' H (n. Clare); PB (s. Tipperary); JL (w. Cork); Wm. Carleton, *Phelim O'Toole's Courtship* 2, 199: 'who should be sthreelin' across the hill but an ould baccagh' (Tyrone). 2. 'An ignorant person, a boor' MS (e. Limerick); JL (w. Cork). 3. 'A churlish, mean person. Not lame' TOM (s. Tipperary). 4. 'A bacach: a horse suffering from lameness caused by laminitis' RBB (s. Kilkenny); PB (s. Tipperary).

Bacaide n. 1. (State of) being lame. As **bockedy, boghedy**. James Joyce, *Ulysses*, 243: 'Poor old bockedy Ben'; P. J. McCall, *Fenian Nights Entertainment* 84: 'I don't like the way she knocked poor boghedy Kyra Koun around'; ibid. 93: 'an used to be as boghedy as a night bee' (Wexford). 2. As **bocky**. 'A pet-name for a young pig' *CBE* 266 (mid-Tipperary).

Bacán n. Also as **bawcan, bowcaun, buckawn**. 1. 'A bawcan is a stick with which to make the hole for planting cabbages' FF (Monaghan); ER (Louth). 2. 'A bacán is a crook' G (n.w. Donegal). 'Buckawn, a hinge' PLH (n. Roscommon). 3. 'The amount of turf etc. one can carry in the crook of an arm is a bacán' S (n.w. Donegal). See *bacóg*. 4. 'A peg driven into the ground and used as a tether post' ER (Louth); 'Your bacán is sunk – you are pegged down, married' MG (n.w. Donegal). 5. 'A bowcaun is an L-shaped iron bar from which a door or pier of a gate is hung' OC (Monaghan); *CBE* 104 (Leitrim). 6. 'A bacán is the step of a spade' JL (w. Cork).

Bach interj. 'Said when calling pigs to food' *IG* (Kilkenny).

Bachall n. Also as **bahal**. Diminutive, **bachaillín**, as **boghaleen**. 1. 'A crozier, and by extension, a hooked nose, is a bahal' PC (n. Clare). 2. 'A bachall is a curl, a ringlet' RBB (s. Kilkenny). 3. 'A bachall is a beetle or pounder' MS (e. Limerick); *EASI* 243: 'boghaleen, from Irish **bachall**, a staff: a stick with a flat cross piece fastened at bottom for washing potatoes in a basket' (Limerick). See *croisín*. 4. 'Bachall, a knob on the head of a stick' *CBD* (n. Kerry).

Bachlóg n. 'The sprout which comes on potatoes in a pit, or is specially sprouted on seed potatoes before setting, to hasten their growth' *An Cho* (w. Mayo); MF (Westmeath); *CBE* 104 (Leitrim).

Bachram n. 1. 'Boisterous behaviour' RBB (s. Kilkenny). 2. 'A sudden downpour' NB (w. Limerick). 3. 'A thunder peal' DOH (e. Limerick).

Báchrán n. Bogbean, *menyanthes trifoliata*: MG (n.w. Donegal).

Bacla n. Bent arm; crook of arm. 'Bring in a bacla of turf' RBB (Waterford).

Bacóg n. An armful. 'The amount of turf, stones etc. that can be carried on one arm piled from the wrist to the shoulder' *CBE* 104 (Leitrim). [See *bacán*.]

Bácús n. As **baakooze**. *Poole* (s.e. Wexford): 'A room or house containing an oven; a bakehouse; a public bakery'. [< Old English *bacan* + *hus;* Middle English *bakhouse*.] 'A bakery' PD (s. Carlow).

Badán n. As **boodawn**. A tuft. 'The crop is in boodawn, we say about corn breaking into ear' D (Kildare).

Badara búidín n. As **boddera boodeen**. 'A blindfold fitted to a thieving cow'. S (s. Wexford).

Badhb n. As **bow**; **babow**. The banshee. 'Be in before dark or the babow will catch you' MF (Westmeath); 'You look like the bow. Comb your hair' D (s.e. Wexford). In compound **badhb chaointe**, in form **bocheentha** in Michael Banim, *Crohoor of the Billhook* 1, 64: 'The mournful wail of the bocheentha, come to predict the sudden death of himself, or of some dear member of his family' (Kilkenny).

Bágún n. Also as **bawkoon**, **bawgoon**. Bacon. 'There's nothing like the home-cured bágún' JL (w. Cork); 'Shandrum bawgoon' Crofton Croker, *Popular Songs of Ireland* (Cork); *Poole* (s.e. Wexford) 'bawkoon'.

Baic n. 1. A crook; a bend on an object. 'A person not standing erect would have a baic on him' H (n. Clare). 2. In phrase **baic talk**. 'Crooked, perverse reasoning' RBB (s. Kilkenny). 3. 'A kind of hurley' PB (s. Tipperary). 4. As **bwaig**. 'A person who is guaranteed to put his foot in his mouth every time he opens it' D (Wexford). [*baic-bhéarla*, a solecism, crooked reasoning Dinn.]

Baicle n. 'A band of people, such as a crowd of children' *IG* (Monaghan).

Baidhgín n. As **byegeen**. 'A wedge, a stopper. "Put a little byegeen in the hole in the gallon"' *CBE* 266 (mid-Tipperary).

Bail n. Success, prosperity, luck. 'There's no bail on him' *IG* (Kilkenny). In phrase **Bail ó Dhia ort**, prosperity from God on you. The usual answer is **an bhail chéanna ort**, the same prosperity to you. 'Considered by the older people as an incomplete blessing because the Blessed Virgin is not mentioned in it' NB (w. Limerick). In phrase **Bail ó Dhia oraibh** (plural), as **boloeeriv** in George Fitzmaurice, *The Pie-Dish* (Kerry): 'Bail ó Dhia oraibh is the greeting given to working men. Sometimes given as **Bail ó Dhia ar an obair**, God's blessing on the work' *An Cho* (w. Mayo).

Bailbó n. 'A person who has a large, foolish looking head' NB (w. Limerick).

Bailc n. Also as **balc**. 'A downpour, a sudden heavy shower' G (n.w. Donegal); 'The rain will be falling in balcs by now about Dunlewey' S (n.w. Donegal).

Baileabhair n. *al.* **bail odhar**. Also as **bau-liore, balyore, balour**. Hence **balourin', ballowrin'**. 1. 'A sorry plight; a state of frustration of helplessness. Note the proper usage: "You are in a bail odhar", or "this bail odhar is on you"' *An Cho* (w. Mayo). 2. In phrases 'You made a baileabhair of it', meaning you made a hash of it; 'You are an awful baileabhair', meaning an unmethodical bungler H (n. Clare); Wm. Carleton, *The Midnight Mass* 1, 328: '... the girsha's makin' a bauliore of herself' (Tyrone). 3. 'Balyore is an uproar, confusion' D (s.e. Wexford); Michael Banim, *The Croppy* 2, 112: '... there's no use balourin' this way'; Glossed as 'making a noise' (Kilkenny); 'You'd hear him ballowrin' in the Domhan Thoir' (q.v.) *CBE* 98 (Kilkenny).

Báinín n. As **bawneen, bauneen**. 'The term is applied loosely now to mean any garment knitted or woven from home-spun white thread e.g. báinín socks, báinín cap, báinín pullover. The proper use of the word in an earlier generation was the jacket of like material worn by a man' *An Cho* (w. Mayo); Somerville and Ross, *Lisheen Races, Second-hand* 77: 'Maybe you'll lend her the loan o' thim waders when she's rinsin' your bawneen in the river' (w. Cork); James Joyce, *Finnegans Wake* 394: '... slooping around in a bawneen and bath slipper ...' (Gen.). **Báinín brocach**: 'speckled homespun cloth' MG (n.w. Donegal).

Bainne n. Milk. In compounds **bainne géar**, sour milk; **bainne nua**, fresh, or new milk; **bainne ramhar**, thick or sour milk *CBD* (n. Kerry); **bainne buí**, yellow milk, beestings *CBE* 34 S (Galway).

Bainne-bó-bleacht n. Also as **bonny o block**. The primrose, *primula vulgaris*: MS (e. Limerick); NB (w. Limerick).

Bainseach n. As **bansha**. 'A small, stout girl' Mac C (Monaghan).

Báinseog n. Also as **bawnshuk**. 1. 'A green, a lawn' TB (Cavan). 2. 'A bunch of anything growing close and level on the top, such as a báinseog of shamrocks or a báinseog of potatoes' *IG* (Cavan); 'Potatoes in bloom. A bawnshuk of spuds' FF (Monaghan).

Bainsín n. 'A self-possessed young woman' RBB (Waterford).

Baintreach n. 'A widow' *CBD* (n. Kerry).

Báire n. Also as **baury, baura, baur-ya, bairy, baaree**. 'A báire is a goal in football. It is dying out since the introduction of the modern football, and the English terminology of goals and points' *IG* (Monaghan); *EASI* 214: 'baury, baura, baur-ya, bairy'; *Poole* (s.e. Wexford): 'Baaree: rod, barrier, a goal at the game of hurley'.

Bairín breac n. As **barnbrack, barney brack, barmbrack**. (Gen.). Speckled loaf. A loaf of bread with currants in it. 'The barnbracks were usually bought, not made at home, for some reason' PD (s. Carlow); 'We used to call them barney bracks' J (s.e. Wexford); James Joyce, *Clay* 110: 'The fire was nice and bright and on one of the side-tables were four very big barmbracks.'

Báirne n. Also as **barnyeh, baurna**. 'Any supernatural thing seen, a báirne' *CBE* 104 (Leitrim); 'My father often saw the barnyeh at the river' TB (Cavan); 'Look out for the baurna' AM (Leitrim).

Báirneach n. Also as **baurnagh, barneagh**. 1. A limpet. 'You can't beat báirneach soup'; 'You old báirneach eater' *CBD* (n. Kerry); 'You may wait till the barneaghs grow on you' H (n. Donegal); *Poole* (s.e. Wexford): 'baurnagh'. 2. 'A native of Kilkee, Co. Clare, as opposed to rúcach (q.v.), a summer visitor' PC (n. Clare).

Báirseach n. In forms **bawrshuch, bawshuk, barsa, barsaun**. A scolding woman, a shrew. 'Everybody can put manners on the báirseach except the man that's married to her' JL (w. Cork); PB (s. Tipperary); Patk. Kennedy, *Legendary Fictions of the Irish Celts* 250: 'I'll get you married to a tay-drinking bawrshuch of a woman' (Wexford); 'She was a ferocious bawshuk of a woman' D (s.e. Wexford); *EASI*: 'barsa, barsaun' (Kildare and Ulster).

Báisleach n. Rain. 'It looks like báisleach' FF (Monaghan); Con (Louth).

Baisleog n. *al.* **baiseog**. 'A splash of water. "Throw a baisleog on that apron and leave it out to dry"' *IG* (Monaghan); 'A baiseog, the full of your hand of water' *CBE* 104 (Leitrim).

Baitín n. Also as **bockeen**. 'A small stick. In compounds **baitín bréagach**, a trap-stick, part of a trap to catch birds; also known as **baitín trá**.' *CBD* (n. Kerry). As **bockeen** MF (Westmeath).

Balbh adj. 1. Dumb. JL (w. Cork). 2. Stammering, faltering in speech. 'He's very balbh, the poor man' *CBD* (n. Kerry). 3. 'Incoherent due to drink' H (n. Clare).

Balbhán n. Also as **ballawawn 1**. 'A dumb person' JL (w. Cork); Smy (n. Clare); J (s.e. Wexford). 2. 'In our inverted kind of charity we seldom use this of a person who is literally or permanently dumb; we keep it for those who are occasionally silent – especially if the silence is blameworthy. "Why didn't you speak up instead of sitting there of a balbhán." Note the idiom "of a balbhán"' *An Cho* (w. Mayo). 3. 'A prattler talking nonsense' MF (Westmeath). 4. 'A stutterer' H (n. Clare); *CBD* (n. Kerry); 'Ballawawn, a fool' PLH (n. Roscommon).

Balcaire n. 'A fine strong lump of a young fellow' JC (w. Cork); 'A strong, well-built man. "He's a right balcaire of a man"' *CBD* (n. Kerry).

Balcais n. Also as **bolkish** *pl.* **bolkishes**. 1. A rag; an untidy garment. 'You're not going to wear them bolkishes to mass, are you?' PD (s. Carlow); *IG* (Kilkenny). 2. 'A balcais is a person who wears ragged clothes' G (s. Kilkenny).

Balcaiseán n. As **bulkyshan**. Ragwort, *senecio* PON (n. Co. Dublin).

Balcán n. 'A short, strong block of a man or beast' JL (w. Cork).

Balctha pp. As **bolked**. Pressed down. 'The meadow is bolked from the floods' PD (s. Carlow).

Baldún n. 1. 'A tomcat' J (s.e. Wexford). 2. 'A man who acts like one' D (s.e. Wexford).

Ball odhar n. 1. A birthmark. 'They can do very little to remove those ball odhars, as far as I can see' PC (n. Clare). 2. 'A mess' *CBE* 34 S (Galway).

Ball séir' n. 'A person acting in a clowning fashion; e.g. he is making a ball séir of himself' MF (Westmeath); G (n.w. Donegal).

Ball seirce n. Place of love. Love spot; beauty spot. 'I like the television woman with the ball seirce on her cheek' JL (w. Cork).

Ballán n. Also as **byan**. Ballan wrasse. *Labrus bergylta*. 'A rock fish, speckled in colour' MC (w. Clare); 'A rock fish we called ballán or byan' S (n.w. Donegal).

Bámhar adj. 'Kindly, agreeable, generous. "He was a bámhar poor man, God rest him"' RBB (Waterford).

Bán adj., adv. Also as **bawn**. 1. White. (Gen.). 2. Fair-haired. 'Paddy Bán' (Gen.). 3. Hypocoristic: **Cailín bán > colleen bawn**, darling girl; James Joyce, *Finnegans Wake* 397: 'girleen bawn asthore ...' 4. Wild, crazy. 'He's gone clane bawn after her' Dee (Waterford).

Bán n. Also as **bawn**. 1. Lea; grassland. Seamus Heaney, *Wintering Out*: 'Not to speak of the furled/ consonants of lowlanders/ shuttling obstinately/ between bawn and mossland' (Derry); *CBD* (n. Kerry). 2. A herd of cattle. 'He has a fine bán of cattle' *CBD* (n. Kerry).

Bánaigh v. As **baany**. Caress. 'To rub softly and gently, and with the grain: as "to baany the poor cat"' *IG* (Monaghan).

Banbh n. As **bonive, bonham**. *dim.* **boneen, bonyeen**. 1. A piglet. J.M. Synge, *The Playboy of the Western World* 98: '... and shying clods against the visage of the stars he'd till put the fear of death into the banbhs and the screeching sows' C.J. Kickham, *Knocknagow*: 'Not a pig, not a bonive' (s. Tipperary); James Joyce, *Ulysses* 428: '... but in the convex mirror grin unstuck the the bonham eyes and fatchuck cheekchops of Jollypoldy the rixdix doldy';

Joyce, *Finnegans Wake* 105; Mrs S. C. Hall, *Irish Life And Character* 106: "'Boneen gra", she continued, addressing the animal' (Wexford); Charles James Lever, *Charles O' Malley*: 'What's that you have dragging there behind you? – A boneen, sir' (Connacht); A. Hume, *Characteristics of the People of Down and Antrim:* 'The boneens are squealing behind'; Emily Lawless, *Grania*: 'The relative number of cows, turkeys, feather-beds, boneens, black pots and the like ...' (Connacht); C. J. Kickham, *Knocknagow*: 'Phil carried a boneen under his arm' (s. Tipperary); Patk. Kennedy, *The Banks of the Boro*: 'Who owns the bonyeens, my brave boy?' (Wexford). 2. In card-playing: 'banbh is the Ace of Hearts' *CBD* (n. Kerry).

Banbhán n. 'A pig nearly two months old' G (n.w. Donegal).

Bandairne n. A disappointed person; one 'stood up' on a date. 'I hear she made a bandairne of you again' JL (w. Cork).

Banlámh n. A measure used at fairs by dealers in flannel, frieze, etc. [An Irish measure of two feet in length. Ash 1775; so Blount, *Law Dictionary* 1681; Cockeran, 1637: *Bannlámh*, a cubit; *O'Reilly: Bann* is the same word as band, string, rope, chain, measure of land, + *lámh*, hand *EDD*.]

Bannach n. As **bonnock**. Same word as Scottish bannock. 'A thick round cake made of oatmeal, baked on the clear turf coal.' As 'bonnock' *EDD* (Ulster).

Bannóg n. 'A cake of home-made bread' Mac C (Monaghan).

Bánóg n. As **banoge, bannoke**. 1. 'A bánóg is a green patch of ground' RBB (s. Kilkenny). 2. *EASI* 214: 'A dancing green, banoge', attributed to P.J. MacCall (Wexford). 3. A small, enclosed field. Ben Jonson, *The Irish Masque*: 'and vil runne t'rough fire, and vater for tee, ouer te bog and te bannoke ...'

Banráinteacht n. 'An expressive word for gibberish or senseless talk' *An Cho* (w. Mayo).

Baoth-ghlór n. 'Empty talk, foolish words. "That's all baoth-ghlór, I'm afraid. Sheer nonsense"' PB (s. Tipperary).

Barr n. 'A layer of uncut turf in a bog. "They got seven barrs out of that bank"' H (n. Clare).

Barr n. As **bar**. Addition, excess, special. Phrase *barr nuachta*, special news, used in attenuated form: 'Have you any big bars?' and 'Wait till I tell you the bar' M Nic M (Derry).

Barra brúcht n. phr. Profit, gain. 'The shopkeeper must have his barra brúcht out of it too' *CBD* (n. Kerry).

Barra bua n. phr. 'In phrase, "blowing your own barra bua": blowing you own trumpet' *CBD* (n. Kerry).

Barra corcáin n. phr. The top of the pot. 'The best of anything' *CBD* (n. Kerry).

Barra n. 1. 'A barrow' RBB (Waterford). 2. 'A wedge' NB (w. Limerick).

Barrach n. In form **borrach**. 1. Tow. In phrases, 'it would light like barrach'; 'he would light like barrach', meaning he is quick-tempered; 'I will give you barrach, meaning, I'll give you a hiding' H (n. Clare); Patk. Kennedy, *Legendary Fictions of The Irish Celts* 130: 'I don't care a wisp of borrach for your politeness' (Wexford). 2. 'Turf from the top spit of the bog. "They gathered in the barrach while it was still dry"' MC (e. Mayo).

Barraí n. 'An arrogant person, a bully' MF (Westmeath); 'A litigious person, a bully' *IG* (Meath).

Barraibín n. 'The toe cap of a boot' *CBE* 34 S (Galway). See *barraicín*.

Barraicín n. Also as **boorakeen**. 1. 'The top ridge of a stack of turf-that's the barraicín' JL (w. Cork); 'The top of a fence, or of a house' MC (e. Mayo). 2. A toe-cap. 'A barraicín in the backside would do him good' JL (w. Cork); *CBE* 104 (Leitrim); 'He hit the ball a boorakeen – a drive with the toe-cap' PD (s. Carlow). See *barraibín*.

Barrathóir n. 'A talkative person' NB (w. Limerick).

Barrdóg n. As **bardogue, bardoch.** 'A pannier with a removable bottom for carrying and depositing farmyard manure. is called a bardogue' O'K (Tyrone); FF (Cavan). 'An ass and bardoch' JB (s. Armagh & n. Louth).

Barrliobar n. 'Numbness of the fingers' CBD (n. Kerry).

Barróg n. 1. In form **brogue.** The dialectal accent used by the Irish when speaking English. George Farquhar, *The Twin Rivals*: 'Tho' this fellow travell'd the world over he would never lose his brogue nor his stomach'; John Durant Breval, *The Play is the Plot*: '... about thirty, and has very much of the brogue'; ibid. 'Arrah and is not the brogue upon your tongue Joy?'; Thomas Sheridan, *The Brave Irishman:* 'Capt: I am an Irishman. Sconse: An Irishman! Sir, I should not suspect that; you have not the least bit of the brogue about you. Capt: Brogue! No, my dear; I always wear shoes, only now and then when I have boots on.' [For a conjecture as to whether the English *brogue*, meaning an Irish accent, comes from *barróg* or from *bróg*, shoe, see G. Murphy, *Eigse* 3, 1941, 2.] 2. 'Sacking made from tow yarn' G (n.w. Donegal). 3. 'A hug, a squeeze' CBE 104 (Leitrim).

Barúil n. Opinion. In phrase **tá barúil agam,** I'm of the opinion. In Wm. Carleton, *The Poor Scholar* 2, 264: as **ta barlhum.** (Tyrone).

Bás gan sagart n. Literally, death without a priest. 'A cudgel used in faction fighting' PB (s. Tipperary).

Bas n. As **boss, bosh, baush, bash.** 1. The palm of the hand. 'I gave him a boss across the face' LB (s.w. Dublin). 2. The blade of a hurling stick; the part that strikes the ball (Gen.); 'Bosh is the face of a spade' D (s.e. Wexford); *Poole* (s.e. Wexford) 'bash, baushe).

Bás n. Death. 'A bird or beast that is sickly and looks close to death.' "Oh, he's a poor bás."' *IG* (Monaghan); 'Here used in refer-ence to a person of sickly appearance: 'He's gone in a bás."' CBE 266 (mid-Tipperary). Hence **básing.** "The hen is básing., meaning dying' Mas (mid-Tipperary).

Básán n. *al.* **básachán, basaí, básánaí, básálaí.** 'A sickly person or animal' CBD (n. Kerry). Variants common all over Munster.

Bastún n. In forms **bostoon, bosthoon.** A lout, a poltroon, a blockhead. James Joyce, *Grace* 181: '"Is this what we pay rates for?" he asked. "To feed and cloth these ignorant bostoons ..."'; Joyce, *Ulysses* 240: 'Some Tipperary bosthoon endangering the lives of the citizens'; Joyce, *Finnegans Wake* 273: 'Curragh macree, me bosthoon fiend' (Gen.).

Bata boilg 'A stick used to fasten a door on the inside when the door is not provided with a lock' *IG* (Kilkenny).

Batal n. As **bottle.** 'A bundle of hay or straw' OC (Monaghan).

Bathallach n. A hovel. 'Twas an old bathallach of a house' CBD (n. Kerry).

Bé léise n. 'A fat woman' *IG* (Kilkenny).

Beacán n. As **bocan.** 'A mushroom' MG (n.w. Donegal).

Beacán bearraigh n. As **bocan barra.** 'A bocan barra is a puffball' MG (n.w. Donegal); O'K (Tyrone); OC (Monaghan). See *beacán.*

Beada interj. Also **beadaí.** 'Call to geese, for food, etc. Repeated – beada! beada!' MF (Westmeath); 'beadaí' PB (s. Tipperary).

Beadaí n., adj. Also as **beddy.** 1. 'A fastidious person in the matter of food' PC (n. Clare); 'Breeding wives are aye beddy' Kelly, *Collected Proverbs* (Scotland); 1751; 'A menial servant who would reject food served up a second time, on the grounds that it was not considered good enough for him, would be considered beddy' *N&Q* (1878); 'A bed-rid or sick person is sometimes seized with an earnest longing for particular kinds of food; so that any person with such a longing is beddy' *UJA* (1859). 2. 'A woman you couldn't please' G (n.w. Donegal). 3. 'A person with a sweet tooth' PB (s. Tipperary). 4. 'A conceited, forward, self-sufficient person' *UJA* (1858); 'As beadaí as a duchess' S (n.w. Donegal). 5. 'A coaxer, a pet' *CBE* 266 (mid-Tipperary).

Beag adj. As **beg**. Little, not much. Anon., *Captain Thomas Stukeley*: 'Slawn lets Rorie beg' [for *slawn lets* see *slán*]; Seumus MacManus, *The Bend in the Road* 40: 'Small grass grows under his feet' < *Is beag féar a fhasann faoina chosa* = Not much grass. (Donegal).

Beag an mhaith n. Also as **beg a voh**. 'A useless person, one who is lazy or has no energy *IG* (Kilkenny); PB (s. Tipperary); 'Go away, you beg a voh' *CBE* 266 (mid-Tipperary).

Beagán rath ort interj. phr. Little luck on you! *CBD* (n. Kerry).

Béal bán phr. Literally, white mouth. Soft talk. 'All you'll get from them is the béal bán' JL (w. Cork. Gen.).

Béal bocht phr. In translated form **poor mouth**. 'Persistent complaint of poverty. "I'm tired of him and his béal bocht"' H (n. Clare); 'You'd think they hadn't a penny to their names, with the poor mouth they'd give you' PD (s. Carlow. Gen.).

Béal gan scoith phr. 'An over-communicative person' PB (s. Tipperary). [Literally, mouth without speech, utterance; an irony.]

Béal na céille phr. Literally, mouth of sense. 'A sensible, discreet talker' *IG* (Meath).

Béal scaoilte phr. Open mouthed, unable to keep a secret. 'She's nice, but unfortunately, béal scaoilte' H (n. Clare); 'She was a right oul' béal scaoilte' *CBD* (n. Kerry).

Béalóg n. 'A road-mouth leading to a strand' MC (w. Clare).

Bealtaine n. In form **Beltany**. The first of May; the beginning of Summer. 'Bunches of wood anemone are tied to a pole and left outside the door on May-eve for the Beltany, that's the Irish word' H (n. Donegal).

[For a description of this feast see Kevin Danaher, *The Year in Ireland*.]

Bean a' leanna n. In form **bannalanna**. Ale-woman; bar-maid. In phrase, 'He was as drunk as bean a' leanna' NB (w. Limerick); PB (s. Tipperary); *CBE* 98 (Kilkenny). James Joyce, *Finnegans Wake* 100: 'bannalanna'.

Bean a' tí n. As **vanithee, woman of the house**. Housewife. James Joyce, *Finnegans Wake* 220: 'woman of the house'; William Carleton, *The Poor Scholar* 2, 277: 'In the meantime, the good woman, or vanithee, had got the pot of water warmed ...' (Tyrone); Patk. Kennedy, *Legendary Fictions of the Irish Celts* 61: '... the Vanithee washed their feet' (Wexford).

Bean chaointe n. Keening woman. A professional who recited traditional praise poetry while weeping over the dead. 'She never stops complaining. She'd make a fortune as a bean chaointe a few years back' JL (w. Cork).

Bean sheoigh n. In form **beansho**. Literally, sporting woman. A loose woman. Patrick MacGill, *The Rat Pit* 4: 'I'm not the beanshee, I'm the beansho' (Donegal).

Bean sí n. In form **banshee**. Literally, woman of the fairies. A being whose wailing was thought to predict a death in Irish families. Maria Edgeworth, *Castle Rackrent* vol. iv. 8: 'I warned him that I heard the very banshee that my grandfather heard, under Sir P's window a few years before his death.' (Longford); W. B. Yeats, *Fairy and Folk Tales of the Irish Peasantry:* 'The banshee was heard keening around the house' (Connacht). See *badhb*.

Beannacht Dé orainn interj. As **banaght dhea orrin**. Wm. Carleton, *Phelim O'Toole's Courtship* 2, 202: '"Banaght dhea orrin!", he exclaimed, starting back; "the blessin' o' God be upon us!"' (Tyrone).

Beannacht leat interj. Literally, blessing with you. In forms **banaght lhath; banaght laght, ma bannaght laht, beanacht lath**. Wm. Carleton, *Going to Maynooth* 2, 142: 'banaght lhath'; Carleton, *Fardorougha*

The Miser 386: 'banaght laght'; ibid. 388: 'ma bannaght laht', my blessing with you (Tyrone); Patk. Kennedy, *Legendary Fictions of the Irish Celts* 44: 'beanacht lath' (Wexford).

Bearach n. 'A heifer' *CBE* 104 (Leitrim).

Bearad n. In forms **beriad, berrad, barrhad, bharradh**. Dimunitive **bearadán**. Lady Morgan, *The Wild Irish Girl* 140: 'I never wear my poor old grandfather's beriad but on the like occasions'; ibid. 141, footnote: 'A few years back, Hugh Dugan, a peasant of the County Kilkenny, who affected an ancient Irish dress, seldom appeared without his berrad' (Leinster); Wm. Carleton, *The Midnight Mass* 1, 356: 'Since the barrhad fits you, wear it ...'; Carleton, *Fardorougha the Miser* 273: ' "... what is the worst?" "The bharradh dhu", replied the man, alluding to the black cap which the judge puts on when passing sentence of death' (Tyrone); 'Bearadán is a dowdy old cap' Mac C (Monaghan).

Béaraí n. Tussle, struggle, contest. 'We'll have a béaraí with him again – said in reference to breaking in a colt' MF (Westmeath).

Bearna n. As **barna**. 1. A gap, breach. 'Put a bush in the barna' PC (n. Clare). 2. The pudendum of a cow. PJG (mid-Donegal).

Bearrthachán n. 1. 'A person with close-cropped hair' *CBD* (n. Kerry); JC (w. Cork). 2. 'A child who cries frequently' *CBD* (Kerry).

Beart n. Also in form **barth**; diminutives, **birteen, berkeen**. 1. A bundle. 'Bring the horse a beart of hay' MS (e. Limerick); *CBD* (n. Kerry); JL (w. Cork); *CBE* 266 (mid-Tipperary); (Gen.). 2. A big woman. 'A beart of a woman the full of your arms' H (n. Clare); *EASI* 214: 'barth'; 'A birteen of hay will do him no harm' C (Limerick); PD (s. Carlow); 'A berkeen of hay' MF (Westmeath).

Beathach n. 'A horse' TB (Cavan).

Béic n. A shout. 'He left an almighty béic out of him when he saw Dracula come in the window' C (Limerick; Gen.).

Béiceachán n. 1. 'A calf which is constantly looking for milk' *CBD* (n. Kerry). 2. 'A prematurely born calf' *CBD* (n. Kerry).

Beilisteáil n. Blabbing, boastful talk. 'All you'd ever hear from them is oul' beilisteáil' RBB (s. Kilkenny); AOL (mid-Waterford).

Béitín n. In form **bayteen**. 1. 'Grass and weeds burned to clear the tillage field. In the past the surface of boggy and hilly land was frequently burned so that the ashes would manure the land. A great deal of land was injured by this practice' *CBE* 266 (mid-Tipperary). 2. 'Grass withered by a heavy frost is called bayteen by the older people' FF (Cavan).

Bhicsín n. 'Vixen' *IG* (Kilkenny).

Bhrille-bhreaille n. Nonsensical talk. 'I never heard such bhrille bhreaille in all my life' PC (n. Clare).

Bí i do host! interj. Also in forms **bedahusht, bedhu husth, be dhe husth**. John Boyce, *Mary Lee, or The Yank in Ireland* 285: 'Whist, bedahusht, I say' (Donegal); Wm. Carleton, *Phelim O'Toole's Courtship* 2, 232: 'Bedhu husth, man!'; Carleton, *Fardorougha the Miser* 21: 'Be dhe husth, Vread' (Tyrone). [Vread= *a Bhríd*, (voc.), Brigid.]

Bia n. Food. 'A call to poultry – bia, bia! H (n. Clare); *IG* (Kilkenny); *CBD* (n. Kerry).

Biliúradh vb. n. 'Calling, ordering or arguing loudly and angrily, as a master to his servants' *IG* (Kilkenny). [Variant of *baile-abhair* ?]

Billeog n. 'A leaf' NB (w. Limerick).

Binneog n. Also as **binnogue**. 'A headscarf' *An Cho* (w. Mayo); Lady Morgan, *The Wild Irish Girl* 69: 'Binnogues: handkerchiefs lightly folded round their brows, and curiously fastened under the chin' (Leinster).

Bíodán n. Gossip, slander. 'Especially women's gossip' *An Cho* (w. Mayo).

Bíodh ciall agat interj phr. 'Have sense!' *CBD* (n. Kerry).

Bíodh sin ag Dia phr. 'Leave that to God; let's not pass judgement. "His wife goes out working and he stays at home and gets the meals. But bíodh sin ag Dia"' *An Cho* (w. Mayo).

Biolar n. 'Watercress' MG (n.w. Donegal).

Bíonn v. Reflected in **he does be**, a literal translation of the Irish habitual present of the verb to be – **bíonn**. James Joyce, *Grace* 174: I know you're a friend of his, not like the others he does be with'.

Bior n. Diminutives, **brawn, brawneen. 1.** 'Bior: pointed rod, iron spike, pin etc.' *Pe* (Wexford); 'Aren't you leaving things to chance, holding your skirt up with a little brawn?' MW (s. Wexford). **2.** Sharpness. 'The wind had the bior of the rain in it' OCn (Laois). **3.** A thin mouth. 'A pipe stuck in the bior by him' *CBD* (n. Kerry). **4.** 'Brawneen is a single stick of kindling' J (s.e. Wexford).

Biorach n. In form **birragh**. 'A muzzle-band with spikes on a calf's or colt's muzzle to prevent it sucking its mother' PD (s. Carlow).

Biuránach n. 'A young brat' NB (w. Limerick); 'A rogue, an untrustworthy person' *CBD* (n. Kerry); PB (s. Tipperary).

Biordóg n. 'A cow that doesn't give much milk' SOM (e. Kerry). [Cf. *biorach*, a heifer *Dinn.*]

Birín n. 'A piece of meat boiled on Shrove Tuesday, attached to the thatch with a sally rod, and eaten on Easter Sunday' MS (e. Limerick).

Bísí bogha n. A child's name for a tiny fish left stranded in a pool on the sea shore. 'I saw a child attempting to catch one. He slid his hand slowly into the water while he said: "Bísí, bísí bogha, come to me to-day and I will go to you to-morrow"' *CBD* (n. Kerry).

Bithiúnach n. In form **vehoon**; vocative, **a bhithiúnaigh**, as a **veehonee. 1.** 'A

scoundrel' JS (w. Kerry); JL (w. Cork); PB (s. Tipperary); Michael Banim, *Crohoor of the Billhook* 1, 20: 'Did you hear me spakin to you a vehoon grawna?' Glossed as 'ugly wretch' (Kilkenny); Wm. Carleton, *Phelim O'Toole's Courtship* 2, 232: **a veehonee** (Tyrone). **2.** 'The devil is sometimes called the Bithiúnach' DOC (Limerick).

Blabaire n. *al.* **blobaire. 1.** 'A braggart, or one who talks a lot. "He's an awful oul blabaire"' NB (w. Limerick). **2.** 'A stammerer' KB (e. Limerick).

Bladar n. As **blather. 1.** Smooth talk, cajolery, flattery. (Gen.). **2.** Talk for talk's sake. 'Ara, bladar!' – retort to a person who is talking nonsense' MF (Westmeath); J.M. Synge, *The Well of the Saints* 24: 'If it is can't you open the big slobbering mouth you have and say what way it'll be done, and not be making blather till the fall of night'; Eric Cross, *The Tailor and Ansty* 102: 'Hould your blather, you ould shtal, and drink it up' (w. Cork). Jane Barlow, *Kerrigan's Quality*: 'Jim Gallaher had been blatherin' about goin' after the macker'l' (Ulster). **3.** 'A person with too much talk' MS (e. Limerick). [< Old Norse *blaðra*, to talk indistinctly, to talk nonsense *EDD*.]

Bladaráil vb. n. As **bladaráling.** 'Talking in a nonsensical manner. "Stop you old bladaráiling."' *CBD* (n. Kerry).

Bladarálaí n. 'A person given to talking nonsense' *CBD* (n. Kerry).

Bladhmann n. Boasting, bombast. 'He'd deafen you with his bladhmann' H (n. Clare); *CBD* (n. Kerry).

Bladhmannach adj. **1.** Boastful, proud. *CBD* (n. Kerry). **2.** Deceptive. ' "It's very bladhmannach" – said about a rick of turf which is not as big as it appears' ibid.

Blaispínteacht n. '(Act of) nibbling at dainty foods' *An Cho* (w. Mayo). [Cf. *Blaistínteacht:* sipping, nibbling, testing by taste *Dinn.*]

Bláith adj. 'You'd call a beautiful young woman bláith' PD (s. Carlow); S (n.w.

Donegal). [Literary use: Smooth, delicate, beautiful *ODON.*]

Blas n. 1. Taste, flavour. 'You haven't a blas of sense' PC (n. Clare); 'I still have the blas of garlick on my breath' DOH (e. Limerick). 2. Accent, mode of pronunciation. 'He speaks Irish with a good blas' RBB (mid Waterford; Gen.).

Blastóg n. In forms **blasthogue, blastogue, blostogue.** 1. Flattery, delusive talk, blarney. Samuel Lover, *Legends and Stories of Ireland,* 201: 'He has a power of blasthogue about him'; 'I've heard too much of your blastogue a'ready' P.J. McCall (Wexford, *EDD).* 2. 'A blostogue is a woman who likes to flatter men' J (s.e. Wexford).

Bláth n. Luck, prosperity. '"God put bláth on your efforts." Used similarly in Donegal' *CBE* 104 (Leitrim).

Bláthach n. Also as **blagh.** 1. 'Buttermilk' *CBD* (n. Kerry); MG (n.w. Donegal); RBB (s. Kilkenny); JL (w. Cork). 2. Figurative, flower. 'He married the blagh of the family: the best looking' MG (n.w. Donegal). 3. Of articles: new or fresh appearance. 'He took the blagh off the new shirt by wearing it in bed' S (n.w. Donegal).

Bleachtán n. *al.* **bleachtóg.** As **blithan.** 'A milk-thistle or sow-thistle' OC (Monaghan); 'The bleachtóg or sow-thistle' *IG* (Monaghan).

Bleitheach n. 'A big, hefty fellow' H (n. Clare); 'A fat person' *CBE* 34 S (Galway).

Bligeárd n. 'A blackguard' NB (w. Limerick); JC (w. Cork); PC (n. Clare); (Gen. Munster).

Bliústar n. A fool; a simpleton. 'Good man yourself! Sending a bliústar on a man's errand' JL (w. Cork).

Bloc Nollag n. 'Block of Christmas. Yule Log' H (n. Clare); MJD (w. Cork).

Blogam n. A mouthful. 'Will you have a blogam of whiskey?' JC (w. Cork); NB (w. Limerick); JS (w. Kerry).

Blúire n. In form **blooreh.** A morsel. '"Mister, give us a blooreh of bread and a weeshy biteen of butter", said a tinker girl begging' *CBE* 266 (mid-Tipperary).

Bó interj. As vo. Alas! Gerald Griffin, *The Collegians* 50: 'Oh vo, vo, Eily, asthore, oh wirra, Eily!' (Limerick).

Bobailín n. 'A tuft, tassel; pompon' LOS (w. Clare)

Boc n. Diminutive, **boicín.** As **buck, buckeen.** 1. 'A well-to-do farmer; a young dandy' FF (Cavan, Monaghan). Hence **boc seó,** 'a man who shows off' JL (w. Cork); Patk. Kennedy, *Evenings in the Duffrey* 355: 'You half-sirs, or buckeens, or squireens' (Wexford). 2. 'A male goat' *CBE* 104 (Leitrim). [Early Irish *bocc;* Old English *bucca,* a he-goat; related to Old Norse *bukkr;* Old High German *bock.*]

Bocaí n. 'A ghost' *IG* (Cavan); 'A fairy' Con (Louth). See *bocán.*

Bocaileaidí n. 'A playboy, a wild man. "I'd say now that some of them pop-stars are right bocaileaidís"' Dee (w. Waterford).

Bocaire n. 'A cake of home-made bread' RBB (w. Waterford).

Bocán n. In form **bocaun.** 1. A goblin. A term of endearment. Wm. Carleton, *Going to Maynooth* 2, 153: 'Oh, you bocaun of the wide earth, to come home with a long face upon you, telling us that you were rejected ...' Carleton glosses the word in *Fardorougha the Miser* 366 as 'a soft, innocent fellow' (Tyrone). See *bocaí.* 2. 'A toadstool' McK (Leitrim).

Bochtán n. 1. 'A very poor person' NB (w. Limerick); *CBD* (n. Kerry). 2. 'A very mean person' *CBE* 266 (mid-Tipperary).

Bod a' bhóthair n. phr. 1. 'A churlish fellow' H (n. Clare). 2. 'A rural roué, Don Juan' DOC (Limerick). 3. 'It means the public ... Mrs Grundy; the man-in-the-street' *An Cho* (w. Mayo).

Bod a' ghlogair n. phr. In form **bud a glugger.** The yellow rattle, *rhinanthus* *minor.* 'Applied also to a good-for-nothing fellow and to poor hay' *CBE* 266 (mid-Tipperary). [Cf. *bodach glogair Dinn.*]

Bod n. Diminutive form **boidín**, as **budion**, **budjeen**. 1. 'Budion is a word for the penis' O'K (Tyrone). 2. 'Budjeen is a spike used in thatching' TB (Cavan).

Bodach n. In forms **boddagh**, **bodeaugh**, **buddogh**, **bodagh**, **badach**. Diminutive form **bodaichín**. 1. Boddagh, a churl, PLH (n. Roscommon); Anon., *Captain Thomas Stuckley*: The play has the phrase **bodeaugh breene**, rotten lout; Jonathan Swift, *A Dialogue in Hybernian Stile*: 'Why, a mere buddogh'; Charles Kickham, *Knocknagow* 353: 'To put himself in the way of being insulted by any old bodagh' (Tipperary); Seumus MacManus *Bold Blades of Donegal* 158: 'And when Magistrate Reddington ... demanded why he didn't touch his hat to him ... your grandfather hurled a bolt of Latin at the bodach, that nearly knocked him out of the saddle'; James Joyce, *Ulysses*, 320: '... badachs from the county Meath...' 2. One of the gentry. Wm. Carleton, *The Geography of an Irish Oath* 25 (footnote): 'The word is used in Ireland sometimes in a good and sometimes in a bad sense. For instance the peasantry will often say in allusion to some individual who may happen to be talked of, "Hut!, he's a dirty bodach"; but again, you may hear them use it in a sense directly the reverse of this; for instance, "He's a very decent man, and looks the bodagh entirely"; *Bodagh*, signifying churl, was applied originally as a term of reproach to the English settlers' (Tyrone); 'A miserable little bodaichín' JL (w. Cork).

Bodaire n. Plural **bodairí**, as **buddaree**. 'An ignorant, vulgar man. I've only heard the word applied to farmers' JS (e. Limerick); James Joyce, *Finnegans Wake* 100: 'buddaree.'

Bodalach n. 1. 'Part of calf's intestines hung up in chimney and kept for greasing boots' MS (e. Limerick). 2. A paunch. 'Look at the big bodalach on him' *CBD* (n. Kerry). 3. 'A big udder on a cow' *CBD* (n. Kerry). 4. 'A big, ungainly youngster' JPL (w. Cork); PB (s. Tipperary).

Bodarán n. A clumsy person. 'The poor bodarán can't get out of his own way' AM (Leitrim).

Bodhar adv. As **boorotie**, **bothered**. 1. Deaf. 'I'm a bit boorotie since I had the flu' TB (Cavan); James Joyce, *Ulysses* 262: 'To the door of the waitingroom came bald Pat, came bothered Pat'; 'Are you bothered, or what?' J (s.e. Wexford). [Cf. the Early Irish *bodar*. 'Amal nathracha bodra' is glossed as 'sicut aspides surdae' in the *Turin Glosses on St Mark*. See *R.I.A. Dictionary*] 2. Numb. 'My shoulder is bodhar with the rheumatism' PD (s. Carlow).

Bodhdán n. As **boudhawn**. 'A fool' PLH (n. Roscommon).

Bodhrán n. In forms **booran**, **booraan**. 1. 'A deaf person' McK (Leitrim); *CBE* 104 (Leitrim); 'Often applied to a heedless one. It is very often used in the second and third person singular as a sarcastic comment on someone who was called on for help and did not respond. "then I saw Tom walking in the road, but if I was to be shouting there yet, he wouldn't heed me. The bodhrán" *An Cho* (w. Mayo). 2. 'A bore' MP (mid Tipperary). 3. 'A fool' PLH (n. Roscommon). 4. 'A shallow vessel, similar in shape to a riddle, with goat-skin bottom, used for lifting oats' MF (Westmeath); Patk. Kennedy, *Legendary Fictions of the Irish Celts* 160: '... the fire is getting low. Take that booran out to the clamp, and bring in the full of it of turf'; Glossed as 'domestic article shaped like an over-grown tambourine' (Wexford). 5. A kind of tambourine used by traditional musicians (Gen.); *Poole* (s.e. Wexford): 'Booraan: a drum, tambourine'.

Bodóg n. 1. 'A heifer' MC (w. Clare); S Ua G (s. Tipperary). 2. 'A strongly built young woman, good for working' JL (w. Cork); S Ua G (s. Tipperary).

Bog n., adj. 1. Soft. Hence, wet place where peat, or turf, is cut (Gen.). 2. In translated form, **soft**. Tender, young. Mrs S. C. Hall, *Tales of Irish Life and Character* 210: 'The woman cuts and sets the pratees; the children are too soft to put a hand to anything' (s. Leinster); 'The children are too soft to go to school' JA (s. Wexford). 3. In term bog-spavin, 'a soft spavin on the front of a horse's hock' MM (e. Wicklow).

Bogadúradh n. (Act of) trifling, footling about. 'What bogadúradh have you anyway?' R (s. Galway). Hence **bogadoorin'** 'He never does a stroke of work, only bogadoorin' around all day' JG (Westmeath).

Bogaide n. 'A soft-made person' *IG* (Meath).

Bogha ceatha n. The rainbow JM (w. Cork). See *bogha síne*.

Bogha síne n. The rainbow DOH (e. Limerick). See *bogha ceatha*.

Boghaisín buí n. 'Ring around the moon' CBD (n. Kerry). [Alternatively **bogh síne buí**, yellow bow of the weather.]

Bogóg n. *al.* **bogán**, as **bogawn, bogan**. 'A bogóg is an egg without a shell; figuratively, a soft person intellectually' MC (e. Mayo); 'It's neither an egg nor a bogawn – neither one thing nor another' OCn (Laois); MS (e. Limerick); H (n. Clare); James Joyce, *Finnegans Wake* 198: 'bogans'.

Bogúrach adj. 'Soft and warm, as applied to clothing' *IG* (Meath).

Bóic n. 'A boastful person. "That bóic would give you the pip, with his "when I was in America"' RBB (s. Kilkenny).

Boilg n. 'A colic in calves' CBD (n. Kerry).

Boilsín n. 'Sirloin meat' *IG* (Meath).

Boinneán n. 'An ash plant' PB (s. Tipperary).

Bóirdréis n. 'A woman who dresses in the height of fashion, or what she thinks is the height of fashion' JL (w. Cork).

Bóisteálaí n. 'A boaster' DOC (Limerick).

Boiteán n. In form **batten**. 'A small bundle of straw' Mac C (Monaghan).

Bóithreán n. As **bowshawn**. 'Dried cowdung, formerly used as fuel' *Pe* (Wexford); RBB (s. Kilkenny, Waterford); PB (s. Tipperary); 'I was often sent gathering bowshawns when I was young' OCn (Laois); MS (e. Limerick).

Bóithrín n. In forms **bosheen, boreen, bohereen**. Wm. Carleton, *Going To Maynooth*, 2, 142: 'I see somebody... ridin' down the upper end of Tim Marly's boreen' (Gen.); John Banim, *Crohoor of the Billhook* 1, 185: 'I went down the bosheen yesterday' (Kilkenny); J. M. Synge, *The Playboy of the Western World* 111: 'She's in the boreen making game of Shaneen Keogh'; M. J. Mulloy, *The King of Friday's Men* 94: 'There's no road or boreen but has enemies his father scolded' (Galway); James Joyce, *Ulysses* 445: '... while in the boreens and green lanes the colleens with their swains strolled'; Somerville and Ross, *Put Down One and Carry Two* 405: 'What it took me to was, as might been forseen on any Co. Cork bohereen, a pole jammed across it from wall to wall and reinforced by furze bushes' (w. Cork); 'They say that the bosheen is haunted' FM (Wexford); 'The cows are in the bosheen' G (Kilkenny); 'I must mend the pot-holes in the bóithrín' JL (w. Cork). See *bóthar*.

Bóitseach n. Diminutive, **bóitseachán**. 1. 'A dressed up fellow, perhaps overdressed; a swank' H (n. Clare). 2. 'A sturdy, thick-set person' CBE 266 (mid-Tipperary); PB (s. Tipperary).

Bolastar n. 1. 'A big, hefty lout' MKN (Wexford); Ham (e. Clare); RBB (s. Kilkenny). 2. 'A strong, stout child or a lusty young animal' CBE 266 (mid-Tipperary).

Bolg n. Belly; stomach. Appears to mean anger in Michael and John Banim, *John Doe* 148: '... what bolg is on you now, Black Jack?' (Kilkenny). [Cf. Latin *stomachari*, to be angry.]

Bolg le gréin phr. Also in form **bullagh lea greehan**. Belly to the sun. Sunbathing. 'Summertime is the time for bolg le gréin' MC (e. Mayo); JL (w. Cork); Michael Banim, *The Croppy*, 1, 284: 'playing, as the Irish term it, bullagh lea greehan. Glossed as 'breast to the sun' (Kilkenny).

Bolg mór n. 'Applied to a corpulent person' *CBE* 104 (Leitrim).

Bolg uisce n. Water-bag, 'which precedes the birth of a calf' *CBE* 104 (Leitrim).

Bolgadán n. 1. 'A fat man with a large paunch' DOC (Limerick); LOS (w. Clare); AG (s. Tipperary). 2. The puff-ball fungus, *Lycoperdon* C (e. Limerick).

Bolgán béice n. 1. Puff-ball *CBD* (n. Kerry). 2. (Of a person) 'A windbag' JL (w. Cork).

Bolgshnáth n. As **bollog snaw**. 'The belly thread of a herring. Supposed to do injury and cause terrible thirst if eaten' *CBE* 266 (mid-Tipperary).

Bollán n. 'A large round boulder' PC (n. Clare).

Bolscaire n. In form **bolsker**. 'An unfriendly person' D (s.e. Wexford).

Bomannach n. 'A person given to boasting about himself, his relations, etc.' Mac C (Monaghan).

Bonn n. Bottom, depths. In phrase, 'he cried ó bhonn'. From the depths, with sincerity NB (w. Limerick)

Bonnbhallaibh n. pl. 'Stone bruises in children's feet' *CBE* 104 (Leitrim). See *bonnbhualadh; bonnleac*.

Bonnbhualadh n. 'A stone bruise that festers on the sole of the foot' IG (Meath). See *bonnleac, bonnbhallaibh*.

Bonndalán n. 'A stout person. "He married a small bonndalán of a woman"' JL (w. Cork).

Bonnleac n. In form **bownlock; bine-lock**. 'Bonnleac: a callus on the sole of the foot' *CBD* (n. Kerry); PB (s. Tipperary); MS (e. Limerick); *EASI 222:* 'bownlock; bine-lock'. See *bonnbhallaibh, bonnbhualadh*.

Bonnóg n. 1. 'A sudden leap, a jump' PB (s. Tipperary).

Bonnsach n. 1. A rod, a sapling. 'What the hooligan needs is frequent applications of a bonnsach across the ass' JL (w. Cork). 2. 'A strapping young girl' NB (w. Limerick).

Bórach adj. Diminutive, **bóraichín**, n., as **boarakeen**. 'Bandy, bow-legged' BOD (s.w. Cork); JH (Limerick) 'A little boarakeen of a man, built like a champion jockey' JL (w. Cork).

Bóraic n. 'A piece of timber used to fasten a spancel' NB (w. Limerick).

Bord a stracadh phr. Literally, to tear the table. 'We had bord a stracadh: everyone for himself eating at the table' *CBD* (n. Kerry).

Borr n. 'A lump. "A hardy borr of a man"' Mac C (Monaghan).

Borraic n. Also in form **borick**. 'A borraic – a home-made hurling ball' JL (w. Cork); *EASI* 220: 'A borick: a small wooden ball used by boys in hurling or goaling, when the proper leather-covered ball is not at hand'.

Bos n. 'A pad of hay or straw used by colliers to protect the shoulders and knees in the Arigna mines' *CBE* 104 (Leitrim).

Bosach adj. 'Flat-footed. Curiously another school of Louisburgh interpretation would say that bosach means bow-legged, but dictionaries give *bórach* (q.v.) as the proper term for this' *An Cho* (w. Mayo).

Bosachán n. 'A flat-footed person' *An Cho* (w. Mayo). See *bosach*.

Botán n. 'A small bundle of straw' IG (Cavan).

Bothán deataigh n. A cabin of smoke. 'A small, low house, always full of smoke' *CBD* (n. Kerry).

Bothán n. 'A cabin, a hovel' MJD (w. Cork); (Gen.). See *bothóg*.

Bothánaí n. 'A person who spends a lot of time in neighbours' houses, gossiping' *CBD* (n. Kerry).

Bothántacht n. (Act of) 'Visiting cabins for gossip' *CBE* 266 (mid-Tipperary); 'Bothántacht is a thing of the past around here' RBB (s. Kilkenny).

Bóthar n. In forms **batter, boker, bater, boagher. 1.** A road. 'I'd better be hittin' the batter for Sligo' PG (s. Donegal); 'There used to be a boker between here and the churchyard' MW (s. Wexford); *Poole* (s.e. Wexford): 'Bater: 'A lane leading to a high road. Boagher: a road; Mucha boagher, a big or high road'. **2.** 'In the phrase **on the batter**, meaning, not on the beer, but on the go, active, out and about. The opposite is **off the batter**. She's not keeping very well. "She's been off the batter these three weeks"' O'K (Tyrone). **3.** Phr., **an bóthar amach**, the road out. '"He gave him the bóthar amach" – he sent him packing' CBD (n. Kerry). See *bóthairín*.

Bothóg n. A cabin, hovel. Peadar O'Donnell *Adrigoole* 79: 'to pay rent for a bothog' (Donegal). See *bothán*.

Botún n. **1.** A mistake. 'He pulled across him with the hurl, and that was a grave botún' PC (n. Clare); PON (n. Dublin); CBD (n. Kerry); AG (s. Tipperary). **2.** 'An unfledged bird' IG (Kilkenny).

Brabach n. Surplus. 'Full and plenty and something over; something to spare. "Have you enough there? I have, and brabach"' H (n. Clare).

Brabhsach adj. 'Jovial, merry' CBD (n. Kerry).

Brablach n. In form **brablagh**. Rubbish, rabble. '"If the brablagh of the country would leave Johnny alone"' Mac C (Monaghan). *See rablach*.

Bráca n. **1.** In form **brake**. 'A double harrow. You would need a pair of horses to pull it' G (n.w. Donegal). **2.** 'A bráca is a very small house' NB (w. Limerick).

Bracach adj. 'Pock-marked' IG (Monaghan).

Bracálaí n. 'A rough, awkward person' NB (w. Limerick); 'A hard-working man. It is sometimes implied that his work is slovenly' CBD (n. Kerry).

Brach n. 'Matter formed on the eyes after sleep' CBD (n. Kerry).

Brachadh n. In form **braw**. 'Matter discharged from a sore or boil' BASJ (Cavan).

Brachán n. In form **brochan**. 'Thick oatmeal porridge' G (n.w. Donegal); 'There is a saying, "never bless brochan", i.e. brochan is not worth saying grace for' EDD (N. Ireland). **2.** 'Applied only to very thin porridge, contemptuously' MF (Westmeath).

Bradach adj. In form **bradagh, braddy**. Thieving. 'That bradach bitch of a cow is in the cornfield again' JL (w. Cork); 'A bradagh cow is a thieving cow' OC (Monaghan); 'In the Listowel district of north Kerry this word has been corrupted into *braddy*, used as an adjective, as, for instance, a braddy cow. One also hears of a braddy moon, meaning a very bright moonlit night when an animal given to wandering is, as it were, facilitated by the moon's brightness' Lys (n. Kerry); NB (w. Limerick).

Braebaire n. 'An insolent person. "The judge gave that braebaire his come-uppance"' RBB (w. Waterford).

Brágadán n. **1.** 'A cow with long horns' PC (Clare). **2.** 'An old yellow cow' NB (w. Limerick).

Braidhleog n. In form **brylogue**. 'A small branch, a twig' CBE 266 (mid-Tipperary).

Brais n. In form **brash. 1.** A bout, a turn at some activity. A turn at churning. 'It was unlucky to leave a house without taking a brash' OC (Monaghan). **2.** 'A brais of sickness' MF (Westmeath). **3.** In comp. **water brash**. EASI 223: 'Severe acidity of the stomach with a flow of watery saliva from the mouth' (Munster).

Braiste n. 'Cockle, or wild mustard' CBE 34 S (Galway).

Bramaire n. **1.** 'A farter' JL (w. Cork). **2.** 'A boaster; a bumptious, officious person' RBB (s. Kilkenny); CBE 266 (mid-Tipperary). **3.**

'A big, strong fellow' H (n. Clare); NB (w. Limerick); PB (s. Tipperary).

Bramalach n. Rubbish. 'Their garden is a pile of bramalach, full of weeds, hedge cuttings and similar rubbish' O'K (Tyrone).

Branar n. Broken lea, grassland. Figuratively, 'hard work, excellently done. "He made branar altogether"' RBB (n. Waterford); *CBD* (n. Kerry); JL (w. Cork); PB (s. Tipperary). **2.** A row, ruction. 'There was branar when he heard about it' *CBD* (n. Kerry).

Braon n. Diminutive, **braoinín**. A drop. 'Will you have a braon?' JL (w. Cork); 'Let me put a braoinín of water in that' D (Kildare). In phrase, **droch bhraon**, translated as **bad drop**. Bad breeding, bad blood. 'He has the droch bhraon in him' JL (w. Cork); William Carleton, *The Poor Scholar:* 'They always had the bad drop in them' (Tyrone); Samuel Lover, *Rory O'More* 234: 'The dhirty dhrop was in her'.

Brat n. **1.** A swathe of hay *CBD* (n. Kerry). **2.** A cloak. Hence **brat ceatha**, rain cloak *CBD* (n. Kerry). Diminutive, **bratóg.** 'A covering put over a ewe's quarters to prevent a ram from covering her' PJG (mid-Donegal). **3.** 'A number of bags sewn together and put under corn when threshing' *CBE* 47 S (Galway). **4.** A film on the eye. 'She has a brat on the eye this while back' G (s. Kilkenny); RBB (w. Waterford), who has note in *Seana-Chaint na nDéise 2*: 'See *R.I.A. Dict.* s.v. 3. (Col. 143), the relevant excerpt being from a medical MS (O'Grady Cat. 229) in which hare's blood is prescribed as a cure for this eye condition'. **5.** 'A snowflake' PJG (mid-Donegal).

Bratach n. 'Green scum on water ina boghole' H (n. Clare).

Brath n. In forms **brock, broch.** Dependence. 'He's no great brock: he can't be depended on' *CBE* 266 (mid-Tipperary). 'The phrase, **maith an brath,** a good standby, one who can be depended on, in form **smock-a-brock** This is heard only in a sarcastic vein, and carrying the idea that the person in question is untrustworthy"'

CBE 266 (mid-Tipperary). Hence **broching.** "He was broching on getting a lift" – depending on it' TOM (s. Tipperary).

Bráthair n. 'A big, rough fellow' *CBD* (n. Kerry).

Brathal n. 'An untidy person' *IG* (Cavan).

Breá adj. In form **braw.** Fine, handsome. 'That's a fine braw colt' PJG (mid-Donegal).

Breá breá n. Literally, lovely, lovely. **1.** 'A dandy, a fop' *IG* (Meath). **2.** A plaything. 'She's only a breá breá by him' JL (w. Cork).

Breac adj., n. In forms **brack, brackies, bracked, brackit, brackly. 1.** A mark or blemish. 'I bought it at an auction and there wasn't a brack on it' AG (s. Tipperary); James Joyce, *Ulysses* 358: 'Three and eleven she paid for those stockings ... and there wasn't a brack on them and that was what he was looking at ...' **2.** 'Brackies are mountain sheep. I think they are called that because they are often breac, speckled or dappled' MG (n.w. Donegal). **3.** 'Bracked means speckled. Applied to cattle, also to shins bracked from the fire' MF (Westmeath); *IG* (Monaghan). 'Her legs were brackit from sitting too close to the fire' NB (w. Limerick); 'Brackly: Traces left by the heat of the fire on legs and arms' PLH (n. Roscommon).

Breacast n. *al.* **brucaist.** Breakfast. 'They eat potatoes for breacast' RBB (w. Waterford). 'What's for brucaist?' JC (w. Cork).

Bréagán n. 'A toy, plaything' *CBD* (n. Kerry).

Breall n. Diminutive, **breallán,** in form **brallion. 1.** 'A stupid, blundering gamall' (q.v.) JL (w. Cork); RBB (s. Kilkenny, Waterford); PB (s. Tipperary); Dermot O'Byrne, *Children of the Hills* 85: 'So he rigs himself out like an old breallan of a tramp' (Donegal); 'A brallion is a stupid person who is bone lazy, a good for nothing oaf. A hugely contemptuous term' O'K (Tyrone); McK (Leitrim). **2.** 'A gloomy look on a person's face. "Such a breall as he had on him"' *CBD* (Kerry). 3. 'A six months old bull calf' *CBE* 104 (Leitrim).

Breicíní n. As **breckins**. 'Freckles' G (s. Kilkenny).

Bréidín n. In form **braygeen**. 'A fold of hay to which the súgán (q. v.) is tied at the foot of the haycock' TOM (s. Tipperary).

Breill n. A pout; a moue. 'Look at the breill on her. She's trying to make up to him' PC (n. Clare); NB (w. Limerick).

Breillic n. 1. A lout. 'You could expect nothing else from that ill-bred breillic' MS (e. Limerick); *CBD* (Kerry). 2. A fool. 'Whisht, you brellic of a fool' JL (w. Cork); *IG* (Kilkenny).

Breillis breaillis n. 'Nonsensical talk' *CBD* (Kerry).

Breisin n. 'An armful, especially an armful of turf. An average breisin is the amount of turf put on the open fire at each fixing during the day. Hay, straw or grass is never taken in breisins; but one quotation does add to the description: "The spuds are so big with us that we're picking them in breisins"' *An Cho* (w. Mayo). [May be related to *breis*: sometimes = a great deal *Dinn*]

Brian breá n. The purple loostrife, *Lythrum salicaria* PJG (mid-Donegal).

Brian óg n. In form **breen ogue**. 1. 'A young scamp. A wild young fellow like myself' PJG (mid-Donegal). 2. An eligible young man. John Boyce, *Shandy Maguire*, 325: 'But bedad, sir, it wasn't so when I was a breen ogue an' that same's a good feck i' years ago' (Donegal).

Bríc n. Diminutive, **brícín**. 'A loaf of shop bread' RBB (s. Kilkenny); 'A loaf of bread' PB (s. Tipperary); 'Brícín is a little loaf' NB (w. Limerick).

Brícín n. Diminutive of **breac**, trout. 'A tiny fish found in streams. A pinkeen' AG (s. Tipperary); DOH (e. Limerick). See *pincín*, *lúóg*.

Bricne coll. n. In form **brickens**. 'Freckles' TB (Cavan).

Brídeog n. In form **breedogue**. 1. Ceremonial image of St Brigid (Gen.). 2. 'Rush cross made and placed in the rafters on St Brigid's Eve' PC (n. Clare). 3. 'A band of masked roisterers in fancy dress who appear uninvited at weddings and make mischief. "There was a breedogue at the wedding last night"' OCn (Laois).

Bríleach n. 'Old rotted timber' *CBD* (Kerry). [Cf. *briseach Dinn.*]

Briollán n. In forms **brillauns**, **brill-yauns**. 'Old clothes, furniture, bits and pieces of farmyard implements regarded as rubbish' RBB (s. Kilkenny); GC (Laois, n. Kilkenny); *EASI*: 'Applied to poor articles of furniture in a peasant's cottage'; 'Dick O'Brien and Mary Clancy are getting married as soon as they can gather up a few brill-yauns of furniture' (s.e. Leinster).

Bríomhar adj. Lively. 'Isn't she a fine, bríomhar little girl, God bless her' MS (e. Limerick).

Briosc adj. 'Brittle, easily broken' *CBD* (Kerry).

Briosclán n. Silverweed, *Potentilla anserina*. 'The bulbous root of silverweed, used as food' *IG* (Meath); Mac C (Monaghan); *CBD* (Kerry).

Brioscóg n. As **brisgogue**. Sream. 'Brisgogues on the eyes after a heavy sleep' MF (Westmeath).

Briotach adv. Also in form **britagh**. (Of speech) Brokenly, with a lisp, or a stammer. 'He's very briotach in his speech' JL (w. Cork); 'He speaks very britagh' LB (s.w. Dublin).

Bró n. A quern, millstone. 'If you hit him on the head with a bró he wouldn't wake up' JL (w. Cork).

Brobh n. A straw, a stem of grass. 'A little brobh of a woman. A puff of wind would blow her down' G (s. Kilkenny).

Broc n. In form **brock**. **1.** A badger (Gen.) [Old English *brock*. Shakespeare, *Twelfth Night*: 'Marry, hang thee, brock!'] **2.** A ruck. 'A few hurlers rooting for the ball were said to be in a broc' H (n. Clare); 'We went out for a broc' Smy (n. Clare); 'When set dancing takes place in small Clare kitchens, it is common practice for a new set of four to broc the incumbents out off the floor and take their place' Smy (n. Clare). **3.** Refuse, rubbish. Hence 'A rambling speech in which the speaker ploughs his way from one irrelevant matter to the next. A listener might say of this, he was talking a lot of aul' brock' MG (n.w. Donegal); 'Refuse; leftovers such as bruised potatoes given to fowl after dinner' Mac C (Monaghan); *CBE* 104 (Leitrim).

Brocach adj. In form **brockled**. 'Pockmarked' Mac C (Monaghan).

Brocaigh n. In form **brockey 1.** 'A badger's sett' PJG (mid-Donegal). **2.** 'A word for bed when speaking to children' MG (n.w. Donegal).

Brocais n. **1.** 'A fat, gluttonous person' *IG* (Kilkenny); SH (Kerry). **2.** 'A strong, heavy child' PB (s. Tipperary).

Bróg n. In forms **brogue, broge**. Diminutive, **bróigín**, as **brogueeen**. A shoe, boot. Shakespeare, *Cymbeline*: 'My clouted brogues'; Anon., *Purgatorium Hibernicum*: 'I scorn dee, as dirt of me brogue'; Patk. Kennedy, *Evenings in the Duffrey* 291: 'De brogues matched so bad wud the coat' (Wexford); Charles Kickham, *Knocknagow* 283: 'The row of nails he had driven into the toe of his brogue' (s. Tipperary); Anon., *The Pretender's Exercise*: ' She vas go lame since she loose her too fore broge'; Jane Barlow, *Kerrigan's Quality* 105: 'Iligint little high-heeled brogueens' (Ulster). Hence **brogue leather**. Jonah Barrington, *Personal Sketches*: 'Tis me that tans the brogue leather' (Leinster).

Brógadán n. 'A big, heavy cow' *CBD* (Kerry).

Broghach adj. *al.* **bróch**. 'Said of a person. "He's very broghach"' MC (e. Mayo); 'An adjective expressing dislike for a person, i. e.

John bróch. This word is very common in Arigna' *CBE* 104 (Leitrim.)

Broghais n. Also in form **proush**. **1.** 'A fat, lifeless person' JL (w. Cork); *CBD* (Kerry). **2.** 'A big, fat woman' RBB (s. Kilkenny); NB (w. Limerick). **3.** 'A broghais is a dirty, untidy person. Called proush here' *CBE* 266 (mid-Tipperary). **4.** 'The placenta of an animal' RBB (s. Kilkenny).

Broigheall n. The cormorant. *Phalacrocorax carbo* MC (w. Clare).

Broim n. 'A fart' JL (w. Cork); RBB (w. Waterford).

Broimfhéar n. Couch grass, scutch, *Agropyron junceiforme*. 'We'll have to get rid of the broimfhéar before we sow any spuds there' JL (w. Cork).

Bróis n. In form **brose**. **1.** 'A food prepared by pouring boiling water over oatmeal. Special Shrove Tuesday dish: Two or three hens boiled in a pot – the soup poured on a dish of oatmeal – stirred – left over for an hour or two and then eaten' Tr (Donegal). **2.** Figuratively, 'a mess, a job done badly'. 'He made a bróis of it' MG (n.w. Donegal). **3.** Broth. 'In a brose of sweat – bathed in sweat' Tr (Donegal). [Cf. Middle English *browes*, Old French, *broez*, broth.]

Bromach n. **1.** 'A colt' JM (w. Cork); MC (e. Mayo). **2.** 'A strong young man; a youngster feeling his oats' JL (w. Cork); MC (e. Mayo). **3.** 'An awkward young man' S (n.w. Donegal).

Brón n. Grief. 'There is not a brón on her – said of a widow who showed no grief after her husband' MF (Westmeath); *CBD* (Kerry); TOM (s. Tipperary).

Brónach adj. Sorrowful. 'I felt very brónach after they'd left' PB (s. Tipperary).

Broscaire n. **1.** 'Debris; broken turf' C (Limerick). **2.** 'A boastful person' NB (w. Limerick).

Broscán n. 'A heap of fragments' Fin (Mayo).

Brosna n. In forms **brasna, brishna, brois-nín, bresna**. 'Brasna are small dry sticks for lighting the fire with' G (n.w. Donegal); 'She's out gathering brishna for the fire' JS (e. Kerry); 'Bits of broisnín to light the fire' *CBE* 47 S (Galway); Patk. Kennedy, *The Fireside Stories of Ireland* 105: 'A special good bresna of boughs from the forest' (Wexford). See *brus*.

Brothall báistí n. phr. 'The heat that precedes rainfall' *CBD* (Kerry).

Brothall n. 1. (Of weather) Heat. 'There's great brothall in it, thank God' JL (w. Cork). 2. High spirits. Usually of a horse. 'He is full of brothall'; 'There is great bro-thall on him' PC (n. Clare); Ham (e. Clare).

Bruach n. In forms **broo, brough, bruth**. 1. Bank of river, lake. 'The broo gave way and I fell in' G (n.w. Donegal); 'The broo is steep at that point' O'K (Tyrone); 'The bruth of the river' Mac C (Monaghan). 2. *EASI* 226: 'Broo: the edge of a potato ridge along which cabbages are planted' Mac C (Monaghan). 3. *EASI* 226: 'Brough: 'a ring or halo around the moon. It is Irish *bruach*, border'.

Brúcht n. 'A belch' PC (n. Clare).

Brúchtail vb. n. Belching. 'Did you hear the brúchtail of him?' JPL (w. Cork); H (n. Clare).

Brúideáil vb. n. In form **brúideáiling**. Smouldering. 'The fire is only brúideáiling' *CBD* (n. Kerry).

Bruilleam n. A fight, row, commotion. 'He started a bruilleam' MF (Westmeath).

Bruíontach adj. 'Given to fighting or causing rows' *CBD* (n. Kerry).

Brúisc n. 'A lout' PC (n. Clare).

Bruith-bruith n. 'Child's victuals made of boiled white bread and sugar' *IG* (Meath). [*bruith*, act of boiling, cooking *Dinn*.]

Bruithneog n. In form **brunoge**. *EASI* 226: 'A little batch of potatoes roasted in a fire made in the potato field at digging time:

always dry, floury and palatable' (Ros-common). [See *bruith*.]

Brúitín n. In forms **bruteen, brutheen**. 1. Mashed potatoes mixed with butter and onions. 'Bruteen and butter – Irish cheer at old-time weddings. Not much heard of now' H (n. Donegal). 2. A state of confusion; a mess. William Carleton, *The Lianhan Shee* 1,137: 'Squire D's haggard was in such brutheen' (Tyrone).

Brus n. In forms **brish, brishe, briss**. Broken fragments, as small sticks; broken, crumbled bits, dust. Patk. Kennedy, *The Banks of the Boro* 216: 'She let go the saucer ... and down it came ... and was made brishe of in a minute' (Wexford); 'He made briss of the cup' D (s. e Wexford); 'Briss is more refined than brish' *EDD*, quoting P. J. McCall (Wexford).

Bruscar n. Fragments, smithereens. 'It is often applied to the offals of bread and other food which remains after a big meal. In this exact sense it is the word used to describe the fragments of the loaves and fishes in the Gospel. Turf that is not carefully spread becomes bruscar. But perhaps the two most engaging usages of the word are: "All the money I have is five single notes and a couple of shillings of bruscar"; and " Give the men the work to do; and leave the little jobs to the brúscar of children"' *An Cho* (w. Mayo); (Gen. Munster).

Bruth n. In form **bruff**. 'A storm; a heavy sea' PJG (mid-Donegal).

Bruth fá thír n. Sea wrack. 'Something washed ashore. It refers not to seaweed, sea-rods, or such natural growth, but to such things as timber, rubber, barrels of oil or other fuel, which occasionally are washed on to the shore, especially (or our shores) in a west wind. The clear or coloured glass balls-floats for fishing nets (which have been collected on the shore and used as ornaments) are good examples of bruth fá thír' *An Cho* (w. Mayo).

Bruthóg n. 'Roast potatoes' *CBE* 266 (mid-Tipperary).

Bú muc n. In form **bummuck**. The bluebell
or wild hyacinth, *Scilla nutans*: PJG (mid-
Donegal).

Buachaill n. In forms **bouchal, buchel**.
Diminutive, **buachaillín**, as **bouchaleen**.
A boy, a young man. 19th c. ballad, *The
Croppy Boy*: 'To a stranger bouchal I pray
you tell, Is the priest at home ar may he be
seen?'; James Joyce, *Finnegans Wake* 314:
'bouchal'; ibid. 314. Sometimes used in a
derogatory sense. Michael Banim, *Crohoor of
the Billhook* 1,18: 'He looked like the old
bouchal himself (the devil) in the middle of
his own place' (Kilkenny); Wm. Carleton,
Phelim O'Toole's Courtship 2, 199: ' "My
bouchaleen dhas," says he – "my beautiful
boy"...' (Tyrone); Somerville and Ross,
Owneen the Sprat 284: 'Wake up, me
bouchaleen'. **Buachaill bán**, translated as
**fair-haired boy, white-haired boy,
white-headed boy**: the favourite. Sean
O'Casey, *Cock-a-Doodle-Dandy* 147: 'It's
made you a Councillor, a Justice of the
Peace, an' th' fair-haired boy of th' clergy';
Lennox Robinson, *The White-headed Boy* –
title of play. (Cork). **Buachaill báire**,
'rogue, prime-boy' LOS (w. Clare).
Buachaill bréige, 'a bush set in a ditch to
close a gap' *CBD* (n. Kerry); 'A beggar
dressed in straw at a wedding' *IG* (Cavan).

Buachalán n. Also in forms **buachladán,
bólán, boholawn, boouchelawn**. Ragwort,
Senecio Jacoboea. Also known as **buachalán
buí** (Gen.) 'Ragwort is known as bólán' OC
(Monaghan); Jane Barlow, *Lisconnel:* 'And
he about the height of a sizable boholawn'
(Connacht); Poole (s.e. Wexford): 'Boouchelawn'. 'Buachladán is the name given to the
ragworth around Rossmore' AG (s. Tipperary).

Buaic n. 'The top ridge in thatching' KB (e.
Limerick).

Buaiceas n. 1. 'A wick in a candle or oil
lamp' JC (w. Cork). 2. 'A piece of cloth
used to protect the hands while lifting hot
pots etc' *CBD* (n. Kerry)

Buaile n., v. In form **booley**. 1. Milking place
in summer pasturage. *EASI* 220: 'A temporary settlement in the grassy uplands where
the people of the adjacent lowland village
lived during the summer with their cattle,
and milked them and made butter, returning
in autumn – cattle and all – to their lowland
farms to take up the crops'. 2. Used as a
verb also – 'In the summer they used to
booley the cows on the slopes of Brandon
and Mount Leinster' PD (s. Carlow).

Buaileam sciath n. Also as **boulamskeech**.
Literally, let us beat (our) shield. A
braggart. 'There's not much to that fellow,
all talk and no action; an oul' buaileam
sciath' MS (e. Limerick); JL (w. Cork);
CBD (n. Kerry); PB (s. Tipperary); Michael
Banim, *Crohoor of the Billhook* 1, 91: 'the
rustic boulamskeech, whose glory was
gathered by fighting at fairs and patterns,
and drinking inordinate potations of bad
beer, in hedge ale-houses.' A footnote says
'Boulamskeech: Some perversion now
prevails of the use of this word. Its ancient
meaning was fine-shield striker; its present
we have gleaned above' (Kilkenny).

Buailte v. pp. In translated form, **sthruck**.
Mrs S. C. Hall, *Irish Life and Character* 88:
'Sure if I was sthruck, what would keep me
from it?' *Sthruck* glossed by author as 'fell
ill' (s. Leinster).

Buailte amach phr. In translated form **bet
out, beaten out**. 'Extremely tired, exhausted' (Gen. Munster).

Buailteán n. In forms **boltchan, buailtín,
booltin, bóilcín, bolteen, boolkeen**. 1.
The striking part of a flail. ' "There's no
need to hold the buailteán over him: he's
willing enough" – said about a workman'
CBD (n. Kerry); 'boltchan' OC (Monaghan);
'Boolkeen' MF (Westmeath); MS (e. Limerick); 'booltin' JB (s. Armagh; n. Louth);
IG (Cavan): 'bóilcín'. *EDD* (s. Leinster):
'bolteen'. 2. A boulder. 'A big buailteán of a
stone' *CBD* (n. Kerry).

Buailteog n. 'A strong, heavy stick' NB (w.
Limerick)

Buaircín n. 'A piece of stick tied to the nose
of a calf to keep it from the cow' *CBD* (n.
Kerry).

Bualach n. 'A large stone' *CBD* (n. Kerry).

Bualadh bas phr. *al.* **bualadh baise.** 1. (Act of) clapping, applauding. 'Give him a bualadh bas' JL (w. Cork). 2. A beating. 'You'll get bualadh bas from your mother when you get home' *CBD* (n. Kerry); 'Bualadh baise is a game played by the open hands of different persons, placing one hand over another; the hand underneath to be taken out and placed on top. This is done quickly, and anyone making a mistake loses the game and drops out' *IG* (Meath).

Bualadh bata phr. In form **bulliah battha.** Literally, a stroke of a cudgel. Figuratively, a faction fighter. Wm. Carleton, *The Battle of the Factions*, 1, 116: 'He was a powerful bulliah battha in his day, and never met a man able to fight him' (Tyrone).

Bualadh bóthair n. In form **bullia batter.** Literally, a road fight. 'A loud, generalised row that suddenly flares up in a market place or at some such gathering and which is characterised by much noise, dire threats and general mayhem as the circle of participants widens and everyone pitches in. Who, or what, began the bullia-batter is soon forgotten, and in any case irrelevant. One remarkable characteristic of such affrays is that hardly anyone suffers the least physical injury' O'K (Tyrone).

Buarach n. Also as **boragh.** 'A spancel put on a cow being milked' RBB (w. Waterford); JL (w. Cork); Wm. Carleton, *The Midnight Mass* 1, 327 (footnote): 'Boragh: The rope with which a cow is tied in the cow-house' (Tyrone). [< Irish *bó*, cow; Middle Irish *árach*, a tie, binding.]

Búdán n. 'The inside of a cow's horn' *CBD* (n. Kerry).

Buí adj. In form **bwee.** Sallow-complexioned. George Fitzmaurice, *The King of the Barna Men*: 'Donacha Bwee'; 'Cormackeen bwee O'Rourke' (Kerry).

Buicinis n. 'A slovenly-dressed woman. "You'd think she could afford a new dress, the buicinis"' JL (w. Cork).

Buidheach adj. In form **boogh.** Little, tiny. Anon., *Captain Thomas Stukeley*: '... fan we sall be let in at the lettle booygh dore by the abbay'

Builín n. A small cake; a bun. 'We got tea and a few sweet builíns' JM (w. Cork); *CBD* (n. Kerry).

Builín bán n. In forms **boully bawn, bouilly bread, bully bread.** White, homemade bread of wheaten flour, as distinguished from that made with meal. Patk. Kennedy,*The Banks of the Boro:* 'boully bawn' (Wexford); *EASI* 222: As **bouilly bread** and **bully bread** (Wexford).

Buille fé thuairim n. phr. A guess, guesswork. 'There's an acre and a half in it – but that's only a buille fé thuairim' JL (w. Cork); *CBD* (n. Kerry).

Buimiléir n. 'A bumbler; an unhandy workman' Mac C (Tyrone).

Buinne n. Also as **bunnya.** 'The top fringe of a wicker basket or cliabh. The buinne is the hardest part of the cliabh to make' *CBD* (n. Kerry); 'A border or wale on a creel' PLH (n. Roscommon).

Buinneach n. 'Diarrhoea' JL (w. Cork); NB (w. Limerick).

Buinneog n. 'A sudden jump, or plunge.' 'He made a buinneog at me' MF (Westmeath).

Buíochas le Dia interj. Thanks be to God! JL (w. Cork); *CBD* (n. Kerry); Smy (n. Clare).

Búiste n. 1. 'A big, lazy person' *CBD* (n. Kerry); JL (w. Cork). 2. 'An uncouth person; unsociable, uncommunicating, unrefined' *An Cho* (w. Mayo); D (Kildare).

Bulla bogha n. An awkward worker. 'He's some bulla bogha. He put more paint on the floor than he did on the doors I asked him to paint' G (s. Kilkenny); PD (s. Carlow).

Bullabáisín n. Whirligig, revolving motion. 'He went round in a bulla báisín. 'In children's rhyme: "Round a bulla báisín, round Tom Dáisín", recited as they go round in a circle with hands joined' MF (Westmeath); 'My head is in a bullabáisín with you all. Shut up!' C (Limerick); *CBD* (n. Kerry); PB (s. Tipperary); PC (n. Clare).

Bullán n. 'A bullock' MS (e. Limerick); *CBD* (n. Kerry).

Bun n. Bottom, base. Diminutive, **bunán**. 1. A stump. 'The scut of a rabbit' G (n.w. Donegal). 2. *Pe* (Wexford) 'the stem of a plant'; *EDD* (citing P. J. MacCall): 'He hot me wid a cabbage bun' (Wexford); 'Used only in the phrase **cabbage bun**, the part of a head of cabbage where the head meets the stalk' LB (s.w. Dublin); 'A bunán is a cabbage root' JB (s. Armagh & n. Louth).

Bun-ós-cionn adj. Upside down. Awry. 'Things are gone completely bun-ós-cionn with him' PC (Clare).

Bun rua n. In form **bunarua**. 'Light, yellow earth' NB (w. Limerick).

Buncán n. 'A welt on the skin; a hard lump of flesh on any part of the body' *CBE* 104 (Leitrim).

Bundún n. 1. 'The buttocks, hindquarters' MS (e. Limerick); S (s. Wexford); *CBD* (n. Kerry); 'He put out his bundún working = he nearly killed himself' NB (w. Limerick). 2. 'That portion of prolapsed flesh or shin beneath the body of a goose and which corresponds roughly to the dewlap on bovine animals' *An Cho* (w. Mayo). 3. 'An awkward person or implement' MF (Westmeath). 4. 'In our (Louisburgh) language it is often applied to a blunderer, someone who has "flopped" in an undertaking' *An Cho* (w. Mayo). 5. 'A silly person' NB (w. Limerick).

Bundúnaí n. In form **bundie**. 'A bundúnaí is a useless person' RBB (w. Waterford); as 'bundie' *Patterson* (Antrim, Down).

Bunóc n. 'An infant' RBB (s. Kilkenny); NB (w. Limerick); *CBD* (n. Kerry); JC (w. Cork).

Bunóg n. 1. A snack. 'A light meal such as that taken to people working in a bog in summer' MG (n.w. Donegal). 2. 'A sudden start, a jump. "He gave a great bunóg"' *CBE* 266 (mid-Tipperary).

Búraig n. 'A big fire' NB (w. Limerick).

Búrdáil n. A beating. 'He got a right búrdáil' Smy (n. Clare).

Búrdún n. 'A bit of gossip about the neighbours' MS (e. Limerick); 'Always carrying burdúns' *CBD* (n. Kerry). Hence **burdúnaí**, a gossip; **burdúning**, gossiping. 'Women burdúning around the fire' *CBD* (n. Kerry).

C

Cab n. Mouth. 'Mind your cab' PD (s. Carlow).

Cábóg n. 'An ignorant fool of a man' D (s.e. Wexford); G (s. Kilkenny).

Caincín n. 'The nose, especially a snub nose' JL (w. Cork); AG (s. Tipperary); RBB (w. Waterford).

Cáipéis n. A document. 'He had a bagful of cáipéises with him. You'd think he was a judge or something' JH (Limerick).

Caipín n. In form **capeen**. A cap. Patk. Kennedy, *Legendary Fictions of the Irish Celts* 168: '... you are in a strange place without your capeen dearg'.

Cáipis n. A fault, a crime. 'So my ram got in among your sheep. That's no cáipis in me' PJG (mid-Donegal).

Cairde n. Credit; additional time to pay a debt. 'The bank wouldn't give the likes of that boyo cairde' JL (w. Cork).

Cairdeas Críost(a) n. In form **chordius chreete**. A godparent. Michael Banim, *Crohoor of the Billhook* 1, 99: 'Give me your hand, Jack; Dhar law ma chordius chreete! but I'll have a hearty shake at it...' Banim's gloss: 'By the hand of my gossip! a common asseveration among the oldfolk' (Kilkenny).

Cáireábó n. Clamour. Loud noise. 'You should have heard the cáireábó they made when the goal was disallowed' PC (n. Clare).

Cáirín n. 'A smile, but a certain kind of smile. The precise meaning is a little mouth, so it entails a suggestion of a smirk. A cáirín is a smile in which one purses the lips, inhales gently through the nose, and allows a slight, complacent lowering of the eyelids. You compliment a country girl on a cup of tea by saying that she should open a café:

her mother informs you that Kathleen *is* manageress of a leading London restaurant. And then the mother has a cáirín!' *An Cho* (w. Mayo).

Cairiún n. 1. 'A garron, a nag' PD (s. Carlow). 2. 'A lesbian' JL (w. Cork).

Caiscín n. 1. 'Home-made brown bread. It really means the bread baked from home-grown wheat brought to the mill to be ground' *An Cho* (w. Mayo). 2. 'A small bag of wheat for the mill' *CBE* 34 S (Galway).

Caise púca n. 'A fungus resembling a mushroom.' *Calvatia gigantea* MF (Westmeath).

Caiseal n. In form **cashel**. 1. 'An ancient stone fort' MJD (w. Cork; Gen.). 2. 'A clamp of turf sods' R (s. Galway).

Cáisín n. 'The upper part of a churn' *CBE* 104 (Leitrim).

Caisirnín n. A knot or ravel in thread. 'The thread was all caisirníns' *CBD* (n. Kerry).

Caistín n. 'A puny, bad-tempered person. "She is a bad-tempered little caistín"' JL (w. Cork); PB (s. Tipperary).

Cáiteach n. A covering sheet. 'Put a cáiteach over that pile of potatoes' H (n. Clare).

Cáitín n. 'A bag net' *CBD* (n. Kerry).

Cáitín rua n. Literally, Red Kate. Whiskey. 'Enough Cáitín rua to rise my misneach' *CBD* (n. Kerry).

Cál ceannann n. In forms **colcannon**, **kanekannon, kailkannon**. 'Colcannon is a mixture of boiled potatoes, chopped leeks and kale' J (s.e. Wexford; Gen.); James Joyce, *Finnegans Wake* 28: 'kanekannan'; ibid. 456: 'kailkannon'. [< English *kale*, coleworth or cabbage < Old Norse *kal*, a cabbage. *Ceanann*: speckled with white.]

Calán n. 'A pail' *IG* (Kilkenny).

Calcaide n. 'Griddle-baked, doughy bread that doesn't rise like that baked in an oven – "Tis only old calcaide"' *CBD* (n. Kerry).

Caldar n. 'A big pounder of a man or woman' JL (w. Cork); RBB (w. Waterford).

Call n. **1.** Right, claim. Mr and Mrs S. C. Hall, *Ireland, Its Scenery and Character* 1, 205: '... his name is on many a thing he has no call to'; J. M. Synge, *The Well of the Saints* 53: 'She's no call to mind what way I look ...'; ibid. 70: 'You've no call to be talking, for I've heard tell you're as blind as myself'. **2.** Need, occasion. *EASI* 230: 'I have a good call to shout, and that blackguard running away with my apples'. **3.** Relationship. 'They have no call to each another' JL (w. Cork).

Callaire n. **1.** A female scold. 'I don't know how he puts up with that callaire of a wife he have. Nag, nag, nag, from morning till night' JL (w. Cork). **2.** 'A wicked person' NB (w. Limerick).

Cam adj. Crooked. Hence *Poole* (s.e. Wexford) **cambaute**, 'a crooked stick'. [< *cam* + *bata*, stick]. Wm. Carleton, *Shane Fadh's Wedding* 1, 52: 'Beal cam ...' Glossed, correctly, as 'crooked mouth'.

Cam reilige n. phr. As **reel foot**. 'A crooked leg, thought to be induced in pregnancy by walking on graves' *CBE* 98 (Kilkenny). [*cam* + *reilige*, genitive of *reilig*, grave.]

Cam sceabhach adj. phr. In form **cam-scagh**. Contrary, bad-tempered. 'Thon's a camscagh wee man' PJG (mid-Donegal). [*cam* + *sceabhach*, askew.]

Camán n. In forms **comman, commaun, common**. 'Camán is the stick used in the game of hurling' MS (e. Limerick); Ham (e. Clare); *Poole* (s.e. Wexford): 'Comman, commaun: a curved stick used in the game of common, a game resembling hockey'; 'Common: a hurley stick' Mac C (Monaghan). See *camóg*.

Cámar n. A blemish. '"There wasn't a cámar on him.", he wasn't troubled' OCn (Laois).

Camarún n. 'An ignorant person' *IG* (Kilkenny).

Cámas n. Haughtiness. 'She was full of cámas' *CBD* (n. Kerry).

Camharlán n. 'A helpless young family' NB (w. Limerick).

Camóg 1. 'A hurling stick' PB (s. Tipperary); *CBE* 34 S (Galway). See *camán*. **2.** 'A walking stick' *CBE* 47 S (Galway).

Camógaíocht n. In form **camogie**. A form of hurling played by women (Gen.).

Cana n. In form **kana**. A pup, whelp. Anon., *Captain Thomas Stukeley*: '... thou feete lieured kana'. [*Feete* = white.]

Cancrán n. As **ounkran**. A cantankerous person. 'I'm afraid I couldn't deal with that cancrán' JPL (w. Cork). Patk. Kennedy, *Legendary Fictions of the Irish Celts* 102: '... the little ounkran never once thanked them for all the trouble they were taking for him' (Wexford).

Candam n. A part or share of something. 'I got my candam of it' *CBD* (n. Kerry). [< Latin *quantum*.]

Canna crúite n. In form **canna crowta**. 'A milking can' *CBE* 34 S (Galway).

Canrán n. Grumble. 'Stop your old canrán for me' *CBD* (n. Kerry); PB (s. Tipperary).

Canránaí n. 'A grumbler' *CBE* 266 (mid-Tipperary). Hence **canráning**, grumbling' H (n. Clare); NB (w. Limerick); *CBD* (n. Kerry).

Cantal n. Peevishness, crankiness. 'It is also the name given to a habitually cranky person. In the third person, usually!' *An Cho* (w. Mayo).

Cantalach adj. Peevish, contrary, bad-humoured. 'She's a cantalach old cailleach' H (n. Clare); *An Cho* (w. Mayo); *CBE* 47 S (Galway).

Caochánaí n. 'A near-sighted person' *CBE* 266 (mid-Tipperary).

Caochrán n. 'A small clod of turf' *CBE* 104 (Leitrim).

Caoi caoch interj. 'Peep! Said when playing with a child' *CBD* (n. Kerry).

Caoineadh n. In forms **caoine, keen, keenie, caoining, keening.** 1. Lamentation for the dead. Wm. Carleton, *Sir Turlough, or The Churchyard Bride* 15: 'The keen is loud, it comes again' (Tyrone); Patk. Kennedy, *The Banks of the Boro*, 269: 'The name has been enshrined in the caoine of a poor woman' (Wexford). 2. Hence **caoining, keening.** Crying, wailing over a corpse. Patk. Kennedy, *Evenings in the Duffrey*, 83: 'At that time the custom of caoining was still in force' (Wexford); Seamus MacManus, *In Chimney Corners* 190: '... an' both of them keening and ochoning'; MacManus, *Bold Blades of Donegal* 207: 'Three white-capped old mountain women bent over a recently-made mound grave. They were paying their tribute in a soft and gentle caoining'. Hence **keener,** a person who performs the traditional caoineadh over the dead. Eric Cross, *The Tailor and Ansty* 87: '"When a man was dead, the first thing they would do would be to send for the keeners. They were a class of people who would come to the wake, and make a recitation about the man, and kick up the hell of a noise. It was the most pitiful noise in the world. They would tell what manner of person the dead man was; how he lived and how he died, and you would hear them bawl and cry until you thought that the last day had come. If they were not fairly paid, they would dispraise the dead man. They would cut him down to dirt"' (w. Cork); Samuel Lover, *Legends and Stories of Ireland* 2, 360: " I never seen anything finer than a keener at a berrin' (Munster); Jonah Barrington, *Personal Sketches* 2, v: 'Whilst the keeners were washing and stretching the corpse' (Leinster).

Caoinreoirín n. 'A little pet, be it a child or an animal' NB (w. Limerick).

Caointeachán n. In form **keenthecaun.** Act of crying, wailing. 'I'm sick to death of listening to her ladyship's caointeachán all night' JC (w. Cork). Michael Banim, *Crohoor of the Billhook* 1, 2: 'the keenthecaun, or funeral wail ...'; ibid. 1, 252: '... an irregular and dismal song, uttered in many an unequal dhass, (recte *dreas*, q.v.) or verse, his keenthecaun' (Kilkenny).

Caoirliún n. 'A tall man' *IG* (Kilkenny). [Cf. *caoirle*, a reed *Dinn.*]

Caolfhód n. 'The narrow sod turned up by the plough to clear the furrow; the last sod ploughed down the centre of a garden' MS (e. Limerick). [A garden is a potato field.]

Caológ n. In form **keelog.** Water pipit, *Anthus spinoletta spinoletta* TB (Cavan).

Caonach n. 'Moss' (w. Cork); 'The name is applied to the green moss of an unused well' *An Cho* (w. Mayo).

Caonach liath n. In form **keenagh-lee.** 'The fungus which appears on old food is called caonach liath, grey mildew' *An Cho* (w. Mayo); *EASI* 279: 'keenagh-lee' (West and North-West).

Caora aitinn n. The dwarf juniper, *juniperus nana* PJG (mid-Donegal).

Caora bhrocach n. Grey sheep *CBE* 104 (Leitrim).

Caora interj. As **keerie.** 'This is what a sheepman calls to stray sheep: "keerie, keerie!"' PJG (mid-Donegal).

Caorthann n. As **carhan, kitty keeran.** The rowan tree, *Pyrus aucuparia* PJG (mid-Donegal); PD (s. Carlow). 'Caorthann usually called kitty keeran' MF (Westmeath).

Capall corrach n. Also as **copull-hurrish.** 'The game of see-saw we called capall corrach' S (n.w. Donegal). A. Hume, *Irish Dialect* 23 (Down): ' Playing coppul-hurrish with a plank placed over a large stone'. See *cogaltaigh corraigh.*

Capall n. In form **capill.** Diminutive, **capaillín,** as **copalleen.** 1. 'Capill, a horse' JB (s. Armagh & n. Louth); James Joyce, *Ulysses* 423: 'Hand as give me the jady coppaleen'. 2. 'An inedible mushroom' *CBD* (n. Kerry).

Cár n. 'A sneer, grimace of the mouth, often accompanied by a contemptuous gesture' LB (s.w. Dublin); *IG* (Monaghan). Hence **carring**, making a wry face. 'What are you carring at?' MF (Westmeath).

Cár gáirí n. In form **cargary**. A grin. 'He put his cargary on him' – he began to laugh' H (n. Donegal).

Cara mo chroí phr. As **curragh machree**, James Joyce, *Finnegans Wake* 273.

Cara n. A friend. 'We're only caras' *CBE* 266 (mid-Tipperary). See *a chara*.

Caradán n. 'A thin skelper of a boy' PD (s. Carlow). 'A charmer' FF (Cavan).

Caraidh n. In form **corry**. 1. 'A fishing weir in a lake or river' PJG (Donegal). 2. 'A causeway of boulders or stepping stones across a river' G (n.w. Donegal).

Carcas n. 'A marsh' *CBD* (n. Kerry).

Carn n. Also in form **cairn**. A heap. 'That's a fine carn of turnips' Mac C (Monaghan); PB (s. Tipperary); Seamus Heaney, *Wintering Out* 21: '... and gathering stones off the ploughing/ to raise a small cairn'.

Carrach adj. 'Scabby' (referring to potatoes)' MC (e. Mayo).

Carrachán n. 1. 'A small, gnarled fellow. "He's a tough little carrachán"' H (n. Clare). 2. 'An elf-like child' DOH (e. Limerick); 'That precocious kind of child who is so old-fashioned that you would love to pinch him if his mother wasn't looking' *An Cho* (w. Mayo). 3. 'A mitcher' *CBE* 34 S (Galway). 4. 'A mangy dog' JPL (w. Cork).

Carraig n. As **carrick**. A rock. (Gen.). Hence **cargies**, 'rocky fields' JB (n. Louth & s. Armagh.)

Carraigín n. As **carrigeen** in **carrigeen moss**, *chondrus crispus*, an edible seaweed. ['An English term derived from Carraheen

near Waterford' *Dinn.* More probably < *carraigín*, little rock.]

Cársán n. Hoarseness; a wheezing in the chest. 'Honey would be good for that cársán you have' PD (s. Carlow), *IG* (Meath); *JFK* (Mayo).

Cartán n. As **cartan**. 'A tick found on sheep' PJG (mid-Donegal).

Cartóg n. 1. 'Crab apple' *CBE* 98 (Kilkenny). 2. 'Stale bread' (ibid).

Cás n. Case. *EASI* 232: 'Case: The Irish *cás*, and applied in the same way. "It is a poor case that I have to pay for your extravagance." *Nach dubhach bocht an cás bheith ag titim le grá:* "isn't it a poor case to be failing through love" – Old Irish Song. Our dialectal Irish case, as above, is taken straight from the Irish *cás;* but this and the standard English *case* are both borrowed from Latin.'

Cas n. 'A seat made from súgáns' (q.v.) OCn (Laois).

Cas siar n. *al.* **caith siarach**. 1. 'Reclaimed land, such as a drained bog' PC (n. Clare). 2. 'Tillage land allowed to return to grass' *Pe* (Wexford); *IG* (Kilkenny). 'Caith siarach' PB (s. Tipperary).

Casacht n. A cough. Hence **casacht a' reilig**, a cough that presages death. **Casacht an chapaill**, horse cough. **Casacht bog**, soft cough. **Casacht cruaidh**, hard cough *CBD* (n. Kerry).

Casán n. In forms **casan, cashin**. A path. Peadar O'Donnell, *The Knife* 194: 'She has no right to be making a casan over our land' (Donegal); Patrick MacGill, *The Rat Pit* 95: 'The soft cashin wound on' (Donegal).

Casla n. In form **caslagh**. 1. 'A small harbour or creek' PC (n. Clare). 2. 'The sea strand' PC (n. Clare). 3. Low-lying rough ground, especially near the sea. Peadar O'Donnell, *Islanders*, 221: 'She was driving up the ducks from the caslagh' (Donegal).

Casna n. A morsel. 'Shame on her! Not a casna in the house to feed the boyeen' MJD (w. Cork).

Casóg n. 'A jacket' JPL (w. Cork); *CBE* 104 (Leitrim); *CBE* 34 S (Galway).

Casrachán n. 'A coarse-mannered person' *IG* (Kilkenny).

Castóir n. 1. 'An implement used in ringing pigs' MS (e. Limerick); *CBD* (n. Kerry); PB (s. Tipperary). 2. 'A person who habitually insults people' *CBD* (n. Kerry). Diminutive, **castóirín**, 'a twister. A little crank of a person' NB (w. Limerick); *CBD* (n. Kerry).

Cat n. Cat. As **cutch**. 'Only in vocative, when chasing away a cat' MF (Westmeath.

Cat breac n. In form **Cath Breac**. A Bible reader, a proselytising agent. < *Leabhar na gCat Breac*, literally, the book of the speckled cats: 'the proselytising agent, often a fiddler, gathered the people into his house to dance and then entered them into his book as converts' Tr (Donegal); Patrick MacGill, *Glenmornan* 99: 'He had been a Cath Breac in his young days' (Donegal); 'A cat breac is a pervert' S Ua G (s. Tipperary).

Cat caoch n. Literally, blind cat. Hypocrisy. 'You'll get plenty of the oul' cat caoch from that one' FF (Cavan); *IG* (Monaghan).

Catach adj. Also as **kotha**. Curly haired. 1. 'It has shades of usage. One is the natural meaning-naturally curly-haired, though it more properly refers to the hair-type which has very many, very small, curls; and "runs" in certain families. So if there were a number of families of Magees, one of them could be the catach Magees' *An Cho* (w. Mayo); Brian Friel, *Translations*, 38: 'OWEN: Oh, Máire Chatach. YOLLAND: What does that mean? OWEN: Curly-haired; the whole family are called the catachs'. 2. 'A secondary usage of the word is less complimentary – it describes a head of hair that "hasn't seen a comb for a week."' *An Cho* (w. Mayo); 'Kotha, tangled' PLH (n. Roscommon). 3. (Of sheep) 'crop-eared' PJG (mid-Donegal).

Catachán n. 'A curly-haired person; a person with a catach head' *An Cho* (w. Mayo). See *catach*.

Cathairín n. 'A field where there is a lios' *CBE* 34 S (Galway).

Cathaoirleach n. Chairman (of the Senate)

Cathóg n. Also in form **cahag**. 'A little cross-piece on the end of a spade-handle, or the handle of any other implement' *IG* (Monaghan); PJG (mid-Donegal); *EASI* 229: 'cahag'

Cathú n. 1. Regret, sorrow. '"He'll catch cathú yet": he'll pay for it yet' *CBD* (n. Kerry); 'You need have no cathú about that' MW (s. Wexford). 2. Temptation. 'Here's the few pounds I owe you; take it before the cathú comes on me to drink it' R (s. Galway).

Ceach n. 'A dead animal. Carrion' R (n. Clare).

Céad-dlaoi n. Also in form **katchy**. Forelock. 'Céad-dlaoi used in Ulster in speaking English' *Dinn*. 'A great one for pulling the katchy – tugging the forelock' Mac C (Monaghan).

Ceáfráil n. (Act of) cutting capers, acting the fool. 'Cut out that damn ceáfráil and pay attention' JL (w. Cork).

Ceáfrálaí n. 'A fellow who is always acting the flute' JL (w. Cork).

Ceaidé n. 'A rake, roisterer' *CBD* (n. Kerry). Hence **ceaidéing**: 'roistering, playing the rake' *CBD* (n. Kerry).

Ceaifléir n. As **caffler**. 'He's a prime boy, a joker, a real ceáifléir' JL (w. Cork); 'A person who indulges in horseplay; a caffler' TOM (s. Tipperary). [< English dialect *caffle*, to gossip, make mischief.]

Ceailis n. Also as **kalish**. 'A big, fat, useless woman' JL (w. Cork); 'A big strong woman is a kalish' JH (e. Limerick).

Ceailiseog n. In form **kalishogue**. 'A fat little girleen' JC (w. Cork); 'A plump young blowen' JH (e. Limerick).

Ceallaígh n. As **cally**. 'Mashed new potatoes' MC (e. Mayo); 'Colcannon' PLH (n. Roscomon.

Cealdrach n. 1. 'A lazy person; a spiritless cowardly type' O'K (Tyrone); Mac C (Monaghan). 2. 'A fool' OC (Monaghan).

Cealltair n. Facial aspect. 'Look at the cealltair on him. He's as mad as hell' RBB (w. Waterford).

Ceallúir n. 'A large, empty, delapidated house' *IG* (Kilkenny).

Ceallúrach n. In forms **calooragh**, **caldragh**. A place where children who died before baptism were buried. 'There never was a calooragh at St Mullins, as far as I know' PD (s. Carlow); 'They were some Christians, all right, throwing the wee wains into a caldragh' PJG (mid-Donegal).

Ceamach n. 'A slovenly person, a messer' MG (n.w. Donegal). Hence, slovenly, sluttish. 'One of the most ceamach girls I ever did come across' S (n.w. Donegal).

Ceangaltán n. 'A bandage' *CBE* 104 (Leitrim).

Ceann cait n. 'The owl' *CBD* (n. Kerry); JPL (w. Cork).

Ceann Comhairle n. Speaker of the Dáil, the Irish Lower House of Parliament.

Ceann n. 'The head. "Mind the ceann. The door is low"' *CBE* 34 S (Galway).

Ceann fé n. Literally, head lowered. 'A shy person who doesn't talk much' *CBD* (n. Kerry).

Ceannabhán n. As **cannavaun**. Bog cotton, common cottongrass, *Eriophorum angustifolium* NB (w. Limerick); *CBD* (n. Kerry); JL (w. Cork); 'I have often seen the bog white with the ripened down of the cannavaun and it going with the breeze like snowflakes' *CBE* 266 (mid-Tipperary).

Ceannaire n. In form **candary**. Leader. 'The man who led the plough horses while another led the plough handles' H (n. Donegal).

Ceannaitheoir cluaise n. phr. 'A person at a fair who listens to what's going on, and who gets a bargain thereby' *CBD* (n. Kerry).

Ceannóga n. pl. As **ceannógs**. 'The gleanings or stray heads of corn when the harvest is cut down' Always as plural. Rarely used now' *IG* (Monaghan).

Ceant n. Also as **cant**. 1. n. A sale by auction. 'The farm is up for ceant' MS (e. Limerick); *Simmons* (s. Donegal); *EDD* (Cavan, Westmeath): 'cant'. Hence, Jonathan Swift, *A Modest Proposal:* 'They were everywhere canting their land upon short leases'; Wm. Carleton, *Fardorougha the Miser* 3: 'He canted all the world we had at half price and turned us to starve upon the world' (Tyrone); Crofton Croker, *Fairy Legends and Traditions of South Ireland* 312: 'He'll cant every ha'porth we have'; Mr and Mrs S. C. Hall, *Ireland, Its Scenery and Character* 2, 75: 'Every ha'porth upon the lands and in the home was canted' (Leinster). [< English dialect *cant;* French *encant*, Old French *inquant*, Medieval Latin *in quantum*, for how much.]

Ceanúil ort phr. Fond of you. 'I have a feeling he's ceanúil on you' MJD (w. Cork). 'Phrase "tá sé ceanúil ar an bhfearthainn" translated as **it's fond of the rain** in South Kilkenny, meaning, it rains often' RBB (s. Kilkenny).

Ceap n. Bed, plot. In phrase '**to set in ceap**'. 'To plant young trees or plants such as cabbage plants, together in one hole, until one is ready to plant them out properly' JL (w. Cork); *CBD* (n. Kerry).

Ceapaire n. Also in form **capper**. 'Ceapaire is a slice of buttered bread' *IG* (Kilkenny); S Ua G (s. Tipperary). 'When the cow is taken to the bull the usual question asked is: "did you earn the capper?" i.e. were you successful?' Tr (Donegal).

Ceapánta adj. Mean, niggardly. 'Ceapánta isn't the word for that miser' S Ua G (s. Tipperary).

Cearc fhraoigh n. 'The grouse' *IG* (Cavan).

Cearradh n. An inconvenience. 'He put a cearradh on me – he stopped me and delayed me talking to him' *IG* (Kilkenny).

Cearrbhach n. Also as **carroach**. 1. A gambler JM (w. Cork). 2. 'A clever card player' JL (w. Cork); RBB (mid Waterford). Patk. Kennedy, *Legends of Mount Leinster* 149: 'I see the carroachs (card players)' (Wexford). 3. 'A trickster' H (n. Clare); NB (w. Limerick).

Ceartaigh interj. Adjust! 'Said to a cow to get her to stand properly while milking her' MJD (w. Cork); NB (w. Limerick). See *Deisigh*.

Cearthanach n. 'A wizened old person' MC (w. Clare).

Ceathrú chaorach n. Also in translated form **lamb's quarter**. The white goosefoot, a weed, *Chenopodium album* S Ua C (e. Galway).

Céilidh n. Also in forms **kailyee, kaley, caley**. 1. 'A friendly visit, usually at night' G (n.w. Donegal); Seumus MacManus, *A Lad of the O'Friels* 46: 'Uncle Donal seldom or ever went out to ceilidh' (Donegal); Wm. Carleton,*The Lianhan Shee* 2, 77: '... soon afther your other kailyee ...' Carleton glosses kailyee as 'short visit' (Tyrone). 'I made a kaley to Mrs Brady's house and heard about the news' *EDD* (Cavan); 'To go on caley is to go about gossiping' *EDD* (Meath, Dublin, Kildare); *Ballymena Observer* (Antrim). 2. Irish dancing session (Gen.). Also spelled **ceilidhe, céilí**.

Ceiliúr n. In form **kelure**. 1. Greeting. 'I put kelure on her – I greeted her' TB (Cavan). 2. 'Loud conversation' Mac C (Monaghan).

Céirseach n. 1. The hen blackbird, *turdus merula* MC (e. Mayo). 2. Figuratively, 'a talkative woman' S Ua G (s. Tipperary).

Ceirt n. In form **kert**. A rag. 'You'd think she'd wear some decent clothes instead of going around in kerts' G (Kilkenny).

Ceirtlín n. 1. 'A bundle of wool ready for the weaver' *CBD* (n. Kerry); 'A ball of yarn' *IG*

(Meath). 2. 'A plump little woman' *CBD* (n. Kerry).

Céis n. In forms **caish, kesh**. 1. A sow. Gerald Griffin, *The Collegians* 209: 'A small caish to pay the rent' (Limerick). Hence **céis óg**, 'a young sow' McK (Leitrim); NB (w. Limerick). 2. 'Kesh: a fat woman' DOC (Limerick).

Ceis n. In form **kesh**. 'A rough bridge of wattles in a bog or over a stream' PJG (mid-Donegal); OC (Monaghan); Seamus Heaney, *Seeing Things* 102: 'Heather and kesh and turf stacks reappear ... '

Ceithearn n. In form **kerne**. Light-armed infantry. Anon., *Captain Thomas Stukeley*: '... gow make ready oore kerne ...'

Ceithearnach n. 'A derogatory word for an old fellow' H (n. Clare).

Cén díobháil phr. Also in translated form **what hurt?** What harm. 'Cén díobháil, we can finish the job in the morning' H (n. Clare). Translated literally in Gerald Griffin, *The Collegians* 44: 'What hurt' (Limerick).

Ceo gaoithe n. Literally, mist, haze, of wind. A storm in a teacup. 'She was letting the ceo gaoithe blow over, it seemed' BMacM (Kerry).

Ceo n. 1. Fog. 'There's a ceo down on the glen that would keep the púcaí by the fire' MJD (w. Cork). 2. Dust. 'Take the brush to the furniture and wipe off the ceo' RBB (Waterford.); G (s. Kilkenny). 3. Ill-fortune. 'There's some ceo down on top of the whole family' PC (n. Clare). Hence (?) **Ceo-boy** n. 'a wild young fellow, up to all kinds of divilment' PJG (mid-Donegal); OC (Monaghan).

Ceobhrán n. 1. 'Mist' MS (Limerick). 2. 'Light rain' *CBD* (n. Kerry); *CBE* 266 (mid-Tipperary).

Ceochán n. 1. Hoarseness *Pe* (Wexford); NB (w. Limerick); *CBD* (n. Kerry); JL (w. Cork). 2. 'A singer who has a bad voice. "He was a right ceochán"' *CBD* (n. Kerry).

Ceochrán n. 'A shower of rain' *CBD* (n. Kerry).

Ceoil interj. 'A word of praise for somebody who has done something significant, at a hurling match, for instance' *CBD* (n. Kerry).

Ceol n., adj. 'Music' *CBE* 104 (Leitrim). Figuratively, sport, enjoyment. 'He knocks the divil's ceol out of the new bicycle' MJD (w. Cork); PB (s. Tipperary); 'We had a ceol time' *CBD* (n. Kerry).

Ceolán n. 1. 'A miserable, complaining person. "That ceolán of a child never stops bawling"' R (Clare); *Pe* (Wexford); RBB (s. Kilkenny); MS (e. Limerick); PB (s. Tipperary). 2. 'A light-headed person, usually male' H (n. Clare). 3. 'An obstinate person' Ham (e. Clare). 4. 'An idiot' GC (Laois, n. Kilkenny); *CBE* 104 (Leitrim).

Cér chás é phr. 'Means "what harm" – in that ironic kind of phrase "what harm but ..." "The price of eggs is gone sky-high. Cér chás é but we had them to kick when they were cheap"' *An Cho* (w. Mayo).

Chan fhuil phr. In form **ha nihl**. It is not. In Wm. Carleton, *Wildgoose Lodge* 2, 353 **ha nihl anam inh.** (Tyrone). [*recte* chan fhuil an t-am ann; it is not yet time.]

Chugat a' púca interj. phr. The púca (q.v.) is coming to you. 'It could be said to frighten someone, but more usually is heard in the saying, "He never said chugat a' púca to anyone but came in any went out"' *An Cho* (w. Mayo).

Chugat as seo interj. phr. Get out of here! *CBE* 104 (Leitrim).

Cí-cá n. 'A handful of coins scattered at a wedding' *IG* (Kilkenny).

Ciach n. Distress. In phrase, **mo chiach!** – my distress. Often used ironically' RBB (Waterford); JPL (w. Cork).

Ciafart n. In form **cayforth**. 1. 'A dirty person, like a tramp in appearance' PJG (mid-Donegal). 2. 'A confused, bewildered person' Peadar O'Donnell, *Adrigoole*, 230: 'The daft oul' cayforth' (Donegal).

Cianóg n. Also as **keenoge**. A small coin, a mite, a brass farthing. 'Lend you a pound? I couldn't lend you a cianóg' RBB (s. Kilkenny); *IG* (Kilkenny); JL (w. Cork). *EASI* 257: 'keenoge'.

Ciaróg n. The rove beetle, *Ocypus olens* (Gen.). Proverb **aithníonn ciaróg ciaróg eile**. One rove beetle recognises another, or, birds of a feather flock together (Gen).

Cíb n. Also in forms **keeb, keef**. *Carex species*. 'Mountain sedge, the type that was traditionally used for thatching houses in this parish (Louisburgh)' *An Cho* (w. Mayo). As 'keef' OCN (Laois). Hence **cíb dhubh** in form **keeb dhu**: The black bog rush, *Schoenus nigricus* in J. M'Parlan, *Statistical Survey of the County of Donegal*.

Cibeal n. 'A row, a rumpus' DOH (e. Limerick); 'Such cibeal over such a small thing' BMcM (n. Kerry); S Ua G (s. Tipperary).

Cíbleach n. As **keebla**. 'A sedgy place' Con (Louth).

Cídeog n. In form **kidug**. A cape-like covering for head and shoulders. John Boyce, *Shandy Maguire* 203: 'Tied a kidug over hat and under chin' (Donegal).

Cifleog n. As **kifflog**. 1. 'A bumbler, an awkward person' McK (Leitrim); Mac C (Tyrone); *IG* (Monaghan). 2. Tattered clothes. 'You never seen anything like the kifflogs she was rigged out in' PJG (Donegal). Hence **kifflogy**, ragged. 'She was as kifflogy as a scarecrow' AG (w. Donegal).

Cillín n. In form **killeen**. 1. Places where unbaptised children were buried. 'These 'inches of mortality' are buried at night' H (n. Donegal). See *Ceallúrach*. 2. *EASI* 280: 'A nest egg' (Ulster).

Cilpín n. In form **kilpin**. In phrase 'He made a kilpin of him' – he knocked him out: PJG (mid-Donegal).

Ciméara n. 1. 'An aberration or upset of the mind. "Some strange ciméara came on him."' *CBE* 266 (mid-Tipperary). 2. 'Tomfoolery. "Look at the ciméars of him"' MF (Westmeath). [< English *chimera*]

Cimilín n. 'A miserable, insignificant person' PC (n. Clare).

Cincíseach n. Also in form **kingkisha**. 'A cincíseach is a person or animal born at Whitsuntide; an ill-starred person' MJD (w. Cork). As 'kingkisha' FF (Monaghan).

Cineál n. 1. 'Food given to a cow to keep her quiet when you're milking her' AG (w. Donegal). 2. Treat, delicacy, luxury. 'Tea was a cineál in my young days' S (n.w. Donegal); RBB (Waterford). 3. Sort, kind. 'He's a bad cineál' MF (Westmeath).

Cíní n. pl. 'A woman's breasts' CBD (n. Kerry).

Cíoc interj. Peep! JPL (w. Cork); Mac C (Monaghan).

Cíocrach adj. Eager. 'Twas too cíocrach he was' CBD (n. Kerry).

Ciológ n. Bog lark; meadow pippit, *anthus pratensis* IG (Cavan).

Cíonádh n. In form **keenaw**. 'The five of trumps in card games such as "25" and the like' MJD (w. Cork); 'The best trump' Dee (Waterford).

Cíor n. 1. 'A comb' Mac C (Monaghan); TB (Cavan). 2. 'The top of a load of turf' PB (s. Tipperary).

Ciorabúca n. An uproar. 'There was some ciorabúca at the dance last night when the fight started' PJG (mid-Donegal).

Ciotach adj. 1. Clumsy. 'An awkward, clumsy person' PB (s. Tipperary); MJD (w. Cork); OC (Monaghan); OCn (Laois). 2. Unbalanced, untrustworthy. 'That man is ciotach. He'd hit you for no reason at all' RBB (S. Kilkenny).

Ciotóg n., adj. Also as **kethogue, kithogue**. 1. The left hand. John Boyce, *Shandy Maguire* 90: 'I'll run my kethogue down your throat' (Donegal). 2. Left-handed. Wm. Carleton, *The Poor Scholar* 142: '...

appeared to be left-handed or kithogue' (Tyrone); James Joyce, *Ulysses* 425. 3. Hence **ciotógaí**, 'a term of disparagement for an untidy workman' CBD (n. Kerry). 4. Hence **kitter-handed**. Awkward. 'He couldn't get the hang of the machine; he's very kitter-handed' O'K (Tyrone).

Ciotrainn n. Accident, misfortune. 'The poor divil, it's one ciotrainn after another with him' JPL (w. Cork).

Cip n. 'A shoemaker's last' RBB (w. Waterford).

Cíp n. 'Rough grass' CBD (n. Kerry).

Cipeanta adj. Stingy, mean. 'Talk of cipeanta! He never stood a round in his life' S Ua G (s. Tipperary).

Cipil ó cít n. Smithereens. 'He made cipil ó cít of the car on his way home from the dance' RBB (S. Kilkenny).

Cipín n. In forms **kibbin, kippen, kippeen**. 1. A small trowel-like instrument for planting potatoes. J. M'Parlan, *Statistical Survey of the County of Donegal* 43: 'An instrument for planting potatoes. Steveen, which is here called a kibbin, is a wooden pole about four feet long, pointed at the lower extremity within about six inches of which a resting place is made for the foot, to push it into the potato-ridge. The potatoes are dibbled with a Leitrim steveen, or kibbed as they call it, with a kibbin'. 2. A small stick, a twig. Crofton Croker, *Fairy Legends and Traditions*, 39: 'He gave her a little bit of a tip with a kippen' (Munster); Patk. Kennedy, *Evenings in the Duffrey*, 46: 'Just as I am levelling the greeshach with this kippeen' (Wexford); Emily Lawless, *Grania* 1, pt. 2, 2: 'The man that was selling it gave it a now and then a skelp with a bit of a kippeen that he held in his hand' (Mayo); W. B. Yeats, *Fairy and Folk Tales*, 20: 'a lock of dry kippens ...' (Connacht; Gen.). 3. A euphemism for a shillelagh. Wm. Carleton, *Neal Malone* 2, 417: '... and shook his kippeen at the fiercest of his fighting friends ...' (Tyrone).

Circín n. 1. 'A little hen' JC (w. Cork). 2. 'A little girl' MS (e. Limerick).

Circín trá n. Also in form **kirkeen dhra.** Little hen of the shore, the dunlin, *calidris alpina* JS (w. Kerry); Gerald Griffin, *The Collegians* 113: '... kirkeen dhra or little water hen ...'

Círín n. Also as **keereen.** 'The lobe of the ear; the flesh of the jaw. I caught him by the círín' *IG* (Kilkenny); 'The master used to pull the keereens off of us in school' PD (s. Carlow); PB (s. Tipperary).

Círle-má-guairle n. 'Hubbub, hurly-burly' JPL (w. Cork).

Cis n. In forms **kish, kesh.** *Paddiana* 1, 304: 'A large oblong basket, commonly placed upon the rude country car, and used in bringing in baskets of turf from the bog'; M. and R. Edgeworth, *An Essay on Irish Bulls* 180: 'A train of his companions leaving their cars loaded with kishes of turf' (Longford); A. Hume, *Irish Dialects* 23: 'There is an old kish on the ground' (Antrim); Patk. Kennedy, *The Banks of the Boro* 71: 'Sitting on a pillion behind you going to a fair or market to look after your kish' (Wexford); Emily Lawless, *Grania* 1. pt. 2 viii: 'From the time she was the height of that turf kish there, she would not be bid by anyone' (Mayo); Mrs S. C. Hall, *Irish Life and Character* 11: 'An old lady had taken undisputed possession of a kesh of potatoes' (s. Leinster); James Joyce, *Ulysses* 175: 'ignorant as a kish of brogues ...'; 'Durrow must have been always in the heel of the kish = it was never of great account' OCn (Laois).

Ciseach n. 1. 'A big, awkward person' MS (e. Limerick). 2. In phrase 'to make a ciseach' of something, to make a mess of it. 'The cows got into the field and made a right ciseach of the oats' MJD (w. Cork). 3. 'A bridge or path in a bog' H (n. Clare).

Ciseán n. 'A hen's nest hung up with straw ropes' *IG* (Cavan).

Ciseog n. In form **kishogue.** One of a pair of panniers for carrying turf. W. H. Floredice, *Memories of a Month among the 'Mere' Irish* 276: 'Riding all day in a kishogue. (note: turf basket or pannier'. See *ciseán.*

Ciste n. In form **kishtha.** Diminutive, **cisteán,** as **kishtawn.** A chest, coffer, treasury. *EASI* 281: 'Kishtha is very common in Connaught where it is often understood to be hidden treasure in a fort under the care of a leprechaun'; 'Children who had a selection of things such as nuts, apples, pennies etc. were often said to have a right little ciste' Cor (Cavan); 'A purse or pocket full of money is a kishtawn' JB (s. Armagh & n. Louth); 'She gathered a nice little kishtawn of shells' DG (Sligo).

Cístín baise n. Literally, little hand-cake. 'A little cake made on the side of the griddle especially for a child. "Mother, give me a cístín baise" ' CBD (n. Kerry).

Cistineoir n. A cotquean. 'A man who spends a lot of time about the house taking an interest in women's work' CBD (n. Kerry).

Clab n. 1. Open mouth. ' Shut your clab' – shut up. (Gen.) Also as **tlob** MF (Westmeath). 2. 'A person who never stops talking' PJG (mid-Donegal). Hence phrase **clab asail,** an ass's mouth, 'a person who talks too much' CBD (n. Kerry). 3. 'A clab is a soft-minded person' Mac C (Monaghan).

Clab-óinseach n. 'A talkative fool of a woman' DOC (Limerick).

Clabaire n. *al.* **clabachán.** Also in form **clapper.** 'Clabaire, a prattler' CBD (n. Kerry); 'A clapper is an incessant talker. One who has a tongue like the clapper of a blacksmith's bellows' DOC (Limerick); 'That clabachán never shuts up' PB (s. Tipperary). See *Clab.*

Clabairín n. 'Part of a churn. In the old-time "standing-churn", a "churn-dash" was used, and this was raised and lowered through a hole in the lid. To prevent cream being splashed up through this hole, a small six or eight-sided wooden collar or washer was slipped on to the handle of the dash and rested at the hole in the lid. This was the clabairín. It had a secondary purpose: when the churning was made, it was dropped into the churn to help the butter to gather' *An Cho* (w. Mayo).

Clabar n. 'Sour, thick milk' *CBD* (n. Kerry).

Clábar n. In forms **clabber, clauber, tlauber.** 'Clábar is mud' AG (s. Tipperary); PLH (n. Roscommon); Rev William Marshall, *Drumlister:* 'I'm dyin' in Drumlister, in clabber to the knees'; *Patterson* (Antrim and Down): 'They clodded clabber at me'; *Ballymena Observer:* 'Road clabber'; *Simmons* (s. Donegal); Seamus Heaney, *Death of a Naturalist* 48: 'Or in the sucking clabber I would splash/ Delightedly and dam the flowing drain ...'; 'It's hard to keep the house clean and the way he walks in with his brogues all clauber' LB (s.w. Dublin); 'Mud, mire-tlauber' MF (Westmeath).

Clabhaitín n. Also as **tlouteen.** 'A cloth' NB (w. Limerick); 'Tlouteen: a napkin for a baby' MF (Westmeath). [< English *clout.*]

Clabhastar n., v. In forms **clouster, tlouster.** 1. Cumbersome, unshapely object. 'Surely you are not going to wear that old clouster of a hat?' G (s. Kilkenny). 2. To encumber with too many clothes. 'The poor child is tloustered with all the jumpers he's wearing' MF (Westmeath). 3. 'A poultice for a horse's leg' PJG (mid-Donegal). 4. 'Oaten bread, roughly baked, fit only for working sheep-dogs' MG (n.w. Donegal). 5. 'An untidy worker' G (n.w. Donegal). 6. 'To work in an untidy manner. "Stop clousterin' around, and finish one job at a time"' G (n.w. Donegal).

Clabhrán n. In form **klauraun.** 1. 'A small person we called a klauraun' PD (s. Carlow). 2. 'A small potato' RBB (s. Kilkenny); NB (w. Limerick).

Clabhsúr n. 'A party held at the end of harvest work. "We should have the clabhsúr to-morrow"' *CBD* (n. Kerry).

Clabhtóg n. A smack, a light stroke given with the hand, a clout MJD (w. Cork); H (n. Clare).

Clabóg n. 'A woman whose mouth is always open talking from morning till night' DOC (Limerick). See *clab.*

Clachán n. A cluster of houses. 'There used to be a clachán down by the lake shore' G (n.w. Donegal).

Cladach n. The shore. 'A walk along the cladach and a breakfast of buttermilk: the only known cure for a hangover' PC (n. Clare); *CBE* 104 (Leitrim).

Cladhaire n. 1. 'A rogue, a ruffian' BOD (s.w. Cork.); 'A cladhaire is a rogue – in that gentlest and most smiling sense. So it is often used in the vocative to someone who has tried to play a trick on the speaker. Or in card-playing: '"Get away, you cladhaire, you won't fool me"' *An Cho* (w. Mayo). 2. 'A cowardly, spineless person' NB (w. Limerick).

Clafairtín n. In form **clofferteen.** 'A piece of potato without a bud or an eye' MC (e. Mayo).

Clagar n. Very heavy rain. 'I'm drenched to the pelt. I was caught in the clagar' MJD (w. Cork).

Claí teorann n. In form **cly-thoran.** *EASI* 237 'Boundary fence or ditch between two properties' (Roscommon).

Claibín n. In forms **tlabeen, clabeen.** 1. 'Tlabeen, a perforated cup on a churn-dash to prevent splash' MF (Westmeath). 2. 'Clabeen was my mother's word for a latch on the door' MW (s. Wexford).

Claibín muilinn n. 'A person who is always talking' *CBE* 34 S (Galway). [Cf. *clabaire muilinn,* a mill-clapper *ODON.*]

Claibseach n. A big mouth. 'Somebody will close his claibseach for him fairly soon' JPL (w. Cork).

Cláirín n. *al.* **claitín.** 'A cláirín, a scythe-board' JPL (w. Cork); 'Claitín is a tool used to sharpen a scythe' *CBD* (n. Kerry).

Cláirseach n. 1. In form **clairseagh.** A harp. A. Hume, *Irish Dialects* 23 (Antrim): 'They will dance to a clairseagh'. 2. 'A woman with a big, broad face. A cláirseach of a woman' MJD (w. Cork). 3. In form **clarsha.** *EASI* 235: 'A lazy woman' (s. Monaghan).

Clais n. In forms **clash, classy**. 1. A furrow. 'He's some ploughman! Every clash he makes is as crooked as the hind leg of a dog' G (Kilkenny); PD (s. Carlow); NB (w. Limerick); 'A drain running through a farm-yard or a stable is called a classy' FF (Monaghan). 2. A downpour. S (n.w. Donegal) 'I was caught in a clais'. 3. Vulva JL (w. Cork).

Claitín n. 'A bandage' *CBE* 104 (Leitrim).

Claitseach n. In form **klatch**. A slut, a trollop. 'She's a bit of a klatch' Mac C (Monaghan).

Clamhaire n. In form **claura**. A wretch. A person who makes objectionable remarks. 'That claura opened his mouth once too often and somebody closed it with a box' G (s. Kilkenny); RBB (Waterford).

Clamhán n. Dodder, rootless, parasitic plant of the convolvulaceous genus *cuscuta*, with whitish flowers. 'Said with sarcasm, isn't that a grand crop of clamhán?' OCn (Laois).

Clamhsán n. 1. A complaint, grumble. 'I'm fed up with him and his clamhsáns' JL (w. Cork). 2. 'A person who is always grumbling' *CBE* S 34. Hence **clamh-sáning**. 'He's always clamhsáning' *CBD* (n. Kerry).

Clampa n. In form **klaumpa**: 'A clamp (of turf)' LOS (w. Clare).

Clampar n. Also in forms **clam-peer, clamper**. Loud talk, noisy quarrelling. 'I couldn't hear myself with the clampar' McK (Leitrim); 'Nothing but clampar from morn-ing till night in that house' Smy (n. Clare); 'In phrase, Pateen clamper, despicable, trouble-making Pat' PLH (n. Roscommon); Anon., *The Irish Hudibras*: 'Let not dy Ars make a Clam-peer; Lest vid a Fart dou blow it from me ...'; Anon., *Captain Thomas Stukeley*: 'Esta clamper, thoo talkest to much ...' [*Esta clamper = éist do chlampar*, silence your noise.]

Clár n. A board. In phrase **faoi chlár**, in form **under board**. Euphemism for 'dead'. 'In the old times the corpse was laid out under a board, sometimes a door, which was covered with a white sheet. The face was the only part of the corpse to be seen. Plates of tobacco, pipes, and snuff were placed on the sheet above the board' PJG (n.w. Donegal).

Cleabhar n. *al.* **creabhar**. 'The gad fly, horse fly' DOH (e. Limerick); *CBE* 266 (mid-Tipperary); 'The cattle are drove mad by the creabhars' MJD (w. Cork).

Cleamhnaí n. Also as **tlounee**. 1. 'A relation by marriage' *BASJ* (Cavan). 2. A crony. 'They are great tlounees – they are inseparable companions' MF (Westmeath).

Cléibhín n. A hulk. A boat which is falling to pieces. 'They were asking for trouble going to sea in that old cléibhín' RBB (Waterford).

Cleiceán n. 'An earthen fence' NB (w. Limerick).

Cléitheach n. 'A fool' NB (w. Limerick).

Cleithín n. 1. 'A splint, especially a splint applied to a hen's leg' MS (e. Limerick); *CBD* (n. Kerry). 2. 'A dislocation of the breast bone, or as we say, of the spool of the breast. The ailment is fairly common and usually arises from lifting great weights. The old-time cure was a candle on which a breakfast cup was upturned on the breast. The vacuum so formed righted the ailment by suction' *An Cho* (w. Mayo). [Cf. *cleithín uchta*: ensiform cartilage' *ODON*]

Cleithire n. In forms **clehirra, clahirra**. A strong man. 'The strength of that clehirra is something else' PD (s. Carlow; 'A clahirra of a man' MC (e. Mayo).

Cliabh n. In forms **cleave, cleaf, tleev**. Diminutive, **claven**, plural **clavees**. A basket, a creel. Anon., *A Dialogue between Teigue and Dermot*: 'Some butchers say dey did not leave One fellow dat vou'd carry a cleave': 'A large bucket containing a hun-dredweight, for carrying potatoes, is a cleaf' PON (n. Dublin). Also as **claven**, diminutive from *cliaibhín*, O'K (Tyrone). Hence **cliabhaire**, 'a poultry dealer' *IG* (Monaghan); hence **cleaver**, 'a local term for hen-dealers who used to come from Crossmaglen carrying baskets' OC (Monaghan); ER (Louth); 'I remember the women carrying the clavees to Kingscourt' FF (Cavan); 'Wicker basket carried on backtleev' MF (Westmeath).

Cliamhain n. In form **cleeveen**. An indirect relationship, such as a relationship by marriage. Wm. Carleton, *The Geography Of An Irish Oath* 17: '... an' besides, there's a cleeveenship atween your family an' ours'. Glossed by Carleton in *The Midnight Mass* 1, 356 as 'distant relations' (Tyrone).

Cliamhain isteach n. Also in form **clane isteach**. 'Cliamhain isteach is a man who lives with his wife's relations' CBD (n. Kerry); 'A man who marries into a farm' SOM (w. Cork); 'A pejorative term. "He's only a clane isteach man"' AG (s. Tipperary).

Cliathánach adv. Lateral, sideways. 'He walks cliathánach since he had the accident' S Ua G (s. Tipperary).

Clibín n. In form **clibeen**. Plural, **clibeens**, **clibbins**. 'Untidy hair, clibeen' PJG (mid-Donegal). 2. 'Clibeens are lumps of dried dung stuck to a sheep's wool' PJG (mid-Donegal); McK (Leitrim); IG (Cavan). 3. 'Ragged clothes, with loose strips hanging down, are called clibbins' OC (Monaghan).

Climirt n. 'The last part of milking: the "strippings". The word can be applied figuratively to the last part of any supply – most delightfully, perhaps, when one refers to the youngest of a family as "the climirt"' *An Cho* (w. Mayo).

Cliobóg n. Also in forms **clib**, **clip**, **tlib**. 1. 'A colt or filly under a year old is a cliobóg' G (s. Kilkenny); 'A one-year-old horse is called a clib' *Ballymena Observer* (Antrim); 'Tlib: a young horse a year and a half old' MF (Westmeath). 2. Figuratively, 'a rough, unmannerly kind of a man' PJG (mid-Donegal). 3. As **clip**. Figuratively, a forward girl. 'Nothing 'ud be too hot or too heavy for that clip' LB (s.w. Dublin); 'A'll gie it tae ye for that, ye clip' *Ballymena Observer* (Antrim).

Cliotar n. In forms **clitther**, **clatther** 1. A blow. 'He got a bad clitther of a hurl' MS

(e. Limerick); H (n. Clare). 2. 'A talkative person who spreads news is called a clatther' Mac C (Monaghan). 3. 'Cliotar, a racket, noise' CBD (n. Kerry); 'I hear there was the divil's own clitther at the dance last night' FF (Cavan). 4. 'Excitement' PLH (n. Roscommon). Hence **cliotarálaí**, as **clittherawlee**. 'One who makes a lot of noise; an incessant talker' CBE 266 (mid-Tipperary).

Cliste adj. Clever. 'You won't fool me, cliste and all as you are' S Ua G (s. Tipperary).

Cliútach adj. In form **clootough** in Anon., *The Pretender's Exercise*. Deceitful.

Cliútar n. 'A damn fine rogue' JPL (w. Cork).

Clochán n. Also in forms **cloghan**, **cleakawn**. 'Clochán, stepping stones across a river' H (n. Clare); CBE 104 (Leitrim); Michael Harkin, *Inishowen: Its History, Conditions and Antiquities* 129: 'The neat bridge was not there but instead a line of colossal stepping stones ran across the ford, which means of transit was, in the language of the day, termed a cloghan'; George Fitzmaurice, *The Pie-Dish* (Kerry): '... over dykes, ditches, cleakawns...'

Clochar n. 1. In form **clougher**. 'A stony region or shore' H (n. Donegal). 2. 'Round stones cast up on the sea shore' MC (w. Clare). 3. 'The name given to the hollow sound made in a person's throat and regarded as a symptom of approaching death: a death-rattle' *An Cho* (w. Mayo).

Clogaidín n. In form **clugadeen**. 'A small round peck for holding milk' NB (w. Limerick); CBD (n. Kerry).

Cloigeann n. Also as **claggan**. Head. 'As with many Irish words in our parish dialect (of English) it is the less complimentary uses of the words that have survived. A **cloigeann ard** is a "high-head" – one who dreams and floats, with no attention to practical reality. Similarly there are terms: **cloigeann turnap**, turnip-head; **cloigeann éinín**, bird-head; **cloigeann cuasach**, empty-head. And villages are called Claggan, Carrowclaggan, etc., because of the protruding or head-shaped profile of the land' *An Cho* (w. Mayo).

Cluain n. In form **cloon**. 1. A meadow. 2. A plain between two woods. Michael Harkin, *Inisowen, Its History etc.*, 6: 'Between the mountains, or embosomed among them, are glens, cloons, and narrow passes' (Donegal).

Cluais n. In forms **cloos, tloos, cloosey**. 'A fool, a half-wit, a cloos' JM (Westmeath); 'Tloos, a half-wit, a gom' MF (Westmeath); 'He was a right cloosey if he thought he's get away with that' PD (s. Carlow).

Cluiche n. In form **cly**. A game (of cards) Mac C (Monaghan).

Clúideog n. In form **cloodogue**. 1. A batch of Easter eggs. 'The eggs were often covered with straw and hidden around the farm, giving children a good deal of fun in tracking them down' AS (Monaghan); LB (s.w. Dublin). 2. The party connected with the above. 'We always had our cloodogue in our Granny's on Easter Sunday. It consisted in lighting a fire, usually in the paddock where there was a hill, boiling eggs which my aunt had previously painted, and rolling them down the brae. There was lots of tea, with wine and whiskey for the grown-ups' AS (Monaghan).

Clúidín n. 'A rag applied to an infant'; a napkin, diaper' *CBE* 104 (Leitrim).

Clúmh n. Down. 'I think it's time I hit the clúmh' – went to bed. JL (w. Cork).

Clúta n. 'A bandage' *CBE* 104 (Leitrim). [< English *clout*.]

Cluthar adj. In form **cluvver**. 'Comfortable, warm; sheltered' *Pe* (Wexford).

Clutharacán n. Also in forms **cluricaun, cluricaune**. 'A mischievous elf' OC (Monaghan); MS (e. Limerick). Mrs S. C. Hall, *Irish Life And Character* 230: 'How she wished that Harry Connor was little, old and withered as a cluricaun'; Crofton Croker, *Fairy Legends And Traditions* 80 (Cork, Kerry): 'A fairy having the appearance of a tiny old man, supposed to have a knowledge of buried treasure, and to haunt wine cellars ... The Cluricaune of county Cork, the Luricaune of Kerry and the Lurigadaune of Tipperary, appear to be the same as the Leprechan of Leinster and the Logheryman of Ulster.'

Cnádálaí n. A lazy person, a shirker. 'A cnádálaí that would take a week to do a bit of work that another man would do in a day' Smy (n. Clare).

Cnádán n. *al.* **cnáthadán** *An Cho* (w. Mayo). Also in forms **cradan, credan** H (n. Donegal). Bur; head of burdock, *Arctium lappa*.

Cnádanacht n. 'Act of bickering; irritating, disagreeable talk.' Hence **to cnadge** – to beg, insist. OC (Monaghan).

Cnag n. 'A hurling ball' Con (Meath). As **crig**: Mac C (Monaghan).

Cnagachán n. 'A small, hardy person' DOC (Limerick); 'For a cnagachán like him, he has fierce strength' Smy (n. Clare).

Cnagaí n. 'A hard, stunted person' *CBE* 266 (mid-Tipperary).

Cnaig n. 1. A scowl. 'Look at the cnaig of him, just because he didn't get his own way' PC (n. Clare). 2. 'Also applied to a stubborn person who will not fit in with our plans. "Take that cnaig out of my way", "Is that cnaig still in the kitchen?" ' *An Cho* (w. Mayo).

Cnáimhseáil n. *al.* **cnáirseáil, cráinseáil**. In forms **cnaurshaul** G (s. Kilkenny); **crawnshawl** AG (s. Tipperary); **crawshawl, crawshaun** *CBE* 98 (Kilkenny). (Act of) complaining. 'Cnáimhseáil, cnáimhseáil – that's all you'd hear from her from morning till night' JL (w. Cork). Hence **crawshawlin, crawshaunin** *CBE* 98 (Kilkenny).

Cnáimhseálaí n. A complainer. 'A pain here, a pain there; such a cnáimhseálaí' MJD (w. Cork); RBB (mid-Waterford); MS (e. Limerick).

Cnaist n. A big woman. 'A big cnaist of a woman, good for following a plough, I'd say' MJD (w. Cork); RBB (s. Kilkenny).

Cnaiste n. 'The verge of a bed. 'I'm out on the cnaiste. Move in' JL (w. Cork); NB (w. Limerick); *CBE* 266 (mid-Tipperary).

Cnap n. 1. 'A fat fool' NB (w. Limerick). 2. A heap. 'He fell in a cnap' JPL (w. Cork). 3. A lump. 'There was a cnap in my belly when I saw the bull making towards me over the ré' (q. v.) MJD (w. Cork); *CBE* 266 (mid-Tipperary).

Cnapachán n. 'A big-headed person' *CBE* 266 (mid-Tipperary).

Cnapán n. A lump. 'What sort of a cnapán of a fool are you?' JPL (w. Cork).

Cnat n. In forms **kannat, cannat**. A mean, sly person; a rogue; a pedlar, a dealer JS (e. Kerry); J (s.e. Wexford); G (n.w. Donegal); RBB (Waterford); PD (s. Carlow). Patk. Kennedy, *Evenings in the Duffrey* 392: 'A cunning country kannat'; ibid. *Fireside Stories* 98: 'Once he found out you were a cannat he'd outwit you' (Wexford). [< English *gnat* ? *EDD* suggests < Irish *ceannaí*, a merchant, a dealer.]

Cnead n. A groan. 'The cow let a cnead out of her' MC (w. Clare); PB (s. Tipperary).

Cneas interj. 'Said to a hound to incite him in the chase' *CBD* (n. Kerry).

Cniog n. In form **knug**. A sound. 'Sit down there, and not as much as a knug out of you, mind' G (s. Kilkenny).

Cníopaire n. 1. 'A mean rogue' RBB (s. Kilkenny); JPL (w. Cork); *CBD* (n. Kerry); PB (s. Tipperary). 2. 'A person who would annoy you with incessant talk' DOC (Limerick).

Cnoc n. In forms **knock, knaugh, knuck**. Diminutive, **cnocán**, in forms **knaughaan, cnuceen**. 'I must have walked every bog, field and cnocán looking for the pup the time he went astray' JL (w. Cork). Knock is common in placenames: Knockcroghery, the hill of the hangman, in Co. Roscommon. *Poole* (s.e. Wexford): 'knaugh'; diminutive, 'knaughaan'; *Lays and Legends of the North of Ireland* 86: '... set off down the fields till the knuck'; J. M. Synge, *The Playboy of the*

Western World 95: 'She's above on the cnuceen, seeking the nanny goats ...'

Coc n. 'A little tuft of feathers on a hen's head' MS (e. Limerick).

Coc stiúidí n. phr. A conspicuous object. 'She was wearing a right coc stiúidí of a hat' *CBD* (n. Kerry). [Cf. *'stiúidl*, mark or cockshy' T de B, *Eigse V, 200*.]

Cochall n. Also as **coghil**. 1. 'A small compact tuft of anything; generally applied to shrubs' NB (w. Limerick). 2. 'A piece of cloth placed on the head to help carry a load' *CBD* (n. Kerry). 3. 'The rotten core of a potato' *CBD* (n. Kerry). 4. 'A tuft of hair that stands up on the head'. Figuratively used: 'She had a cochall on her: she was cross' *CBD* (n. Kerry). 5. *EASI* 237: 'Coghil: a scoop net, a landing net' (Armagh).

Cochallach adj. 1. 'Combative, quarrelsome' *CBD* (n. Kerry). 2. 'Bushy, thick-set with branches and verdure' *CBE* 266 (mid-Tipperary). 3. 'Well-rounded, buxom. "There's a fine cochallach girl" ' *CBE* 266 (mid-Tipperary).

Cochlán n. 'A little cloak' *CBE* 266 (mid-Tipperary); 'A small cloak with a hood. They're gone out of fashion with years' MJD (w. Cork).

Cocstí n. In phrase, 'To make a cocstaí of it' – to make a hash of it; to destroy it. JPL (w. Cork). [< English *cockshy* ?]

Codaí n. In form **cuddy**. 1. 'A diminutive fellow' *IG* (Monaghan). 2. 'A schemer, a sly fellow' *CBE* 266 (mid-Tipperary). 3. 'A slow, lazy man' MC (e. Mayo)

Codladh driúlaic n. In form **droolacauns**. 'Pins and needles' JV (e. Wicklow); 'Numbness of the hands caused by putting them near the fire when they are very cold' LB (s.w. Dublin).

Codladh go headra n. phr. Literally, sleep until (late morning) milking time. 'This is what a man from Knockavilla parish (a non-Irish speaker) calls any member of his family that lies a-bed to a late hour in the morning: "Are you up at last, codladh go headra?"' *CBE* 266 (mid-Tipperary).

Codladh grifín n. '"Pins and needles"'; numbness' MS (e. Limerick); JPL (w. Cork); *CBD* (n. Kerry).

Codladh ina sheasamh n. phr. Literally, asleep while standing. 'A person who is so lazy that he could fall asleep standing up' DOC (Limerick); 'Look at him leaning on the pike, the bloody codladh ina sheasamh' PC (n. Clare).

Codladh sámh Tranquil sleep! 'Said to children heading for bed' MJD (w. Cork); PC (n. Clare).

Cógaisí n. pl. 'Goods' *CBE* 34 S (Galway). [*Comhgaisí*: fittings, appliances, all things necessary for anything, as a feast, wake, etc. – *Dinn*]

Cogaltaigh-corraigh n. 'A see-saw' Mac C (Monaghan). See *capall corrach*.

Cogar n. Also in form **cugger**. A whisper. 'Cogar here to me' JPL (w. Cork); Michael Banim, *The Croppy* 1, 298: 'Cugger, cugger, a-lanna'; McK (Leitrim); RBB (Waterford, s. Kilkenny). Hence, **cuggering**, whispering. Patk. Kennedy, *Fireside Stories* 94: 'Coshering and cuggering with the woodman' (Wexford). Hence **cogar-mogar**, conspiratorial whispering H (n. Clare). [Cf. English *hugger mugger*]

Cogarnach n. 'A row, a quarrel' NB (w. Limerick).

Coigcríoch n. 'A stranger' *CBE* 266 (mid-Tipperary).

Coigeál n. 'A dirty, untidy person' *CBD* (n. Kerry).

Coileach n. 'A cock, rooster' *CBE* 34 S (Galway); MJD (w. Cork).

Coileán n. Also in form **cullaun**. Diminutive form, **coileáinín**. 1. A puppy (Gen.) 2. A young scoundrel. 'Them young coileáns that attack old people, there's only one thing that will cure them: redden them with the ash plant' JL (w. Cork); PB (s. Tipperary); AK (Kildare); Michael Banim, *Crohoor of the Billhook* 1, 41: 'Myself always had the same mind of the cullaun' (Kilkenny); 'A coileáinín is a clever, sly, forward young person' NB (w. Limerick).

Coilí interj. 'Said when calling a horse or a cow' *CBD* (n. Kerry).

Coimrí n. In form **comree**. Protection, patronage, safeguard. 'Comree: trust, confidence' *Poole* (s.e. Wexford).

Coinicéar n. As **kinnegar**. A rabbit warren C (e. Limerick); H (n. Donegal). [< obs. English *conyger* < Old French *conniniere*.]

Coinín n. 'A rabbit' JPL (w. Cork); *CBD* (n. Kerry); PD (s. Carlow).

Coinleach n. 1. 'Stubble, stubble field' JPL (w. Cork). 2. 'A rough field' NB (w. Limerick).

Coinleog n. 'A stem of a straw used as a tube for drinking out of a well or a vessel' *IG* (Meath). See *coinlín*.

Coinlín n. 1. 'A lighted stick, a torch' McK (Leitrim); DOH (e. Limerick). 2. 'A single corn straw' MS (e. Limerick); NB (w. Limerick); 'A coinlín to free my pipe' *CBD* (n. Kerry). 3. 'A whistle made from a straw' *CBD* (n. Kerry).

Coinlín reo n. As **kinleen roe**. 'An icicle' *EASI* 280 (Limerick.)

Cóir adj. In form **core**. 'Kindly, innocent, good-natured' *IG* (Monaghan); 'Fair, honest. "He's as core as the day is long."' TB (Cavan).

Coircum n. 'A drink made from thin porridge, fresh milk and oatmeal' *CBD* (n. Kerry).

Coirín n. In form **quirren**. 'A small pot or skillet' H (n. Donegal).

Cóiriú n. Arrangement, dressing. In phrase 'She went out in her cóiriú': she went out in her figure' *An Cho* (w. Mayo).

Coirnéal n. In forms **curneale, kurneal**. 'A corner' *Poole* (s.e. Wexford).

Coirpe n. A horse's withers. 'Sixteen hands two to the coirpe' MJD (w. Cork).

Coirt n. A coating, scum. 'There was a coirt on the glass that would sicken you' MC (w. Clare).

Cois n. The second phase of a triple jump, or hop, step and jump as it was formerly known. 'Hop, cois and leap' *IG* (Kilkenny).

Coiseog n. In forms **cushog, cushoge**. 1. A stalk, a blade of grass or corn' ER (Louth); Con (Meath). 2. 'Cushogs are new sproutings of cut rushes. A single cushog may be used as a pipe cleaner' JVD (Cavan); *EASI* 343: 'cushoge' (Munster).

Coisín n. Diminutive of **cos**, foot. 'Sit down by the fire and warm your coisíns' MF (Westmeath); *CBD* (n. Kerry).

Coisinne n. White 'socks' on a horse's legs. 'Coisinne on a horse is a sign of weakness, the old people used to say' MJD (w. Cork).

Cóisir n. Also in forms **cosher, coshur**. 1. 'A cóisir is a friendly visit to a neighbour's house G (n.w. Donegal). Hence **cosherin(g)**, 'visiting a neighbour's house' ibid.; Jonathan Swift, *A Dialogue in Hybernian Stile*: 'He sometimes coshers with me ...' 2. 'A cosy chat, a gossip' S; G (n.w. Donegal). 3. 'A party' RBB (w. Waterford); 'Coshur: a feast' *Poole* (s.e. Wexford). Hence **cóisireáil**, as **cosherawl**, feasting: KB (e. Limerick). 4. A children's Easter party. 'On Easter Saturday children go from house to house asking for eggs ...'; 'Could you spare an egg for my cosher, mam?' S (s. Wexford).

Cóiste bodhar n. Literally, the deaf, or silent, coach: In folklore, a black coach pulled by six black horses and driven by a headless coachman (Gen.).

Cóiste mall n. Slowcoach. 'Used to describe somebody who is late for an appointment, or, more usually, someone who is agonisingly slow in doing a simple task. Did you ever have to wait for a slow cup of tea?' *An Cho* (w. Mayo).

Coite n. In form **cot**. 'A shallow, flat-bottomed boat used in net salmon fishing' FM (s. Wexford); RBB (s. Kilkenny); PD (s. Carlow).

Coiteoir n. 'A herdsman' *CBE* 104 (Leitrim).

Cóitheach n. 'An unconcerned woman. The word is almost impossible to translate, unless, of course, one were to be uncharitable and list some likely qualifiers. To qualify, a female must be strong, uncultivated, swift, and of the "bash-on-regardless" type. Absolutely regardless! One imagines, too, that she is black-haired and with a shaking mane' *An Cho* (w. Mayo). [Perhaps an ironic usage. Cf. *comhthach*: a companion *Dinn.*]

Coll faiche n. In form **coolfaugh**. The nettle, *urtica dioica* H (n. Donegal).

Collach n. Also in form **kiloch**. A boar. 'Getting married again at seventy! Well, isn't he the divil of a collach' MJD (w. Cork). Patk. Kennedy, *Legendary Fictions of the Irish Celts* 12: 'kiloch' (Wexford).

Colmóir n. 1. 'A scoundrel, a prime boy' JS (e. Kerry). 2. 'A frail person' *CBD* (n. Kerry).

Colpa n. 1. In form **collop**. Taken as the unit for grazing animals. Grazing for one cow or eight sheep *Pe* (Wexford); Eric Cross, *The Tailor and Ansty* 39: 'Well, collops was the old style of reckoning for land, before the people got too bloodyful smart and educated, and let the Government or anyone else do their thinking for them. A collop was the old count for the carrying power of land. The grazing of one cow or two yearling heifers or six sheep or twelve goats or six geese and a gander was one collop. The grazing for a horse was three collops'; 'The grazing of two sheep and their lambs; twenty geese' NB (w. Limerick). 2. 'The part of the flail that is held in the hand' *CBD* (n. Kerry); JL (w. Cork). As **collop** in *EASI* 237. Diminutive, **colpán**, 'a strong stick' D (s.e. Wexford); *An Cho* (w. Mayo). 3. A lazy person. 'He's a useless colpa' *CBD* (n. Kerry). 4. Calf of leg *CBD* (n. Kerry). 5. 'A collop is a year-old heifer or bullock' PD (s Carlow); S Ua G (s.

Tipperary). [< Mid. Irish *colpthach*, yearling heifer *RIA Dictionary*]

Colúr n. As **cooloor**. A pigeon *Poole* (s.e. Wexford). [Cf. Old English *culfre*; Middle English *culver*.]

Comaoin n. Compliment, recompense. In forms **comin, common**. In phrase 'to be ill one's common'. 'It was ill your common = it was ungrateful of you' Tr (Donegal). John Boyce, *Mary Lee, or The Yank in Ireland*: 'We're obliged to ye ... for sendin' us over what ye did in our time of need, and ill it'd be our common to forget it'; Seumus MacManus, *Bold Blades of Donegal:* 'It's ill our comin to say a hard word again' the sae'. [Cf. *b'olc an chomaoin ort é*, it would be a poor return to you (for your kindness)]

Comhar n., v. Also in forms **coor, core**. Cooperation; work given as a sort of loan to be paid back. 'They were working in comhar, helping each other in turn' H (n. Clare). 'We always return the comhar' *CBD* (n. Kerry). *EASI* 240: 'I send a man on core for a day to my neighbour: when next I want a man he will send me one for a day in return. So with horses: two one-horse farmers who work their horses in pairs, borrowing alternately, are said to be in core. Very common in Munster'; 'He's not a man who would coor much with his neighbours, I'm afraid' K (Wexford); 'All the Dunmore farmers coor...' 'Where were you to-day?' 'I was coorin' OCn (Laois); *GC* (Laois, n. Kilkenny). Hence **comharing** NB (w. Limerick); MS (e. Limerick); **coorin'** K (Wexford); D (Kildare). [Mid. Irish *comar*, co-tillage, ploughing partnership *RIA Dictionary*]

Comharaíoch n. A person who helps his or her neighbours, who attends funerals etc. 'He was a great comhraíoch' *CBD* (n. Kerry).

Comhartha n. A sign. 'In the phrase **comhartha (na) dtonn**, the distant, dull rumbling of the sea' PLH (n. Roscommon).

Comhchliamhain n. Men married to two sisters. 'They were comhchliamhains' *CBD* (n. Kerry). See *cliamhain*.

Comhluadar n. Also in form **colweddher**. 1. (Social) company. 'He's great comhluadar' MJD (w. Cork). 2. Chat. 'He rambled in to us last night and we had great colweddher' Mac C (Monaghan).

Comhráiteach adv. In conversational mood. 'The two of them were very comhráiteach' H (n. Clare).

Comóradh n. Obsequies. In form **cumra**. 'The house where a corpse is being waked' JB (n. Louth).

Conablach n. 1. 'A person of dirty habits' DOC (Limerick). 2. 'A big, lazy man' *CBD* (n. Kerry).

Conách n. Prosperity. 'In phrase **a chonách sin ort**, said when luck comes the way of a friend' H (n. Clare).

Conán n. A miserable person. 'That conán wouldn't spend Christmas' G (s. Kilkenny).

Conas tán tú? inter. phr. How are you? MJD (w. Cork). **Conas taíonn tú?** *CBD* (n. Kerry). **Conas tá tú?** *CBD* (n. Kerry).

Cóngar n. Short cut on a journey. 'I headed out the cóngar across the ré' (q. v.) MJD (w. Cork).

Conn n. 'The Ace of Diamonds' NB (Donegal).

Consaeit n. A grudge. 'He has some kind of consaeit against me ever since' RBB (s. Kilkenny). [< English *conceit*?]

Constaic n. An obstruction, an obstacle: 'Don't be putting any constaic in it' *CBE* 266 (mid-Tipperary).

Cor n. 1. A twist. 'Give the rope another cor' MS (e. Limerick). 2. A facial grimace, or twist, to show displeasure. 'He put a cor on him' *BASJ* (Cavan, Leitrim).

Cora n. 'Stepping stones across a river' MC (e. Mayo).

Cora n. 1. 'A weir' Smy (n. Clare). 2. 'Stepping stones across a river' MC (e. Mayo). 3. 'The word also refers to the line of turf which, at spreading time, was placed carefully on the brink of the turf-bank and dried so quickly there' *An Cho* (w. Mayo).

Córach adj. Neat, tidy. 'A córach little man' *CBD* (n. Kerry).

Corcach n. In form **kurkas**. A swamp. 'A marsh by the sea' LOS (w. Clare).

Córda an rí n. 'Cord of the king: corduroy' *CBE* 104 (Leitrim).

Cornasc n. 'A horn-and-leg spancel' MC (w. Clare).

Corp n. A corpse. John Dunton, *Report of a Sermon*: '... tis come bourying you are de corp, de cadaver, of a verie good woman...'; Wm. Carleton, *Phelim O'Toole's Courtship* 2, 200: '... only for him you'd be a corp before any relief would a come near you ...' (Tyrone).

Corr riasc n. In forms **grannycoreesk, correesk**. The grey heron, *Grus cinerea*. D (s.e. Wexford).

Corrach n. In form **curragh**. A marsh, a wet bog (Gen.).

Corrachán n. In form **karakawn**. 'A boy who has not developed fully' OCn (Laois).

Corraghiob n. In phrase, 'sitting on one's corraghiob – on one's hunkers' JC (w. Cork).

Corraigh interj. Move! 'Said to hurry a person' *CBD* (n. Kerry).

Corramhíol n. A midge. Plural **corramhíols**. 'The corramhíols would eat you alive' JL (w. Cork).

Corrathónach adj. Restless, fidgety. 'You're as corrathónach as a hatching hen' JC (w. Cork).

Corrlach n. In form **corkluck**. 'A seaweed seen at low tide' D (s.e. Wexford).

Corróg n. 'A bundle of anything tied together' *IG* (Monaghan).

Cortha pp. Exhausted. 'I'm cortha after the day in the meadow' MJD (w. Cork).

Cos interj. 1. 'Said to a cow, requiring her to move a leg during milking' MF (Westmeath). 2. Phrase **cos ar chois**, literally, leg-by-leg, meaning side-by-side. 'She's walking cois ar chois with the gentry now that she's married money' MC (w. Clare).

Cos n. The foot, leg. Plural **cosa**, in diminutive form **coshees**. 'A word used only when speaking to a small child' PD (s. Carlow); MG (n.w. Donegal).

Cosa bacóid n. A long hop or stride. 'He cleared the stream in one cosa bacóid' *CBD* (n. Kerry).

Cosa fuara n. Literally, cold legs. 'Stilts' PB (s. Tipperary).

Cosagán n. 'A spancel between the front and hind legs of an animal' *CBD* (n. Kerry).

Cosair easair n. Trampled matter, litter. 'The cows have a complete cosair easair made of the cornfield' JC (w. Cork).

Cosaráil n. 'Continuous trampling. " There won't be much of a crop left after the cosaráil of the tinkers' horses all night"' JS (e. Kerry).

Cosarán n. As **cusseraane**. 'A path through the fields' R (s.e. Wexford); *Poole* (s.e. Wexford).

Costarnocht n. Barefooted. Figuratively, bare, mere. Phrase **tae costarnocht** in translated form **barefooted tea** – 'tea on its own, without bread, biscuits, etc' MNicM (Down). [Cf. *Barefit broth, kail* – made with a little butter but no meat *Concise Scots Dictionary*.]

Cóta mór n. Also in forms **cothamore, cota-more**. An overcoat, greatcoat G (n.w. Donegal); MS (e. Limerick); Wm. Carleton, *Fardorougha the Miser* v: 'Throw that ould cothamore off o' you'; W. B. Yeats, *Fairy and Folk Tales of the Irish Peasantry* 193: 'What's that rowled up in the tail of your cothamore?'; A. Hume, *Irish Dialects* 23 (Antrim): 'The men wear the cota-more.'

Cothrom n. In form **cowdrum**. Fairness, equity, justice. 'Cowdrum: retribution, usually in the form of a thrashing. "You'll get a cowdrum and a half when when your mother sees what you've done" ' Del (Antrim).

Cothú n. Nourishment, sustenance. 'That calf got damn little cothú, by the looks of him' JL (w. Cork); *CBE* 104 (Leitrim).

Crá croí phr. Distress of the heart. 'He's an awful crá croí to his poor mother; always in trouble' JL (w. Cork); *BASJ* (Cavan, Leitrim).

Crá vb. n. In form **crawbin** in Walter Macken, *Mungo's Mansion*, 74: '... crawbin the life oo'm'. Distressing, agonizing.

Crabachán n. A weak, sickly person. 'What good would that crabachán be in a corn field?' Su (s.e. Wexford).

Crabaire n. 'A youngster that has too much talk out of him and is too grown-up for his years' JL (w. Cork).

Cradán n. Lesser burdock, *Arctium minus*. *An Cho* (w. Mayo); FF (Cavan); *CBE* 104 (Leitrim).

Crág n. In form **crawg**. 'A big, strong hand, well used to work' G (n.w. Donegal); 'For a man with such crawgs, he plays a flute well' R (n. Clare); 'He had two crawgs on him like shovels' O'K (Tyrone); OC (Monaghan).

Craibhtéal n. In form **crahail**. 'A contrary person' D (s.e. Wexford).

Craiceálaí n. 'A person gone in the head; not mad out, but scatterbrained and cracked' JL (w. Cork); BMacM (Kerry), NB (w. Limerick); PC (n. Clare).

Craiceann is a luach phr. Literally, the skin and its price. 'You want craiceann is a luach: you are asking for too much' CBD (n. Kerry).

Craideal n. 'A small, underdeveloped person' *CBE* 104 (Leitrim).

Craidheal n. 'Tragedy, misfortune, loss, pity' H (n. Clare).

Cráigeog n. 'A small fistful of anything' *CBE* 104 (Leitrim).

Cráin n. A sow MJD (w. Cork). Figuratively, 'a dirty woman' JL (w. Cork); 'A hag' *IG* (Cavan).

Craindí n. In form **crandy**. 'A bed made of planks or cut boughs on which a good soft mattress of down was put. You'd never see one nowadays' AOL (mid-Waterford).

Cráinín n. 1. The willy wagtail, *motacilla* JS (e. Kerry). 2. 'A file used to sharpen a scythe' *CBD* (n. Kerry).

Cráinseálaí n. 'A constant grumbler' PB (s. Tipperary).

Cráintín n. 1. 'A hatching goose' NB (w. Limerick). 2. 'An old, withered woman' ibid. 3. A small plump bird, especially a goose. 'I'll have a cráintín of a goose for you at Christmas' *CBD* (n. Kerry).

Craist n. A bang. 'I heard the craist as he fell off the ladder into the glasshouse' RBB (w. Waterford).

Cráite pp. Also in form **crawtha**. 1. Tormented, annoyed. 'I'm cráite by you' BOD (s.w. Cork); *CBE* 266 (mid-Tipperary); MS (e. Limerick); MC (w. Clare); *CBE* 98 (Kilkenny). *EASI* 241: 'crawtha.' 2. Sick. 'I'm feeling very cráite' SOM (w. Cork).

Cráiteachán n. 'A miserable person or animal; a person who worries continually – usually about trifles' NB (w. Limerick); 'Give some milk to that cráiteachán of a cat' H (n. Clare); 'A person impossible to satisfy' PB (s. Tipperary).

Cramhóg n. In form **cravog**. Refuse, residuum. 'Pig's liver and black pudding is cravog to us' JB (s. Armagh & n. Louth).

Crampán n. Cramp. 'I do be killed with the crampáns in the wet weather' MJD (w. Cork).

Cránaí n. A sow. 'Applied to a clumsy woman' Mac C (Monaghan).

Crandaí bogadaí phr. Also in form **wady buckety**. A see-saw. 'I'll make a crandaí bogaidí for you, to keep you quiet for an hour' G (n.w. Donegal); 'Wady buckety: a see-saw' LB (s.w. Dublin).

Crann cumair n. Literally, the tree of the ravine. The trailing willow, *Salix repens*: S (n.w. Donegal).

Crannaí n. In form **cranny**. 'A small, miserable-looking person' PJG (mid-Donegal); Kiv (Sligo).

Crannda adj. In form **cranned**. 'Dwarfed, stunted, shrivelled' H (n. Donegal).

Cranndúir n. 'A man shrivelled up with old age or some disease like arthritis' MJD (w. Cork).

Crannóg n. Also in form **crannogue**. 1. 'A beehive' JC (w. Cork). 2. An ancient lake dwelling; an artificial island in a lake. A. Hume, *Irish Dialects* 22 (Antrim and Down): 'There was a crannogue in an adjoining lake; *EDD* (Antrim): 'Such crannogues are now generally found in peat bogs because the lake which existed in former times has been filled up by the formation of peat.'

Craobh n. 'A branch of a tree' H (n. Clare); 'Cut up a few craobhs for the fire' C (Limerick).

Craoibhín n. 'A little branch' *CBE* 104 (Leitrim).

Craorac adj. Blood-red, crimson. 'Easily ruffled – "She is very craorac"' NB (w. Limerick).

Craosghalar n. 'Thrush; a disease of the throat' *CBD* (n. Kerry); NB (w. Limerick).

Crastaí n. 'A big corpulent fellow' *IG* (Monaghan).

Cratair n. 'An old coat, full of patches, like you'd see on a bacach. "Have you nothing to wear going to Mass but that damn old cratair?"' MJD (w. Cork).

Crátaire n. 'A weary, worn-out person' MJD (w. Cork).

Cré n. 1. 'A wretch' *IG* (Kilkenny). 2. 'A poor, hard-working man' ibid.

Creabhar n. 1. 'A small cock of hay' NB (w. Limerick). 2. 'The woodcock' MJD (w. Cork).

Creabhdéis n. A mixture of dulse and limpets. 'We had creabhdéis for the dinner' *CBD* (n. Kerry).

Creach n. Also in form **creagh**. A raid, robbery; ruin. 'The Guards found the poitín still and they did clean creach altogether' JL (w. Cork); Patk. Kennedy, *Legendary Fictions of the Irish Celts* 76: '... a creagh was made on my land in my absence' (Wexford); 'The cows are making a creach' Mac C (Monaghan).

Creachán n. Also as **crahaun**. 1. 'A small potato' MC (Limerick); PB (s. Tipperary); *EASI* 241: 'crahaun'. 2. Figuratively, 'a small, weak kind of a man' JL (w. Cork).

Créadóir n. A potter. 'But here used for a lounger – one who sits down most of the day, just as an olden time potter had to remain seated at his work: "The lazy créadóir" or "Sitting down all day in his créadóir"' *An Cho* (w. Mayo). [*in his*: direct translation of Irish idiom, *in a*.]

Creag n. 'A high rocky place' MJD (w. Cork). See *creig*.

Creamh n. 'Wild garlic' PC (s. Galway; n. Clare).

Creannthach n. 'An edible seaweed. This is a bluish black weed which is gathered at spring-tide in places along the shore. When dried and saved, it makes a salty, tasty leaf which is a rare treat' *An Cho* (w. Mayo).

Creathan n. 'We get so much rain around here that we have to put a creathan on the cocks of hay to protect them. A bit of light polythene, or some such material' MG (n.w. Donegal).

Creathnach n. 'Tiny shelled dulse' *CBE* 104 (Leitrim).

Créatúir n. In forms **cratur, craythur, cra-thur**. 1. Creature. Mrs S. C. Hall, *Tales of Irish Life And Character* 83: 'It's little pleasure they see, the craturs' (s. Leinster); Wm. Carleton, *The Poor Scholar* 2, 275: 'Bekase he's far from his own, the craythur!' (Tyrone); James Joyce, *Finnegans Wake* 4: ... the little craythur'. 2. Whiskey. 'A drop of the crathur is good for the heart' R (n. Clare); FF (Cavan).

Créice n. A wizened person or animal. 'You can get good money nowadays for any old créice of a beast' R (n. Clare).

Creig n. In form **crig**. 1. 'A rock' O'K (Tyrone). 2. Figuratively, 'in describing a person, a ballocks' O'K (Tyrone). See *creag*.

Criocaid n. 'A cricket' *IG* (Cavan).

Críochnúil adj. 'Tidy in doing work. "Seldom you'll get a críochnúil workman nowadays"' BOD (s.w. Cork).

Críochtóir n. 'A stick used by fishermen to kill fish' *CBD* (n. Kerry).

Criog n., v. In form **crig**. 1. To strike against; knock. 'I crigged my toe on a stone' MG (n.w. Donegal); OC (Monaghan). 2. To crush, kill. 'I'll crig them clegs as fast as they come' H (n. Donegal). 3. 'A mallet for beating flax' H (n. Donegal).

Criogar n. 'A small, light, tough person' DOC (Limerick).

Críon v. 'To age; to shrink, shrivel through washing (of cloth), or by action of the sun (on peat or wood)' H (n. Donegal).

Críonna adj. Also in form **creina**. 1. Old. 'I don't know what age he is, but he's very críonna' JC (w. Cork); Gerald Griffin, *The Collegians* 17: 'Nora Creina' (Limerick). 2. Wise. 'He's too young to be críonna' JL (w. Cork); *IG* (Cavan).

Crios n. 'A belt, girdle' PC (n. Clare).

Críosta interj. Christ! FF (Cavan); Mac C (Monaghan).

Criotóg n. 'A fragment of turf that has broken off' *IG* (Monaghan). [Cf. *crod*: a piece, a patch; diminutive, *crodóg O'R*]

Crithlaí n. In form **crilly**. 'A shivering sort of person: one who appears to be cold and bent down with misery: "Nora is gone in a rale oul crilly"' *CBE* 266 (mid-Tipperary).

Cró n. Also in forms **crow, craw**. Diminutive, **cróitín**. A pen, fold, for sheep and pigs; a coop for fowl. 'A pig crow and a duck crow' FF (Cavan); Seumas Mac Manus, *Bold Blades of Donegal* 307: 'He made his home in a sheep's craw on the north side of Sliabh Mór'. 2. A hovel. 'You could only describe her house as a cró, it's that dirty' G (n.w. Donegal). Diminutive, 'cróitín' *CBD* (n. Kerry); BMacM (n. Kerry).

Cró isteach interj. Into the pen! 'Said to geese when trying to get them into a pen' *CBD* (n. Kerry).

Crobhnasc n. In form **crounosk**. 'A cow's fetter, one that goes from her head to a leg' *CBE* 266 (mid-Tipperary).

Cróca n. 'A crock, jar' RBB (w. Waterford).

Croch n. The gallows. In phrase **croch ard chugat** – a high gallows to you! H (n. Clare).

Crochadh n. 'A pot rack; the contraption over an open fire from which pots are hung' *CBE* 104 (Leitrim).

Crochaire n. 'A hangman, or a gallows bird. "A right crochaire, that fellow"' PB (s. Tipperary).

Crochán n. In form **cruckaun**. 'A type of straw bed on which a dying person was laid' MC (e. Mayo).

Croí cráite n., adj. phr. Also in form **cree crawcha**. 'A plaintive person' LB (s.w. Dublin); 'A real cree crawcha' TOM (s.

Tipperary); 'Cree crawcha, very unhappy' PLH (n. Roscommon).

Croí maith mór phr. A good, big heart. 'He did it with a croí maith mór, this is, willingly' Mac C (Monaghan).

Croibhín n. In form (plural) **crivvins**. A finger. 'This word is seldom heard except in the plural, crivvins. No doubt from *crobh* a hand, paw' *IG* (Monaghan).

Croichtín n. 'A small croft; a small field' *IG* (Kilkenny).

Croíleacán n. 'The heart of a head of cabbage' *CBD* (n. Kerry).

Cróilí n. In form **croil**. Infirmity, disablement. Hence a very weak person. Wm. Carleton, *The Brothers* 168: 'That excuse of a man, little shabby Dan Gallagher! the poor croil, that a dacent man would put in his pocket and not feel 'im in it afther.'

Croiméal n. In form **crommeal**. Moustache. Patk. Kennedy, *Legendary Fictions of the Irish Celts* 234: '... a large cat sitting on his head, and licking his greasy chin and crommeal' (Wexford).

Croíncín n. 'A pain in the neck' *CBD* (n. Kerry).

Cróinín n. 'First run of small Autumn salmon' PB (s. Tipperary).

Crois n. Cross. In interj. **An Chrois orainn**, as **chrosh orrin!** in Wm. Carleton's *Phelim O''Toole's Courtship* 2, 226. Carleton's gloss: 'The Cross be about us' (Tyrone). **Crois Chríosta** interj., Cross of Christ, in form **chrosh Christa**. Michael Banim, *Crohoor of the Billhook* 1,72: '... only give me time to scrape my senses together ... oh, Chrosh Christa!'

Croisín n. In forms **crisheen, crusheen**. 1. 'The crosspiece at the top of the shaft of a spade' PJG (mid-Donegal). 2. 'A crutch' D (Kildare); *Simmons* (s. Donegal). 3. *EASI* 243: 'A stick with a flat crosspiece fastened at the bottom for washing potatoes in a basket. Also called a **bachaillín**, from Irish bachall, a staff' (Limerick). 4. 'A burial ground for unbaptised children' MC (e. Mayo).

Cromóg n. 'A heavy walking stick' *CBE* 98 (Kilkenny)

Crompán n. 'A grumpy person' *CBE* 266 (mid-Tipperary).

Crónán n. Also in forms **cronaune, cronaan, croniawn, cronane, crooniawn.** Hence **cronauner, crónaí.** 1. Eugene O'Curry, *Manners and Customs of the Ancient Irish*: 'The low murmurings or chorus to each verse in choral singing'; Jonah Barrington, *Personal Sketches of his Own Time* (Laois): 'The cronaune had no words ... executed by drawing in the greatest possible portion of breath, and then making a sound like a humming-top.' 2. A murmured song, as a lullaby. Anon., *The Irish Hudibras*: 'But sing dyselfe de sweet cro-naan'; Lady Morgan, *The Wild Irish Girl* 191: '(A nurse) hums old cronans or amuses me with what she calls a little shanaos'. See *sean nós.* (Leinster). Patk. Kennedy, *Legendary Fictions of the Irish Celts* 234: '... the dwarf in a far-off cell, rocking himself and singing a cronane.' (Wexford); Charles Lever, *The Martins of Cro' Martin* (Connacht): 'Warbled out a ditty ... your stupid old croniawn about dimples'; Crofton Croker, *Fairy Legends and Traditions* 228: 'It kept up a continuous cronane like a nurse hushing' (s.w. Munster). 2. 'An old song' H (n. Donegal). Hence 'cronauner, one who hums or sings the cronaune'. 'Whoever could hum the longest, was accounted the best cronauner' Barrington, op. cit. Hence also 'crónaí, one who hums a song; one who is always complaining' *IG* (Kilkenny). 3. 'Crónán: the purring of a cat' *IG* (Kilkenny); JL (w. Cork). 4. '"Potato fadge and crooniawns", descriptive of a good concert programme; good entertainment' H (n. Donegal).

Crosach adj. Cross or cross-looking. 'He's a crosach old devil' H (n. Clare).

Crosachán n. 'A cross or ill-tempered person' H (n. Clare).

Crosóg n. 'A rope used to tie a load of hay on a man's back' PJG (mid-Donegal).

Crosta adj. In form **crusty**. 'Hot or ill-tempered people were said to be crusty' Cor (Cavan).

Crostálaí n. 'A belligerent person' *CBD* (n. Kerry).

Crot a' chomhraic phr. 'Literally appearance of fighting or hostile intention. "He had a fearful crot a' chomhraic on him"' S Ua G (s. Tipperary).

Crot n. Shape, appearance. 'Put some crot on yourself' RBB (s. Kilkenny); NB (w. Limerick); *CBD* (n. Kerry).

Crotal n. 1. The lichen *parmelia omphalodes*, commonly used to make a reddish brown dye G (n.w. Donegal). 'The lichen from which litmus and orchil [i.e. archil] are prepared; also used to dye feathers and wool orange for tying fishing flies' H (n. Donegal); O'K (Tyrone). 2. 'A small potato' MS (e. Limerick). 3. 'The dregs of milk' *CBD* (n. Kerry).

Crothán n. A cluster, bunch. 'A crothán of blackberries' RBB (s. Kilkenny).

Crothóg n. 'Old worn-out clothes. "You'd pity her, to see her in crothógs, with all the money the husband have"' JL (w. Cork).

Cruachán n. 1. 'A miserly person' *CBD* (n. Kerry). 2. 'A little rick or stack' MJD (w. Cork). 3. 'A heap; a good measure' *IG* (Cavan).

Cruachás n. Difficulty. 'I'm in a right cruachás' *CBE* 266 (mid-Tipperary); JC (w. Cork).

Crúb n. 'The hoof or paw of an animal' JPL (w. Cork). 'Large hands or feet' H (n. Clare)

Crúbach adj. 'Club-footed' *IG* (Cavan).

Crúbadán n. In form **croobadan**. A distorted person or animal. 'He knocked John into a croobadan at the first blow' *Dinn* (Donegal).

Crúbóg n. 1. 'The spider crab' MC (w. Clare). 2. 'An awkward person' *IG* (Cavan); FF (Monaghan).

Crúibín n. In form **crubeen**. 1. A pig's trotter. Somerville and Ross, *A Misdeal* 96: 'vendors of crubeens, alias pigs's feet, a grizly delicacy peculiar to Irish open-air holiday-making' (w. Cork); Patk. Kennedy, *The Banks of the Boro* 120: 'My crubeens will be just the thing.' (Wexford); *Paddiana* 2, 87: 'It isn't aisy to rake out the marks o' crubeens like them'; George Fitzmaurice, *The King of the Barna Men*: '... and she dozing over the fire after her bully feed of crubeens' (Kerry); James Joyce, *Ulysses* 146: 'Florence MacCabe takes a crubeen and a bottle of double X for supper every Saturday.' 2. 'Used endearingly: a child's foot' PON (n. Dublin).

Cruiceog n. 'A heap of footed turf, set to dry' JL (w. Cork)

Cruicín interj. 'A harmless expletive' MC (Cavan).

Crúiscín n. In form **cruiskeen**. A jug. James Joyce, *Ulysses* 293: 'There he is, says I, in his gloryhole with his cruiskeen lawn ...' i.e. full jug. Also the title of a drinking song, *An Crúiscín Lán*.

Cruit n. Also in forms **cruiht, crith, crutch.** 1. A hump. 'He has a cruit on his back, the poor man' McK (Leitrim); Wm. Carleton, *Shane Fadh's Wedding* 1, 64: 'cruith'; Carleton has (footnote): 'The hump, which constitutes a round-shouldered man' (Tyrone); James Joyce, *Finnegans Wake* 111: 'crith'; 'Look at the crutch on him walking. He has a quare crutch on him' OCn (Laois).

Cruiteachán n. 'A hunchbacked person' JL (w. Cork). *al.* **cruipeachán** *CBD* (n. Kerry). Also in form **crootyer** *EDD* (Antrim).

Crupais n. In form **cruppy**. 'A wasting disease in animals, due to lack of food' JB (s. Armagh & n. Louth.)

Crupán n. A disease in cattle: cramps, *aphosphorosis* G (n.w. Donegal); *CBE* 104 (Leitrim).

Crústa n. A crust. 'Mind your ass. There's a fine crústa of frost on the póirse' (q.v.) JL (w. Cork).

Crústa n. As **croosht**. A strong blow. 'I gave him a croosht in the ear' JM (w. Cork); CBD (n. Kerry). Hence **crooshting**. They were crooshting me with stones' CBD (n. Kerry); JM (w. Cork).

Crústóg n. 1. 'A crust, an overdone rasher' S Ua G (s. Tipperary). 2. 'The solid residue after lard has been melted' MS (e. Limerick); NB (w. Limerick).

Cuach n. 'A bowl' Cor (Cavan).

Cuachán n. In form **coohan**. A state of entanglement. 'When a speller (the long line used in fishing turbot or other flat fish) gets entangled, it is called a coohan' Tr (Donegal); 'The wool is in a right coohan' S (n.w. Donegal).

Cuachóg n. 'A ball of thread' S (n.w. Donegal).

Cuairt n. *al.* **cuaird.** 1. A visit, especially an evening visit. 'I went on cuairt to Seán's house' H (n. Clare); 'He came on his cuaird and stayed until ten o'clock' IG (Kilkenny). 2. 'A round of stitches in knitting' Del (Antrim).

Cual n. Diminutive, **cuailín**, in form **gooleen**. 'A faggot; bundle, heap' IG (Wicklow; n. Wexford); 'She threw a gooleen of furze on the fire, and I thought she'd put the house on fire' MW (s. Wexford).

Cuansóg n. In form **coonsog**. A bees' nest. *EASI* 239 (Cork). [< *cuansa*, a haven?]

Cuarán n. In form **coorawn**. A sandal. 'Jocosely, a big, clumsy boot' Mac C (Monaghan).

Cuardaíocht n. Visiting a neighbour's house. In forms **koorjeek, koojeek, koorjeekin**. 'We went for a koorjeek, koojeek' OCn (Laois). Hence, 'We go koorjeekin' every Saturday night' ibid.

Cuardaithe v. pt. In form **coardhed**. Searched. 'Coardhed an recoardhed': searched and researched' *Poole* (s.e. Wexford).

Cuas n. *al.* **cuais**. In form **coose**, plural **cooses**. 1. A small bay, a cove, a creek.

Emily Lawless, *Grania*, ii. 31: 'The cooses and small bays on the west and north-west were astir with the hissing waves' (Mayo). 2. A cave, cavern. 'The cuais was alive with seals' RBB (w. Waterford).

Cuasán n. In form **cousaane**. A cavity; a hole as in a fence. *Poole* (s.e. Wexford): 'Eee crappes o' shearde ich had a cousaane' (In the bushes of the gap I had a hole to go through).

Cúb n. 1. 'The space beneath the stairs' MW (s. Wexford). 2. 'Space under the kitchen dresser' NB (w. Limerick). 3. 'A hen coop' CBD (n. Kerry); PB (s. Tipperary). 4. A bend. 'There's not enough of a cúb in that ash to make a good hurl' PC (n. Clare).

Cúbóg n. 1. 'A place where hens lay' CBE 34 S (Galway). 2. 'Easter eggs given as a present' Sy (Monaghan).

Cúibín adj. Hooked, bent. 'A cúibín nose' CBE 104 (Leitrim).

Cuid oíche n. In forms **cuidhich, cudeehih**. A night's lodging and food. 'Cuidhich' EDD (Antrim). [Evening portion, properly a supper and night's entertainment due to the lord from his tenant. Among the customary services cudeehih is mentioned by Spenser in *A View of the State of Ireland* EDD]

Cuideog n. 1. A wrap for the shoulders. 'Better a cuideog on your back than the doctor's horse in the street' G (n.w. Donegal). 2. A helping hand; a leg-up. 'I gave him a cuideog up on the horse' G (n.w. Donegal).

Cuigeal n. 'A yoke that ties two goats together by the neck' H (n. Clare). Hence **cuigealed**, tied together, married. 'I heard the O'Brien one got cuigealed to some fellow from Limerick' PC (n. Clare).

Cúigleáil v. In form **coogil**. To cheat at cards, embezzle. 'He'll take all he can coogil out of the place. He was cooglin' all he could' CBE 266 (mid-Tipperary).

Cuilceach n. A prime-boy; a trickster. 'Why should I vote for a cuilceach like you?' S (n.w. Donegal).

Cúilchearrbhach n. Literally, back-gambler. Onlooker at card game, often giving unwanted advice. Hence any pundit. 'The government is in no want of cúilchearrbhachs' MJD (w. Cork).

Cuileachta n. Company, a sociable person. 'He's great cuileachta, especially when he has a sup in' JC (w. Cork). A variant of *cuideachta*.

Cuileann n. 1. Holly, *ilex aquifolium* H (n. Donegal); JM (w. Cork). 2. 'Rough grass' NB (w. Limerick).

Cúileann n. In form **coolin**. Fair maiden. Song, *An Chúileann*, translated as *The Coolin*.

Cuileat n. *al.* cuileata. In form **quilt**. 1. A knave, a blackguard. 'A mischievous, conniving person' PON (n. Co Dublin). 'I'd expect no more from that quilt' ON (n. Dublin). 2. 'The knave in card-playing is the cuileata' MJD (w. Cork).

Cuileog lín n. In form **gallogleen**. Literally, flax fly. 'The earwig' PJG (mid-Donegal).

Cúilín n. 1. In form **coulin**. A forelock, especially on a boy's head. R. S. Brooke, *The Story of Parson Annaly* 50: 'With a grin and a pull at his coulin or forelock, he turned' (Ulster). 2. 'A little field' NB (w. Limerick); 'a small paddock field' AG (s. Tipperary). 3. 'The corner in a field' CBD (n. Kerry); PB (s. Tipperary).

Cuimil a' mháilín n. Literally, the rubbing of the bag. To toss about, to make a rag of something, or somebody. 'Kerry made a right cimil a' mháilín of us last Sunday' JL (w. Cork).

Cuimín n. As **cummeen**. 'A field separated from the farmhoiuse by other people's land' PLH (n. Roscommon).

Cuimireacht n. 'The endless litany of household chores, indoors and outdoor – such as milking, cleaning byres, foddering, cutting mangolds for cattle, digging to-morrow's dinner etc. A variant of *timireacht*' *An Cho* (w. Mayo).

Cuing n. Corner. In form **quing**. 'The swingle tree, with which the horses were yoked to the plough' MS (e. Limerick); 'He not pulling his quing; he's not doing his share of the work' NB (w. Limerick).

Cúinne n. 'The corner of a field' CBD (n. Kerry). 'He took the cúinne too fast once too often' MJD (w. Cork).

Cuinneog n. In forms **quingokee, khuingokee**. A churn: *Poole* (s.e. Wexford).

Cúinseach n. 'Flax tow' CBD (n. Kerry).

Cuíosach adv. Middling. 'How are you?' 'Cuíosach is all' BOD (s.w. Cork).

Cúiréib n. 'A riotous, obstreperous person. Usually applied to a woman' NB (w. Limerick).

Cuirim mo chos phr. As **kara magus**. Literally, I place my foot (probably taking up some formal pose to start dancing). Anon., *The Welsh Embassador*: 'EDM: kara magus. CLO: This dauncinge ioggs all my dynner out of my belly.'

Cuirim ort interj. I challenge you! 'Challenge spoken by a hurling captain before a match. The answer: **Tigim leat**, I accept' H (n. Clare).

Cúirliún n. 1. The curlew, *numenius arquata* MJD (w. Cork); CBD (n. Kerry). 2. 'A simpleton' NB (w. Limerick). 3. 'A bad singer' JL (w. Cork). 3. 'A tall, thin person' CBD (n. Kerry).

Cuiscreach n. In form **cushkina**. 'Reeds' H (n. Donegal).

Cuiseog n. In form **cushog**. 'A slender stem of grass or reed' O'K (Tyrone); OC (Monaghan).

Cuiteog n. 1. 'A worm' G (n.w. Donegal). 2. Perjorative, penis. 'Sure you're not afraid of that little cuiteog of a man' PJG (mid-Donegal).

Cúithín n. *al.* **cuaichín**. 'A rope used laterally at the top end of a rick of straw or hay' *CBD* (n. Kerry).

Cúl báire n. Also in form **cool-baury**. 1. 'A reserve of skilful players placed near the báire, (q. v.) or goal, in the game of hurling' *EDD*; 'Jack and I will stand cool – baury' P.W. Joyce quoted in *EDD*. 2. In the modern games, the goalkeeper in both Gaelic football and hurling.

Cúl fionn comp. n. In form **coolfan**. 'A thick beef sinew formerly given to teething babies to suck' LB (s.w. Dublin)

Cúl n. Also in form **kules** (pl.) 1. 'Back of head, poll' MF (Westmeath). 2. 'A head of hair' *CBE* 104 (Leitrim). 3. 'The goal in hurling and Gaelic football' Smy (n. Clare); James Joyce, *Finnegans Wake* 178: 'on akkount of all the kules in Kroukaparka ...' 4. A 'wide' in hurling. ''Twas only a cúl' *CBD* (n. Kerry).

Cúlán n. Also in form **coolaan**. 1. 'A secluded place' PD (s. Carlow). 2. 'A sheltered little field' McK (Leitrim). 3. 'A lane' Kiv (Sligo). 4. 'Coolaane is the back of the neck' D (s.e. Wexford); *Poole* (s.e. Wexford).

Culcais n. 'A spiritless person' Mac C (Monaghan).

Cúlóg n. 1. In phrase, **riding cúlóg**: riding behind another' *CBD* (n. Kerry). 2. 'Riding side-saddle' ibid.

Cúlóg riabhach n. Meadow pipit, *anthus pratensis*. 'To refer to somebody as a cúlóg riabhach is to say that he is a lackey for someone else. The primary meaning of the name is the little bird which is often seen following in attendance on the cuckoo when she is in flight. By a delightful metaphor the phrase is then applied to such as a president's aide-de-camp; a county councillor travelling with a TD; a bishop's secretary' *An Cho* (w. Mayo).

Cuma n. 1. Shape, form; appearance, look. 'He put a good cuma on the work' OC (Monaghan). 2. In form **cumas** 'I don't like the cumas of him ... Look at the cumas of him! ... He hasn't the cumas of a workman on him' OCn (Laois). [*Cuma* and *cumas*, capability, are confused here.]

Cumann n. Association, club, society. As in **Cumann Lúthchleas Gael** (Gaelic Athletic Association). As **cumman** in James Joyce, *Finnegans Wake* 228.

Cumar n. Also in forms **cummer, commer**. 'The ravine, made by streams running down the face of a hill or cliff. 'Don't stop the horse there, or she'll go into the commer' OCn (Laois); 'The cows are in the shade at the foot of the cumar' JL (w. Cork); *CBE* 266 (mid-Tipperary); Daniel Corkery, *Carraig-an-Aifrinn* 37: 'I thought maybe music might come rising up to me out of the cummer' (w. Cork).

Cumas n. Capability, competence. 'There's no cumas in me for that job' NB (w. Limerick).

Cúnach liath n. Grey mould. 'There was cúnach liath on the bread' H (n. Clare).

Cúnamh n. In form **coonagh**. Literally, help. 'Money put aside; savings; a nest egg' O'K (Tyrone).

Cupánach n. 'A little pig taken from the sow and reared on cow's milk, which he drinks from a cup' *IG* (Monaghan).

Cupóg n. In form **cappog**. Dock, *rumex*. 'Dig 'em out: that's the only way to get rid of the cupógs.' JL (w. Cork); G (n.w. Donegal); 'Cappogs, dock, are noxious weeds' ER (Louth).

Cur isteach n. phr. Interference. '"He puts no cur isteach on her": he doesn't interfere in her work. "He'd always put some cur isteach on it": if something was to be agreed, he'd interfere. "He put no cur isteach on me": he didn't question me; he accepted the story as I told it' *CBD* (n. Kerry).

Cur n. 'Clamp or outer layer of sods in a turf stack' MF (Westmeath).

Curach n. Also in forms **curragh, corragh, curagh** A light coracle used on the western coast (Gen.). Jane Barlow, *Kerrigan's Quality* 110: 'A bit of carved wood needed for the dislocated frame of his curragh' (Connacht); Emily Lawless, *Grania* 1, 4: 'She was about to step on board her curragh for the mainland' (Mayo); J. M. Synge, *The Well of the Saints* 24: 'I'm after bringing in a little curragh into Cashla Bay'; Charles James Lever, *The Martins of Cro' Martin* 2, xvi: 'Seated beside him, she learned to steer a corragh through the wild waves' (Connacht); Crofton Croker, *Fairy Legends and Traditions*: 'Jack put out his little corragh' (Munster); James Joyce, *Finnegans Wake* 131: 'curach'; J. M. Synge, *The Playboy of the Western World* 110: 'I've nice jobs you could be doing – gathering shells to make a white-wash for our hut within, building up a little goosehouse, or stretching a new skin on an old curagh I have ...'

Cúram n. 1. Family, dependants. 'How's the cúram?' G (s. Kilkenny); MS (e. Limerick). 2. Care. 'They have cúram on that baby: they look after her well' Mac C (Monaghan).

Cúramáboc n. Noise, clamour. 'The meeting got out of hand. Such cúramáboc you never heard in all your life' PC (n. Clare).

Cúramach adj., n. Also in forms **cooramuch, cooramagh, cooramuck**. 1. Careful, thoughtful, provident. 'He's a cúramach man; he won't go astray in matters of money' JL (w. Cork); Michael Banim, *The Croppy* 3, 60: '... bless the providhers for the cooramuch fire.' Glossed by Banim as snug (Kilkenny). *EASI* 239: 'No wonder Mrs Dunn would look well and happy with such a cooramagh husband.' 2. n. A fuss. Patk. Kennedy, *Fireside Stories*, 48: 'There was a great cooramuck made about the youngest boy next day' (They held a party for him.) (Wexford).

Curasán n. 1. 'Asthma' *CBE* 104 (Leitrim). 2. 'A person suffering from asthma' ibid. (Leitrim).

Curca n. In form **kurk**. 1. 'A little tuft of feathers on the crown of a bird's head' *IG* (Monaghan); G (n.w. Donegal). 2. (Of hair) 'A topknot' JL (w. Cork); RBB (s. Kilkenny).

Curcaí n. Also in form **kurky**. 1. 'A bird having a curc' *IG* (Monaghan); G (n.w. Donegal) 2. 'A woman who wears her hair in a topknot was called a kurky' RBB (s. Kilkenny). 3. 'A kurky is also a smartly dressed young woman, irrespective of how she wears her hair' RBB (s. Kilkenny).

Curcóg n. 'A heap of footed turf' RBB (w. Waterford).

Cutaí n. 'A short, worn-out article, such as a pipe, pencil, spade etc' *IG* (Monaghan). [< Scots *cutty*.]

Cúthail adj. Shy. 'She's a cúthail little girleen' MJD (w. Cork); *CBD* (n. Kerry).

D

Dá chomhartha sin phr. In consequence; it shows itself in the result. In translated form as **sign's on it**: 'He was always attentive to his work and sign's on it he is well-to-do' LB (s.w. Dublin; Gen.).

Daighsín n. *al.* **daighdín**. In forms **dydee, dydy**. 'A trinket, bauble, a worthless ornament' JFK (Galway); OD (Clare); RBB (s. Kilkenny).

Dáil n. The lower house of parliament. As **doil** in James Joyce, *Finnegans Wake* 256.

Dailc n. Diminutive, **dailcín**. Also in form **doulsheen**. 1. 'A strong, well-made person or animal. "A fine dailc of a woman, God bless her"' JPL (w. Cork); *CBD* (n. Kerry). 'He's a tough little dailcín' FF (Monaghan); 'He's an able doulsheen' NB (w. Limerick). 2. 'A large amount of anything valuable, such as coal, money, etc.' *CBE* 104 (Leitrim).

Dailtín *al.* **dailthín**. n. 1. 'An impudent young dailthín of a pup' JC (w. Cork); 'A well-dressed good-for-nothing' MS (e. Limerick); H (n. Clare); JL (w. Cork); *EASI* 245: 'Originally from **dalta**, a fosterchild. The diminutive, dailtín was first applied to a horseboy, from which it has drifted to its present meaning'. 2. 'You'd hear young fellows calling young women and girls dailtíns; stuck-up posers' PD (s. Carlow).

Daingean Uí Chúise n. Placename, anglicised Dingle, Co. Kerry. As **Dingley-couch** and **Dinglety-cootch**. 1. In phrase 'He's gone to Dingley-cooch': he's done something discreditable *EDD*. 2. In phrase 'to send a man to Dinglety cootch': to send him to Coventry; *EDD*: 'Quite common in Ulster'. [< 'the remoteness and inaccessibility of the Co. Kerry town' *EDD*]

Dáith Dubh n. phr. Literally, Black David. In phrase, 'He's a match for Dáith Dubh': he's very sly *CBD* (n. Kerry).

Dalbach adj. Bold, naughty. 'Especially used of a child, and particularly so if he or she persists in the boldness' *An Cho* (w. Mayo).

Dalcán n. A load, heap, amount. 'I hear she was left a fine dalcán of American money' H (n. Clare). See *Dailc* 2.

Dall adj. Also in form **dhoul**. 1. Blind. J. M. Synge, *The Well of the Saints*: Martin Dhoul and Mary Dhoul. 2. Ignorant. 'As regards the sums, I was dall in school, and I still am' G (Kilkenny).

Dallacáil n. (Act of) fumbling. 'What dallacáil have you? What are you looking for?' S Ua G (s. Tipperary).

Dallachán n. 'A person with poor sight' DOC (Limerick).

Dalladh púicín n. In form **dallapookeen**. Blind man's buff. *EASI* 245: 'dallapookeen'.

Dallán Dé n. comp. 'The magpie moth' Del (Antrim).

Dallán n. 'A standing stone or pillar stone' H (n. Donegal).

Dallóg n. 'Any kind of covering to blindfold the eyes;; a veil put over the eyes of troublesome cows' *IG* (Monaghan); McK (Leitrim); Mac C (Monaghan).

Dalta n. 1. A child. In plural form **daltaís**. 'Such a pack of pampered daltaís' *CBD* (n. Kerry). 2. 'A female good-for nothing' ED (s. Tipperary). See *Dailtín* 2.

Dámh n. Affection, liking. Peadar O'Donnell, *Adrigoole* 109' 'There was always dámh between her people and yours.'

Damhán alla n. 'The spider' *CBD* (n. Kerry).

Damnú síorraí ort interj phr. Literally, eternal damnation on you! In form **damnho sherry orth** in William Carleton, *Phelim O'Toole's Courtship* 2, 193 (Tyrone).

Daoine maithe n. The fairies. In translated form **good people** in James Joyce, *Finnegans Wake* 221. As **daoine matha** in Patk. Kennedy, *Legendary Fictions of the Irish Celts* 81: '... (propitiating) the fairies by addressing them as the daoine matha' (Wexford).

Daol n. The stag-beetle, *lucanus cervus*: Mac C (Monaghan).

Daol dubh n. As **dowlduff**. Ground beetle, *carabus*. Jane Barlow, *Irish Idylls* 277: 'If it had been any of them black bastes of dowlduffs, now, there'd ha' been some raison it it; I'd put me fut on one of them fast enough' (Connacht).

Dar an leabhar fhéin interj. In forms **dher a Lorha Heena, dher a larna heena.** By the Book itself. Wm. Carleton, *Phelim O'Toole's Courtship* 2, 230. Carleton has 'Dher a larna heena' in *The Party Fight and Funeral* 1, 190. He glosses the phrase thus: 'By the *very* book – meaning the Bible, which, in the Irish, is not simply called *the* book, but the *very* book, or the book *itself*' (Tyrone).

Dar an leabhar so interj. phr. In forms **dhar-a-loursa, leursuh.** By this book! Michael Banim, *The Croppy* 1, 305: 'dhar-a-loursa' (Kilkenny). Anon., *A Dialogue between Teague and Dermot*: 'leursuh you shud have cut deir troats ...'

Dar an Sprid Naomh interj. phr. In form **dhar an sphird Neev.** By the Holy Ghost! In Wm. Carleton, *Fardorougha the Miser* 377 (Tyrone).

Dar Críosta interj. phr. By Christ. In form **dar Chriastha** in Wm. Carleton, *Fardorougha the Miser* 121 (Tyrone).

Dar Dia interj. phr. By God. In form **Dar dhea** in Wm. Carleton, *Fardorougha the Miser* 120 (Tyrone).

Dar m'anam interj. phr. In form **dher manim.** By my soul. Wm. Carleton, *Going to Maynooth* 2, 182: 'Dher manim, if I was near you I'd put your bones through other ...' (Tyrone).

Dath n. Colour. In phrase **scéal gan dath**, 'a story without colour, a story without the appearance of probability' S Ua G (s. Tipperary).

Dathúil adj. Handsome. 'Present-day criterions of beauty may not concur, because *dath* is the Irish word for colour. *Dathúil*, then, means coloursome' An Cho (w. Mayo); JC (w. Cork).

Dé bheathsa interj. Welcoming salutation. 'You are welcome' JM (w. Cork); *CBD* (n. Kerry).

Deabhal n. The devil. In form **deawle** in Anon., *Captain Thomas Stukeley*. In form **diouol** in Wm. Carleton, *Phelim O'Toole's Courtship* 2, 189: 'To the diouol I pitch your half-acre, man' (Tyrone). In *phr.* **deabhal scéal**, and its translated form, **devil the story**. 'Have you any news?' 'Deabhal scéal': devil the story, not a bit of news: *CBE* 34 S (Galway).

Dealg n. In form **dawk**. A thorn. 'There's a dawk hidden in every compliment that one would give you' PD (Carlow); 'There's a dawk in my finger' J (s.e. Wexford); Dee (w. Waterford).

Dealramh n. In form **dowra**. A sign, appearance, resemblance. 'He had no dowra of work on him' *IG* (Kilkenny).

Dealús n. Dire poverty, destitution. 'You'll tell me next that there's no dealús in America' JPL (w. Cork).

Deamhan n. Devil. 'Deamhan take you!' G (s. Kilkenny).

Deán n. In form **dhan**. An estuary. An inlet of the sea; especially one that can be crossed at low tide. Patrick MacGill, *The Rat Pit*, 10: 'The woman on the verge of the channel (dhan they called it) stood ... looking at the water'; 'Why did ye let yer clothes drop into the dhan?' (Donegal).

Deannach n. 1. Dust. *EASI* 245: 'Mill-dust and mill-grains for feeding pigs' (Carlow and Tipperary); *CBE* 98 (Kilkenny); 'Basically this is the ordinary dust or ashes which may be raised by a gust of wind, or has to be dusted off the furniture from time to time. But the more usual meaning of the word in our locality is the figurative, not the basic meaning. So if a child spends a lot of money foolishly on a nonsensical toy, his mother might say "Take it out of my sight or I'll make deannach of it." One occasionally hears a mid-day gossip session being brought to an abrupt end by: "I must go in. I put on the potatoes half an hour ago and they'll be in deannach"' *An Cho* (w. Mayo); Con (Meath). See *cacallach*. 2. 'Light, sparse, downy hair' *CBE* 104 (Leitrim).

Dearagán n. The fish, bream RBB (w. Waterford).

Dearg adj., n. 1. Red. Patk. Kennedy, *Legendary Fictions of the Irish Celts* 168: 'capeen dearg', red cap (Wexford). 2. A red cow. 'Did you milk the dearg yet?' *CBD* (n. Kerry).

Deargadaol n. In forms **dardeel, daradeel.** FF (Monaghan, Cavan). 1. The rove beetle, *Ocypus olens.* 2. Figuratively, 'a wicked, evil person' *CBE* 34 S (Galway). 3. 'A term of affection applied to a little child' PON (n. Co. Dublin).

Dearóil adj. In forms **darrol, droll.** Small, puny, insignificant. *EASI* 246: 'darrol' (Mayo); 'Poor, wretched: droll' DOH (e. Limerick.)

Deas adj. In form **dhas.** Nice, pretty. Wm. Carleton, *Fardorougha the Miser* 5: '... mo colleen dhas': my pretty girl (Tyrone).

Deas anall interj. phr. 'If the cows did not stand for the women long ago they used to say "deas anall," and then they would stand' *CBE* 34 S (Galway).

Deas do chos interj. phr. Literally, settle your leg. 'Said to a cow to induce her to lift her hoof off something' *CBE* 104 (Leitrim).

Deascáin n. 'Gleanings' DOH (e. Limerick).

Deaschaint n. Sweet, insincere talk. 'Give over your old deaschaint for me' *CBD* (n. Kerry).

Deasóg n. 'The right hand' *CBE* 34 S (Galway).

Deatach n. Smoke. In expression 'to knock deatach out of a person, to give him a roasting, a hard time' H (n. Clare).

Deil n. Also in form **dell.** A turning lathe. *EASI* 246: 'dell'. Phrase **ar deil**, and its translated form, **on dell.** 1. In good working order. 'He's on his feet again after the accident, on dell, thank God' JC (w. Cork). 2. Splendidly finished. 'Everything he does is ar deil. Look at that for ploughing; a work of art' JL (w. Cork).

Deileadóir n. 'A complainer, of any size or age or state in life. The kind of person who has the complaints lined up so that when one source of complaint is removed he has another ... and another ... and another' *An Cho* (w. Mayo).

Deiliús n. Impertinence. 'That's enough of your deiliús, boy' JL (w. Cork).

Deimheas n. A pair of shears. Figuratively, a sharp tongue. 'Her ladyship have a deimheas of a mouth when it suits her' MJD (w. Cork).

Deirim v. In form **dherum.** I say. Wm. Carleton, *The Lianhan Shee* 2, 78: 'Husht, husht, dherum!' (Tyrone).

Deisigh interj. Adjust! 'Said to a cow, before sitting down to milk her' H (n. Clare).

Deocán n. 'A reed pipe; a drinking straw' NB (w. Limerick); PD (s. Carlow).

Deoch an dorais n. In forms **dhoch in dorris, duchan-dhurruss, deoc an doruis, duc an durras.** *Deoch*, drink + *dorais*, *gen.* of *doras*, door. John Boyce, *Mary Lee or The Yank in Ireland:* 'You'll take a dhoch in dorris (stirrup cup) with us' (Donegal); Wm. Carleton, *The Illicit*

Distiller 259: 'Oh, isn't it a thousand pities that you should be the first of the Duchandhurruss family that ever died and was buried without it' (Tyrone); Crofton Croker, *Fairy Legends and Traditions* 80: 'Tak a duc an durras before you go; you've a cold journey before you' (s. Munster); James Joyce, *A Little Cloud* 87: 'Let us have another one as a deoc an doruis – that's good vernacular for a small whisky, I believe.'

Deoch n. Also in forms **guck, gyuck**. 1. A drink. 'Have a deoch' H (n. Clare); 'You got two gucks and I only one' PON (n. Dublin); 'Give us a gyuck' PD (s. Carlow). 2. 'A call to pigs' PB (s. Tipperary).

Deoiricín n. In form **doorakeen**. A little drink. 'I had a few doorakeens too many last night' PC (n. Clare).

Deor n. Also in form **dyor**. A tear. Figuratively, a small quantity of liquid. Seumus MacManus, *A Lad of the O'Friels*, 14: 'That one deor (drop) of intoxicatin' liquids' (Donegal); Patterson: 'A wee dyor is the same as a wee drop' (Antrim).

Deoraí n. Also in forms **dorry, dyorrie**. 1. 'Deoraí: A miserable-looking person or animal' Mac C (Monaghan). 2. 'The dorry is the smallest pig in the litter' MG (n.w. Donegal); *Patterson* (Antrim): 'If a young pig in a litter is smaller than the rest it is called a wee dyorrie.'

Dia dhuit interj. Literally, God to you. Still a common greeting. The answer is **Dia is Muire dhuit**, God and Mary with you. Also in forms **Dieu-a-uth; Dieu-as-mayu-uth**. Michael Banim, *Crohoor of the Billhook* 1, 138: '"Dieu-a-uth", said the astonished stranger. "Dieu-as-mayu-uth", answered Pierce' (Kilkenny).

Dia leat interj. Literally, God be with you. (*singular*). 'You'd say it to someone leaving your house' JL (w. Cork); 'Said instead of "good luck!"' *CBE* 266 (mid-Tipperary).

Dia libh interj. Literally, God be with you. (*plural*). In form **Dieu liuve** in Michael Banim, *Crohoor of the Billhook* 1, 212: 'Dieu liuve a-vouchaleen'. Glossed by Banim as 'God speed you lads' (Kilkenny).

Dia linn interj. Literally, God with us! 'Said when one sneezes. To which is replied **Dia linn is Muire!**, God and Mary with us!' H (n. Clare); *IG* (Kilkenny); JL (w. Cork).

Diabhal n. Also in forms **deel, dheel**. The devil. In interjections th'anam 'on diabhal – your soul to the devil! (Gen. Munster); **an diabhal**, a minor expletive: 'An diabhal, but I think it's time we were going home' JL (w. Cork). Phrase **don diabhal amach**, translated as **to the devil out**. 'How are you?' 'I'm to the devil out', meaning very well: JL (w. Cork).

Diachairt n., interj. Euphemism for *diabhal*, devil DOH (e. Limerick); NM (w. Cork).

Dias n. An ear of corn. *al.* **déas** *IG* (Kilkenny). In form **discorn**: 'An ear of wheat' D (s.e. Wexford.)

Did n. In form **diddy**. A woman's breast. *EASI* 347: 'A baby sucks its mother's diddy'; James Joyce, *Ulysses* 546: 'Cuts off their diddies when they can't bear no more children'; also in Joyce, *Finnegans Wake* 179 (Gen.).

Dil n. A drop. Diminutive, **dilín**. 'There was no drink to be got at the wake, would you believe it? Not a bloody dil' PC (n. Clare); 'He had more than a dilín taken, I'd say' RBB (s. Kilkenny).

Díle n. Also in form **deela**. A deluge. 'That was some díle last night' S Ua G (s. Tipperary); 'The rain came down in a deela' G (s. Kilkenny).

Dílis adj., adv. 1. Faithful. 'He's not very dílis to her, I'm afraid' PC (n. Clare). 2. Soundly, steadily. 'He beat him go dílis' J (s.e. Wexford); 'The horses were working away go dílis' MW (s. Wexford).

Dílseog n. In forms **deelshog, dilsie**. 'A pretty girl they call a deelshog' FF (Cavan); 'A good-looking woman is a dilsie' TB (Cavan); Mac C (Monaghan).

Ding n. 1. A wedge. 'Make a ding of that beer-mat and put it under the leg of the table' R (n. Clare). 2. 'A strapping young man. "A fine ding of a young fellow"' MW (s. Wexford).

Dinnéar n. Dinner. In special sense, the potatoes for the meal. 'Dig the dinnéar' S Ua G (s. Tipperary).

Dioc n. 1. Set or inclination of the head. 'Look at the dioc of him' MF (Westmeath) 2. 'A stooped or bent appearance. "He has a dioc on him"' IG (Kilkenny).

Díocas n. Zeal. 'The horse showed no great díocas to jump the big fences' H (n. Clare).

Díocasach adj. Eager. 'He is very díocasach for the drink' H (n. Clare).

Díog n. 'A ditch or drain' BMacM (Kerry); NM (w. Cork).

Díolúnach n. 'A young hooligan; a bad pill. "He's a right díolúnach, that fellow"' MJD (w. Cork).

Díomá n. Disappointment. 'The díomá was a fright when Kilkenny lost' G (s. Kilkenny).

Dírigh interj. Straighten up! 'Said to a cow before milking her' PD (s. Tipperary).

Diúc interj. *al.* **diúcaí.** 'A call to hens at feeding time, and to which they answer' IG (Monaghan); TB (Cavan).

Diúch n. In form **gyuck.** The windpipe, gullet. '"I'll drink it by the gyuck", meaning from the bottle, without a glass' PON (n. Dublin).

Diúg n. In forms **doog, joog, jube.** A drop. 'Would you like a doog of water in your whiskey?' G (Kilkenny); OCn (Laois); 'There isn't a joog of milk in the house' DC (Galway); 'There wasn't a jube left in it' AG (s. Tipperary).

Diúgadh vb. n. In form **jooging.** To drain dry. 'Said of a bad milker: she was jooging at the cow' GC (Laois).

Diúlach n. Also as **joolyuck.** 'A lad, chap, "boyo"' CBE 104 (Leitrim); 'Joolyuck: a curious fellow, a fellow' PLH (n. Roscommon).

Diúraicín n. 1. 'An ugly, mis-shapen animal' NB (w. Limerick). 2. 'The last banbh born. It is often the smallest in the litter' DOC (Limerick). 3. 'A little fairy of a man or woman; a very small person' PB (s. Tipperary).

Dlaoi n. In form **dlee.** 'A wisp of straw, or hay, or hair' TH (s.e. Wexford); 'The first fistful of straw the thatcher uses' PB (s.e. Wexford).

Do féin a h-instear é phr. 'Translated as **to itself be told,** a sort of obsit omen, may it happen to no one else! – after narrating a misfortune that has happened to someone' H (n. Donegal).

Dó gréine n. 'Discoloration from sunburn on the part of a potato not covered by soil' MC (e. Mayo).

Dobhar chú n. Also in form **dhorko.** Literally, water hound. 1. 'The otter, or as we say, dobhar chú' S (n.w. Donegal). 2. 'A fabled monster; the Phooka or lake-seal of Lough Gartan' H (n. Donegal); Seumus MacManus, *The Leadin' Road to Donegal* 73, 4: 'If you ask me what is a Dhorko, I will tell you that a Dhorko is an amphibious animal, shaped much like a greyhound, with this one material difference, that the snout of the Dhorko is prolonged, running with a straight hand, very hard, sharp-pointed horn, some two feet or more in length, with which weapon it is enabled to execute fearful vengeance on its foes. This Dhorko was at one time ... common to all the lakes of Ireland; but at the present time – owing, I presume, to the hostile and intolerant spirit fostered towards him by unbelievers – is to be found only in the numerous lakes in the remote districts of Donegal, as well as, I daresay, of Connemara and parts of Kerry.'

Dobhrán n. 1. 'A stupid, dull person' MC (e. Mayo). 2. 'A weak animal' ibid.

Dochar n. Harm. In phrase **what dochar** JPL (w. Cork).

Dóib bhuí n. 'Viscous yellow clay from lake or river' H (n. Clare); *CBE* 34 S (Galway).

Doicheall n. Churlishness, inhospitality. 'I thought they had a doicheall before me, i.e. I thought they weren't too glad to see me' MG (n.w. Donegal); 'You'd get nothing in that house but the doicheall' *CBD* (n. Kerry); MS (e. Limerick); H (n. Clare); NM (w. Cork).

Doicheallach adj. Inhospitable, hostile. 'He's a very doicheallach man, a real begrudger' H (n. Clare).

Dóideog n. 'An awkward lump, especially a large, ungainly sod of turf. But it could be an outsize boot, or word, or person' *An Cho* (w. Mayo).

Doighear n. 1. 'A dart of pain. "The doighear hit me all of a sudden"' NM (w. Cork). 2. Ill-feeling. 'He said what he had to say to me with great doighear' H (n. Clare).

Doirb n. 'A water beetle' PJG (mid-Donegal); *CBE* 104 (Leitrim). Figuratively, 'a spiteful little person' ibid. (Leitrim).

Dol n. In form **dull**. 'A loop, a running noose, a snare for catching rabbits' McK (Leitrim); Mac C (Monaghan); FF (Cavan); G (n.w. Donegal); AM (Leitrim); 'A horse-hair noose and snare for catching trout; also applied to a noose in a rope or cord; the phrase "put a dull on the rope" is frequently heard' *Patterson* (Antrim). Hence **dulling**, a method of catching sheep by means of a noose G (n.w. Donegal). Hence also **dulling-boat**: 'one man stands on the shore holding the end of the net while the boat on the sea moves about' Tr (Donegal); Seumus Mac Manus, *Bold Blades of Donegal* 55: 'It was lurch and lumber forward he did, like an Inver dulling-boat tacking in a gale of wind'; ibid. 260: 'The thrill of steering a dulling-boat round and round the rushing herring shoals.'

Domhan Thoir n. *al.* **Domhan Toir**. The Eastern World. In expression, 'You'll be heard in the Domhan Thoir' MS (e. Limerick); H (n. Clare); *IG* (Kilkenny); PB (s. Tipperary); 'At the Missions long ago you'd hear the roars of the Redemptorists in the Domhan Toir' PD (s. Carlow).

Domhnach deireannach n. phr. As **Donagh-dearnagh**. Literally, last Sunday. *EASI* 248: 'Last Sunday of the period before the first of August; the Sunday before Lammas' (Ulster).

Donaí adv. In forms **dunny, dawny**. Sickly, wretched. Richard Head, *Hic et Ubique*: 'The donny fellow make buse for my moister'; 'He's donny, the poor man, since his fall' OC (Monaghan); MF (Westmeath); 'Indeed he's dawny enough' LB (s.w. Dublin); 'Pat is dawny with the cold in his head' *EDD* (Cavan).

Dónal gorm n. 'A name for the sea in north Antrim and Rathlin island' O'K (Tyrone).

Donán n. Also in forms **dhonan, dunnan**. A weak person or animal PJG (mid-Donegal); R (n. Clare); JPL (w. Cork); Wm. Carleton, *The Lianhan Shee* 1, 77: 'There now, ye dhonans ye, ye can't say that ye're ill-thrated here ...'; 'The poor dunnan!' JB (s. Armagh & n. Louth).

Donas n. Also in form **dhunnus**. Misfortune, mischief. 'Isn't he the donas' *IG* (Dublin); Michael Banim, *The Croppy* 1, 139: '... pitch 'em all to the dhunnus' (Kilkenny). Hence **donaisín**, as **dunisheen** in *EASI* 253: 'a small, weakly child' (Carlow).

Donasaí adv. In form **donsy**. Sick-looking, weak. 'I wish I could say she was better nor donsy' PD (Carlow); FF (Cavan).

Donn adj. In form **dhun**. Brown; brown-haired. William Carleton, *Fardorougha the Miser* 6: 'God bless her anyway, an' mark her to grace and happiness, mo colleen dhas dhun' – My pretty brown-haired girl (Tyrone).

Donnsa n. 'A big lazy boy or girl: "He's going around in a donnsa". Note the idiom "in a". " That big donnsa should be sent to work"' *CBE* 266 (mid-Tipperary).

Dorc n. 1. 'A surly, ignorant, silent person' DOC (Limerick) 2. 'A big, awkward lump of a man or woman' JL (w. Cork).

Dorcha adj. In translated form **dark**. 1.
Blind. Mr and Mrs S. C. Hall, *Ireland, Its
Scenery and Character* 1, 11: 'Look at the
poor that can't look at you, my lady, for the
dark man can't see if yer beauty is like yer
sweet voice'; J. M. Synge, *The Well of the
Saints* 36: '... and it's more joy dark Martin
got from the lies we told of that hag is
kneeling by the path than your man will get
from you, day or night, and he living by
your side'; ibid. 35: 'Why should he be
vexed, and we after giving him great joy and
pride, the time he was dark?'; James Joyce,
Ulysses 181: 'Dark men they call them'. 2.
Secretive. 'He wouldn't tell you the time,
he's that dorcha' Dee (w. Waterford).

Dorchas n. 'Dark-textured bread, owing to
bad baking; considered unsatisfactory' Cor
(Cavan).

Dorn n. Also in form **dhorrug**. Diminutive
forms **dornán, doirnín, dornóg, dornogue, dúirnín. 1.** A fist. 'A dorn of flour'
CBD (n. Kerry); 'A dornán of corn' *An Cho*
(w. Mayo); JL (w. Cork). 2. *EASI* 249:
'Dornóg, as dornogue: 'a small round lump
of stone, fit to be cast from the hand'. 3 'A
strong leather glove, used on the left hand
by faggot cutters' ibid. 253 (Wexford). 3. 'A
dornóg is a small, sturdy woman' PJG (mid-
Donegal). 4. 'The handle of a scythe – is
called doirnín' H (n. Clare); *EASI* 253:
'One of the two handles of a scythe that
project from the main handle'; 'I heard
them call the grip of a scythe a dúirnín'
NM (w. Cork); PB (s. Tipperary); MS (e.
Limerick). 5. As **dhorrug**. 'I gave him a
dhorrug in the ribs' OC (Laois).

Dornfhásc n. In form **dornasking**. Act of
feeling with hands, groping; hand-fishing,
trout-tickling. 'There he was, dornasking his
way up the stairs in the dark' SOB (s.
Tipperary).

Dorr interj. 'An expression of encouragement
used to a dog' Q (Donegal); 'Said in daring,
or inciting butting or wicked rams' *IG*
(Meath); 'We used to say this to a bull. We'd
be safely up a tree or sitting on the pier of a
gate at the time, of course' JL (w. Cork).

Dorránaí n. Also as **durawny**. A surly,
grumpy person. 'You'd never hear a civil
word out of his mouth, the old dorránaí' JS
(e. Kerry); George Fitzmaurice, *The King of
the Barna Men:* '... an old durawny of sixty
...' (Kerry).

Dos n. 1. 'A bush' PC (n. Clare). 2. 'A mop
of hair' MC (e. Mayo).

Dosachán n. 'A boy who acts like a man. An
impertinent youngster' DOC (Limerick).

Dosaire n. Also in forms **dussy, dussyeh. 1.**
'A dosaire is a person who never stops
talking and who thinks himself fierce wise
altogether' JL (w. Cork) 2. 'A young man
who apes the manners of his elders' PB (s.
Tipperary). 3. 'A brat' *CBE* 266 (Tipperary); 'A dussy, or dussyeh is a forward
young person, usually a girl' TOM (s.
Tipperary).

Dosaireach n. Courage. '"Show dosaireach":
said when challenging in a card game' *CBD*
(n. Kerry).

Dosán n. In form **dossan. 1.** A small bush
PJG (mid-Donegal). 2. 'A forelock' ibid. 3.
'A tassel' MG (n.w. Donegal).

Drabhlach n. In form **drowluck**. 'A deep
tub, a "cool"' S Ua G (s. Tipperary).

Drabhsóg n. 1. 'An insignificant person.
A small person' NB (w. Limerick). 2.
'A talkative, boastful woman' *CBD* (n.
Kerry).

Dráchaí adj. In form **drawky**. 'A drawky
day, wet, miserable and depressing' AM
(Leitrim)

Drad n. 'Mouth, showing teeth or gums in a
smile or grimace' MS (e. Limerick). In
phrase "he's the old drad" – said of a
winning, smiling baby' MF (Westmeath).

Dradaire n. 'A sneering person' *CBD* (n.
Kerry); *Sguab* (w. Cork).

Drádamán n. Hubbub, commotion. *al.* **drálamán** *CBD* (n. Kerry).

Draighneán n. In form **dreenan**. The blackthorn. 'Fairy thorns, sloe bushes, dreenans'
JB (s. Armagh & n. Louth.)

Dráinín interj. As **drawneen** 'A word said to pet a cow while being milked.' PD (Carlow); *CBE* 98 (Kilkenny).

Draíochta adj. In form **draghy**. Literally, magical, enchanted. Of a road, or journey: 'one which is deceptive in the sense that it is really longer than it appears to be. A draghy road' Tr (Donegal).

Drálamán n. 'Work and its accompanying noise' NB (w. Limerick).

Dramhaíl n. 1. 'Refuse, trash, inferior stuff' NB (w. Limerick). 2. 'The smallest animal in a brood or litter' PJG (mid-Donegal); MS (e. Limerick).

Dránaí n. 'A delicate person' *CBE* 34 S (Galway).

Drancaid n. 'A flea' *CBE* 104 (Leitrim).

Drann n. 'A grin' H (n. Clare). Hence **drannaíl**, (act of) grinning. 'I don't like the drannaíl of him. He's up to no good' H (n. Clare). Hence also **drannachán** *al.* **drann-aire**. 'A drannachán: one who is half-grinning or half-laughing' *IG* (Kilkenny); 'A drannaire is a person given to laughing at others; a grinner, a sneerer' PB (s. Tipperary).

Drantán n. *al.* **drandán**. 'Humming, crooning of a song' MF (Westmeath); 'Drandán' *IG* (Cavan).

Draoib n. Mud. 'You couldn't see the colour of her dress from the draoib' JPL (w. Cork).

Draoiblín n. 'A person whose clothes are wet and/or muddy' FF (Cavan); *CBE* 104 (Leitrim).

Draois n. 'A laughing expression on the face' *CBE* 104 (Leitrim).

Dréacht n. In dimunitive form **dréachtín**, as **drachteen**. 'A story' KB (e. Limerick).

Dream n. In form **dhroum**. 'A class, coterie or clique. I don't know them. I was never one of that dhroum' PC (n. Clare); S Ua G (s. Tipperary).

Dreamadaire n. 'A hunchback' NB (w. Limerick). [< English *dromedary*?]

Dreas n. Also in forms **dhrass, drass, grass, dhass**. 1. A trip or jaunt in a vehicle' MF (Westmeath). 2. Spell, bout, turn. 'I took a dreas at the churning' MS (e. Limerick); 'Give me a dreas of your pipe'; 'I fell asleep for a dreas' H (n. Clare); Patk. Kennedy, *Legendary Fictions of the Irish Celts* 161: 'I wasn't after cryin' a second dhrass when I heard steps outside' (Wexford); 'Drass, grass' LB (s.w. Dublin): 'to give a drass of the churn dash is good manners when one enters a house where churning is going on'. 3. A section, such as a section of a long poem. Michael Banim, *Crohoor of the Billhook*, 1, 252: '... an irregular and dismal song, uttered in many an unequal dhass, or verse, his keenthecaun'.

Dréimire Muire n. Literally, Mary's ladder. The centaury or pink gentian, *Erythroea centaurium*: MG (n.w. Donegal).

Dréimire n. A ladder. 'Watch yourself. I wouldn't trust the rungs of that oul dréimire' S Ua G (s. Tipperary).

Dréimire na mBodóg n. Literally, the ladder of the heifers. 'The path or ladder made by cows' hooves in passing out muddy gaps' S Ua G (s. Tipperary).

Dreoilín n. 1. 'The wren' AOL (mid-Waterford); JC (w. Cork). 2. Figuratively, 'a tiny child, man, or woman' Mac C (Monaghan); J (s.e. Wexford). 3. Figuratively, 'a weakling' NB (w. Limerick).

Dreoite pp. In n. form **droit**. Decayed, withered. Hence 'a small, deformed piglet' O'K (Tyrone).

Dríodar n. Dregs, rubbish. 'They are only the dríodar of the parish' MS (e. Limerick); 'The dríodar of a bottle' H (n. Clare); 'The horse drank the water to the dríodar' MC (e. Mayo).

Driog n. In forms **drig, drigeen, drooigeen, drooig**. 'A droplet. A small quantity of liquid' D (s.e. Wexford).

Driongán n. 'A small, miserable person' MS (e. Limerick); 'An animal in a poor condition' NM (w. Cork); KB (e. Limerick).

Driopás n. Hurry. 'That kind of hurry which causes pressure or anxiety. Driopás could be associated with preparing for a cow to calf, or preparing for the arrival of the Yanks. The state of driopás is seldom admitted in the first person: it frequently arises in a question: "What driopás is on you now?"' *An Cho* (w. Mayo).

Driseachán n. 'The rectum' PB (s. Tipperary).

Driseóg n. Also in form **drishog**. The common bramble or blackberry, *rubus fruticosus*. 'May hands are scrawbed by them driseogs' PB (s.e. Wexford); AOL (mid-Waterford); 'The ram has a ten foot drishog hanging from his tail' MG (n.w. Donegal).

Drisín n. In form **drisheen(s)**. The intestine of a pig, stuffed with blood and other ingredients, and cooked as a pudding. Associated with Cork. James Joyce, *A Portrait of the Artist as a Young Man* 91: 'Mr Dedalus had ordered drisheens for breakfast and during the meal he crossexamined the waiter for local news'; Joyce, *Finnegans Wake* 164: 'Correspondents, by the way, will keep asking me what is the correct garnish to serve drisheens with. Tansy Sauce. Enough.'

Driuch n. In form **drukt**. Sickly appearance. 'He is drukt in himself lately' OCn (Laois).

Driúrac n. 'Pins-and-needles' R (n. Clare). *al.* **druarthach** *CBD* (n. Kerry).

Drobhailín n. In form **druvaleen**. 'A tub' PD (s. Carlow).

Droch adj. In form **drogh**. Bad, evil. *EASI* 251: 'The worst and smallest bonnive in the litter' (Armagh).

Droch rath ort interj. phr. 'Bad luck to you!' *IG* (Cavan).

Drochmheas n. Contempt. 'Twas with drochmheas they used to put nicknames on people' *CBD* (n. Kerry).

Droichidín n. 'A little bridge' PB, AG (s. Tipperary).

Droighean bán n. 'The whitethorn' PJG (mid-Donegal).

Droighean dubh n. Also as **dreenan**. 'The blackthorn' PJG (mid-Donegal). Also as **droighneán donn** (Gen. Munster). 'Dreenan is the blackthorn tree' JB (s. Armagh, n. Louth.'

Droimín drú phr. Also as **drimmy drew**. 'Despondent, down-in-the-mouth. "He's looking very druimín drú"' MF (Westmeath); 'A man speaking critically about his wife called her a drimmy drew' MC (Cavan). [Cf. Donegal phrase *ag tuitim i ndruim dubhach* – becoming dejected.]

Droinneach adj. In form **drimeck**. Humped, arched. Of animals, sickly. 'She looks drimeck.' Of the weather, inclined to deteriorate. 'The day is very drimeck-looking' OCn (Laois).

Drólainn n. 'A weak old man. "He's gone in a drólainn. He's barely able go go for a walk' JPL (w. Cork).

Drólásach adj. 'Bad tempered, nasty. 'For neighbours, they were ever drólásach' NM (w. Cork). Variant of *drabhlásach*.

Drom n. In form **drum**. 'The ridge of a hill' MG (n.w. Donegal); DOH (e. Limerick); TB (Cavan); FF (Monaghan); Con (Louth, Meath).

Drom taoide n. Literally, top of tide. 'High water mark' *CBD* (n. Kerry).

Dromán n. *al.* **dromaide**. 'Leather back band of plough traces' *Pe* (Wexford); MF (Westmeath); 'That harness needs a new dromán' MJD (w. Cork); 'I'd call the back band the dromaide' PJG (mid-Donegal).

Dronnachán n. 'A hunchback' R (n. Clare).

Drúcht n. 1. Dew. 'The drúcht is bad for shoe leather' JPL (w. Cork); MC (e. Mayo). 2. Euphemism for light rain. 'Tis only drúcht' PB (s. Tipperary).

Drúchtín n. Also as **drutheen**. 1. 'Light dew' MC (e. Mayo). 2. A snail, slug, without a shell. 'Women used to go out early on May Morning to find a drúchtín. Whatever colour was on the first drúichtín they found would be the colour of their true love's hair' G (Kilkenny); Crofton Croker, *Fairy Legends and Traditions* 296: 'The young girls go looking after the drutheen, to learn from it the name of their sweethearts'; ibid. 302 (note): 'A small white slug or naked snail sought by young people on May Morning, which, if placed on a slate covered with flour or fine dust, describes, it is believed, the initials of their sweethearts' (s. Munster). 3. A penis. 'An Drúchtín': title of a bawdy 18th century macaronic song about same. 4. **Gearradh drúchtín** 'Soreness under the toes from walking on dewy grass, barefooted' MC (e. Mayo).

Drud n. A squeak; the least noise. 'I gave him his answer, and there wasn't a drud out of him after that' MJD (w. Cork).

Druid v. Close. In phrase **druid do bhéal** – close your mouth Mac C (Monaghan).

Drúisc n. 'A long dejected face, such a face as tells a story of misery better than any words of its owner' *An Cho* (w. Mayo).

Duailín n. 'A horse's forelock' CBD (n. Kerry).

Duarcán n. A moody person, given to depression. 'He never laughed in his life, that duarcán' JPL (w. Cork).

Duartan n. 'A heavy downpour of rain. 'You couldn't hurl on that pitch after the duartan we got' Smy (n. Clare).

Duasmánaí n. In form **doosamauny**. 1. 'An undependable person' CBE 266 (mid-Tipperary). 2. 'A gloomy person' ibid.

Dúchal n. 'A large rectangular pile of farmyard manure built, mostly without supporting walls, to a height of several feet and with the sides neatly trimmed. At the lower end is a channel to catch effluent. Now largely displaced by slurry pits' O'K (Tyrone).

Dúchán n. 'A small clamp of turf' MC (e. Mayo).

Dúchas n. Inherent characteristic or trait. 'That's a dúchas in him, to be fond of the drink' PJG (mid-Donegal); 'Twas his dúchas to be bald' CBD (n. Kerry).

Dúd n. 'Craning of the neck with head to one side, in a listening attitude. He had a dúd on him. He had a dúd of divilment on him' MF (Westmeath).

Dúdach adj., n. 1. 'Foolish looking' PON (n. Co. Dublin). 2. 'A fool' ibid.

Dúdaire n. 1. 'An incessant pipe-smoker' NB (w. Limerick); S Ua G (s. Tipperary). See *dúidín*. 2. 'An inquisitive person, an eavesdropper' RBB (w. Waterford).

Dúdálaí n. 1. 'A shy, self-conscious person' NB (w. Limerick). 2. 'A dunce, a dolt' S Ua G (s. Tipperary); AOL (mid-Waterford).

Dúdóg n. 1. A blow. 'A dúdóg across his pus would do him a power of good' G (Kilkenny); PON (n. Dublin); NB (w. Limerick). 2. *EASI* 248: 'A big pinch of snuff' (Limerick). 3. A short smoking pipe CBD (n. Kerry); CBE 104 (Leitrim). See *dúidín*. 4. 'A drop of whiskey' PB (s. Tipperary).

Dúidín n. A short smoking pipe. Also in forms **doodeen, dhudeen, dudeen, dudheen**. *Paddiana* 1, 65: 'The tobacco smoke ascended from the bowl of his doodeen'; *N&Q* 1873: 'The legend of old Donnybrook Fair, describing the conventionally pugnatious Irishman as with caubeen adorned with dhudeen stuck in the band on his head'; Crofton Croker, *Fairy Legends and Traditions* 87: 'A dudeen in his mouth' (s. Munster); Patk. Kennedy, *The Banks of the Boro* 174: 'Their hands went into their pockets more than once in search of the treacherously consoling dhudeen' (Wexford); As 'dudheen' in James Joyce, *Finnegans Wake* 200 (Gen.).

Dúig n., v. 1. A drop. 'He didn't leave a dúig in the glass' NB (w. Limerick). 2. Empty. 'Dúig it out well' ibid.

Dúil n. Also as **deul**. Desire. 'He have a great dúil in the porter' C (Limerick); S Ua G (s. Tipperary). In footnote to Anon., *The Irish Hudibras:* 'deulmore, Iricism, great eye, great desire'.

Duileasc n. *Rhodymenia palmata*. In forms **dulse, dulsk, dillesk, dilse.** *EASI* 247: 'A sort of sea plant growing on rocks, formerly much used when dried as an article of food, and still eaten in single leaves as a sort of relish. Still sold by the basket-women of Dublin. (Gen.). Hence **dulse-man; dulse-wife**, sellers of dulse. RS (Antrim).

Duine n. Person. In phrase **mo dhuine**, literally, my person. 'Look at mo dhuine making an ass of himself' H (n. Clare). Phrase **duine gan dadaidh**, literally, a person without anything, and figuratively, 'a thin insignificant person' *CBE* 104 (Leitrim). Phrase **duine uasal**, noble person, gentleman, in form **dinnha ousahl** in Wm. Carleton, *Phil Purcel, the Pig-Driver* 1, 417 (Tyrone).

Dúirt sé dáirt sé allit. couplet. *al.* **dúirse dáirse**. Also as **doorshay-daurshay**. 1. 'A bearer of hearsay tales' MS (e. Limerick); *CBD* (n. Kerry). 2. Hearsay, gossip. *EASI* 249: 'Doorshay-daurshay: often used by Munster lawyers in court, whether Irish-speaking or not, in deprecation of hearsay evidence in contradistinction to the evidence of looking-on. "Ah, that's all doorshay – daurshay"'; 'Dúirse dáirse' *GC* (Laois).

Dúisc n. A boor; a stupid, backward person LOB (s.w. Dublin); *IG* (Carlow).

Dúiseacht n. An awakening, an arousing. 'Great punishment or hardship' *IG* (Kilkenny). 'You'll get dúiseacht when you get home' PB (s. Tipperary).

Dul amú n. < vb. n. In form **dulamoo**. Literally, going astray. 1. 'An odd person' J (s.e. Wexford). 2. 'An effeminate man' D (s.e. Wexford). 3. 'A person given to bouts of depression' MW (s. Wexford).

Dul ó mhaith phr. Translated literally as **to go away from good** i.e. to deteriorate.

'He's gone away from good since he came out of the hospital' J (s.e. Wexford).

Dúlachán n. 'Lake trout'. *Salmo ferox* G (n.w. Donegal).

Dúlamán n. Channel wrack, *pelvetia canaliculata*. An edible seaweed, in season in March S (n.w. Donegal).

Dúlán n. Two handfulls. 'A few dúláns of oats would do that horse no harm' R (n. Clare).

Dúr adj. 'Stupid' Ham (e. Clare); 'That boy is as dúr as Jack's ass' PD (s. Carlow).

Dúradán n. 1. A particle of dust. 'There's a dúradán in my eye' JC (w. Cork). 2. 'The mote in your brother's eye. That meaning has practically died here now, but a much more poetic usage remains. Dúradán is now a term of endearment, especially used by parents of their offspring. It pictures a small, and therefore harmless, helpless child. Tautology goes mad in its most endearing (diminutive) form: "My little dúradáinín"' *An Cho* (w. Mayo). 3. 'A stupid person' NB (w. Limerick).

Dúrálaí n. 'A boor. A person who wouldn't return a greeting' NB (w. Limerick).

Dúrdálaí n. 'A stupid person; one rather slow to grasp an idea' NB (w. Limerick).

Dúrdán n. 'A deaf person' NB (w. Limerick).

Durm n. In forms **dhirum, dharum**, in phrase **to say neither dhirum nor dharum**, to say nothing. Seumus MacManus, *The Leadin' Road to Donegal*, 13: 'Neither of them said dhirum or dharum'; ibid. 153: 'Without saying dhirum or dharum she ups with her fist'; Seumus Mac Manus, *Bold Blades of Donegal:* 'You've come in our absence, and without dhirum, dharum or by-your-laive, ate up our ten thousand dinners.'

Dúrtam dártam phr. Gossip. 'Don't believe what that one would tell you. Probably its only oul' dúrtam dártam' R (n. Clare).

Dúsmánaí n. 'A silent person who listens attentively, nevertheless, to all that is being said around him' MP (mid Tipperary).

Dúthracht n. Also in forms **dhuragh, dooracht. 1.** Wm. Carleton, *The Battle of the Factions* 1, 141 (footnote): 'An additional portion of anything thrown in from a spirit of generosity, after the measure agreed on is given. When the miller, for instance, receives his toll, the country people usually throw in several handsful of meal as a Dhuragh' (Tyrone); MG (n.w. Donegal). **2.**

Simmons (Donegal): 'Used in a somewhat different sense in southern Ireland. When you pay great attention to a person, pet him, feed him with goodies, take care of him in ever way, this is called dooracht'; *EASI* 249: 'Tender care and kindness shown to a person. This word in the sense of kindness is very old; for in the Brehon Law we read of land set aside by a father for his daughter through dúthracht' **3.** Energy. 'He put dúthracht into it' MF (Westmeath; H (n. Clare).

E

Eachlais n. A filthy person. 'An oul tramp of a woman, a dirty eachlais she was' R (n. Clare).

Éadáil n. A stroke of good fortune. 'It's a great éadáil to me' IG (Kilkenny); 'He's a poor éadáil: he's not much to write home about' MC (e. Mayo).

Ealaíonadóirí n. pl. In form **alleenadhores**. Literally, Artists, meaning con-artists. 'Three-card trick men and the like, seen at fairs, races etc.' DOC (Limerick).

Earc n. Diminutive, **earcán**. A lizard. 1. In compound **earc luachra**: a newt, in form **dark lyooker** GC (Laois). 2. Figuratively, a small child, man or woman. 'You wouldn't believe it, but Dolly Parton is only a little earc of a woman' R (n. Clare); 'Earcán: a brat' Mac C (Monaghan).

Éarlais n. Also as **earls, airles**. Earnest money, a deposit paid on purchase, money given to a servant when hired, as a sign of good faith. 'I wouldn't trust him if I were you. Don't give him any éarlais, anyway' JPL (w. Cork); 'He paid five pounds of earls at the auction' O'K (Tyrone); *Patterson*, 'Airles' (Antrim). [< English. 'Arles: Argentum Dei, money given in earnest of a bargain' *Blount's Law Dictionary* (1691); 'Arles penny: earnest money given to servants' *Bailey's Dictionary* (1755); 'This ure lauerd giueth ham as an erles of the eche mede that schal cume therafter' *Hali. M.* (c. 1220), *EDD*]

Earrach an áir n. phr. Literally, the Spring of the slaughter. 'As bad as earrach an áir: extremely bad. Said of the weather' *CBD* (n. Kerry).

Earrach n. Spring. As **arraugh** in phrase **arraugh curthere** *Poole* (s.e. Wexford). [*Curthere:* season. *Arragh curthere*, spring season.]

Easair n. 1. 'Bedding, litter, for animals' NB (w. Limerick). 2. 'A bundle of sheaves of oats laid down for threshing' IG (Cavan).

Eascaidh n. Also as **askeen**. 'A slough, a quagmire' *CBE* 104 (Leitrim); *EASI* 212: 'askeen – wet, sedgy bog' (Kildare).

Eascann n. In form **ascon**. The eel. 'As slippery as an ascon in a kitchen sink' TB (Cavan).

Easnamh n. A want, deficiency. A shortage in a measure. 'There is an easnamh in the measure he is pleased to call a glass of whiskey' JPL (w. Cork); 'He's not entirely mad, but there's an easnamh in him' RBB (s. Kilkenny); NB (w. Limerick).

Easóg n. 'A stoat' Mac C (Monaghan); IG (Cavan). Figuratively, 'a spitfire of a woman' MJD (w. Cork).

Easpag speatháin n. As **espibawn**. Ox-eyed daisy, *Chrysanthemum leucantheum*. *Patterson* (Antrim). [*easpag*, bishop; *speatháin*, genitive of *speathán*, stalk of burned heather; thin, shrivelled stem *ODON*.]

Éillín n. In form **ailian**. A brood. Patrick Mac Gill, *Maureen*: 'A fine ailian of ducklings'.

Éinín n. 'Generally used for the tit-lark' *CBE* 266 (mid-Tipperary).

Éinín cois na mbó n. The tit-lark. 'A little bird that follows the cows' S Ua G (s. Tipperary).

Éinín giolcaí n. 'Reed bunting' *CBD* (n. Kerry).

Eireog n. 1. 'A pullet' HG (n.w. Donegal). 2. 'A good-looking young woman' PJG (mid-Donegal).

Éirí amach v. To move out, to travel forth. Direct translation **to rise out**. Peadar O'Donnell, *Adrigoole* 82: 'Ye take no interest in the neighbours, Mary Nabla, Hughie said, except for our house ye usen't rise out'; 'He was a man that never rose much out among the neighbours' ibid. 143 (Donegal). (Common in Ulster, Connacht.)

Éirí as v. To give up some activity. In translated form **to rise out**. 'We used to have cattle but I rose out of them when I got old' DM (w. Cork).

Éirí in airde phr. 'Airs and graces; upishness' H (n. Clare); 'It's a divil altogether the éirí anairde that came on them when they fell into the few American dollars' MJD (w. Cork).

Éirigh suas interj. phr. Get up. 'Said to a cow to get her to stand' CBD (n. Kerry); In Wm. Carleton *Tubber Derg* 2, 390 (Tyrone).

Eiris n. 'A rope put in a basket or cleeve, for carrying on the back' *IG* (Meath).

Eisc n. 'A small cave or a fissure between cliffs by the sea' CBD (n. Kerry).

Eiscir n. As esker. A long, winding ridge of sand or gravel, originally deposited by a meltwater stream flowing under a glacier. Wm. Carleton, *Shane Fadh's Wedding* 2, 54: '... it's not upon them seven acres of stone and bent, upon the long Esker, that I'd let my daughter go to live'. Carleton's gloss: 'A high ridge of land, generally barren and unproductive, when upon a small scale. It is also a ridgy height that runs for many miles through a country' (Tyrone). Jane Barlow, *Idylls:* 'A sunbeam, glinting across some little grassy esker, strikes out a strangely jewel-like flash of transparent green' (Connacht).

Éist do bhéal interj. 'Shut your mouth' NB (w. Limerick); CBD (n. Kerry; JM (w. Cork); *IG* (Cavan).

F

Fabhtach adj. Also as **fouty**. 1. Faulty, unsound. 'That potato is fabhtach – that is, rotten in its core' *IG* (Limerick); S Ua G (s. Tipperary). 2. 'Fouty, negligent' PLH (n. Roscommon).

Fada adj. In forms **fadh, foddhah, fadow.** Long, tall. Wm. Carleton, *Shane Fadh's Wedding* 1, 55: 'But I was something for a woman to look at then ... standing six feet two in my stocking soles, which, you know, made them call me Shane Fadh' (Tyrone); John and Michael Banim, *Peter of the Castle* 3, 90: 'Thomaus Foddhah', glossed as 'long Tom'. (Kilkenny). The dance called **Fadow**, mentioned in Ben Jonson's *The Irish Masque* is probably *rince fada*, long dance, a form still popular in the 19th century.

Fadálach adj. Tedious, drawn out. 'He'd bore you to tears with his fadálach old stories' H (n. Clare).

Fadharcán n. 1. 'A lump on the knuckle, usually caused by rheumatism or arthritis' MS (e. Limerick); PB (s. Tipperary). 2. 'A knot in timber' RBB (s. Kilkenny); NB (w. Limerick); JJH (w. Waterford); *CBD* (n. Kerry). 3. 'A stubborn, troublesome, hot-tempered person' JL (w. Cork). 4. 'A corn on the foot' NM (w. Cork) 5. 'A welt on the palm of the hand or on the base of the fingers, caused by continued work with spade or sleán' *An Cho* (w. Mayo).

Fadhbáil vb. n. 'Searching for something about a room and creating disorder; fumbling' *IG* (Kilkenny).

Fadhbóg n. 'A lie. A tall tale' McK (Leitrim).

Fág an baile interj. phr. Leave the town! Get out!' *IG* (Kilkenny). Possible a confusion with **fág an bealach!**, clear the way, a phrase commonly used in faction fighting.

Fág marbh é phr. 'Literally, leave it dead. Let it rest. "Didn't that crowd do something mean to us one time about the land we have near them?" – "Listen, John, fág marbh é. Don't bring it up again"' *An Cho* (w. Mayo).

Fág san interj. phr. Leave that! JL (w. Cork).

Faic n. Also as **fock**. (with negative in Irish) Nothing. 'There's not a faic on him': there's nothing the matter with him: *IG* (Kilkenny); 'He hadn't a faic: he had nothing' *CBD* (n. Kerry); 'They made a fock of him: they made nothing of him' *CBE* 266 (mid-Tipperary).

Fáideog n. 'The wick of a candle or lamp' NB (w. Limerick).

Faideog n. 1. 'A faggot' *CBE* 104 (Leitrim). 2. 'A straw used in drawing lots' FF (Monaghan).

Fail n. 1. A sty. 'A dirty hovel' NB (w. Limerick). 2. 'A doss, a dirty, untidy bed' *IG* (Kilkenny).

Failbó n. 'A big, fat, idle person' NB (w. Limerick).

Failm n. A heavy blow. 'He hit him a failm with the hurl' Smy (n. Clare).

Failp n. A blow. 'He hit him a failp, and he deserved it' NB (w. Limerick); 'He got the divil's father of a failp off the ground' NM (w. Cork). Hence **failping**. 'He got a failping' *CBD* (n. Kerry).

Fáilte n. interj. Welcome. Also in phrases, **fáilte is fiche**, a welcome and twenty; **fáilte is céad**, a welcome and a hundred; **céad fáilte**, a hundred welcomes. **Céad míle fáilte**, a hundred thousand welcomes in Wm. Carleton, *The Poor Scholar* 2, 276, as **Kead millia failta**. As failtah in Carleton,

Shane Fadh's Wedding 1, 73 (Tyrone). Lady Morgan, *The Wild Irish Girl* 82, 3: 'You are welcome and 100,000 welcomes, gentleman'; In footnote: '*Failte agus cead ro ag duine uasal.*' (*recte* 'fáilte agus céad romhat, a dhuine uasail' – a welcome and a hundred before you, gentleman.) (Leinster). In form **cead nillia fealtha** in Gerald Griffin, *The Collegians* 115 (Limerick). As **cead mealy faulty** in James Joyce, *Finnegans Wake* 57.

Fáiméadrach n. 'A big fat woman' NB (w. Limerick). *al.* **fáiméadaí** – 'A lazy, incapable girl' *CBD* (n. Kerry); **fáiméara** NB (w. Limerick).

Fáinne óir ort phr. Literally, a gold ring on you. 'Phrase used to praise a good card player, Fáinne óir on you!' MS (e. Limerick); 'A question put in card playing. "Fáinne óir ort?" – Have you the ace to rob with?' Ham (e. Clare); 'Said to a person who holds the ace' *CBD* (n. Kerry).

Fainneal n. 'A straw pad placed under his knee by a thatcher' MF (Westmeath).

Fáintiún n. In phrase, 'going like fáintiún: going like the wind' *CBD* (n. Kerry).

Faire interj. Fie! Dear me!: Ham (e. Clare); JL (w. Cork).

Fáisceán n. A bandage, tourniquet. 'The vet. did nothing but put a fáisceán where the horse cut himself, and charged me ten pound for a job I could have done myself, and better' JL (w. Cork).

Fáisleog n. 'A small, low-lying, marshy plot in a bog' *IG* (Monaghan).

Faiteach adj. 'Frightened, but it means a continuing state of being easily frightened. The quality is to be expected in children; in adults it becomes more blameworthy. It appears, too, to run in certain families: "They were always faiteach." And the fear entailed doesn't refer only to ghosts, banshees, etc.: one could also be faiteach of a teacher, a priest, a stranger, even of electricity' *An Cho* (w. Mayo).

Falaing n. In form **phalang**. A cloak, mantle. Gerald Griffin, *The Collegians* 46:

'Undyed black wool formed the texture of the phalang' (Limerick).

Falaire n. 'A mean person' NB (w. Limerick).

Falamar n. 'A foolish person' DOH (s. Tipperary).

Falbó n. 'A big, lazy girl' *CBD* (n. Kerry).

Falcaire n. 1. A big, strong man. 'For such a big falcaire of a man, you'd think he'd be some use in a hay-field' R (n. Clare); *CBD* (n. Kerry). 2. 'The old seed potato found when digging the new potatoes' AOL (mid-Waterford).

Falmaire n. Also as **folmorra**, **follomer**. A big, strong man. 'She married a fine falmaire of a man from Lismore' AOL (mid- Waterford); 'A fine follomer of a man' *CBE* 266 (mid-Tipperary); 'A strong folmorra of a young lad' G (s. Kilkenny).

Falsa adj. Lazy. 'He's so falsa that he wouldn't bother to get out of bed if he knew that there was a bomb under it' PD (s. Carlow).

Falsóir n. 'A lazy person' *CBE* 104 (Leitrim).

Fámaire n. 1. 'A big, hefty man' MS (e. Limerick). 2. A visitor. 'September is the time for the fámairís in Lisdoonvarna' H (n. Clare); *An Cho* (w. Mayo).

Fánach adj. 1. Aimless, purposeless, careless. 'A person who has little order or method in his life is fánach. It's very fánach of you to have your children wandering about aimlessly, for instance; or your hay left in the meadows until September; or your purse left on the counter of the post office while you have gone down the town' *An Cho* (w. Mayo). 2. Haphazard, odd. (Of places.) '"That was a fánach place to leave a man's scythe when you got a lend of it." Unscrupulous hens lay their eggs, and careless mothers leave their prams in fánach places. A proverb says: "it's a fánach place you'd find a lobster!", that is, they turn up in unexpected places' *An Cho* (w. Mayo). 3. 'Mentally retarded, not all there' MF (Mayo).

Fánas n. 'A gap between the front teeth' Mac C (Tyrone); TB (Cavan); *IG* (Monaghan). See *séanas*.

Fanc n. *al.* **feanc**. As **founk**. A start, upset. 'It didn't take the slightest founk out of him – it didn't upset him in the least' G (s. Kilkenny).

Faobhar n. Also as **fweer, fware**. 1. Energy. '"Put faobhar in him" means smarten him up' MF (Westmeath). 2. 'Edge, eagerness for wordly goods, food etc. "He's all right but for the fware he has for the money"' S Ua G (s. Tipperary); 'He has the divil's own fweer for the drop' DC (Galway).

Faochán n. 'The perriwinkle' *An Cho* (w. Mayo).

Faoileán n. Also as **fweelaun, faoileog**. The seagull H (n. Clare); *CBD* (n. Kerry); 'By some obscure reasoning the word is also used of somebody who is temporarilly insane: "She is seeing faoileáns"' *An Cho* (w. Mayo); George Fitzmaurice, *The King of the Barna Men*: 'Likewise it's no voice you heard but a fweelaun ...' (Kerry); as 'faoileog' in *CBE* 104 (Leitrim).

Faraoir interj. In forms **fareer, fahreer**. Alas! Woe! John Boyce, *Shandy Maguire* 295: 'Then he's not at home? Noa, noa, fareer, sir, he's not' (Donegal). Also in phrase **faraoir géar**, bitter woe, as **fahreer gairh** in Wm. Carleton, *Going to Maynooth* 1, 185 (Tyrone).

Fardoras n. 'The lintel of the door' MC (e. Mayo).

Fásach n., v. As **whassah**. *EASI* 347: 'To feed cows in some unusual place, such as along a lane or road; to herd them in unfenced ground. The food so given is also called whassah' (Monaghan).

Fáslach n. The 'floor', or cut-away portion of a bog. 'On which is spread the turf which is cut at the lower level' *An Cho* (w. Mayo); MC (e. Mayo). See *fáisleog*.

Fastaím n. Nonsense. 'Arrah, fastaím! What do you know about football?' JPL (w. Cork).

Fastúch n. 'A big, useless person' NB (w. Limerick); *CBD* (n. Kerry).

Fathach n. 'A giant; a big awkward fellow' H (n. Clare); PB (s. Tipperary); 'Used in derision: "what a fathach he is!"' *IG* (Kilkenny).

Feac n. In form **fack**. A spade *Pe* (Wexford); 'Dig the spuds with a fack, not a shovel' D (Kildare); OCn (Laois).

Féach interj. Look! In form **feagh** in Anon., *Captain Thomas Stukeley*: '... loke, feagh bodeaugh dost thou see any thing?'

Féachadóir n. 'A man who oversees the work of making a hay-rick, etc.' *CBD* (n. Kerry).

Feadhain n. 'A band, troop. Referring to children: "She landed and the feadhain with her"' MC (e. Mayo).

Feadhnóg n. In form **finog**. 'A pannier basket for carrying turf on a horse or an ass' PJG (mid-Donegal).

Feadóg n. 1. In form **fadoge**. The waterpipe, *equisetum limosum* H (n. Donegal). 2. The snipe, *gallinago gallinago*: *CBE* 104 (Leitrim).

Fealltach adj. Treacherous, deceitful, dangerous. Peadar O'Donnell, *The Knife* 104: 'There's men like Billy ... and when they're roused they're fealltach, dangerous' (Donegal).

Feam n. Sea rod; stipe, *laminaria cloustoni* MC (w. Clare); 'The seaweed was all feams' *CBD* (n. Kerry).

Feamainn n. In form **famin**. Seaweed. D. Deeney, *Peasant Lore From Gaelic Ireland*, 67: 'To see the women gather the famin off the bleak rocks'.

Feamnach na gclog n. Bladder wrack, *fucus vesiculosus* MC (w. Clare).

Feanc n. In form **founk**. Twist, jolt PB (s. Tipperary). 'It never knocked a feanc out of him, i.e. it had no effect on him' MF (Westmeath).

Fear an tí n. Also as **farithee** and in translated form, **man of the house**. Master, householder. As such in James Joyce, *Finnegans Wake* 101: 'bondwoman of the man of the house ...' Wm. Carleton, *The Poor Scholar* 2, 280: 'farithee' (Tyrone).

Fear bocht interj. Poor man! 'Said to a child when he cries after a fall or the like' JC (w. Cork); PB (s. Tipperary).

Fear bréige n. Also in form **farh breeacha**. Literally, false man. 'A scarecrow' RBB (s. Kilkenny); *CBD* (n. Kerry); PLH (n. Roscommon); John Banim, *Peter of the Castle* 3, 256: '... he'd lose six inches of his ungainly hoith if a fahr-breeacha only wagged the caubeen at him' (Kilkenny).

Féar gortach n. Also in forms **fairgurtha, feargartha, fairgarta, féur gortach**. Commonly known as the hungry grass. Quaking grass, a mountain grass supposed to have the effect of making those who come near it weak and hungry by the power of the fairies. Seumus MacManus, *Bold Blades of Donegal*, 89: 'Had he not taken the feur gortach and dropped from weakness...'; ibid. (note): 'feur gortach is the sudden hunger-weakness that befalls one who steps upon a patch of fairy-stricken "hungry grass" – a spot whereon, once, some greedy one ate and neglected to leave a bit for the Gentle People'; Black, *Folk Medicine* 1: 'Feargartha, fairgurtha, hungry grass'; *Simmons* (s. Donegal): 'fairgarta'.

Fearabán n. Also in form **farawaun**. The creeping buttercup, *ranunculus repens CBE* 104 (Leitrim). As 'farawaun' *BASJ* (Cavan); PC (s. Galway; n. Clare).

Féasóg n. 'A beard' *CBE* 104 (Leitrim).

Feic n. Also as **feck**. A sight, spectacle; an object of derision. 'Are you trying to make a feic of me?' DOH (e. Limerick); 'Stop making a feck of yourself' *CBE* 266; AG (s. Tipperary).

Feileastram n. Also as **felistrum**. The wild iris, or yellow flag, *iris pseudacorus*: Ham (e. Clare); JM (w. Cork); *CBD* (n. Kerry); AG (s. Tipperary); George Fitzmaurice, *The Pie-Dish*: 'felistrum' (Kerry).

Féin emphatic adj. Reflected in the intensifier **itself**. J.M. Synge, *The Well of the Saints* 52: 'And why wouldn't she, if she's a fine woman itself'. Direct translation of '... *dá mba bean bhreá féin í.*' James Joyce, *Ivy Day in the Committee Room* 142: 'Is there any chance of a drink itself?' Direct translation of '*an mbeadh seans ar bith ar dheoch féin ?*'

Feirbín n. 'That green sod of earth which is turned by a spade on lea-land to form the brow of the future potato ridge. So one of the first proofs of oncoming spring is a man turning feirbíns' *An Cho* (w. Mayo).

Feirc n. Also **ferk**. Diminutive, **feircín**. 1. 'Rakish angle of a man's hat' MS (e. Limerick). 2. A comical appearance. 'You should see the feirc of him!' H (n. Clare). 3. 'A quiff in one's hair' LOS (Clare). 4. 'A small man' NB (w. Limerick); 'A strong, thick-set little man' PC (n. Clare). [< English *firkin*.] 5. 'A little protuberance. A pejorative word. "A right little ferk"' AG (s. Tipperary). 6. 'The hilt of a knife, spade etc. A descriptive word in recounting a scene of violence; a fiercely belligerent and intimidating word if used threateningly in verbal combat' *An Cho* (w. Mayo).

Féirín n. Also in form **fairin**. 1. A present. 'He bought that watch for me as a birthday fairin' J (s.e. Wexford); 'Women cost a lot nowadays, what with buying drink for them and fairins and all' R (n. Clare); H (n. Clare); O'K (Tyrone). In phrase, **féirín tickles**, freckles; **féirín tickled**, freckled *IG* (Monaghan). [*Féirín*: fairing, gift, present; keepsake; reward; valuable acquisition *ODON*. [< English *fairing*, a gift bought at a fair *EDD*.] 2. ' A lasting injury of any kind' FF (Cavan). 3. A fright. 'You'd get some féirín in that place. It's haunted' DOH (e. Limerick).

Feis n. Festival. Somerville and Ross, *Poisson d'Avril* 202: 'A Feis, I should explain, is a Festival, devoted to competitions in Irish songs and dances' (w. Cork; Gen.).

Feochadán n. The thistle, *circsium*: Lys (Kerry); NB (Limerick). See *geosadán*.

Feoil capaill n. 'The type of turf which slips away from the sleán (q.v.) MC (e. Mayo).

Feorainn n. Creeping bent grass, *agrostis stolonifera*. 'Stretched out on his back on the feorainn I found the lazy bastard' JL (w. Cork). See *Fiorthann*.

Fiaga n. As **feeha**. 'Rushes' PJG (mid-Donegal).

Fialthach n. 'A wild looking man' JL (w. Cork). *al.* **fialach** *CBD* (n. Kerry); **fialtach** PB (s. Tipperary); H (n. Clare).

Fíbín n. 'The running of cattle caused by stings of gad-fly. There's fíbín on the cattle with them cleabhars' (q.v.) MS (e. Limerick).

Fíbín n. Also as **faoibín, feebeen**. 1. Fit of excitement; gadding. 'What fíbín is on you?' JL (w. Cork). *al.* **faoibín** PB (s. Tipperary). 2. (Act of) acting capriciously. Hence 'Don't be making feebeen of me, don't be making little of me' PB (s. Tipperary).

Fideog n. 'A small flute or whistle' *Sguab* (w. Cork); *IG* (Meath).

Fídire n. Diminutive, **fídirín**. 'A silly, flippant person' *GC* (Laois; n. Kilkenny).

Fige fíge phr. The least thing. 'He was a nasty bit of work for a teacher. He'd murder you for fige fíge' AOL (mid-Waterford).

Filibín n. In form **filibeen**. 1. The lapwing: MF (Westmeath). 2. 'A sod turned with a spade on the outer part of a ridge' MC (e. Mayo). [See *pilibín*.]

Fínic interj. 'Exclamation used when calling ducks' R (n. Clare).

Fiodán n. 'A mountain stream. Often a mearing or boundary between villages or townlands. By a kind compensation of nature the best solvent for removing turf-stains off the hands at spreading-time is the soft, brownish water of the fiodán' *An Cho* (w. Mayo).

Fionna-mhóin n. Bog moss, *sphagnum* LOS (w. Clare).

Fionnán n. Purple moor grass, *Molinia coerulea* Lys (Kerry); NB (w. Limerick). *al.* **fionnánach** MC (w. Clare).

Fionndruine n. In form **finndrinn**. White bronze. A literary term. James Joyce, *Finnegans Wake* 52: 'finndrinn'.

Fionntarnach n. The purple melic-grass, *molinia coerulea*: PJG (mid-Donegal).

Fíonóg n. Also in form **feenogue**. 'Fíonóg is a mite found in hay' *CBE* 104 (Leitrim); 'Courting in a hayshed and eaten alive by feenogues' JK (Kildare); MF (Westmeath).

Fíor adj. Also in form **feer**. 1. True. In phrase **fíor duit** – true for you! H (n. Clare). 2. Edge, furthest point. 'The feer top of the house; the feer end of the boreen' *CBE* 266 (mid-Tipperary).

Fíor mhóin n. In form **firwoan**. Literally, true turf. 'The best turf, the bottom layer of a bog' PJG (mid-Donegal).

Fiorthann n. Creeping bent grass, *agrostis stolonifera*: G (n.w. Donegal). See *Feorainn*.

Fiosrach adj. Inquisitive. 'Yes, she was good and fiosrach about you' H (n. Clare).

Fir fia n. Also in form **fer fia**. The bog asphodel, *narthecium ossifragum*: J.M. Parland, *Statistical Survey of the County of Donegal*.

Firín n. 'A small man' NB (w. Limerick). 'Usually a contemptuous term. "A mean little firín"' PC (n. Clare).

Fírinne n. Truth. In phrase of M. J. Mulloy, *The Wood of the Whispering* 24: 'You have the truth.' Direct translation of *Tá an fhírinne agat.*

Fisire n. 'A person having a troubled expression' NB (w. Limerick).

Físte fáiste phr. 'A mess, a mix-up. "He made a físte fáiste of the job"' NB (w. Limerick).

Fít interj. 'A call to ducks, to gather them together' *IG* (Monaghan).

Flaith n. Ruler, prince. Seumus MacManus, *Bold Blades of Donegal*, 339: 'Ride the world round and fare like a flaith.'

Flaithiúil adj. As **flahool, flahoolagh, flockool, flockooluck**. Generous. 'Flahool is not the word for that man' McK (Leitrim); James Joyce, *Ulysses* 309: 'flahoolagh entertainment'; 'Flahool, flockool, flockooluck' PON (n. Dublin). Hence **flahooler**. 'A generous, good-natured man' HG (n.w. Donegal).

Fleadh n. Festival. In phrase **fleadh cheoil**, festival of traditional music.

Fleaite adv. 'Exhausted, famished' BOD (s.w. Cork).

Fleascach n. 1. 'A stripling, a young person' DOH (e. Limerick). 2. 'A wild young fellow from the hills' S Ua G (s. Tipperary).

Flíoch n. Common chickweed, *stellaria media*: MC (w. Clare.)

Flíp n. As **fleep**. A heavy blow; a swipe. 'She made a fleep at him with the brush' JPL (w. Cork).

Fliuchtín n. 'A little bit of material you might find on your face after drying it with a towel' S (n.w. Donegal). [< *fliuch*, wet]

Flúirse n. Plenty. 'Thank God, we were never in want. We always had flúirse' BOD (s.w. Cork).

Flúirseach adj. Also in form **flureshuk**. 1. Abundant, plentiful. 'The blossom was poor; the apples won't be flúirseach this year' MJD (w. Cork); AG (s. Tipperary). 2. Generous. 'He is very flureshuk with his money. The money is very flureshuk with him' OCn (Laois).

Flústar n. As **floosther**. 1. Flattery. 'Flooster will get you anywhere' TB (Cavan). 2. A flatterer. 'Applied to a dog etc. much given to fawning' Mac C (Monaghan).

Fo-ribín n. As **forrabeen**. 'A ribbon for an undergarment' KB (e. Limerick).

Focal bog phr. Literally, soft word. 'Plausible talk; a promise that cannot be fulfilled' H (n. Clare).

Fód ar boir n. 'The broken ground found on the edge of a boghole' McK (Leitrim).

Fód n. Sod, earth. Corrupted as **foot** in phrase **fairy foot**. 'Ground controlled by fairies' JB (s. Armagh & n. Louth).

Fód seachráin n. Literally, Sod of straying. 'It is said that if persons walk on it they'll go astray' IG (Cavan); 'The fairies are said to put a spell on these sods to lead people astray; they do it for fun and no harm comes of anyone who goes astray by night' TB (Cavan). See *fóidín mearathail*.

Fodar n. 1. Bustle, activity. Hence **fodarer** n. ' A good, honest footballer who mightn't be brilliant, but plays his heart out' PJG (n.w. Donegal). 2. 'Fodder' G (n.w. Donegal).

Fogha n. 1. A sudden attack. We made only two foghas in towards their goal in the second half MS (e. Limerick); PB, AG (s. Tipperary). 2. A resolve. 'I took a fogha'; 'There's a good fogha in him: he would do a good turn if he took the notion' IG (Kilkenny).

Foidhir n. 'A gully made by floods. The word is used throughout west Waterford' RBB.

Fóidín mearathail n. phr. As **fodheen marahull**. A place where one's sense of direction tends to go awry, so that one goes astray. Michael Banim, *Crohoor of the Billhook* 1: 'bewildered by the Fodheen-Marahull ...' Glossed by Banim as 'Will-o'-the-wisp' (Kilkenny). *al.* **fóidín mearaí**, 'a spot in a field where you tend to go around in circles at night' MC (e. Mayo). See *fód seachráin*.

Fóidín n. Diminutive of **fód**. 1. 'A small sod' JPL (w. Cork). 2. 'A small farm' McK (Leitrim). 3. 'A heap of surface sods formerly burned and scattered on the land as manure' PLH (n. Roscommon.)

Fóill interj. Easy! Gently! NM (w. Cork).

Fóir n. 'The outer, regular wall of a turf rick.' Hence, **fóiring**. 'I was fóiring turf all day' H (n. Clare).

Fóirneach n. 'An awkward woman. "He married a big fóirneach of a Kerrywoman"' MJD (w. Cork).

Fóirnéal n. 'A small egg' PB (s. Tipperary). In forms **fortnail** OR (Tipperary); **fóirtnéal** *IG* (Kilkenny); **forneal** OR (Kilkenny).

Fóisc n. 1. 'A year old ewe' PB (s. Tipperary). 2. 'A fat, lazy girl' *CBD* (n. Kerry); PB (s. Tipperary). *al.* **fóisce**, 'a big, dirty woman' DOC (Limerick). 3. 'A fine young girl' JL (w. Cork).

Foiscealach n. 1. 'A large measure (of hay, meal etc.)' JPL (w. Cork); 'As much meal etc. as can be taken between the two hands' *IG* (Kilkenny). 2. 'A small sum of money' *CBD* (n. Kerry).

Fóisí n. 1. 'A person who works by fits and starts' G (s. Kilkenny); 'A loiterer' *CBE* 266 (mid-Tipperary). 2. 'An inquisitive person, a cabin hunter who comes uninvited for something to eat, drink or gossip' S Ua G (s. Tipperary).

Fonsín n. As **foonsheen**. 'The circular band of a stocking' NB (w. Limerick).

Foradh n. In form **forrah**. A shelf. 'The space overhead on either side of the chimney, between the beam called the mantle-tree and the wall is the forrah, and within this space may be found many articles of household and farm use, embraced under the term triosgan' *BASJ* (Cavan, Leitrim).

Fórán n. 'Hemlock' MF (Westmeath).

Forbhán n. 'A rough mountain-side' *CBE* 104 (Leitrim).

Forgach n. 1. 'A tall man' *IG* (Kilkenny). 2. 'A cow that has not been in calf for more than a year' RR (Galway).

Forgan n. Also as **forracan**. 'A large quantity of food and drink. "She's gone home with a fine forgan of stuff for the funeral" MC (w. Mayo); 'They had a right forracan at the wake' AM (Leitrim).

Formán n. As **furamaun**. 'A sudden blast of wind which sometimes sucks the corn up into the sky' MC (e. Mayo).

Forrach n. Violence, fury. In phrase 'the forrach was lit' – the row had started: MF (Westmeath).

Forrán n. As **furrawn**. Used in phrase *forrán a chur ar dhuine*, to accost, address, a person. Wm. Carleton, *The Three Tasks* 1, 25: 'Arragh, Jack Magennis, how is every tether-length of you?' says the old fellow, putting the furrawn on him ...' Glossed by Carleton as: 'that frank, cordial manner of address which brings strangers suddenly to intimacy'; ibid. *Fardorougha the Miser* 24: 'He used to stare her out of countenance ... and struv to put the furrawn on her' (Tyrone).

Foscaí n. In form **fuskey**. 'A forrager; a thieving animal' *CBE* 266 (mid-Tipperary).

Fostúch n. A grown yougster; a boy of employable age. Depreciatory, 'a big, clumsy, or lazy fellow' MP (mid-Tipperary); *Sguab* (Cork); NB (w. Limerick); JS (e. Kerry).

Fothanán n. 1. The colt's-foot, *tussilago farfara*: PJG (mid-Donegal). 2. The common thistle: MJD (w. Cork).

Fotharach n. 'A wet marsh' *CBD* (n. Kerry).

Fotharaga n. Also as **fotherough**. 1. Hurry, fuss, confusion. George Fitzmaurice, *The Pie-Dish*: 'What a fotherough was on that loobera, Jack, going for the priest!' (Kerry). 2. 'A fussy person, a fuss-pot' *CBD* (n. Kerry). 3. Uproar, confusion. 'Such fotharaga as they had' *CBD* (n. Kerry).

Fothrach n. 'An old house' *CBD* (n. Kerry); 'A ruin' JL (w. Cork); PB (s. Tipperary).

Fraeic n. A notion. 'We took the fraeic to go to Cork for the match' RBB (s. Kilkenny).

Fraoch n. Heather, *calluna vulgaris*: JB (s. Tipperary); *An Cho* (w. Mayo); *CBE* 47 S (Galway); 'I had a few rolls in the fraoch with her in my time' JL (w. Cork).

Fraocháin n. pl. In forms **fraughans, fragh-ans, frockans, frughans, frawhawns, frauns.** The bilberry, or whortleberry, *vaccinium myrtillus.* Jonathan Swift, *A Dialogue in Hybernian Stile*: 'in summer we have the best frawhawns in all the county'; Threlkeld, *Essays*: 'They grow in wet, boggy ground ... the poor women gather them in the Autumn and cry them about the streets of Dublin by the name of fraghan'; Patk. Kennedy, *Evenings in the Duffrey* 208: 'fraughans in the woods' (Wexford); Jane Barlow, *Bogland Studies* 109: 'Wee frauns, each wan stuck twixt two leaves on a grand little stem of its own' (Ulster); *Patterson* (Antrim, Down): 'frughans, frockans'.

Fraoichín n. In form **freeheen.** 'This used to be the name the townspeople in Cashel and other towns used call the people from our local bogs who used to sell loads of turf in the towns. The tops of the loads were bound with heather, *fraoch*, hence the name. "The freeheens from the bogs of Ballymore" ' *CBE* 266 (mid-Tipperary).

Frasóg n. The corn marigold, *chrysenthemum segetum*: O'K (Tyrone). See *Geal gabhann.*

Frithir adj. 'Sore, painful. 'This is still frithir''' S (n.w. Donegal).

Frois-frais n. Also in form **frish-frash.** 1. A mixture. J.M. Synge, *The Playboy of the Western World* 100: 'and when it's dead he is they'd put him in a narrow grave, with cheap sacking wrapping him round, and pour down quicklime on his head, they way you'd see a woman pouring any frish-frash from a cup.' 2. A bad job, fiasco. 'You've a real frois-frais made of the story' R (n. Clare); 'They kept changing the team and made a frois-frais of it' Smy (n. Clare).

Fú fá phr. Faux pas NB (w. Limerick).

Fuachais n. 1. A lair, burrow, den. 'Used to describe a dirty house' JPL (w. Cork). 2. 'A dirty woman' DOC (Limerick).

Fuachtán n. 'A chilblain' *IG* (Kilkenny); JL (w. Cork); *CBD* (n. Kerry).

Fuadar n. Haste, hurry. 'He's in a divil of a fuadar this morning' MS (e. Limerick);

'What fuadar is under you, airiú?' MJD (w. Cork). [Note translation of Irish idiom, *cad é an fuadar atá fút*.] Hence **footering.** Brian Friel, *Translations* 16: 'That aul drunken schoolmaster and that lame son of his are still footering about in the hedge school ...'

Fuaice n. A miksop. 'Would you think there's the making of a hurler in that fuaice?' RBB (s. Kilkenny).

Fuaiceas n. 'A cloth placed under the fire-crane in an open fire, to help lift a pot' *CBD* (n. Kerry).

Fuaidrín n. As **foodereen.** 'A fussy woman' R (n. Clare).

Fuairneach n. 1. A barren animal. 'I'm afraid the cow is a fuairneach by me' JL (w. Cork). 2. 'A cold, calculating person' JS (e. Kerry.)

Fuairnéal n. 'A cold person who likes to sit by the fire day and night' MJD (w. Cork).

Fuairnimh n. *al.* **fuairneamh, fuairne, fuairleam.** 'Numbness of fingers due to cold' *Sguab* (Cork); PC (n. Clare); NB (w. Limerick); H (n. Clare); 'Young people like you don't get the fuairneamh; it comes, like pains in the bones, with age' JL (w. Cork); 'Fuairne, fuairleam' *CBD* (n. Kerry).

Fuairthé n., adj. 1. 'A listless person' NB (w. Limerick); 'an idle, thriftless farmer' BOD (s.w. Cork); 'that fuairthé hasn't his hay saved yet' JPL (w. Cork). 2. Laziness and tardiness in farmwork. 'He hasn't the hay saved yet; sure how could he with the fuairthé?' *CBD* (n. Kerry). 3. adj. Lazy, slow in farmwork. 'He was only a fuairthé farmer' *CBD* (n. Kerry).

Fuarán n. As **foorawn.** 'An herb used as food for fowl' PLH (n. Roscommon). Unidentified.

Fuarthach n. 'Pins-and-needles' *CBD* (n. Kerry). See *codladh grifin.*

Fuasálaí n. 'A careless, easy-going fellow' *CBE* 266 (mid-Tipperary).

Fuascar n. In form **foosten**. Terror, panic. 'Such a foosten came on me when he jumped out of the dark towards me' W (s.e. Wexford.)

Fuath n. Hatred. 'He failed his exams again. He has a fuath for the books' MG (n.w. Donegal).

Fuil Dé interj. Blood of God! As **Ful Dea** in Anon., *Purgatorium Hibernicum.*

Fuílleach n. 'The remains of something – the "lavins". Perhaps the most frequent use nowadays (in Louisburgh) is the rather peculiar one, "We didn't see a fuílleach", when asked how did a day's hunting go' *An Cho* (w. Mayo).

Fuinseog n. In form **whinshag**. 'The ash-tree' H (n. Donegal)

Fuire faire phr. In form **firra farra**. 'A cow without apparent economic purpose, neither rearing a calf or milking, but a permanent fixture on the farm due to her popularity or antiquity' O'K (Tyrone).

Fuirseadh fairseadh phr. A mess; slovenly work. 'He made a complete fuirseadh fairseadh of it' JL (w. Cork); BOD (s.w. Cork).

Fuirseadh n. Literally, harrowing. Figuratively, high jinks, especially among the young. 'Enough of your fuirseadh, boys, for one night' JL (w. Cork).

Fuirseálaí n. 'A clumsy person' PB (s. Tipperary).

Fuirseoir n. 'A fumbler who does his best but gets nowhere' JPL (w. Cork).

Fuiseog n. The lark. 'He rises with the fuiseog' R (n. Clare).

Fulach n. 'A soreness of the forearm' OCn (Laois). See *trálach.*

Fústar n., v. 1. Fuss, fidgetiness. Hence **foostering**. 'He broke the chain of my bike whatever foostering he had with it' S (s.e. Wexford); James Joyce, *Ulysses* 75: 'What is he fostering over that change for?' *Fostering* is a misprint of *foostering.* 2. Courting: 'They're foostering now for years' J (s.e. Wexford).

Futa-fata n. 1. 'Confused talk, babble of excitement, bustle' MS (e. Limerick). 2. 'The gossip of the countryside. "That story is futa fata by now"' MJD (w. Cork).

Fútar n. A faux pas. 'Don't do the fútar – don't make a faux pas' MF (Westmeath).

G

Gabaire n. 'A prattler' MS (e. Limerick); *JCHAS* (Cork).

Gabáiste n. As **gaubbach**. Cabbage. *Poole* (s.e. Wexford).

Gabh amach as sin interj. In forms **gho-moch-a-sinn; go mah a shin**. Get out of that. Michael Banim, *Crohoor of the Billhook* 1,133: ' gho-moch-a-sinn! piped the imp' (Kilkenny); Wm. Carleton, *Tubber Derg* 2, 390: 'go mah a shin' (Tyrone).

Gabh aníos interj. phr. Come up: *CBE* 104 (Leitrim).

Gabh anseo interj. phr. Come here! In form **gutsho** in Wm. Carleton, *Tubber Derg* 2, 403 (Tyrone).

Gabh anuas interj. phr. 'Come down' *CBE* 104 (Leitrim).

Gabh ar ais interj. phr. 'Come back' *CBE* 104 (Leitrim.)

Gabh craobh interj. phr. Literally, come to branch. 'Said to a swarm of bees when trying to coax them to perch' *IG* (Kilkenny).

Gabh isteach n. phr. Come in. 'He gets his gabh isteach: he gets his bit and sup' *IG* (Kilkenny).

Gabha n. As **gow**. Blacksmith. Michael Banim, *The Croppy* 1, 33: 'Shaun-a-Gow': John the smith (Kilkenny); Patk. Kennedy, *Legends Of Mount Leinster* 165: '... the good-hearted but bibulous gow' (Wexford).

Gabhairín n. Also in form **goureen**. The herring, *clupea harengus*. 'I heard old fellows from the Ballinskelligs district call the herring gabhairín' PBB (w. Kerry); 'The fishermen by whom they were known as and called goureens' *EDD* (Kerry). [The *EDD*

speculates that the word may not be Irish, but originates in Gourock, a fishing town near Greenock in Scotland. Cf. the slang expression 'a Gourock ham' for a salt herring. PBB said that this is nonsense.]

Gabhairín an bhainne bheirithe n. Literally, the goat of the boiled milk. The jacksnipe S Ua G (s. Tipperary). See *gabhairín reo*.

Gabhairín reo n. Also in form **gowereen roe**. Literally, the little goat of the hoarfrost. The jacksnipe. 'The jacksnipe is only known by his Gaelic name when he is heard drumming his mournful descent at Summer dusk; at other times he is simply called a snipe' Lys (Kerry). See *gabhairín an bhainne bheirithe*.

Gabhal n. Also as **goul**. Diminutive, **gabhlóg**, also in forms **gowlogue, gawlogue**. 1. 'A forked stick for gripping furze' JL (w. Cork; Gen.). 2. Crotch. 'If you fall off that branch you'll break your gabhall' ibid; PB (s. Tipperary); Smy (n. Clare). 3. 'A gabhal or goul is a road-branch' S Ua G (s. Tipperary); 'Gabhlóg, gowlogue is a two-pronged fork, used to support a cage in trapping birds' S Ua G (s. Tipperary). 4. A four-pronged pike for cleaning out a stable' JPL (w. Cork). 5. 'A field is said to be in gabhlógs when it is ploughed parallel with two fences meeting in a V. The V is left untilled' MF (Westmeath). 6. A prop or support. 'The gabhlóg was used to prop the bastable at the correct distance above the open fire' DA (e. Cork). Hence a stiff drink. Michael Banim, *The Croppy* 1, 311: 'Maybe your reverence 'ud try a gawlogue'. Glossed 'a guzzle' (Kilkenny); MG (Kilkenny). See *gabhlán, gáilleog*.

Gabhál n. Diminutive in form **goleen**. An armful. 'Give the horse a a gabhál of hay' MS (e. Limerick); JM (w. Cork); *CBD* (n. Kerry). Somerville and Ross, *The Whiteboys*

307: 'Having immured them in an inner room she withdrew, muttering something about another goleen of turf ...' (w. Cork); *EASI* 270: 'In Carlow and Wexford, "goleen"'.

Gabhal-luachair n. Jointed rush, *Junctus articulatus*: Lys (Kerry).

Gabhar n. A goat. 'Used only in the phrase **hi gabhar!** said when driving goats' MF (Westmeath).

Gabhlán n. 'A prop' DOH (e. Limerick). See *gabhlóg*.

Gabhshnáth n. 'Strong thread for sewing, pack thread' *EASI* 266; MS (e. Limerick).

Gad n. 1. Osier withe. 'A ring made of sally rods' McK (Leitrim); HG (n.w. Donegal); 'As tough as a gad' OCn (Laois); 'Some old Cavan farmers never let out their cows to pasture on May Morning unless there was twisted on each cow's tail a gad of rowan tree twigs. This ensured milk and butter against all malign influences for the ensuing season' *BASJ* (Cavan, Leitrim); Somerville and Ross, *Lisheen Races Second-hand* 74: 'One side of her mouth is as tough as a gad' (w. Cork); 'Cut the gad next the throat – afford relief where it most urgently needed' MF (Westmeath). 2. 'A knot in timber' MS (e. Limerick).

Gadaí n. 'A robber' *CBE* 98 (Kilkenny); *IG* (Louth).

Gadarálaí n. 'A tough, stubborn, reluctant person' NB (w. Limerick). See *gadrach*.

Gadhar n. 1. 'A dog' NM (w. Cork); MC (e. Mayo); 'A hound of doubtful pedigree' AG (s. Tipperary). Figuratively, 'a rough, uncouth person. "That fellow is a right gadhar"' ibid. 2. 'A crying child' MC (e. Mayo).

Gadrach adj. 'Tedious, long, protracted. "A gardach céilí"' *IG* (Meath).

Gadrach n. 'A tough, uncompromising person' NB (w. Limerick). See *gadarálaí*.

Gaeltacht n. Irish-speaking areas. As **Gaeltact** in James Joyce, *Finnegans Wake* 87.

Gág n. In form **gawg**. 1. Crack, crevice. 'The ground is all cracks and gaws with the dry weather' OCn (Laois). 2. Crack in skin, chap (Gen.). Hence 'sand gawg, sand crack in a horse's hoof' Su (s. Wexford). 3. 'A splinter' D (s.e. Wexford).

Gaibheal n. In form **gavell**. 'Fun, enjoyment. "There was great gavell at the dance." "Such a night's gavell!"' *CBE* 266 (mid-Tipperary). [Cf. *gáibhéireacht*: taking recreation, sporting. *ODON*]

Gaibín n. 'A short pipe' PB (s. Tipperary). See *dúidín*.

Gáifeach adj. Of sound, loud, wild. Hence n. **guythock**. 'A craver, a useless whiner' *CBE* 266 (mid-Tipperary).

Gaige n. Dandy, fop. 'How did they think they could make a hurler out of that gaige?' PC (n. Clare); PB (s. Tipperary; JL (w. Cork). Hence phrase **gaige na maige**: the toss-of-the-head dandy RBB (Waterford).

Gáileán n. 'An inexperienced person. The word is often used by a town tradesman of a country tradesman' *An Cho* (w. Mayo).

Gáille n. As **gallya**. 'The full of two hands' PLH (n. Roscommon). PLH's headword is *gáille(óg)*.

Gáilleach n. 'A rod on which fish are carried' McK (Leitrim).

Gáilleog n. *al.* **gailleog**. 'A jorum of whiskey or punch' *IG* (Kilkenny); MC (e. Mayo). 'He has a good gáilleog taken: he is under the weather' Kiv (Sligo).

Gailseach n. The earwig. As **coltshogue** D (s.e. Wexford); as **tailseog** *CBE* 98 (Kilkenny).

Gaimbín n. In forms **gombeen, gombeen man**. Usurer, money-lender at exorbitant interest. Somerville and Ross, *The Finger of Mrs Knox*, 321: '"I suppose that's Goggin, the Gombeen?," said Mrs Knox; "how were you fool enough to get into dealings with him?"' (w. Cork); Bram Stoker, *Snake's Pass*, 2: ' A gombeen man, is it? He's the man that linds you a few shillins or a few pounds ... and then niver laves ye till he has tuck all ye've got' (Mayo); James Joyce, *Ulysses* 243: 'A certain gombeen man of our acquaintance'.

Gáinne n. A reed. 'As straight as a gáinne' FF (Monaghan); *CBE* 104 (Leitrim).

Gáir n. In form **gar**. 1. A cry, a shout. 2. A rumour. Seamus MacManus *A Lad of the O'Friels* 187: 'He says there's a great gar out that Con MacCadden's cow ... had a calf with two heads on it' (Donegal).

Gáirdín n. 'A garden. Usually a small garden' H (n. Clare); 'A potato garden' JC (w. Cork).

Gaisce n. *al.* **gaisc**. Also as **gaisca**. 1. Deed of valour. 'Yerra man, you did great gaisce' *CBD* (n. Kerry); PB (s. Tipperary); JM (w. Cork); 'It isn't any great gaisc to do what he did' H (n. Clare); 'He made a great gaisc out of visiting the son in America' C (Limerick). 2. Hero. Often used in sarcasm. 'You're a great gaisce now, aren't you!' *CBD* (n. Kerry); 'A man who is doing great gaisc is generally regarded as attempting more than he is able to do; and incidentally, he is raising the standard of performance on the neighbours! For this reason there is often more than a little irony in the the use of this word; and a demolishing kind of tolerance in the verdict: "He's a bit of a gaisc"' *An Cho* (w. Mayo); Patk. Kennedy, *The Amadhan Mór* 61: 'If you have liquor in that cup worthy of a gaisca, let me take a drink' (Wexford).

Gaiscíoch n. Hero. Often used in derision. 'Aren't you the great gaiscíoch to make a little girl cry' MJD (w. Cork); PB (s. Tipperary).

Gaiste n. In forms **gask**, **gassick**. A trap set for birds. A noose of wire, a snare. W. H. Floredice, *Memories of a Month among the 'Mere' Irish*: 'Take a hare out of a gassick' (Ulster).

Gal daighre n. Literally, the smoke of (or blown by) a blast of wind. Figuratively, an awkward, ungainly person. 'Will you leave my way, you big gal daighre!' MF (Westmeath).

Gal soip phr. Literally, smoke of a wisp. Something of no consequence; a flash in the pan. 'They had a disagreement; airiú, it was only a gal soip' JL (w. Cork).

Galamaisíocht n. 'Playfulness, capers' MC (e. Mayo). 'Pretence – of a very particular kind. It is pretending to be ignorant of the reason for a compliment, or pretending to be ignorant of the good news which will benefit oneself. An example may clear up the meaning. A middle-aged man is congratulated on the news of his oncoming marriage. He says he hasn't heard anything about it, suggests that it must be someone else, and asks who would marry *him*, anyhow. The man might then be told to "stop your galamaisíocht"' *An Cho* (w. Mayo).

Galar n. Disease. 'He has a galar of some kind.' Mac C (Monaghan). Hence **galarachán** n. A sickly animal. 'He got a hell of a price for that oul' galarachán of a cow' PC (n. Clare).

Galdar n. 1. Loud talk. 'I couldn't hear my ears with the galdar' TB (Cavan). 2. 'Cackle of geese' McK (Leitrim). 3. 'A roar, a screech. 'She let a galdar out of her' FF (Monaghan).

Gallach n. In form **gallagh**. A catch of fish. 'That's a nice gallagh you have there, if they're small itself' PJG (mid-Donegal).

Gallagún n. 1. A tadpole. 2. 'A long, tapering worm found in mud' MF (Westmeath).

Gallán mór n. In form **gallon**. The butterburr, *Petasites vulgaris*: *EDD* (Antrim, Down).

Gallán n. Also in form **gallaun**. A standing stone, menhir. 'He's about as agile as the gallán wesht in the field' JL (w. Cork); Eric Cross, *The Tailor and Ansty* 84: 'My father used to tell me of an Englishman who dug up a gallaun at Rosbeg years ago' (w. Cork).

Gallfheabhrán n. In form **gunshelawn**. Wild angelica, *angelica sylvestris*: J (s.e. Wexford).

Gallóglach n. In forms **gallowglass, gallinglasse, galloglass**. Literally, foreign soldier. Heavily armed foot-soldier. Anon., *Captain Thomas Stukeley*: '... gow make ready oore kerne and gallinglasse against the night ...'; Spenser, *A View of the State of Ireland* (1596): 'It is worne of a footeman under a shirt of mayle, the which footeman they call a Galloglass'. For *kerne* see *ceithearnach*.

Galún Uí Dhónaill n. In translated form **O'Donnell's Gallon**. A large quantity of drink. 'He'd drink O'Donnell's gallon and Dunlewey Lake after it' G (n.w. Donegal).

Gam n. Also as **gám**. A person innocent to the point of foolishness: FM (s. Wexford); PD (s. Carlow); RBB (s. Kilkenny); 'The exact phraseology to use can be noted in the following (historical) admission: "When I first came to New York, straight from Louisburgh, I was standing *of a gám* – looking at Central Station until the roof of my mouth got sunburnt"' *An Cho* (w. Mayo).

Gamach n. In forms **gommach, gommagh**. A simpleton, clown. Samuel Lover, *Legends and Stories of Ireland* 4,176: 'The big chap turned out a gommach'; ibid. 1, 80: 'Don't be making a gommagh of yourself' (Connacht); Somerville and Ross, *Major Apollo Riggs* 381: 'What ails ye ... ye old gommach, that ye'd let the dog kill me chickens?' (w. Cork); Jane Barlow, *Irish Idylls* 37: Mrs Brian was inwardly calling herself a big, stupid gommach for alluding to Thady' (Connacht).

Gamal n. Also as **gommula**. Gomeral, fool. 'You wouldn't mind what that gamal would say to you' JL (w. Cork); PB (s. Tipperary); Smy (n. Clare); Patk. Kennedy, *Fireside Stories* 27: 'Oh, but you're the divel's own gommula of a Jack, for taking such wages' (Wexford).

Gamalóg n. Also as **gommologue**. 'A breall (q. v.) of a fool' JL (w. Cork); *CBD* (n. Kerry); George Fitzmaurice, *The King of the Barna Men*: "Listening to you I am, you pair of gommologues ..." (Kerry. Gen. Munster).

Gamba n. 'A lump of bread, meat, or the like' R (n. Clare)

Gamhain gairí n. In form **gown gree**. 'A heifer calving at two years old' *CBE* 266 (mid-Tipperary); 'A calf mated before she was a year old' PB (s. Tipperary). Figuratively, 'a well-made girleen of about sixteen' JC (w. Cork).

Gamhain rua n. Also in form **goon roo**. 'A two-year old in-calf heifer' PLH (n. Roscommon); MF (Westmeath);

Gamhain samhraidh n. Literally, a summer calf. Such was considered soft and delicate, being reared on an abundance of milk. Figuratively (of person), a milksop JL (w. Cork); RBB (w. Waterford).

Gamhnach n. 'A stripper cow' *CBE* 104 (Leitrim).

Gan dabht phr. Without a doubt. As **gondoutha** in Gerald Griffin, *The Collegians* 83 (Limerick). Phrase, **Gan dabht ar domhan**, without a doubt in the world: *CBD* (n. Kerry).

Gan rath air interj. In corrupted form **gon rahid**. Bad luck to it! Eric Cross, *The Tailor and Ansty* 70. Glossed, inaccurately, as 'Gan raht ... May you have no luck.' The Tailor would have used the correct Irish form; the corruption is Cross's.

Gandal 1. 'A gander' JC (w. Cork). 2. Figuratively, a simpleton. NB (w. Limerick); NM (w. Cork); *CBD* (n. Kerry).

Ganfhiosaíocht n. 'Conspiracy' *CBD* (n. Kerry).

Ganga n. Also as **gongy**. 'A long-legged person' *IG* (Kilkenny). Hence noun and adjective 'gongy, a lanky person; lanky' FM (Wexford).

Gaorthadh n. 'A wooded river valley' JL (w. Cork); *CBD* (n. Kerry).

Gaota n. 1. 'A windbag' Con (Meath). 2. 'A fool' ibid. (Louth).

Gaoth n. Wind. Figuratively, boastful talk. 'You'll hear plenty of gaoth from your man after his trip to see the son in New York' JL (w. Cork); PB (s. Tipperary).

Garbhán n. 1. 'A loutish man' DOC (Limerick). 2. The stonecrop, *sedum Anglicum*: DOC (Limerick).

Garbhánach n. In form **garvan**. The sea bream, *pagellus centrodontus*. Michael Harkin, *Inisowen, Its History etc.*: 'A very nutritious little fish which the people call the garvan' (Donegal).

Garbhóg n. 1. As **gorravogue**. 'A gorravogue is a large, rough stone' S Ua G (s. Tipperary). 2. 'A sally rod used in the old days for making baskets' MJD (w. Cork).

Garda n. Guard; member of the Irish police force. James Joyce, *Finnegans Wake* 197: 'Garda Crowley or the Boy with the Billy-club'.

Gárlach n. 1. Brat, urchin. 'He wouldn't spend a penny, and him not having a wife or a gárlach' R (n. Clare). 2. 'An unmarried mother's child' DOC (Limerick).

Garr n. 1. 'Turf mould' *IG* (Kilkenny). 2. 'Soft turf, useless for burning' RBB (mid-Waterford).

Garraí n. Also as **garry**. 'A plot of potatoes' RBB (Waterford); 'A garry is a garden' JB (s. Armagh & n. Louth).

Garrán n. 'A grove of trees' NB (w. Limerick).

Garsún n. Also as **gar-soon; gorcoon; goson; gossan, gossoon; gawsan**. 1. A boy. 'Good garsún' JL (w. Cork); JS (e. Kerry); S Ua G (s. Tipperary). Anon., *The Irish Hudibras*: ' My gar-soon'; John Banim, *Peter of the Castle* 35: 'When the gorcoon is settlin' his oats ...' (Kilkenny); Maria Edgeworth, *Castle Rackrent* 33: 'The little gosson was sent to his neighbours'; James Joyce, *Finnegans Wake* 271: 'gossan'; Mrs S. C. Hall, *Tales of Irish Life and Character* 15: 'Come here, do, you little gossoon'; James Joyce, *Ulysses* 54: 'I was a strapping young gossoon at that time, I tell you'; 'He was a

wild little gawsan' ER (Louth). [< French *garcon*] 2. 'The thatcher's quiver in which the scollops are stuck' S Ua G (s. Tipperary).

Gas n. 'A stalk of corn' Ham (e. Clare); PB (s. Tipperary).

Gasta interj.; adj.; adv. Also as **gastha, gosther**. 1. Quickly! 'You'll be late for school. Out you go. Gasta! Gasta!' MG (n.w. Donegal). 2. Crafty. 'He'd buy and sell you, young as he is. Be talking of a gasta boy!' AOL (mid-Waterford); Wm. Carleton, *The Geography of an Irish Oath* 2, 59: 'By the hole o' my coat, Parra Gastha.'... crafty Paddy; 'He's as gosther as be damned' J (s.e. Wexford). 3. Soon. 'It's three o'clock. He should be here gasta' ER (Louth).

Gastar n. 1. 'A prattler' MF (Westmeath). 2. 'Idle talk, gossip' Wm. Carleton, *Larry M'Farland's Wake* 1,110 (footnote).

Gastóg n. 'Cabbage stalk' *BASJ* (Cavan, Leitrim); Con (Meath).

Gasúr n. Also in forms **gasair** (pl.), **gosur**. A boy. Patrick MacGill, *The Rat Pit*, 41: 'Bringing ruin to the gasair' (Donegal); Dermot O'Byrne, *Children of the Hills*, 85: 'Yon poor gossur' (Donegal).

Gátaire n. As **gawther**. 'A small, thin cake baked in a hurry. "Slap down a gawther for the tea"' *CBE* 266 (mid-Tipperary).

Gátar n. Need, distress. 'He was a good friend in the time of gátar' NM (w. Cork).

Gátarán n. 'A poor little boy left to his own shifts' *IG* (Meath).

Geab n. Also in form **gab**. Talk, chat. Samuel Lover, *Handy Andy* 13: ' He has the power and prate and gift of the gab'; 'She has the divil's own geab' H (n. Clare; Gen.)

Geabaire n. Also as **gabster**. A prater, a chatterbox. 'Imagine being married to that geabaire. She never shuts up' H (n. Clare); S Ua G (s. Tipperary); 'She's a bit of a gabster, that woman' BOD (s.w. Cork.); Mac C (Monaghan).

Geabanta adj. Cheeky, ill-mannered. 'Don't correct them and they'll turn out geabanta' S Ua G (s. Tipperary).

Gead n. 'A blaze, a white mark on a horse's face' RBB (w. Waterford); R (n. Clare).

Geadán n. Buttock(s), bottom. ' Put your geadán under you there, for a minute and rest yourself' R (n. Clare).

Geáitse n. Also as geáits, gauch, garsh. 1. Antics, showing off. 'Look at the geáits of her' RBB (s. Kilkenny); J (s.e. Wexford). Plural geaitsí H (n. Clare); PB (s. Tipperary); JC (w. Cork); George Fitzmaurice, *The King of the Barna Men*: 'by the gauch of her ... I'm thinking it isn't unknown to her'. 2. A show-off. 'He's only an oul' geáits' MW (s. Wexford); 'A bit of a garsh' TOM (s. Tipperary). Hence 'garshing, showing off' ibid.

Geal gabhann n. The corn marigold, *Chrysanthemum segetum*. Also called geal seed PJG (mid-Donegal).

Geal n. Also in form gale. The common wild rape, *Brassica campestris*: H (n. Donegal).

Gealach na gcoinleach n. *al.* gealach na gcoinlíní. The moon of the stubbles – the harvest moon. 'A cold moon, gealach na gcoinleach' PJG (mid-Donegal); 'They say that young women would want to be careful courting under gealach na gcoinlíní. A dangerous time, by all accounts' JL (w. Cork).

Gealán n. 'A sunbeam' *IG* (Kilkenny).

Gealóg n. 1. 'A pretty little girl' RBB (s. Kilkenny). 2. A small potato: JC (w. Cork).

Gealtán n. 'A foolish, giddy person without much sense. "A cracked gealtán of a girl"' *CBD* (n. Kerry).

Geamhar n. 'Young corn, grass, young foliage on root crops' RBB (w. Waterford).

Geamp n. 'A jagged cut. A slovenly dressmaker would leave a garment full of geamps. The word can be applied to any irregularity in somethink that should be regular-even a haircut' *An Cho* (w. Mayo).

Geanc n. A snub nose: *CBD* (n. Kerry); NM (w. Cork); H (n. Clare); NB (w. Limerick).

Geancach n., adj. Turned up, cocked. 'An ugly little geancach' H (n. Clare); NB (w. Limerick); JPL (w. Cork); *CBD* (n. Kerry); 'He had a geancach nose' *CBD* (n. Kerry).

Geancánach n. As gancanagh, gankeynogue, gankey, gankinna, ganconer. 'A gancanagh is a fairy man, a leprechaun' TB (Cavan); *EDD* (Louth): 'A kind of fairy said to appear in lonesome valleys, making love to milkmaids &c'; ibid. 'Extremely common, especially near Drogheda'; B. Hunt, *Folk Tales of Breffny* 189: 'the gankeynogue or gankey'; *EASI* (Monaghan): 'gankinna'; W. B. Yeats, *Fairy and Folk-Tales of the Irish Peasantry:* 'What would he see but a whole lot of ganconers dancing!'

Geantaraí n. 'A cow in calf' *CBD* (n. Kerry).

Gearán vb. n. In form gearning. Complaining. 'He never stops gearning' Mac C (Monaghan).

Gearrabhreac n. The oystercatcher H (n. Donegal). H quotes *Manx Birdnames* (*Zoologist*, Feb. 1897): '*Gearra- breac*: oystercatcher and also black guillemot.'

Gearrach n. 'A short potato ridge or drill' *IG* (Kilkenny); PB (s. Tipperary).

Gearrach n. 1. 'A short ridge in ploughing' S Ua G (s. Tipperary). 2. A short cut. 'I took the gearrach home' ibid. See *giorrach*, *gearóg*.

Gearradh vbl. n. In translated form cutting. 1. A pain in the stomach, bowel; diarrhoea H (n. Donegal). [*Gearradh*, diarrhoea, literally, the cutting.] 2. Gearradh, 'cutting', substance, lasting power. Peadar O'Donnell, *The Knife* 188: 'It's a wonder he had that much cuttin' in him', Molly grumbled' (Donegal).

Gearrán n. In forms garron, garon, garran, garrane, garraane. 1. Gelding. 2. A nag. Anon., *The Welsh Embassador*: 'garron';

Gerald Griffin, *The Collegians* 108: 'Get up there, you old garron' (Limerick); Mrs S. C. Hall, *Tales of Irish Life and Character* 9: 'Sure it isn't such a garron as that you'd put before his honour' (s. Leinster); William Carleton, *The Party Fight and Funeral* 1, 197: 'Would you have me for to show the Garrane-bane, and lave them like a cowardly thraitor ... ?' Carleton's gloss: 'The white horse, i.e. wanting in mettle. Tradition affirms that James the Second escaped on a white horse from the battle of the Boyne; and from this circumstance a white horse has become a symbol of cowardice' (Tyrone). As **garraane bane** in Richard Head, *Hic et Ubique.* As **garrane baun** in *Poole* (s.e. Wexford): 'An a priesth o parieshe on his garrane baun.' As **garrane dough** [*dubh*, black] in Head, *op. cit.* As **garon-reagh** [*riabhach*, roan], in John Durant Breval, *The Play is the Plot.*

Gearrcach n. 1. A fledgeling, nestling *CBD* (n. Kerry); Smy (n. Clare). 2. A small child. 'She died and left a houseful of gearrcachs after her' NB (w. Limerick).

Gearrchaile n. Also in forms **geachaile, gahilla, gahalla.** 'A young girl, a female infant; a daughter' MF (Westmeath); 'A good-looking young gahilla' FF (Cavan); 'She's the only gahalla in the family' Mac C (Monaghan); 'A fine geachaile of about eighteen' McK (Leitrim.)

Gearrlomán n. 1. An untidy person S Ua G (s. Tipperary). 2. A closely-cropped head ibid.

Gearróg n. Also as **geerogue.** 'A gearróg is a short drill in an irregularly shaped field' OC (Monaghan); 'A geerogue, a short drill in the corner of a field' D (s.e. Wexford). See *giorrach.*

Geataire n. Also in form **gatherie.** 1. *EASI* 260: 'A splinter of bog deal used as a torch' (Carlow). 2. ibid. 260: 'A small cake, commonly smeared with treacle, sold in the street on market days'. 3. 'Geataire: a tall rush' *CBD* (n. Kerry).

Geidimín n. 'An unlikable character; generally a social nuisance ... there is no known female specimen' *An Cho* (w. Mayo).

Géillín n. Chin support for a person learning to swim. 'Rest your chin in my cupped hands. The géillín will keep your head above water' MS (e. Limerick); *CBD* (n. Kerry); JPL (w. Cork).

Geilt n. As **gelt.** A madman. 'Here used for a ragged, half-wild person. "He was going round in a gelt with his old clothes hanging half-off of him"' *CBE* 266 (mid-Tipperary).

Géim n. Game. **To make game of,** to make sport of. Translation of Irish phrase **ag déanamh géim.** J. M. Synge, *The Well of the Saints* 39: 'Ah, you're thinking you're a fine lot ... to be making game of myself and the woman I've heard called the great wonder of the west.'

Geis n. As **gesh.** Taboo or prohibition. 'It is a gesh to cut down fairy bushes' *BASJ* (Cavan).

Geit n. A sudden start. 'The horse took a geit' LOS (w. Clare); RBB (s. Kilkenny).

Geocach n. Also in forms **geoceogh, geoch-ach** 1. A rascal: *Pe* (Wexford); 'A young, foolish person' MS (e. Limerick). 2. 'A tinker, a vagrant' J (s. Wexford); *IG* (Kilkenny); PB (s. Tipperary); Gerald Griffin, *The Collegians* 38: 'Give you my sister, you keowt of a geoceogh ...' (Limerick); Patk. Kennedy, *Legendary Fictions of the Irish Celts* 11: '... come, be off, you lazy geochachs!' Glossed as 'greedy strollers' (Wexford).

Geocán n. Also as **jokawn.** 'Geocán is a reed of straw' *CBD* (n. Kerry); *EASI* 278: 'Jokawn: An oaten stem cut off above the joint, with a tongue cut in it, which sounds a rude kind of music when blown with the mouth' (Limerick).

Geois n. A belly, paunch. 'Look at the geois on your man' PD (s. Carlow); *IG* (Kilkenny); PB (s. Tipperary).

Geonail n. *al.* **giúnáil.** Whimpering, whining. 'The dog is at the geonail again.' 'Stop your giúnáil' MC (e. Mayo).

Geosadán n. 1. 'Ragweed' MS (e. Limerick); Ham (e. Clare); *CBD* (n. Kerry); PB (s. Tipperary). 2. 'A half-witted person' Ham

(e. Clare). 3. 'A thin, weedy person' C (Limerick). See *feochadán*.

Gibiris n. As **gibberish**. 'Unintelligible speech' BOD (s.w. Cork).

Gile geal phr. In form **gilla gal**. Tautological, bright brightess. 'Said only to little children. "Whisht now, gilla gal, see what I have for you"' *CBE* 266 (mid-Tipperary).

Gillimín n. 'A small, active little boy or girl' *IG* (Meath).

Gillín n. 1. 'A spirited horse' PC (n. Clare). 2. A gelding. 'He's married with a bit and no sign of a child. He's a gillín, I'm thinking' JL (w. Cork). 3. 'A flighty young woman' PD (s. Carlow). 4. 'A featherheaded young man' MW (s. Wexford).

Gilmín n. As **gilmeen**. 'A tiny fish seen in streams. A pinkeen' RBB (mid-Waterford).

Giob n. A bit, a morsel. 'The horse is fine. He didn't leave a giob of his feed after him' PJG (Donegal).

Giob v. Also as **gib**. 'To trim cocks of hay at ground by pulling out all the loose hay; e.g. go and giob the cocks' MF (Westmeath); 'Some people don't even bother to gib the cocks of hay' MW (s. Wexford); PD (s. Carlow).

Giob-geab n. 1. Inconsequential talk. 'All you ever hear from the minister is giob-geab' PC (n. Clare). 2. 'Type of communication between birds in flight, especially wild geese. "You could hear the giob-geab of birds across the sky"' MC (e. Mayo).

Giobach n., adj. Also in form **geobgah**. 1. 'A rag' *Pe* (Wexford). 2. Tattered, ragged in appearance. 'You're looking very geobgah, if you don't mind me saying so' JB (s. Armagh & n. Louth).

Giobadán n. As **gibbadaun**. *EASI* 216: 'A frivolous person' (Roscommon)

Giobal n. Also **gibble**. A rag, a torn garment. 'You'd think she'd be ashamed going around in them giobals' MS (e. Limerick); 'She has a lot of giobals hanging to her' NB (w. Limerick); H (n. Clare); *CBD* (n. Kerry); PB (s. Tipperary); *An Cho* (w. Mayo). 'Her clothes were in gibbles' AG (s. Tipperary).

Giobalach adj. Untidily dressed. 'A giobalach girleen like you won't be the belle of the ball' H (n. Clare); PB (s. Tipperary).

Gioblachán n. 'A person whose clothes are in tatters' PB (s. Tipperary).

Giobóg n. A tiny bit, a scrap. 'Look at the giobóg of a dress that Swede has on her' R (n. Clare).

Gioda gioda interj. 'Gioda gioda is said to a child when one tickles him to make him laugh' S Ua G (s. Tipperary).

Giodach n. In cardplaying: 'If you'll come into me I'll put the giodach on you: I have a card to beat yours' *CBD* (n. Kerry).

Giodam n. 'Friskiness, liveliness' OCn (Laois); 'He's full of his giodam' Mas (mid-Tipperary); H (n. Clare); PB (s. Tipperary); *JCHAS* (Cork).

Giodán n. Buttock. 'Sit there on you giodán' JF (n. Wexford).

Giodóg n. A blow. 'I'll give you a giodóg in the ear' *CBD* (n. Kerry).

Giodramán n. 'An unreliable, flighty person' MC (e. Mayo). *al.* **giodamán** PC (n. Clare).

Giodróg n. As **gidrog**. 'A flighty, skittish girl' FF (Cavan); Mac C (Monaghan).

Gíog n. Also in forms **geeg**, **gig**. A squeak, the smallest sound. 'There wasn't a geek out of him' G (s. Kilkenny); 'There was neither gig nor gag in him' Mac C (Monaghan).

Giolcach n. 1. 'Reeds' JL (w. Cork) 2. Broom, *cytisus scoparius*: *CBE* 98 (Kilkenny); PB (s. Tipperary).

Giolla guaille n. In form **gilly gooly**. 'A silly, light-headed person. "He's going round every day in a gilly gooly"; "Don't be such a gilly gooly"' *CBE* 266 (mid-Tipperary).

Giolla n. In form **gillie**. Attendant, man-servant. M. J. Mulloy, *The King of Friday's Men* 16: 'The rent for his potato patch he pays by serving his landlord ... as gillie on his fowling and fishing occasions' (Galway).

Giolla rua n. In form **gillarue**. 'Brown trout' H (n. Donegal).

Giorrach n. 'A short drill in a ploughed field' *CBD* (n. Kerry); RBB (s. Kilkenny). See *gearróg, gearrach*.

Giorria n. The hare, *lepus timidus hibernicus*: *CBE* 104 (Leitrim).

Gíoscán n. Any creaking, squeaky noise. 'That gíoscán would addle you' *CBD* (n. Kerry). As vb n. **gíoscáning**. 'What sort of fiddler is he?' 'Muise, only gíoscáning' *CBD* (n. Kerry).

Giostaire n. In form **gistra**. 1. 'A chatty old man. Also a precocious, loquatious child' OC (Monaghan); MF (Westmeath); *EASI* 262: 'A sturdy, active old man' (Ulster). 2. 'A young person who talks too much' PJG (mid-Donegal); 'A brat of a child' ER (Louth).

Giota n. Also as **bit, piece, giteen**. 1. The lunch brought to school by children. 'You went to school without your giota to-day' MG (n.w. Donegal); Seumus MacManus, *Bold Blades of Donegal* 6: 'The only thing I had in my pocket was my bit, which Uncle Donal told me not to eat till the middle of the next day'; 'Bread and jam is not much of a piece for a growing boy' MG (n.w. Donegal). 2. Bit of anything. 'He dug his giteen of spuds in no time' MC (e. Mayo).

Giotarlóg n. 'A small piece of something – of bread, of cloth etc. The word is obviously related to *giota* (q.v.), but it is not included in the modern Irish dictionaries. A particular Louisburgh usage refers to a small or young person who is inadequate for some responsibility. "What could you expect from a giotarlóg of a girl!"' *An Cho* (w. Mayo).

Girseach n. Also in forms **girsha, geirseach, giorseach, girsah**. A young girl. Wm. Carleton, *The Poor Scholar* 2, 276: '... an' whin the girshas are done milkin'; ibid. *Fardorougha the Miser* 21: 'A girsha's as well entitled to a full glass as a gorsoon' (Tyrone); Seumus MacManus, *A Lad of the O'Friels* 17: 'I'll make the little geirseach as happy as she was in Sent Pether's pocket' (Donegal); Dermot O'Byrne, *Children of the Hills* 51: 'The giorseach must be getting used to it' (Donegal); John Boyce, *Shandy Maguire* 211: 'The girl was a wee girsah' (Donegal); Patrick MacGill, *The Rat Pit* 3: 'Who is the girsha who is out so early?' (Donegal); Emily Lawless, *Grania*, 2, 243: 'Your poor Grania, that's loved you all her life long, since she was a little bit of a girsha' (Mayo).

Giuc n. A 'jump' in the light of an oil lamp. 'There's a giuc in the light' *CBD* (n. Kerry).

Giúis n. Pine, fir, Scotch fir: NM (w. Cork); JS (e. Kerry).

Giúrnáil n. Light work, chores. 'She's much better; she's able to do some giúrnáil around the house now' BOD (s.w. Cork). Hence, **giúrnáiling**. 'She's giúrnáling in the kitchen' JL (w. Cork).

Giúsachán n. A downy growth. 'He's young and soft, the poor boy. Look at the giúsachán of a beard on him' R (n. Clare).

Glac n. In form **glack**. A recess. Michael Harkin, *Inisowen, its History* etc.: 'Between the mountains, or embosomed among them, are glens, cloons (valleys), glacks (secluded nooks) and narrow passes' (Donegal).

Glac n. In form **lock**. A small amount of anything. Patrick Gallagher, *My Story* 55: 'We had a good many locks of whiskey' (Ulster).

Glac v. In form **glak**. Take, accept. In phrase **glac seo** – take this, written as **glak shogh** in Wm. Carleton, *Fardorougha the Miser* 21 (Tyrone).

Glafaire n. Also as **glaffer, glaff.** 1. 'One who shouts instead of talking. It is a common occurence with people – usually men – who spend all day in the open having to shout loudly at neighbours, to passers-by, to cattle, dogs etc., and who forget later that they have to come indoors. Women, who do not appreciate the boon of a Sunday match broadcast, frequently refer to a commentator as a glafaire' *An Cho* (w. Mayo). 2. 'A glaffer is a bad-tempered person who would snap at you' FF (Cavan). 3. 'A glaff is a foolish person who talks nonsense all the time' S (n.w. Donegal).

Glagaire n. 'A very talkative woman' *GC* (Laois, n. Kilkenny); *IG* (Meath). See *gliogaire.*

Glaicín n. A fetter *CBE* 104 (Leitrim).

Glaise n. 1. A stream DOH (e. Limerick); JL (w. Cork); *CBD* (n. Kerry); PB (s. Tipperary); 'Take the cows down to the glaise' Mas (Tipperary). 2. Wet, marshy land *CBD* (n. Kerry).

Glam n. A howl. 'The dog let a glam out of him' RBB (w. Waterford); JL (w. Cork). [Cf. Old Norse *glamm*, noise.]

Glám n., v. As **glaum.** 1. Grab, clutch, grope. John Banim, *Peter of the Castle* 3, 4: 'glaums of wool' (Kilkenny); 'He made a glaum at me' C (Limerick); 'He never stops glauming women, the oul' ram' R (n. Clare); James Joyce, *Ulysses* 664: ' whenever he was there meaning him of course glauming me over ...' 2. A blow. George Brittaine, *Irishmen and Irishwomen* 129: 'Oh, sorrah foot will I go where Mrs B. could give me a glaum.'

Glamóg n. As **glamoge.** 'A handful' PLH (n. Roscommon).

Glamaire n. A loudmouth. 'I don't know what she needs a phone for. That glamaire could be heard in Cork without one' JL (w. Cork); AOL (mid-Waterford).

Glamaisc n. A gluttonous person *CBD* (n. Kerry).

Glámhán n. '(Act of) complaining, scolding' PB (s. Tipperary).

Glámhánaí n. A complainer, grumbler. 'A young person who always has the béal bocht' (q.v.) DOC (Limerick).

Glanadh amach phr. Cleaning out. 'They got a great glanadh amach during the war: that family was well-scattered through death, emigration or marriage' *CBD* (n. Kerry).

Glantóir n. Cleaner, dusting rag DOH (e. Limerick). Now common through school usage.

Glár n. In form **glar.** Silt, alluvium. 'Oozy mud' ER (Louth); *CBE* 104 (Leitrim); Seamus Heaney, *Fostering*: 'I can't remember never having known/ The immanent hydraulics of a land /Of glar and glit and dailigone'.

Glas gaoithe n. In form **glasgeehy.** 'A white sea eel, smaller than conger' H (n. Donegal).

Glasair léana n. Literally, the plant of sorrow. 1. Spearwort PJG (Donegal). 2. The bog asphodel, *narthecium ossifragum*: MG (n.w. Donegal).

Glasán n. The coalfish, *Merlangus carbonarius.* Also in forms **glashan, glassan, glassin:** M'Parlan, *Statistical Survey of the County of Donegal; IG* (Meath, Louth).

Glé n. 'Virgin soil; a newly laid down field' *IG* (Meath).

Gleabhac n. Peering expression, often one of belligerence. 'You should have seen the gleabhac on him when I took the trick with the Ace of Hearts' R (n. Clare).

Gleacaí n. 'A smart fellow with an element of trickery' H (n. Clare). 'The word has little of a condemning sense. It is more often used in a playful way to show that one has one has unearthed an ingenious trick or practical joke conceived by a younger person. When the ruse is exposed one says to the trickster, "Ha, a ghleacaí!" (The initial *g* changes to *gh* in the vocative.)' *An Cho* (w. Mayo).

Gleadhrach n. 'A big fire, like you see on St. John's Eve; a bonefire' R (n. Clare); *CBD* (n. Kerry).

Gleamaighdear n. 'A senseless person' NB (w. Limerick).

Gleann n. 'A glen' *CBE* 104 (Leitrim).

Gleic n. (Act of) wrestling. Hence **gleeks**, 'a grip in wrestling' PON (n. Co. Dublin).

Gléic n. As **glake**. A fool, a clown. 'There he goes, making a glake of himself as usual' PD (s. Carlow).

Gléireán n. 1. 'An empty or light sensation in the head' Con (Meath). 2. 'A light, giddy-headed person' *IG* (Meath).

Gleo n. Also as **glow**. 1. Noise. Patk. Kennedy, *Legendary Fictions of the Irish Celts* 86: 'the glows and the moans were never out of his mouth' (Wexford). 2. Lively fun. 'We had the divil's own gleo after the match, singing and dancing' AOL (mid-Waterford). 3. Fighting. 'There's always gleo at the matches between those two parishes' PC (n. Clare).

Gleoisín n. 'A girl without much sense' NB (w. Limerick); *CBD* (n. Kerry).

Gleoite adj. 1. Neat. 'You are really gleoite' JC (w. Cork). 2. Plausible. 'He's really gleoite, that fellow. He'd charm the birds off the boughs' H (n. Clare).

Gleoiteog n. 'A type of small, west-coast, open-decked sailing boat' PC (n. Clare).

Gleorán n. 1. Hogweed, *Heracleum sphondylium* NB (w. Limerick). 2. 'Loud, discordant talk, din' PB (s. Tipperary).

Glib n. 1. A lock of hair, especially on the forehead; a forelock. (Gen.). Richard Stanyhurst, *Chronicles*: '... proud of long crisped bushes of heare which they terme glibs'. 2. Untidy hair. 'That's an awful glib of a head' *CBD* (n. Kerry). 3. A person whose hair is unkempt, untidy' *CBD* (n. Kerry).

Glic adj. Crafty, cunning. 'As glic as a vixen' H (n. Clare).

Glifín n. 'A silly person' H (n. Clare). See *glig, gligín, glincín*.

Glig n. Literally, a bell. Also in diminutive forms **gligín, gligin, gligeen**. Used figuratively. 'A glig is a woman who can't keep her mouth shut, always ready to talk about things she knows nothing at all about. We'd say a gligín too' JL (w. Cork); Peadar O'Donnell, *The Knife* 235: 'They won't let a priest near us except gligins like themselves' (Donegal); 'A gligeen is a person who babbles nonsense mostly' PB (s. Tipperary).

Glig gleaig phr. Silly talk. 'All you'll ever hear from him is old glig gleaig' MJD (w. Cork).

Glincín n. Also as **glinkeen**. 1. 'A rattle-brained person' H (n. Clare); *CBE* 34 S (Galway); 'A depreciatory term used of a girl' *EDD*; Patk. Kennedy, *Evenings in the Duffrey* 375: 'Such a glinkeen of a girl' (Wexford). 2. A gossip. 'She have the news of the country, that glinkeen' JM (w. Cork); PB (s. Tipperary); PC (n. Clare). See also *glig, gligín, glifín*.

Gliogaire n. 'A talkative person, a rambling prattler' *Sguab* (w. Cork). See *glagaire*.

Gliogar n. Also as **glugger**. Gurgling or squelching noise. James Joyce, *Finnegans Wake* 222. Hence **gluggerin'**. 'The water was gluggerin' around in his boots when he came out of the swamp' OCn (Laois.)

Gliomach n. 'A lobster' *An Cho* (w. Mayo).

Glisín n. 'A small, slim, thin woman' *CBD* (n. Kerry).

Gliúcach n. 1. 'A person whose sight is defective' NB (w. Limerick); *CBD* (n. Kerry). 2. 'A person who is inquisitive about other people's business. "A right old gliúcach"' *CBD* (n. Kerry).

Glóire do Mhuire interj. Glory to Mary! As **glorhia wurrah!** in Wm. Carleton, *Lachlin Murray* 341.

Glórach adj. 'Noisy. 'He's a bit too glórach for my liking' NB (w. Limerick).

Glothar n. In form **gluher**. 'Frogspawn' *CBE* 266 (mid-Tipperary).

Glug n. 'The rattle of a rotten egg when shaken, or noise in the belly of a horse after drinking' *IG* (Meath).

Glugar n. 1. 'An addle egg' AOL (mid-Waterford; Gen.). 2. A stupid person. 'He's only a glugar of a fool; listen to the nonsensical talk of him' JPL (w. Cork).

Glúiníneach n. 'A crippling disease in the legs of sheep or calves. Also used in relation to humans. 'He was bet at half-time, running around like an oul' ewe with the glúiníneach' RBB (s. Kilkenny); PB (s. Tipperary).

Glúnach n. A disease in the legs of poultry. A form of *glúiníneach* (q. v.) In expression 'He/she would give you the glúnach, that is, would give you the pip' MW (Wexford)

Glúracáin n. In form **glooracks**. 'Numbness in the fingers from the cold' Con (Meath).

Gnúis n. As **grush**. Face, appearance. 'An unpleasant face' Mac C (Monaghan).

Go bhféacha Dia oraibh interj. May God look upon you. In form **go vioch a Dieu uriv** in Michael Banim, *Crohoor of the Billhook* 1, 194. Glossed, inaccurately, by Banim as 'God look down on us.'

Go bhfóire Dia orainn interj. God help us! MJD (w. Cork); RBB (w. Waterford); Ham (e. Clare); NB (w. Limerick). **Go bhfóire Dia ort** interj. (singular), God help you! as **Gho wori dhe orth** in Wm. Carleton, *The Dream of a Broken Heart* 320 (Tyrone).

Go deimhin interj. Indeed. As **ghe dhiven** in Wm. Carleton, *Phelim O'Toole's Courtship* 2, 241 (Tyrone). As **go deine** in Patk. Kennedy, *Legends of Mount Leinster* 120 (Wexford).

Go leor phr. In forms **galore, gillore**. Wm. Carleton, *Shan Fhad's Wedding* 1, 57: 'You all know that the best of aiting and dhrinking is provided when a runaway couple is expected; and indeed there was galore of both there.' Glossed by Carleton as 'more than enough-great abundance' (Tyrone); Tennyson, *To-Morrow*: 'To be there wid the blessed Mother, an' saints an' Marthyrs galore'; Anon., *The Irishman's Prayers*: 'Dat ve should have Lands and Livings gillore'.

Go mbeannaí Dia dhuit interj. May God bless you. In Wm. Carleton, *The Lianhan Shee* 2, 78 as: **Gho manhy dhea ghud**; Carleton, *The Midnight Mass* 1, 353, as **gho mhany Deah ghud** (Tyrone).

Go raibh ádh ó Dhia orainn interj. May we have luck from God! 'Said as a remark at something extraordinary' *IG* (Meath).

Gob n. Also as **gub, gob**. 1. Beak, bill, mouth. Wm. Carleton, *Phelim O'Toole's Courtship* 2, 200: 'Open your purty gub' (Tyrone); J. M. Synge, *The Playboy of the Western World* 106: 'An ugly young streeler with a murderous gob on him'; 'He has his gob up to her, i.e. he was chatting with her' MF (Westmeath). 2. 'A portion of land extending into water. "Tony's gub"' MC (e. Mayo). 3 In comp. **gobshell**. *EASI* 263: 'big spittle direct from the mouth' (Limerick). [< *gob* + *seile*, spittle.]

Gobach adj. Clever. 'She has a mind for the books: she's very gobach' NB (w. Limerick).

Gobach n. 'A small, lightly-built person' *CBD* (n. Kerry).

Gobadán n. The sandpiper, *tringa glareola*: D (s.e. Wexford). There is an Irish saying, *ní féidir leis an ngobadán an dá thrá a fhreastal*, the sandpiper cannot attend to two strands; this is probably the origin of Boyle Roche's famous bull, 'I cannot, unlike the bird, be in two places at once.'

Gobán n. 1. 'A tin or porringer with breathing holes in the bottom, tied on a calf's snout to prevent it from sucking the cow' OC (Monaghan). 2. 'A bad tradesman.' From the mythical Irish builder, the Gobán Saor' PON (n. Co. Dublin); H (n. Clare). 3. 'A handyman' *CBE* 34 S (Galway). 4. 'One who pretends to have a deep knowledge of things, and has a lot to say' MF (Westmeath).

Gobóg n. The spur dog-fish, *Squalus acanthius*: H (n. Donegal); *Patterson* (Antrim, Down).

Gog n. 1. A sound. 'The child is asleep. There isn't a gog out of him' NB (w. Limerick). 2. 'A child's name for an egg' SF (Wexford).

Gogaí n. As **guggy**. 'A child's name for an egg' Mac C (Monaghan; Gen.).

Gogaire n. 1. 'One who puts seed potatoes into their holes' S Ua G (s. Tipperary). 2. 'A midwife' ibid.

Gogalach n. 1. 'The noise made by a grouse; the noise made by a crow when feeding its young etc. The word may be a borrowing of English gaggle, possibly influenced by other words like gobble' RBB (w. Waterford); 'The cackling of a goose or the gibble of a turkey' JC (w. Cork). 2. *EASI* 264: 'A dotard' (Limerick).

Goic n. 'A person is said to have a goic on him if his head is not in an upright position, but slanted towards the shoulder, due to a hurt or a crick' PJG (Donegal.

Goidé deir sé inter. phr. What is he saying? As **gho dhe dirsha?** in Wm. Carleton, *The Poor Scholar* 2, 264 (Tyrone).

Goidé mar tá tú inter. phr. How are you? As **ghud dhemur tha thu** in Wm. Carleton, *Wildgoose Lodge* 2, 351 (Tyrone).

Góilín n. Also in form **gullion**. 1. 'Góilín: a lakelet' *CBD* (n. Kerry). 2. 'A small inlet' Mac C (Monaghan). 3. 'A gullion is a muddy, soggy place' PJG (mid-Donegal).

Goirge n. A dolt *IG* (Monaghan); FF (Cavan); Mac C (Monaghan).

Goirt n. In form **girt**. Literally, salt. Figuratively, pain, trouble. 'Campbell, speaking of a sister-in-law's illness, said, "it's a great girt entirely"' H (n. Donegal).

Goirtín n. 'A small garden' NB (w. Limerick); PB (s. Tipperary).

Góislín n. 'A gosling' JC (w. Cork).

Goldar n. As **gulder**. A shout, a roar. 'He let an awful gulder out of him when he fell off the horse' G (n.w. Donegal); JB (s. Armagh

& n. Louth). Hence **gulderin**, 'shouting, roaring' G (n.w. Donegal).

Gonc n. In form **gunk**. A snub, rebuff. 'A set-back, a sobering collision with reality; a richly deserved disappointment. "He'll get some gunk when he finds out the whole story is only nonsense"' O'K (Tyrone); FF (Cavan); Mac C (Monaghan); Gen.

Gor n. As **gurr**. The condition of a broody, or hatching, hen. 'The hen is on gurr' G (s. Kilkenny). Hence **to gurr, gurrin**: 'the hen is about to gurr'; 'All my hens are gurrin' *CBE* 266; AG (s. Tipperary). Hence **gurry hatch**: 'a person who spends too long on the toilet' AG (s. Tipperary).

Gorán n. 'A live coal' *Pe* (Wexford).

Gorb n. Diminutive, **gorbán**, as **gorban**. 'A glutton' JB (s. Armagh & n. Louth). 'In Belfast, the boys of any one school call the boys of another gorbs'; 'That kitten is a greedy gorb'; 'Anybody eating more than his share would be called a greedy gorb' *Ballymena Observer;* James Joyce, *Finnegans Wake* 31: 'gorban'.

Gort n. 'A cultivated field' JL (w. Cork; Gen.).

Gorta n. 'Want; of food in particular *CBD* (n. Kerry); PC (n. Clare); MS (e. Limerick).

Gortach adj. Miserly. 'She keeps a gortach house' J (s.e. Wexford); Mac C (Monaghan).

Gotha n. 1. Appearance. As **gothaw**. ' "You have not the right gothaw of work on you" is a reprove often earned by one not over-fond of his business' *BASJ* (Cavan, Leitrim). 2. Plural **gothaí**, 'Flirtatious antics; showing off. "Look at the gothaí of your man"' FF (Monaghan); PB (s. Tipperary).

Grá n. Also as **grádh, grah, gragh, graw**. Love. In phrase **a ghrá**, a term of endearment. Seamus MacManus, *A Lad of the O'Friels* 51: 'But, a gradh, it's what he didn't do, that I despise Dan for' (Donegal); Wm. Carleton, *Phelim O'Toole's Courtship* 2,188: 'Throw the grah an' love I once had for you in my teeth now' (Tyrone); James

Joyce, *Finnegans Wake* 317: 'gragh'; Flann O'Brien, *The Dalkey Archive* 87: 'The Irish people have a great graw for the horse.'

Grá Dé n. Literally, love of God. An act of charity. 'That's a grá Dé to give her a bag of spuds' MG (n.w. Donegal); RBB (w. Waterford).

Grá mo chroí phr. Love of my heart. As **gra-ma-cree**, **gra machree**. Anon., *Purgatorium Hibernicum*: 'For old acquaintance, for it's thee Dat is mee only gra-ma-cree'; 'A "grá mo chroí man" is a plausible man; "grá mo chroí talk" is soft talk' H (n. Clare); NB (w. Limerick); MP (mid-Tipperary): 'It's all grá mo chroí with him and nothing behind it'; Wm. Carleton, *Phelim O'Toole's Courtship* 2, 237: 'gra machree' (Tyrone).

Grábach adj. 'Soft, pliable' MP (mid-Tipperary).

Grabach adj. (Of land) 'rough, stony, difficult to cultivate' FF (Cavan).

Grabaire n. 'A talkative person' *IG* (Kilkenny); PB (s. Tipperary).

Grabaireacht n. (Act of) 'prattling' *IG* (Kilkenny).

Grabhar móna n. Turf mould. Peat moss. 'If you told the old people that they could sell grabhar móna for big money they'd have a good laugh at you' G (n.w. Donegal).

Gradam n. Affection. 'I have a great gradam for him' Mac C (Monaghan).

Grafán n. 1. 'A grubbing-hoe, scuffle-hoe' RBB (s. Kilkenny); MS (e. Limerick); JL (w. Cork). 2. 'A rake' DOH (e. Limerick).

Grág n. A howl; hoarse, raucous cry. 'You should have heard the grágs of him when he fell into the bog-hole' R (n. Clare).

Grágán n. In form **gragan**. 'An untidy head of hair' H (n. Donegal).

Graidhin n. In phrase **mo ghraidhin tú** 1. Bravo! Good man! JL (w. Cork). 2. Poor

fellow! 'An expression of sympathy, or mock sympathy' JL (w. Cork).

Gráig n. In form **grag**. Tree stumps found in bogs. Patrick Gallagher, *My Story* 15: 'A fine lot of grags fencing his field'; 'A fire of grags is better than any turf fire' G (n.w. Donegal).

Gráin n. 1. Disgust. 'He'd put gráin on you' *IG* (Carlow, Wexford); MW (s. Wexford). 2. 'Enmity. "The gráin was in her laugh"' MC (e. Mayo). With intensifier, **gráin dearg**, red enmity ibid.

Gráin n. Little love. 'Said to a cow' *IG* (Kilkenny); 'Cows being milked are soothed with this word' *CBE* 266 (mid-Tipperary).

Gráinne n. 'A man who goes to weddings uninivited, dressed as a woman in straw, in order to get free drink' TB (Cavan). [? < personal name Gráinne, wife of Fionn Mac Cumhaill and lover of Diarmaid in the old Fenian story.]

Gráinneog n. 1. The hedgehog, *Erinaceus europaeus*: G (n.w. Donegal); *Pe* (Wexford); MF (Westmeath); PB (s. Tipperary). 2. 'A quick-tempered person' MC (e. Mayo).

Gráinseachán n. Also as **graanshaghaun**. 1. 'Boiled corn, frumenty, usually served with butter' MS (e. Limerick); *CBD* (n. Kerry). *EASI* 267: 'In my early days what we called graanshaghaun was wheat in grains, not boiled, but roasted in an iron pot held over the fire, the wheat being kept stirred till done' (Munster). 2. 'A hearty meal. 'We had great gráinseachán' *CBD* (n. Kerry).

Graithin n. In form **grahin**. 'A swarm, a mob. Generally used in a derogatory sense: "They have a grahin of childer"' *CBE* 266 (mid-Tipperary); 'He should have known better than to marry into that graithin' MJD (w. Cork); AOL (mid-Waterford).

Graitseachán n. 'A wizened little man' PB (s. Tipperary).

Gramaisc n. Rabble. 'They are only the gramaisc of the street' JPL (w. Cork); PB (s. Tipperary); RBB (s. Kilkenny)

Grámhar adj. Also as **grauver**. 'A lovable, kindly, grámhar person' JL (w. Cork); DOC (Limerick); 'A grauver man' TOM (s. Tipperary); Somerville and Ross, *Poisson d'Avril* 200: 'they told me in return that I was a fine grauver man, and it was a pity there weren't more like me' (w. Cork).

Gramhas n. 1. 'A little weazened face' RBB (w. Waterford). 2. A grimace. 'I knew by the gramhas on him that he was in pain' *Sguab* (w. Cork). 4. 'A sulking expression' MW (s. Wexford); PD (s. Carlow); G (s. Kilkenny).

Grán bruite n. In forms **graanbroo, brootheen**. Literally, boiled grain. *EASI* 267: 'Wheat boiled in new milk and sweetened: a great treat to children, and generally made from their own gleanings or liscauns, gathered in the fields. Sometimes called brootheen' (Munster).

Grán buí n. As **granbuidh**. Yellow grain. Maize. Food of the poor, when available, in mid-19th century Ireland. Patk. Kennedy, *Legends of Mount Leinster* 63: 'I saw some of the granbuidh (yellow grain, boiled wheat) in a pot' (Wexford).

Grán tonóg n. Duckweed, *Lemna minor*, an aquatic plant with small leaves that cover the surface of the water: FF (Monaghan; Con (Meath).

Gránlach n. Smithereens. 'They made gránlach of it' *CBD* (n. Kerry).

Gránna adj. Ugly. In form **grawna**. Michael Banim, *Crohoor of the Billhook* 1, 21: 'Did you hear me spakin' to you a vehoon grawna?' See *Bithiúnach* for *vehoon*. In compounds **cangrane** and **kingrann**, < *ceann gránna*, ugly head, in Thomas Sheridan, *The Brave Irishman*.

Gráscar n. Fighting. 'There was a fierce gráscar between them' *CBD* (n. Kerry); MJD (w. Cork).

Greadadh n. A trouncing. 'He'll get some greadadh when he gets home' S Ua G (s. Tipperary).

Greadóg n. A slap, stroke. 'A few greadógs

on the ass would do him the power of good' NM (w. Cork); *CBE* 266 (mid-Tipperary).

Greamaisc n. 'Rabble. People of no account' RBB (w. Waterford).

Grean n. Sediment. In form **gran**. 'You'd find a lot of gran at bottom of the bottles of ale they used to make before they pasteurised it. That gran would give you severe diarrhoea if you weren't used to it' PD (s. Carlow).

Greanthamh n. A grunt *An Cho* (w. Mayo).

Greim an fhir bháite phr. Also as **greim an fhir bhá'**. The grip of the drowned man. 'A tight grip' MJD (w. Cork). 'He had greim an fhir bhá' on every shilling' *CBD* (n. Kerry).

Gríobach n. A fight. 'The gríobach started over politics, of course' PJG (mid-Donegal).

Gríobh n. As **greeve** KF (Mayo). 'A clamp, the outside binding sods of a stack of turf in Mayo, where it is used even in English' *Dinn*.

Gríofóg n. 'A woman who hasn't a word to throw to a dog' JPL (w. Cork).

Griog v. In form **grig**. Tantalise, provoke. 'He was griggin' him' OCn (Laois); PB (s. Tipperary); PD (s. Carlow); FM (s. Wexford.); JV (e. Wicklow); James Joyce, *Ulysses* 110: 'Desire to grig people. Molly wanting to do it at the window ...'

Gríosach n. Hot ashes, embers. Also in forms **greeshick**, J (s.e. Wexford); **greeshah, greeshee** Mac C (Monaghan). Hence **greeshing** – 'sitting over the embers' J (s.e. Wexford).

Gríosóg n. 'A spark from embers' *Pe* (Wexford).

Gríscín n. In forms **grishkin, griskin, greeshteen**. 1. Broiled meat PB (s. Tipperary); Gerald Griffin, *The Collegians* 136: 'He whips them till their backs is all one grishkin'; Samuel Lover, *Legends and Stories of Ireland* 3, 48: '... as raw as a griskin'; OCn (Laois): 'That rasher is burned into a greeshteen. My face is roasted into a greeshteen from standin' at the fire all day.' **2.** Pork steak from an unsalted flitch: MF (Westmeath); 'pork steak received from a neighbour' MS (e. Limerick). **3.** Giblets: Ham (e. Clare). [Cf. *grisken* in *EDD:* 'We be gwyne to kill a pig a Vriday, an we shall hay zum grisken vor dinner Zunday' Isle of Wight; common in English dialects. English dialect *grice*, a young pig; in Scotland, *gryce*. < Old Norse *griss*, a pig, a young pig.]

Gró n. 'A crowbar' *IG* (Kilkenny); *CBE* 266 (mid-Tipperary).

Grog n. In form **grug**. A haunch. 'The dog was on his grug' H (n. Clare); NB (w. Limerick); Mac C (Monaghan); AG (s. Tipperary).

Gróigín n. A small heap of footed turf. 'Four sods standing up together and one on top' *CBE* 34 S (Galway).

Groiseog n. 'A gooseberry' S (n.w. Donegal).

Gruagach adj., n. In form **gruggy**. Hairy. As a noun, person with curly hair' H (n. Donegal).

Gruagach n. 'A magician; a very clever fellow' Con (Meath, Louth).

Gruagán n. Also **grogan, grogin**. 'A gruagán is a small pyramid-shaped heap of turf-sods set on end to dry' MC (w. Clare); 'Grogin, grogan: footed turf' S Ua G (s. Tipperary); Hence, 'to grogue turf' D (Kildare); *EASI* (Leinster, Munster).

Gruama adj. Sad, morose. 'He's a gruama kind of man' MJD (w. Cork). Used to describe dull, overcast weather: 'That's a gruama kind of a day' JL (w. Cork). Also in form **gruamach** MF (Westmeath); 'Gruamach means churlish. It is applied usually to men or to children, and refers as much to appearance as to manners' *An Cho* (w. Mayo). Hence, **grumach** – 'A morose person' Pe (Wexford); 'He's a grumach old divil' J (s.e. Wexford).

Gruaspaire n. 'A hard, cold-hearted person' JC (w. Cork).

Grug n. A frown, a scowl. 'Look at the grug of him' PD (s. Carlow); PB (s. Tipperary).

Grugán n. A hump, a ridge. As **gruggans**: 'Bad land yielding few crops' JB (s. Armagh & n. Louth).

Gruideog n. Sediment *IG* (Cavan); 'There's too much gruideog in Bass for my liking' TB (Cavan).

Grúidil n. In form **grudels 1.** 'Tea leaves left in the bottom of the cup. You'd hear people say they were good at reading the grudels' PD (s. Carlow). **2.** 'Scraps left on plate after porridge' RBB (Waterford, s. Kilkenny); *JCHAS* (Cork)

Gruth buí n. **1.** Beestings *An Cho* (w. Mayo). **2.** A food made from same. 'Literally, the words mean yellow curds. Recipe: Take one cow approximately two days after calving. Milk her into a sterilised vessel and strain yellow liquid so obtained. Measure twice the required amount into a saucepan and, stirring all the while, heat until breaking-point. Decant measures of whey into several large bowls; add curds to re-establish natural consistency' ibid.

Guaigín n. Also **googeen**. *EASI* 265: 'Googeen, a simple-minded person' (Carlow); 'A foolish woman. "It's only a guaigín that would do that"' MC (e. Mayo).

Guaireach n. Hair from a horse's tail. 'Felix Doran, the piper, used to collect guaireach from the farmers' R (n. Clare).

Gúcá n. An ugly old man. 'They were married to old gúcás' *CBD* (n. Kerry).

Gúgán n. 'The two posts on which the rail-gates of a cart are hung. Each one is called a gúgán' *CBD* (n. Kerry).

Guilpín n. In form **gulpin**: 'A lout' JB (s. Armagh & n. Louth); G (n.w. Donegal).

Gúngín n. 'A narrow fundament on a person or animal' *CBD* (n. Kerry).

Gurrán n. ' The noise made by suckling pigs'. Hence **gurry**: 'A pig' JB (s. Armagh & n. Louth).

Gustalach adj. 1. Garrulous 'I can't stay long in her company. She's too gustalach altogether for my liking' NB (w. Limerick). 2. Self-important. 'Oh, the airs and graces. A gustalach little óinseach' (q.v.) JL (w. Cork).

Gustóg n. 1. 'A thick-bodied or clumsy girl' Con (Louth) 2. 'A thick, badly-made cake' *IG* (Meath).

H

Hab nó hé phr. A move, a squeak. 'There was neither hab nó hé out of him' *Sguab* (w. Cork).

Heiseach interj. 'Said to the horse on the left when ploughing with a pair' *IG* (Meath).

Heit interj. Be quiet! shut up! – 'Heit, for the love of God!' JL (w. Cork).

Hí cearc interj. 'Said to hens when trying to direct them into the hen house' McK (Leitrim).

Hí gé interj. 'Used when trying to direct a flock of geese' McK (Leitrim).

Hí muc interj. 'Said to pigs when trying to get them into, or out of, a sty' McK (Leitrim). As hi moox *GC* (Laois).

Hó bhó interj. 'Said to cattle by a drover' JC (w. Cork).

Hob interj. 'Said to a horse to keep him to the right in ploughing' *IG* (Meath). As Hob off D (s. e. Wexford).

Holc n. 'An unruly child' NB (w. Limerick).

Holla holla hussaí interj. 'Exclamation on the occasion of lighting bonfires or torches' *IG* (Meath).

Hólum hó n. *al.* hólam tró. Fun and games; high jinks. 'We had some hólam hó at the dances in the old days' AOL (mid- Waterford). *Díolaim Dhéiseach* has hólam tró.

Hububú n. As hubbubboo, hubbubbo, hububoo, hubbabowe. A confused crying or wailing. Spenser, *A View of the State of Ireland:* 'hubbabowe'; Crofton Croker, *Fairy Legends and Traditions*: '"Hubbubboo", cries Jack, "now I know how it is"' (Cork, Kerry); Emily Lawless, *Grania*: 'Och, Mary, Queen of Heaven, but there was a hububoo' (Mayo).

Húla má boc phr. 'Tumult, confusion' Mac C (Monaghan).

Hulla abhaile interj. Hulla home! 'Said when driving cattle home' *CBD* (n. Kerry).

Hurra gabhar interj. 'A call to frighten a goat' Ham (e. Clare). *al.* huis gabhar *CBD* (n. Kerry).

Hurra gé interj. 'A call to frighten a goose' Ham (e. Clare).

Hurrais interj. Also as hurrish. 'A call to pigs' MF (Westmeath); Mac C (Monaghan); *CBE* 34 S (Galway). 'A call to a cow to keep still for milking or to a pig to approach' PLH (n. Roscommon).

Huth muc interj. As hummuck. 'A call used when driving pigs' PLH (n. Roscommon).

I

Iarlais n. 1. An elf-child, a changeling. 'You'd say it to a tiny child' JC (w. Cork). 2. 'A good-for-nothing person. "He's only an old iarlais"' *CBD* (n. Kerry). 3. 'A sick, woe-begone person' DOH (e. Limerick)

Iarmhar n. The hindmost. 'The smallest pig in the litter' MS (e. Limerick). *EASI* 253: 'This bonnive being usually very small and hard to keep alive is often given to one of the children for a pet; and it is reared in great comfort in a warm bed by the kitchen fire, and fed on milk' (Munster).

Iarracht n. A try, turn. 'I'll bring the turf in in a couple of more iarrachts' *CBD* (n. Kerry).

Iarsma n. Remainder, remnant. 1. Figurative, 'a very small person' PB (s. Tipperary); 'A wretched little child. "You little iarsma"' AG (s. Tipperary). 2. An encumbrance. 'God help us, but the old mother is an iarsma by him' JL (w. Cork).

Íde n. Ill usage. 'A hearty scolding' IG (Meath); 'She gave him the divil of an íde, and he deserved it all' JC (w. Cork).

Íde ort interj. phr. Ill usage on you' *CBD* (n. Kerry).

Imeacht vb. n. Going, meaning living, in existence. James Joyce, *Ivy Day in the Committee Room* 143: 'What kind of people is going at all now?' Translation of *cén sort daoine atá ag imeacht anois* ?

Imleacán n. 'The hub of a wheel' *CBD* (n. Kerry).

In ainm an Athar interj. In form **nhanim an airh**. In the name of the Father. Wm. Carleton, *The Lianhan Shee* 1, 78: 'Nhanim an airh ... and she forthwith proceed to bless herself' (Tyrone).

In airde adv. phr. As **in ordha**. High up. Michael Banim, *The Croppy* 1, 207: 'my-lady-in-ordha'. Glossed as 'my high lady-one assuming a station unfitted to her.'

Iníon n. Daughter. 'In phrase **iníon ó**, darling daughter' NB (w. Limerick).

Inse n. Also in form **inch**. 1. 'Inse: a water-meadow' NB (w. Limerick). 2. 'Inse here is a green field in the midst of rough land on a hillside or a stretch of land beside a stream or along the edge of a cliff' RBB (w. Waterford). Crofton Croker, *Fairy Legends and Traditions* 60: 'The big inch near Bally-hafaan ford' (Cork, Kerry); Patk. Kennedy, *The Banks of the Boro* 225: 'The big inches by Boro's side' (Wexford); George Fitzmaurice, *The King of the Barna Men*: ' that variegated vagabone of a duck ... after coming out of her hiding down in the inch' (Kerry).

Íocainn n. *al.* **níocainn**. 'The bottom of a woman's dress' NB (w. Limerick); 'Put a níocainn on the petticoat' *CBD* (n. Kerry).

Íochtar n. 'The youngest of a litter; the weakest in a litter; a weak piglet' *CBD* (n. Kerry).

Iodhán n. 'An idiot' *CBE* 104 (Leitrim).

Iog n. A notch *CBE* 104 (Leitrim); DK (Kerry).

Iomar n. A large skillet. 'An iomar of a saucepan' *CBD* (n. Kerry).

Iompar n. In forms **umper, umperin**. Transport; a lift, a ride. Michael Banim, *Crohoor of the Billhook* 2, 47: '... fen tis so very asy to get an umperin' all de way home for nothing' (Kilkenny); 'Will you come for an umper, Joe? = will you accept a lift?' O Cn (Laois).

Ioscar n. 'A jot of sense' *IG* (Kilkenny).

I rith phr. In the course of. Translated direct-ly: M.J. Mulloy, *The King Of Friday's Men* 39: 'twill dry in the run of a few minutes'.

Iris n. 'The rope or straps of a basket for carrying turf on a person's back' PJG (mid-Donegal); MF (Westmeath); PC (s. Galway).

L

Lá bog phr. Drizzly, damp day. In translated form **soft day**. James Joyce, *Ulysses* 37: 'Soft day, sir John. Soft day, your honour ...'

Lá crosta na bliana phr. 'Cross or contrary day of the year. Only the Irish form is used. The day of the week on which December 28 falls is regarded as the unlucky day for the following year. One would be loath to marry on that day, or to launch a new project' H (n. Clare).

Lab n. 1. 'A useless thing. "What a lab it is!"' H (n. Clare). 2. 'A considerable amount, lump.; e.g. you have a lab of money.' [Cf. English dialect *lob*.]

Lábán n. 1. 'A rotten egg' OC (Monaghan). 2. 'Mud, clabber' G (n.w. Donegal).

Lách adj. Also in forms **lawk, laughey, lawky, láchaí.** 1. Pleasant, affable, friendly *CBE* 104 (Leitrim). 'He a nice lawk man' PD (s. Carlow); John Boyce, *Shandy Maguire* 388: 'He was the laughey kind of uncle to me' (Donegal); Patrick MacGill, *Glenmornan* 108: 'Both of them laughey cutties' (Donegal). 2. As **láchaí.** Awkward. He was a láchaí hurler' MS (e. Limerick).

Láchán n. 'The youngest child in the family' PB (s. Tipperary).

Lachtar n 1. 'A clutch of eggs at the incubation stage' O'K (Tyrone). 2. 'A brood of newly hatched chicks, generally hens or turkeys' ibid. Hence **Cuckoo's lachtar:** 'an only child' ibid. [Old Norse *latr*, also *lattr*, the place where animals have their young.]

Ladar n. Also as **lather.** Literally, ladle. Unwanted intervention. 'To put your ladar in a conversation is to put your oar in, so to speak' MF (Westmeath); H (n. Clare). 'You don't be putting in your lather' PON (n. Dublin).

Ladhar n. 1. 'The hands with fingers extended. Used in the phrase **leathadh ladhair.** '"He fairly had a leathadh ladhair on him for the food", literally he had his hands held, or spread out to receive the food' S Ua G (s. Tipperary). 2. A handful. 'Throw a ladhar of corn to the hens' MS (e. Limerick); JC (w. Cork); *CBD* (n. Kerry).

Ladhróg n. 'A short drill in the corner of an out-of-square field. "Twenty drills and a few ladhrógs"' *CBD* (n. Kerry).

Ladús n. 1. 'Nonsense, silly talk' MS (e. Limerick). 2. Mildly flirtatious, mildly erotic talk. 'She's no angel, that one, to judge from the ladús she had with an old dog like myself' TM (w. Cork).

Ladúsach adj. 'Smug, cheeky' H (n. Clare).

Ládúsaí n. 1. 'A person who engages in risque talk' DOC (Limerick); TM (w. Cork). 2. 'A cheeky, pert person' LOS (w. Clare).

Lag n. 'A hollow' RBB (w. Waterford).

Lagachar n. Weakness. 'There's a lagachar on me because I haven't had a bite to eat since my breakfast' S Ua G (s. Tipperary).

Lái n. In form **loy.** A long narrow-bladed spade. J. M. Synge, *The Playboy of the Western World* 84: 'I just riz the loy and let fall the edge of it on the ridge of his skull, and he went down at my feet like an empty sack, and never let a grunt or groan from him at all'; James Joyce *Finnegans Wake* 545: ... the loy for a lynch ...'

Laidhricín n. The little finger. 'The word recalls a most imaginative description of a public figure. The judgement was that he "hopped about" a great deal, yet did nothing. This was put in two words, **laidhricín píobaire.** It means "a piper's little finger". (which is not used in the playing of the uileann pipes)' *An Cho* (w. Mayo).

Láimhín n. 1. 'A withered or defective hand' PB (s. Tipperary); H (n. Clare). 2. 'A nickname given to a man who has lost an arm, *e.g.* Láimhín Donohoe' ibid.

Laincis n. Also as **langish**. 'A fetter, hobble on animals' MJD (w. Cork). 'He has a tight langish on him now that he got married' PD (s. Carlow).

Laingeal n. In form **langel**. 'A side-spancel on animals' MF (Westmeath); Mac C (Monaghan).

Láithrigh n. pl. In form **lawshigs**. Places, sites. '"Put the hay in lawshigs first" – the hay is first raked with a horse rake and left in rows, lawshigs, ready to be made into small cocks' OCn (Laois).

Lámh n. The hand. Also in forms **law, lauv**. 'Give me a lámh with this' MS (e. Limerick). **Lámh cham**, crooked hand. Corrupted by Michael Banim, *Crohoor of the Billhook*, 1, 301, to **law-thcaum**: '... if it isn't Shaun-law-thcaum, every inch iv him'; Wm. Carleton, *The Station* 1, 178: '... wus dha lauv...' Glossed by Carleton as 'give me your hand' (Tyrone). [*Wus = abhus*, hither.]

Lámh shábhála phr. In translated form **mending hand**. M.J. Mulloy,*The Wood of the Whispering* 17: 'She's on the mending hand surely'. < *Tá sí ar an lámh shábhála*, i.e. recovering, safe.

Lámhán n. (Act of) complaining. 'You're always lámháning' Mas (mid-Tipperary).

Lámhghad n. Hand-withe. 'The handle of a basket, made of twisted rods' CBD (n. Kerry).

Lampaire n. 'A lame person. Not very lame, though; not someone who neds a stick or walking aid. A lampaire is well able to walk about but in doing so rises and falls rhythmically because of a slight impediment, permanent or temporary, in one foot' *An Cho* (w. Mayo).

Lán a' mhala phr. Also as **launa wallya**. The full of the bag. 1. 'Abundance to eat and drink at a feast' MF (Westmeath); H (n. Clare). 'There was always lán a' mhála in that house' SOM (w. Cork). 2. 'Something

to think about, a bellyful. "I gave him launa wallya"' PON (n. Dublin).

Lána n. 'A lane' Mac C (Monaghan).

Langa n. In form **langel**. 'A tall, spindly man or boy' O'K (Tyrone). 'A long, lanky, lazy, useless man' G (n.w. Donegal).

Langaide n. A spancel to tie an animal's legs together. 'He'd still score even if you put a langaide on him' AOL (mid-Waterford).

Langal n. In form **langle**. 'A spancel from the front to the hind leg of a cow or horse.' '"You're well langled now" – said to a newly-married person' G (n.w. Donegal); PD (s. Carlow).

Langán n. In form **langen**. 'That part of a seed potato which is not used' PJG (mid-Donegal).

Laoidheán n. As **leeawn**. 'The remains of a potato when the seed is cut out' *CBE* 104 (Leitrim); PLH (n. Roscommon); 'I've heard the word used of women who are past the marrying age' AM (Leitrim).

Lapa n. A paw. 'Also a little hand' JM (w. Cork); RBB (w. Waterford). *al.* **lapaire**, as **loppara** *CBE* 266 (mid-Tipperary). Diminutive, **laipín**, as **loppeen** MS (e. Limerick).

Lapadáil n. (Act of) Paddling, wading, splashing. 'He thinks he can swim; that's only lapadáil' JL (w. Cork).

Lapadálaí n. 'A slatternly, clumsy person' *Sguab* (w. Cork); MF (Westmeath).

Lapadán n. 1. 'A whale' JS (w. Kerry). 2. 'A very big, clumsy man' RBB (w. Waterford); DOC (Limerick). 3. 'A wee man who walks like a duck' G (n.w. Donegal). 4. 'A lame person or animal' CBD (n. Kerry).

Laparóg n. 'One who creeps on all fours. A waddler, a flat-footed person' *CBE* 266 (mid-Tipperary).

Láragán n. 1. 'A square of hay' NB (w. Limerick). 2. 'A tall man' ibid.

Lasadh n. 'A sudden blaze of light from a fire made with grags' G (n.w. Donegal).

Lasc n. 1. 'A whip' NM (w. Cork). 2. A strong, heavy blow. 'He gave the ball a great lasc' *CBD* (n. Kerry).

Lasóg n. Also as **lassog, lossoge**. 1. A blaze of light. *EASI* 282: 'lassog' (Monaghan). 2. 'Lossoge: A handful or little bundle of sticks for firing' MC (e. Mayo).

Latarach n. A swampy place in a bog. 'As happy as ducks in a latarach' RBB (Waterford).

Leábharaic n. 'A tricky person, a rogue' JS (w. Kerry). [< English *laverock*.]

Leabhó n. 'A big fuss about a trifle. "They made a great leabhó about it"' NB (w. Limerick).

Leac liath n. Grey rock. 'Heavy grey subsoil in wet, low-lying land' MF (Westmeath); *IG* (Meath)

Leac n. In forms **lock, lick**. A flagstone, a slab. '" It remained in a lock in his stomach: he found it indigestible." "We put it out on the lick for him": we made it quite clear to him that he could not do something or other' *CBE* 266 (mid-Tipperary).

Leac stámair n. An idler; a person who stands idly about MS (e. Limerick). *al.* **leaicsteámair**. 'A big lazy woman' *CBD* (n. Kerry).

Leaca n. 1.'A stretch of pasture on the side of a hill, or on the top of a cliff' RBB (n. Waterford); JL (w. Cork). 2. 'The side of a hill' JM (w. Cork); NB (w. Limerick); *CBD* (n. Kerry); *Sguab* (Cork).

Leacht n. As **laghta**. A pile of stones in memory of the dead. *Folk-Lore Rec.* 1 iv, 120 (1881): 'They erect laghtas, or pillars of loose stones, on the road to the graveyards, each family having its own laghta. Three stones are placed at a time, in the names of

the Father, Son and Holy Ghost, by the head of the family or the principal representative present.'

Leadhb n. Also as **libe**. 1. A piece, a slice *Pe* (Wexford). 2. A deep sod. 'He turned up leadhbs of land, i.e. he ploughed too deeply' MF (Westmeath). 3. 'A rag' *IG* (Kilkenny). 4. 'A slovenly woman' RBB (s. Kilkenny). 5. 'A libe is a foolish person, with no self-control' J (s.e. Wexford); 'A leadhb is a half-wit. It conjures vague images of a large man (not a woman) who has been sent on an important errand but wanders round bewilderedly not knowing where to begin or whom to ask. Note the usage: 'he's there *of a leadhb* with his mouth open' *An Cho* (w. Mayo).

Leadóg n. Also in forms **lidogue, leedogue**. A hard blow. 'A good leadóg would do him good' CW (Wicklow); J (s.e. Wexford); *CBE* 34 S (Galway); 'He gave him a leedogue (lidogue) with the stick' OCn (Laois).

Leadradh n. A beating. As **leathering**. 'I gave him a good leathering.' Hence, 'to leather, to beat soundly' MF (Westmeath). [Leathering is not derived from English 'leather', but from Old Irish 'letrad', glossed as 'act of wounding, lacerating, hacking, mangling, rending' in *RIA Dictionary*.]

Leadramach n. 'A big awkward man' Con (Louth).

Leadránach adj. Tedious, long-winded. 'That's a leadránach old song' MS (e. Limerick); H (n. Clare).

Leadránaí n. 'A longwinded person' DOC (Limerick).

Leaintí leabhraí n. A useless cow. 'An old leaintí leabhraí of a cow' *CBD* (n. Kerry). [*leabhraí*, a lanky person – *Dinn*.]

Leamh adj. 'Insipid. Porridge without salt, chips without vinegar, or cabbage without bacon – these are all leamh. So too is a party without music, a game without scores, or conversation without a joke. Within the last year a parishioner passed judgement on her first artichoke: "All right, but very leamh"' *An Cho* (w. Mayo). MS (e. Limerick); JL (w. Cork); MC (Clare).

Leamhnacht n. 'Fresh milk' JM (w. Cork); *CBD* (n. Kerry).

Leamstar n. A thick slice of bread, cake, meat etc. 'She gave us tea and a big leamstar of bacon' JS (e. Limerick).

Léana n. **1.** As **lanny**: 'A meadow by a river or stream' Con (Meath). **2.** As **lanna**: 'Hillside meadowland' JB (s. Armagh & n. Louth).

Leang n. 'A blow, a slap' PB (s. Tipperary).

Leangaire n. **1.** 'A tall, thin man or boy' MS (e. Limerick); PB (s. Tipperary). **2.** A blow, a slap. 'He hit him a leangaire with the hurl across the legs' Smy (n. Clare). See *leang*.

Leann beach n. Bees' ale. Drink made from honeycombs placed in a vessel containing some water, after the honey has been squeezed out of them: *IG* (Meath).

Leannán Lover. In phrase **leannán sí**, fairy lover. In form **Lianhan Shee**, title of Wm. Carleton story (Tyrone) As **lianhan sighe** in Patk. Kennedy, *Legendary Fictions of the Irish Celts* 81 (Wexford).

Leap dearg n. Great trouble. 'I'm in some leap dearg now' NB (w. Limerick).

Léaróga n. pl. In form **larrogs**. 'A horse's winkers' JON (Armagh).

Léas n. **1.** 'Corn stalk, with its ear' MS (e. Limerick). **2.** 'A blister on a cow's tongue, far back at the throat, which can cause death if not promptly cut' *IG* (Kilkenny).

Léasadh n. As **lacing**. A beating. 'He deserves the father and mother of a lacing' TB (Cavan); Mac C (Monaghan); DOH (e. Limerick). Hence, **lace**. 'I'll lace the arse off you' PC (n. Clare); *CBE* 266 (mid-Tipperary).

Leastar n. An indolent person. 'A useless leastar' *CBD* (n. Kerry).

Leathach n. 'A wide field' NB (w. Limerick).

Leathaill n. 'A steep field by a river' AG (s. Tipperary).

Leathamadán n. 'A half-wit (male)' *An Cho* (w. Mayo).

Leathanóg n. 'A corpulent person, as broad as he is long' S Ua G (s. Tipperary).

Leathbhaic n. In expression, 'He had a leathbhaic on him with the cold', meaning he was very bent' H (n. Clare).

Leathbhreis n. As **lafresh**. 'A "drag" to one side on a dress. "There's a lafresh on your dress." The use of this word, leathbhreis, seems to be confined to the Galtee region. Speakers from West Cork and southern Déise appear unacquainted with the word. A streel of a woman would have a lafresh on her dress' S Ua G (s. Tipperary).

Leathcheann n. In form **leckan**. Tilt of head. 'Look at him. He has a leckan on him trying to overhear what we're saying' PJG (mid-Donegal).

Leathdoras n. A half-door. 'He went for him like a pig going for the leathdoras' JL (w. Cork).

Leathgháire n. A half laugh. 'A cynical smile' H (n. Clare).

Leathóg n. 'A miserable animal affected by the cold' JC (w. Cork).

Leathóinseach n. 'A half-wit, female. *al.* **leathóinsín** *An Cho* (w. Mayo).

Leathphingin n. Halfpenny. In plural form **laffenas** in Michael Banim, *The Croppy* 1, 137:' 'My mother didn't give me any laffenas' (Kilkenny).

Leathroinn n. As **lafferin**. 'The upper part of a flail' JB (n. Louth).

Leatromach adj. Afflicted, distressed. 'She's leatromach since the sister died' HG (n.w. Donegal).

Leibhit n. A severe reprimand. 'I stayed out a bit late, and got some leibhit when I came home' AOL (mid-Waterford).

Leibide n. 1. 'An untidy person' MS (e. Limerick); *CBD* (n. Kerry). 2. 'A fool' NB (w. Limerick).

Léice n. 'A fool, a stupid person' Con (Louth). See *léiceach*.

Léiceach n. 'A soft, harmless person' *IG* (Meath). See *léice*. Soft is an Irish euphemism for 'slightly retarded.'

Leiceachán n. 'A weak, sickly person' DOC (Limerick). *al.* **leicneán** *CBD* (n. Kerry).

Leicneach. n. 'Mumps' *IG* (Kilkenny; Cavan); Con (Meath).

Leid n. 'A permanent disfigurement' *IG* (Kilkenny). Diminutive, **leidín**. 'He hit him a paste of the stick and he'll have the leidín on him for the rest of his life' Dee (w. Waterford).

Leidhbín n. In form **lybeen**. A tattered thing. 'A thin, bad shoe that lets in the wet; light, poor clothes. "She had only a thin lybeen of a coat on her that wet day"' *CBE* 266 (mid-Tipperary).

Leidhce n. 'A silly person' RBB (w. Waterford). See *pleidhce*.

Léintín n. 'A chemise' *CBD* (n. Kerry).

Leipreachán n. In forms **leprechaun, lepracaun, lhifrechaun**. A little fairy man. William Carleton, *Fardorougha the Miser* 5: 'Only for the withered ould leprechaun himself, divil a dacenter people ever broke bread' (Tyrone); *Lays and Legends of the North of Ireland* 16: 'The oul' days ... When fairies an' leprechauns frolicked galore'; Bram Stoker, *Snake's Pass* 11: 'Rimimber, wid leprachauns, if ye wance let thim go ye may never git thim agin. But if ye hould thim tight, they must do whatsumiver ye wish' (Mayo); *Century Magazine* (Feb. 1900): 'A lhifrechaun or leprechaun, is a fairy shoemaker. If the reader has ever the good luck to catch a lhifrechaun, then, having presence of mind not to remove his

eyes from him for a fraction of an instant (thereby rendering the little fellow powerless of melting into thin air), he must at once command him to disclose where there is a crock of gold hid. The little scoundrel will first endeavour to trick you into lifting your eyes off him, and, failing in this, will try fifty little dodges; but finding all useless, will discover to you what you want, on condition of being set free.'

Leirg n. 'A large quantity of anything. A leirg of land, corn, time' *CBD* (n. Kerry).

Leis n. In form **lesh**. A permanent disfigurement, such as a scar, or other mark; lameness. '"Look at the lesh of him" – said about a person with a lame step' OCn (Laois); *IG* (Kilkenny); *CBE* 266 (mid-Tipperary).

Leiscire n. 'A lazy person' NB (w. Limerick). *al.* **leisceadóir** *An Cho* (w. Mayo).

Leithead n. 'A dull-witted person' *IG* (Kilkenny).

Leitheadach adv. 'Free and easy; conceited. "Seán was sitting there as leitheadach as you please"' H (n. Clare).

Leithéis n. In form **lahaesh**. Act of joking, teasing, ridicule. 'He has too much lahaesh' LOS (w. Clare).

Léithín n. 'A grey cow' PC (n. Clare).

Leathscéal n. Also in form **leskel**. An excuse. 'One leathscéal after another, that's all you'll get from him' JL (w. Cork). 'He's only a leskel of a man' H (n. Donegal).

Léithuisce n. Watery tea or milk. 'The tea is in a pure léithuisce of water by you' *CBD* (n. Kerry).

Leitreachán n. In form **latragaun**. The smaller or common scallop, *Pecten opercularis*: H (n. Donegal).

Leochaileach adj. 'Lonely after somebody or something' *CBD* (n. Kerry).

Leoiste n. A lazy person. 'If you are a woman, think of him as the languid individual who blocks your way to the oven when you have a cake in your hands. Out of doors he is the lingerer when the men have finished dinner and are back at the hay; or the drooping figure seated on the floor of a cart who doesn't notice that the horse has begun to graze' *An Cho* (w. Mayo).

Liabró n. 'A whetstone' MJD (w. Cork).

Liach n. In form **liagh**. The seaweeds, *Laminariae*: H (n. Donegal). Hence **liagh-knife**: a knife used for cutting seaweed stumps. Seamus MacManus, *Bold Blades of Donegal* 229: 'A man grabbed hold of a big liagh-knife lying in the boat's bottom.'

Liaróg n. 'A short drill in a field' *CBE* 34 S (Galway).

Liathadh n. Milk used in tea. In translated form **colouring**. Hence, J. M. Synge, *The Playboy of the Western World* 95: 'She's above on the cnuceen, seeking the nanny goats, they way she'd have a sup of goat's milk for to colour my tea'; 'I couldn't drink tea without colouring' JL (w. Cork).

Liathóg n. 'A half-circle of potatoes being roasted in the embers.' 'Put down a liathóg of roasters for me' *CBD* (n. Kerry).

Liatraisc n. 'The woodcock' *CBD* (n. Kerry).

Líbín n. Also as **leebeen**. 1. 'A slut' *IG* (Meath). 2. 'A new shoe of soft, bad leather' *IG* (Meath). 3. Wet clothes. 'I'm in a leebeen from the rain' JS (e. Kerry). 4. 'A tiny fish, a minnow' MC (e. Mayo); PLH (n. Roscommon).

Lintéar n. In forms **linthern**, **lenthern**. A gully, culvert. *EASI* 286: 'A small drain or sewer covered with flags for the passage of water, often under a road from side to side' (Munster).

Liobaire n. 'An untidy person' *CBD* (n. Kerry).

Liobar n. 1. 'A pout, a hanging lip' G (n.w. Donegal); MF (Westmeath); *CBE* 104 (Leitrim). 2. 'A limp object, especially *membrum virile pendens*' RBB (Waterford). 3. 'An untidy person' H (n. Clare).

Liobarach n. As **libberoch**. 'A flatulent person' *CBE* 266 (mid-Tipperary).

Liobarnach adj. Untidy. 'She's a very liobarnach person' H (n. Clare); *Sguab* (Cork).

Líofa adj. 'Fluent, persuasive, polished. "He is as líofa as a councillor"' S Ua G (s. Tipperary).

Lionn rua n. In form **linh roe**. Heartburn. Wm. Carleton, *The Lianhan Shee 2*, 76: ' the bogbane for linh roe, or heartburn, grew in their own meadow-drain.' 'Lionn ruadh: red humour, bile, choler; *al.* melancholy, stomach complaint with violent vomitings' *Dinn*. Carleton mistakenly glosses *linh* as 'literally, red water'.

Lios bhocht n. As **lish vocht**. A poor enclosure. 'A dirty farmyard' NB (w. Limerick).

Lios n. Also in forms **liss**, **lish**. Diminutive **lisín**, as **lisseen**, **lisheen**. A ring fort. A lios is popularly believed to be a fairy dwelling (Gen.).

Lioscán n. 1. 'Gleanings' MS (e. Limerick). 2. Savings. 'He had put by a good lioscán of money towards the daughter's fortune' JL (w. Cork); *JKAS* (Kildare).

Lipín n. 'A net used in fishing a stream' *CBE* 98 (Kilkenny).

Lispín n. 'A frog' Kiv (Sligo).

Liú n. 'The lowing of a cow' *Pe* (Wexford).

Liúdaí n. 1. 'An idler, a person who shirks work' RBB (s. Kilkenny); PB (s. Tipperary); *IG* Meath). 2. 'A half-witted lout' MF (Westmeath).

Liúdar n. 1. In form **ludher**. 'A blow, a thrashing' D (s. Wexford). Hence, to beat, thrash. Wm. Carleton, *Tubber Derg 2*, 390: 'Brian, ludher them two lazy thieves o' dogs out o' that' (Tyrone); Seumus MacManus, *Bold Blades of Donegal* 365: 'Come home ... I order ye this instant! Or I'll go myself to Tyrhugh and ludher ye home.' 2. 'A long, shapeless garment. 'Look at the liúdar of a dress on her' PC (n. Clare). 3. 'An untidy man or woman, especially in matters of dress' G (n.w. Donegal).

Liúdramán n. Also as **loodheramaun, luderman, looderamaun**. A drone, an idler. (Gen.). 'It is the correct name for the male of the honey bee. Social historians will be interested to find that the more common use of the word in Louisburgh is to indicate a fool. In other words our ancestors equated the idler and the fool' *An Cho* (w. Mayo); James Joyce, *Ulysses* 304: 'there was an old one with a cracked loodheramaun of a nephew'; Joyce, *Finnegans Wake* 21: 'luderman'; Flann O'Brien, *The Dalkey Archive*, 10: 'I found a looderamaun in Dalkey village by the name of Teague McGettigan.'

Loc isteach! interj. 'Said to geese by a woman driving them in from the fields' JC (w.Cork).

Loch n. In forms **lough, lock**. Diminutive, **lochán**, as **loughan, lochaun**. A lake. (Gen.) 'A lock is small pool of water' LB (s.w. Dublin); 'A loughan is a small lake, a pool' H (n. Clare); 'The ducks are enjoying the lochaun' *CBE* 266 (mid-Tipperary).

Lóchán n. Chaff; waste. 'Tis only old lóchán: there is no substance in it – said by an old woman about baker's bread' *CBD* (n. Kerry).

Lochlannaigh n. As **Lochlanns**. Scandinavians. James Joyce, *Ulysses* 50: 'Galleys of the Lochlanns ran here to beach ...'

Lochta n. The loft. 'You can sleep in the lochta' MJD (w. Cork).

Lochtán n. 'A small height in a field' *CBD* (n. Kerry).

Lodar n. 'A treacherous, boggy place' MJD (w. Cork).

Log n. Diminutive, **logán**, as **logey**. Hollow, pit, depression. 'A pool of water on the road' H (n. Clare); NB (w. Limerick); *CBD* (n. Kerry). In compound **logey-hole**. 'A hollow or hole; a hiding place, such as the cubby-hole underneath the staircase where children might hide during a storm.

Also the fire-pit in a lime kiln' O'K (Tyrone).

Lointheán n. 'A stick used in crushing sloke' *CBD* (n. Kerry).

Lóipín n. 1. 'A cloth fixed on a hen's claws to stop it from scratching the earth' NB (w. Limerick); 'Pieces of jute put on a donkey's hooves to keep them from slipping on frost' MC (w. Clare). 2. 'The sole of a stocking' NB (w. Limerick). 3. 'A filthy, torn stocking. 'Your stockings are in right lóipíns by you' *CBD* (n. Kerry); *Sguab* (w. Cork), DOH (e. Limerick).

Loipiste n. A sloven, a slattern. 'You'd thing she's wear something decent on a Sunday itself, the loipiste' JPL (w. Cork); RBB (w. Waterford).

Loiscneach n. 'Half-burned furze' *Pe* (Wexford).

Lópais n. 'An article of clothing hanging down, such as a slip showing beneath a woman's dress' AOL (mid-Waterford).

Lorachán n. As **lurrahaun**. 'An incapable person, a fool' PLH (n. Roscommon).

Lorgadán n. 1. 'Another name for a leprechaun' MS (e. Limerick); *CBD* (n. Kerry); *IG* (Kilkenny); PB (s. Tipperary). 2. 'A thin-shinned person' NB (w. Limerick). 3. 'A fellow given to wandering' JS (e. Kerry).

Lorgnán n. 'A chain to fetter a horse or an ass' *CBE* 104 (Leitrim).

Losad n. Also in form **losset**. 'A board on which bread is kneaded' MS (e. Limerick); H (n. Clare).

Loscadh n. Burning. In phrase, **loscadh on you** PJG (mid-Donegal).

Loscán n. In form **luscan**. *EASI* 289: 'A spot on the hillside from which the furze and the heath have been burned off' (Wicklow).

Lot n. A congenital defect. 'That sort of a lot (a lazy eye in a child) is nothing. The doctors can fix it no bother at all' JL (w. Cork); RBB (w. Waterford).

Lota n. 'A number of sheep, cattle, etc. "We were held up by a a lota of sheep on the road"' RBB (s. Tipperary). [< English *lot*]

Lóta n. 'A big, overweight person' RBB (w. Waterford).

Lótais n. 'A fat woman' *IG* (Kilkenny).

Luadar n. Vigour, activity. 'I hear she's walking out again. Such luadar for an oul' dame like her' JL (w. Cork); RBB (w. Waterford).

Luadhóg n. 1. 'A pollock' Del (Antrim). 2. As luoge: *EASI* 288: 'The eel fry, a couple of inches long that come up the southern Blackwater in myriads, and are caught and sold as food.' 3. As luadhág. 'A minnow' FM (s. Wexford).

Lúb n. Also as loob. Diminutive, lúbán. A loop. Also a twisted, crumpled object. 'There's a loob in the rope' PON (n. Dublin); 'He pulled the hurl across him and made a lúbán of him' Smy (n. Clare); 'He hit the pier of the gate and made a lúbán of the bicycle' JL (w. Cork); PB (s. Tipperary); RBB (s. Kilkenny); 'A lúb knot': a knot on a shoe lace' OCn (Laois).

Lúb ar lár n. 'A defect, weak point, loophole. "We must see that there is no lúb ar lár in the story"' MC (e. Mayo); JM (w. Cork).

Lúbaire n. Also as loobera. 1. 'A twister; a dangerous person, usually given to much law' NB (w. Limerick); George Fitzmaurice, *The Pie-Dish*: '... that loobera, Jack' (Kerry). 2. 'A strong, supple man' PB (s. Tipperary).

Lúbánaí n. 1. 'A trickster' DOC (Limerick). 2. 'A tall, thin, narrow-shouldered man' ibid.

Lúbóg n. 'A buttonhole. "You should see the Yankee. He had a tom (q. v.) of heather in his lúbóg"' S (w. Donegal).

Luchán n. Little mouse. 1. 'The youngest child in a family' DOC (Limerick). 2. 'The smallest member of litter of pigs etc.' MF (Westmeath).

Lucharachán n. A tiny tot. A term of endearment. 'Aren't you the lovely little lucharachán!' PR (Limerick).

Lucharmán n. Also in form loughreyman. 'An elf, or sprite traditionally believed to inhabit woods and notorious for stealing money' O'K (Tyrone).

Luchtar n. A reaper's handful of corn. 'When grain was cut with the hook and simultaneously gathered in the left hand, the full of that hand was called a luchtar, and three luchtars were a sheaf; nowadays it would be applied to a certain amount (e.g.) a forkful of grain or hay' Tr (Donegal).

Lúdar n. (Act of) fawning; flattery, obsequiousness. 'Lúdar won't get you anywhere with him' DOH (e. Limerick).

Lúdaróg n. 'A blow on the head or face' *IG* (Kilkenny).

Lugán n. 'The sand eel' PW (s. e. Wexford).

Lugún n. 'The clam' PW (s. e. Wexford)

Luichín n. As lucheen. Little mouse. Michael Banim, *Crohoor of the Billhook* 1, 159: '... you haven't the heart of a slucheen!' The intrusive *s* is probably a misprint; Banim glossed the word correctly as 'a little mouse'.

Luid n. As lid. 'A scrap, a rag. "She hadn't a lid on her"' *CBE* 266 (mid-Tipperary).

Luideog n. 'A very small girleen' MJD (w. Cork).

Lúidín n. 'The little finger' Smy (n. Clare); BOD (s.w. Cork); PB (s. Tipperary); RBB (s Kilkenny); FM (s. Wexford); *An Cho* (w. Mayo). *al.* lúdóg PD (s. Carlow); lúdagán FF (Monaghan)

Luifearnach n. Dross, refuse. 'The wasted remnants of hay, etc.' H (n. Clare).

Luifseog n. Also as lifshog. 'An untidy woman' Con (Meath); 'A bad housekeeper' JB (n. Louth).

Lúiricín n. As lurikeen, looracaun. A fairy man, a leprechaun. Patk. Kennedy, *Legends Of Mount Leinster* 176: 'lurikeen' (Wexford); 'A word I heard for a leprechaun is looracaun' D (s. e. Wexford).

Lúragadán n. 'A hole in the bottom of a river pool' *CBD* (n. Kerry).

Lúrapóg lárapóg phr. A nonsense phrase signifying the galloping of a horse MJD (w. Cork).

Lúrapóg n. 'A small, round stone' MJD (w. Cork).

Lus Cholm Cille n. Colm Cille's herb. The yellow pimpernel, *Lysimachia nemorum*: S (n.w. Donegal).

Lus mór n. Also as **lusmore**. The Great herb. Foxglove, *digitalis purpurea*. Seumus

MacManus, *Bold Blades of Donegal* 334: 'Blushin like the lusmore'; RBB (w. Waterford); *EASI* 289: 'Lusmore: An herb of mighty power in fairy lore'. See *méaracán sí.*

Lus na lao n. Herb of the calves. 'Golden saxifrage, excellent for syrups' *IG* (Meath).

Luthairt lathairt adj. Indifferently cooked food. 'We had our dinner in the chip shop. I left half of the luthairt lathairt after me. You wouldn't throw it to a dog' RBB (w. Waterford).

M

Má hé phr. As if. Similar in meaning to **mar dhea**. 'He passed by without speaking; má hé he didn't see me' S (s. Wexford).

Mac n. Dimunitive, **maicín**. Also as **mack**. 1. Son. 'he was a good mac to her' DC (Galway); 'He's the eldest maicín' R (s. Galway); *CBE* 47 S (Galway). 2. Chap, fellow. 'How is my poor mac?' MF (Westmeath). Vocative **a mhic** (Munster); **a mhac** (Connacht). Also **a mac** (Connacht). 'Come here to me, a mac' DC (Galway). 'As **mack** in an address to a male stranger: Hey, mack, Hey, mister' PON (n. Co. Dublin).

Macánta adv. Honest. 'You'd travel before you'd meet anyone as macánta as him' MJD (w. Cork); 'The first time the ball came between us I wound the hurl around him, and he stayed damn fine and macánta after that' RBB (s. Kilkenny).

Macasamhail n. As **mockysowl**. Reproduction, copy. 'He's the very **mockysowl** of his father' T McC (Westmeath); AK (Kildare).

Macha n. 'A farmyard' NB (w. Limerick).

Máchail n. A blemish. 'He has a slight máchail in the eye' MS (e. Limerick); *CBD* (n. Kerry); MJD (w. Cork).

Macht n. An affliction, hoodoo or jinx. 'I'm sorry. There's a macht on me all day' PB (s. e. Wexford). [*ODON* has *macht*, trans. v., kill, slaughter in literary usage. *RIA Dictionary* has *macht*, n., possibly meaning destruction, and probably an abstraction from *machtaid*, a loanword from Latin *mactare*, to slay, smite, afflict punish.]

Macnach n. A term of endearment for a little son. 'Come here to me, macnach' JC (w. Cork).

Macnas n. *al.* **macnais**. 1. Ease; contentment. 'He's living in macnas now that he has the family reared' RBB (e. Waterford). 2. 'Macnais, high spirits' *IG* (Kilkenny).

Madadh n. 'A dog. Also said when calling a dog' *CBE* 104 (Leitrim).

Madadh crann n. Literally, dog of the trees. The marten or pine marten, *Martes sylvatica*: H (n. Donegal).

Madra rua n. Pronounced **madar rua**. Also as **moddhera rua**. Red dog. The fox. 'I never yet could bait a trap that would catch the madar rua' MJD (w. Cork); Patk. Kennedy, *Legendary Fictions of the Irish Celts* 7: 'the moddhera rua' (Wexford).

Madra uisce n. Water dog. 'The otter' RBB (w. Waterford); *CBE* 104 (Leitrim).

Magadh vb. n. As **moguing**. Making fun of; ballyragging. 'We had great sport moguing him about women' AM (Leitrim). As adj. **mocky**. Ridiculous, absurd: 'That's a mocky bicycle' LOS (w. Clare).

Magairlín meidhreach n. Literally, little jolly testicles. As **mogolyeen-mire, mogra myra**. Early purple orchis, *orchis mescula*. *Folk-Lore Record* iv, 117 (1881): 'The early purple orchis is called mogra-myra, and is supposed to be most efficient as a love potion.' 'A love potion. "Oh, they'll catch him yet, even if they have to give him the mogolyeen-mire." Said of a young man frequently visiting a house where there are likely-looking daughters' LB (s.w. Dublin).

Maide n. As **midyee, muddiagh, muddie, waddy**. 1. A stick. 'Give him the waddy' *CBE* 266 (mid-Tipperary). 2. Tongs made of bent rods. A. Hume, *Irish Dialects* 24:

'Another extemporises a pair of midyees' (Antrim); *Ballymena Observer*: 'A pair of muddies'; *Simmons* (Donegal): 'muddiagh'. In combinations. 1. **Maide aráin**, grid-iron, as **muddha arran, mudyarn**. 'The bread stick; a forked stick with three legs, which supports the oat-cake till it is gradually baked' H (n. Donegal); 'He stuck to her like a scone to a maide aráin' *ibid.;* A. Hume, *Irish Dialects:* 'There is bread roasting at the mudjarn' (Antrim, Down); Wm. Carleton, *Going to Maynooth* 2, 113: '... it is aisy known he never was laid to the muddha arran – that is to say, properly baked – or duly and thoroughly educated' (Tyrone). 2. **Maide briste**. 'A bent stick used as a tongs' MG (n.w. Donegal); *CBE* 104 (Leitrim). Also as **maidis, muddie breestie**. 'Maidis are home-made tongs, a bent stick' McK (Leitrim); *Ballymena Observer*: 'Muddie breesties are tongs made from a bent rod' (Antrim). 3. **Maide tochais**, as **modda tuckish**. A scratching post for cattle. 'What d'you want there in a maide tochais?' = 'why are you standing there doing nothing?' *CBD* (n. Kerry). 4. **Maide éamainn, in form modda eamon**. 'A bolt for a door' *CBE* 34 S (Galway).

Maidhm sléibhe n. phr. In form **moom shlay**. 'A sudden flood from the hills caused by a cloudburst: "Do you hear the noise of the river? There's a moom shlay coming"' *CBE* 266 (mid-Tipperary).

Maidrín lathaigh n. phr. Little dog of the mud. A servile person. 'He's a real maidrín lathaigh by the priest' JC (w. Cork); *CBD* (n. Kerry).

Maig n. Also as **mwag**. 'A contemptuous toss of the head. "If you saw the mwag on her"' S Ua G (s. Tipperary). Hence phrase **gaige na maige**, 'A toss-of-the-head dandy. "He's some hurler! A useless gaige na maige' RBB (w. Waterford).

Maighdean n. Maiden, virgin, girl. Used with vocative particle: **A mhaighdean**, as an interjection. Peadar O'Donnell, *The Knife* 214: 'Well, a mhaighdean, they say there were thousands after them.' The allusion is

to the Blessed Virgin, an Mhaighdean Bheannaithe.

Máilín n. Also as **mauleen**. 1. A little bag. John and Michael Banim, *Peter of the Castle* 3, 4: 'If the old folk happen to be stingy, the girls who can do it now embezzle ... mauleens o' corn ...' (Kilkenny). 2. 'A large amount, a hoard. He made a máilín of money' MF (Westmeath). 3. In comp. **máilín sáite**: 'A little bag for holding the potato sets when sowing them with a spade' *IG* (Kilkenny).

Maingín n. A little bag. 'She brought me a maingín of fresh mushrooms' MS (e. Limerick).

Máinneáil vb. n. In form **máinneáling**. Walking with a rolling, lazy gait. 'Look at him máinneáling down the road' JPL (w. Cork).

Maíomh n. Also as **meeve**. 1. A boast. Hence **maíomhing**. 'He was only maíomhing out of it' *CBD* (n. Kerry); AG (s. Tipperary). [*out of it* = Irish preposition *as*] 2. Begrudging, envy. 'Used in sentences such as "not meeving it on you" – not begrudging it to you, a translation of *ní á mhaíomh ort é*' PB (s. Tipperary). 'I wouldn't maíomh it on him' SOM (w. Cork).

Máire fhada n. *al.* **Ceataí Fhada**. The heron, *ardea cinerea* MC (e. Mayo).

Mairg n. Woe, sorrow. 'Mairg that wouldn't have the larnin' MC (e. Mayo). 'I survived without a mairg' BMacM (Kerry).

Máirín a' chlúimh n. 'The caterpillar' MJD (w.Cork).

Máirtín n. In form **Markeen**. March. 'In the story of "the riabhach days", Máirtín skinned the old cow' MF (Westmeath).

Mairtíneach n. 'A cripple' NB (w. Limerick); *CBD* (n. Kerry); *Sguab* (w. Cork).

Máirtíní n. In forms **marteens, markins**. 1. 'Long soleless stockings, with a flap over foot, or a little lop for big toe or toe next to it, worn by youngsters in April and May to prevent their legs being scourged by hard weather' Tr (Donegal). Seumus MacManus, *The Bend of the Road* 129: 'The hottest day in summer never saw the mairtins off him' (Donegal). 2. 'At Carrablagh, coarse gloves worn by one pulling thistles out of the crop' H (n. Donegal).

Maise interj. Also in forms **musha, wisha, 'usha.** James Joyce, *Ivy Day in the Committee Room* 143: 'Wisha!', says I, what kind of people is going at all now'; Ibid. 136: 'Musha God be with them times!' said the old man; Ibid. 137: 'Mean little tinker! 'Usha how could he be anything else?'

Maise n. A becoming act. '"It's a great maise for you" = it's a great action of yours; or, it's great of you to do it. This is the only way I heard this word used, and always ironically' *IG* (Kilkenny).

Maiseach adj. Elegant, beautiful. 'A maiseach young woman' TOM (s. Tipperary).

Maistín n. 1. 'A rude, cantankerous person; a bully' G (s. Kilkenny); MC (e. Mayo). 2. 'A virago' NB (w. Limerick); *CBD* (n. Kerry); *An Cho* (w. Mayo). 3. 'A vicious kind of a dog' JM (w. Cork). [< Late Latin *mastinus.*]

Maistir n. In forms **mawhisdeer, moister, moistere, moistare, moyster.** Master. Thomas Dekker, *The Honest Whore*: 'A mawhisdeer (voc.) a gra, fare de well ...'; Richard Head, *Hic et Ubique*: 'The donny fellow make buse for my moister.' Head also has the forms listed above.

Maith go leor phr. Good enough. A phrase used to describe a person who is half-drunk. 'Drive him home; he's maith go leor' PD (s. Carlow).

Malabhóg v. In form **malavogue.** To beat soundly.

Malafústar v. As **mallafooster.** To beat mercilessly. 'I'll malafústar you' JL (w. Cork); *CBD* (n. Kerry); MH (w. Clare); S

(s. Wexford). 'You'll be mallafoostered when your mother finds out' PD (s. Carlow).

Mallacht n. A curse. In phrase, **mallacht Dé air** – God's curse on it: JPL (w. Cork). As **mallach** in Wm. Carleton, *Fardorougha The Miser* 398: '... oh, ma shaght millia mallach ort, Flanagan'. Recte, *mo sheacht míle mallacht ort*, my seven thousand curses on you.

Mallmhuir n. Neap tide. 'It was well known by wracking men as the least likely time for getting seaweed' *An Cho* (w. Mayo).

Mallréis n. Weakness of intellect. 'Tis terrible the way they go with that Altzheimer's disease. Mallréis like that is a fright to God' G (s. Kilkenny).

Mám n. A handful. 'Put a couple of máms of bran through the horse's feed' MS (e. Limerick); JL (w. Cork); *CBE* 34 S (Galway).

Mamailíneach n. 1. 'A long-backed person with short legs' NB (w. Limerick). 2. 'A waddler; a small, bulky, short-legged person' *CBE* 266 (Tipperary). 3. 'A lazy, useless person' *CBD* (n. Kerry).

Mán mán interj. *al.* **mánaí mánaí.** 'Phrases used when fondling a child or a pet animal' MG (n.w. Donegal).

Mana é seo interj. phr. Literally, this is an omen! 'Welcome! Your coming is the fulfilment of omens' Mac C (Monaghan).

Mangach n. 'The pollock' S (n.w. Donegal).

Mangalam n. 'A miserable-looking, shabby person' MJD (w. Cork).

Mánla adj. Modest, well-mannered, gracious. 'She's a fine mánla girl' JL (w. Cork).

Mant n. 1. Toothless gums. '"Ah, you little mant": said to a toothless child' OCn (Laois). 2. 'A gap in a row of teeth' NB (w. Limerick). 3. A bite. 'He took a mant out of the cake.' Diminutive, **mantóg** *CBD* (n. Kerry).

Mantán n. Also as **manthawn**. *al.* **mantóg**, in form **monthogue**. 'A gap-toothed person' MH (s. w. Clare); 'He was a man-thawn altogether, to day, after getting his teeth out ... He is an ugly little manthawn' OCn (Laois); 'A monthogue: one whose speech is defective' Mac C (Monaghan).

Maoileann n. Also as **mullin**. The brow, summit or ridge of a hill; an eleveted piece of ground. 'You can see Bantry from the top of that maoileann' JL (w. Cork). Seumus MacManus, *A Lad of the O'Friels* 146: 'It was only when thy played caman on Micky Thaig's mullin in summer, or on the frozen loch in winter' (Donegal).

Maol adj. Also in forms **mweel, miel, muil**. Bare, bald; without horns. 'A mweel ditch – a ditch without a bush or a sceach (q.v.) on top.' 'Whose is the mweel bullock?' OCn (Laois); Patk. Kennedy, *The Banks of the Boro*, 307: 'You're like our miel cow that gives a pailful of milk' (Wexford). Used figuratively in W. B. Yeats, *Fairy and Folk Tales of the Irish Peasantry* 150: 'A hammer-less gun has been called a "mweal" gun' (Connacht). Hence **moiled**, hornless, borderless (of a cap), bare: H (n. Donegal); **maolaí**, 'a petname for a cow without horns' JL (w. Cork); as **maoilín** Kiv (Sligo); **moolyeen** G (n.w. Donegal); Wm. Carleton, *The Lianhan Shee*, 2, 77: 'Moolyeen died, any way, soon afther your own kailyee, ye crathurs ye'. Carleton has spelling **moulleen** in *Shane Fadh's Wedding* 2, 54 (Tyrone).

Maolachán n. Also in form **mwaelachaun**. 1. 'A stingy, mean man' CBE 266 (mid-Tipperary). 2. 'A bald man' S Ua G (s. Tipperary). 3. 'An unfinished cock of hay. "With the hurry they were in to the circus they left the cock in a maolachán." That is, not topped off' ibid.

Maothal n. Beestings. 'The first milk given by a cow after calving' MJD (w. Cork).

Mar a chéile é phr. 'It is all the same' CBD (n. Kerry).

Mar atháim phr. In form **miraam**. As I am. 'How are you?' 'Miraam, boy, miraam' D (s.e. Wexford). The phrase means: I'm as you see me, holding my own, reasonably well.

Mar dhea phr. In forms **morya, moryah, moya, muryaa**. As it were, supposedly. Michael Banim, *Crohoor of the Billhook* 1, 106: 'Was it only a morya iv a thigha we seen one night in the ould castle among the hills?' Gloss by Banim: 'a pretended ghost' (Kilkenny); Peadar O'Donnell, *The Knife* 33: 'Godfrey Dhus lead the Lagan, moryah' (Donegal); James Joyce, *Ivy Day in the Committee Room* 138: 'And the men used to go in on a Sunday morning before the houses were open to buy a waistcoat and trousers – moya!'; Flann O'Brien, *The Dalkey Archive* 72: 'He disobeyed God's orders because, muryaa he knew better' (Gen.). See *má hé*.

Marbh adv. Dead. In phrase, **bhfuil tú marbh?**, as **wuil thu marra?** – are you dead? in Wm. Carleton, *The Midnight Mass* 1, 364 (Tyrone).

Marbhán n. Dead person. 'A very listless person' H (n. Clare).

Marbhthásc ort interj. Literally, news of death about you. In form **marafastot** in Anon., *Captain Thomas Stukeley*: '... mara-fastot art thou a feete liuerd kana'. [*Feete*, white; *kana*, see *cnat*.]

Margadh Mór n. Big market. In form **maragah-more, margymore**. Wm. Carleton's *Larry M'Farland's Wake* 1, 85 has footnote: 'There are three of these held before Christmas, and one or two before Easter, to enable the country folks to make their markets, and prepare for the more comfortably celebrating those great convivial festivals. They are almost as numerously attended as fairs; for which they are termed big markets' (Tyrone); 'Off to the margy-more a week before Christmas' Mac C (Monaghan).

Márla buí n. 'The yellow clay or marl found as subsoil in the Glen of Aherlow' AG (s. Tipperary).

Márlachan n. A weak, puny creature. A term of contempt. Peadar O'Donnell, *Storm* 80:

'When that márlachan, Sergeant Arnold, was a-burying'.

Maróg n. 'Sweet food' *CBE* 34 S (Galway).

Mart n. 'A beef' *IG* (Meath).

Más fada n. 'The swingle tree of a plough' MC (w. Clare).

Más fíor phr. If true. 'She's engaged to a fierce rich man, más fíor' JPL (w. Cork); *IG* (Kilkenny).

Más n. Plural, **másaí**, in form **mausey**. 1. 'That part of a plough in which the sock is held' MC (w. Clare). 2. A buttock. James Joyce, *Finnegans Wake* 127: 'mausey'.

Mascáil n. (Act of) 'mixing' *IG* (Kilkenny). Hence, **mascáling** Dee (w. Waterford).

Masla n. 'An insult' *CBD* (n. Kerry); 'We helped him all we could, and after all we did for him all we got was masla' NM (w. Cork).

Masmas n. Nausea. 'The food would put masmas on a duck' RBB (s. Kilkenny); 'It would give you masmas' LOS (w. Clare).

Máthair n. In form **maghair**. Mother. Patrick MacGill, *The Rat Pit* 42: 'It does not matter, maghair, what you say' (Donegal).

Meadalach n. 'A small, paunchy person' NB (w. Limerick).

Meadar n. Also in forms **maddor, madder, mether**. 'A vessel for drinking out of: the original meaning of the word never being altogether lost here' *IG* (Meath). Originally a wooden vessel, or pail. Jonathan Swift, *A Dialogue in Hybernian Stile*: '... we had nothing but a maddor to drink out of'; Lady Morgan, *The Wild Irish Girl* 84: '... the old dame produced what she called a "madder" of sweet milk, in contradistinction to the sour milk of which the rest partook, while the cow which supplied the luxury slumbered amicably...' (Leinster); William Carleton, *The Battle of the Factions*, 130: 'The rain fell as if it came out of methers' (Tyrone); James Joyce, *Ulysses* 323: '... the mether of dark strong foamy ale ...'

Meadóg n. As **meddoag**. A dagger. John Dunton, *Report of a Sermon*: '... another maybe has a trust with a meddoag or sword in his guts'.

Meaig n. Also as **mag**. 'State of exhaustion, collapse. "He fell in a mag"' TOM (s. Tipperary). 'In phrases such as "he's gone off in a meaig": he's fallen asleep; "he fell in a dead meaig": he fainted; "there isn't a meaig left in me": I'm exhausted' *CBD* (n. Kerry).

Meanaithín n. 'A peg in a churn-barrel' *IG* (Kilkenny).

Meann gabhair n. In form **minigower**. 'The jacksnipe' D (s.e. Wexford). [See *meannán aeir*.]

Meannán aeir n. 'The jacksnipe Con (Louth); *IG* (Cavan). *al*. **meannán aerach** MC (e. Mayo). See *meann gabhair*.

Méaracán n. 'A thimble' JC (w. Cork); 'A méaracán of whiskey is all we got' PD (s. Carlow).

Méaracán sí n. Fairy thimble. Foxglove, *digitalis purpurea*: JL (w. Cork). See *lus mór*.

Méarda n. 'Dung' JL (w. Cork). [< French *merde*]

Meas n. Also as **mass**. 1. Esteem, regard. 'He has no meas on money' RBB (s. Kilkenny) (Gen.); 'As in many other cases, the word must be properly built into a sentence. The preposition is all-important, because it must be the one used in Irish. You don't have meas *for* somebody. You have great meas *on* the Westerns, or great meas *on* the people from Side-over' *An Cho* (w. Mayo); George Fitzmaurice, *The Pie-Dish*: '... it's no mass you have on me at all ...' (Kerry). 2. Recollection; opinion. 'I had no meas on where I left the coat, i.e. I forgot where' Tr (Donegal).

Meas a' mhadra *al.* meas madra phr. Also as meas my dog. Respect of a dog, i.e. no respect. 'I haven't meas a' mhadra on him' H (n. Clare); You couldn't have meas madra on the likes of him' RBB (s. Kilkenny); 'He hadn't meas my dog on it' *CBD* (n. Kerry).

Meascán n. In forms miscawn, miscaun, miskin, muskawn. A lump of butter. 'A lump of butter weighing about four pounds' G (n.w. Donegal); Wm. Carleton, *The Party Fight and Funeral* 1, 183 (footnote): 'A portion of butter, weighing from one pound to six or eight, made in the shape of a prism' (Tyrone); *Poole* (s. e. Wexford): 'Aar was a muskawn o' buthther'; W. B. Yeats, *Fairy and Folk Tales of the Irish Peasantry* 271: 'She got the largest miscaun of butter'; *Lays and Legends of the North of Ireland* 71: 'Plates wir heap'd up with miskins av butter, an' praties an' beef'; A. Hume, *Irish Dialects* 24: 'We notice a miscaun of butter' (Antrim and Down); *N & Q.* (1854): 'She tauntingly replied that his large oatcake, his quarter of beef, and his "miscawn" of butter would amply suffice a better man.'

Meata pp. (Of person): In delicate health. 'He's meata, God help him' PB (s. Tipperary).

Meathán n. *al.* meathánaí. 1. 'One of the fibres or strips of wood of which the bottom of a sieve or riddle is made' *IG* (Kilkenny). 2. 'A person in delicate health' G (s. Kilkenny); 'A small person' *CBE* 34 S (Galway); 'A meathánaí is a person in poor health' PB (s. Tipperary).

Meathlóirín n. 'A weak person or animal' NB (w. Limerick).

Meidhreach adv. 'Merry; slightly drunk' LOS (w. Clare).

Meig n. 1. 'The bleat of a goat' S (n.w. Donegal); Smy (n. Clare); PB (s. Tipperary) 2. 'The slightest of human articulations. "There wasn't a meig out of Seán when she accused him; not a word"' H (n. Clare).

Meigeadán n. 1. 'A person who talks and talks. Usually complaining' S (n.w. Donegal). 2. 'A half pint of beer' PB (s. Tipperary).

Meigeall n. 'A goat's whiskers' MS (e. Limerick); H (n. Clare); JM (w. Cork); RBB (w. Waterford); PD (s. Carlow).

Meigeallachán n. Also as megalachaun. 1. 'A long-bearded man' RBB (s. Kilkenny). 2. 'A double-chinned person: "She's in a megalachaun with fat"' *CBE* 266 (mid-Tipperary). 3. A sulk: "She gets into a megalachaun for the least thing"' ibid.

Méirín n. 'Protective covering for a sore finger' MF (Westmeath); *IG* (Kilkenny).

Meirlín n. Dizziness. 'My head is in a meirlín' MF (Westmeath).

Meirliún n. Merlin, *falco columbarius:* *CBE* 104 (Leitrim). [< Old French, *esmerillon*.]

Méirscre n. *al.* meirsire. Chaps on the hands. 'You won't find any méirscre on that lady's hands' MS (e. Limerick); *CBD* (n. Kerry); 'Washing things in cold water would give you méirsire' NB (w. Limerick).

Meisceal n. *al.* maidhsceal. 'A person with a big paunch; a glutton' *CBD* (n. Kerry); 'He's gone in the divil of a maidhsceal' JL (w. Cork).

Meitheal n. Also in forms metheil, mechil. A band of volunteer labourers who cut one another's corn, save turf etc. (Gen.); Seumus MacManus, *Bold Blades of Donegal* 287: 'The Vagabone's mother had a metheil of men, half a dozen, setting potatoes'; ibid. 147: 'As hungry as a mechil o' men coming from the bog'.

Mí-ádh n. Also in forms mí-ádh dearg, miau, meeawe, mee ah. Bad luck. 'There was nothin' in that business ever but mí-ádh' H (n. Clare); 'There is an old saying that when your luck is out your ducks can drown. That would be mí-ádh dearg, red bad luck!' *An Cho* (w. Mayo); Michael

Banim, *Crohoor of the Billhook* 1, 36: 'The miau and the miroch has come over you'. Glossed by Banim as 'sorrow and trouble' (Kilkenny). Walter Macken, *Mungo's Mansion* 27: 'meeawe'; 'Bad luck, mee ah' PON (n. Dublin). [*Mí* is a negative separable prefix.]

Mí-ámharach adj. Unlucky. 'He's a mí-amharach poor devil' *CBE* 266 (mid-Tipperary).

Mí-fhortún n. As **miortún**. Ill-fortune. 1. 'An unfortunate person' NB (w. Limerick). 2. 'A rake' ibid.

Miamhlach n. As **meevluch**. 'An infant's cry' *CBE* 266 (mid-Tipperary).

Mianach n. As **meenach**. 'Stuff, material' MF (Limerick).

Mias n. In form **mease**. A dish. *EASI* 293: 'A measure for small fish, especially herrings. Used all round the Irish coast.'

Micilín n. 1. 'A fairy man' PB (s. Tipperary). 2. 'A penis' JL (w. Cork).

Midilín n. ' The thong of a flail' G (n.w. Donegal); FF (Cavan).

Míle n. In phrase **míle murder**. Also in forms **millia(h)-, melia-, meel a-, mille-, moliamordhar**. A thousand murders. A rhetorical expression to give colour to narrative. Samuel Lover, *Legends and Stories of Ireland* 1, 103: 'Milla murther! cries the King'; Wm. Carleton, *Fardorougha the Miser* 17: 'It 'ud be the milliah murdhers to let the ... villin ... off' (Tyrone); W.B. Yeats, *Fairy and Folk Tales of the Irish Peasantry* 208: 'Poor Shemus roared out "mille murdher"' (Connacht); *Lays and Legends of the North of Ireland* 78: 'Protect us! ... Mille murdher!'; *Century Magazine*, 606 (Feb. 1900): 'Melia murther!, says Billy, and over went two of the skeps' (Donegal); Seumus MacManus, *In Chimney Corners* 239: 'Spitting on the stick and winding it round his head, and fetching it down, oh, melia murdher! that you'd think it wouldn't leave a bone in the poor baste's body it wouldn't knock into

stirabout' (Donegal); James Joyce, *Ulysses* 327: '... he flogs the bloody backside off of the poor lad till he yells melia murder'; Joyce, *Finnegans Wake* 99: 'moliamordhar'.

Milis n. In phrase **a mhilis**, also as **avilish**. My sweet. A term of endearment. Seumus Mac Manus, *Bold Blades of Donegal* 19: 'A mhilis, will ye tell me what they call ye'; T. O'Flanagan ('Samoth') *Ned M'Cool and his Foster Brother* 65: 'But avilish, since ye don't care I'll go my ways again (Donegal).'

Milítheach adj. 'Pale, sickly-looking. "I wonder are you a bit anaemic? You're very milítheach with a bit"' AG (s. Tipperary). [*with a bit*: translation of the idiom *le tamall*.]

Mill v. Destroy. 'When I see him, I'll mill him' TB (Cavan). Hence **mill an maide** n. phr. Literally, destroy the stick. 'A name for a bad carpenter' *IG* (Kilkenny). Perhaps it should have been spelled **milleadh maide**, the destruction of the stick.

Millín n. As **milleen**. A small hill, a knoll. 'He lives east between them two milleens' JL (w. Cork).

Mín n. In form **meen**. 'A smooth green spot in the middle of rough land' MG (n.w. Donegal).

Míneagán n. 'A little fairy' NB (w. Limerick)

Mínicín n. 'A little fellow, a dwarf' *IG* (Meath). [Cf. English *mannikin*]

Mínscoth n. Black knapweed, *Centaurea nigra*: OCn (Laois); *CBD* (n. Kerry); D (Kildare).

Minseach n. *al.* **mínsín, minseog** as **minnshogue, meenshogue**. 1. 'A year-old goat' H (n. Clare). 2. 'A she goat, nanny goat' RBB (s. Kilkenny); JM (w. Cork.); PB (s. Tipperary); NB (w. Limerick): 'mínsín'; Patk. Kennedy, *Evenings in the Duffrey* 361: 'A puchawn and eleven meenshogues' (Wexford); James Joyce, *Finnegans Wake* 37: 'minnshogues'.

Míol an chrainn n. 'Wood louse': MS (e. Limerick).

Míolachán n. 'A low, mean person; a hooligan' PB (s. Tipperary).

Míoltógaí n. Midges. 'Smoke from a pipe is the only cure for the míoltógaí' G (n.w. Donegal).

Mionaerach n. 'A type of fever which affects children' *Béal* XX (Offaly); *JKAS* (Kildare).

Mionnán n. 'A kid goat' PB (s. Tipperary); JM (w. Cork).

Mionrabh n. Fragments, smithereens. 'He made mionrabh of it' *CBD* (n. Kerry); MJD (w. Cork).

Míosach n. *al.* **míosachán**. 'A stunted crop of wheat' PB (s. Tipperary).

Miotán n. 'A withered or otherwise deformed hand' PJG (mid-Donegal).

Mírath n. As **miroch, meeraw**. Bad fortune. Michael Banim, *Crohoor of the Billhook* 1, 36: 'the miau and the miroch has come over you'. Miroch glossed by Banim as 'trouble.' *EASI* 294: 'there was some meeraw on the family' (Munster). For *miau*, see *mí ádh*.

Mise le meas phr. I, with respect. Used to formally close a letter in either English or Irish.

Mismín n. Water mint, *mentha aquatica*: *CBD* (n. Kerry).

Misneach n. Also as **misnach**. 'Courage' *CBD* (n. Kerry). As **misnach** in Patk. Kennedy, *Legendary Fictions Of The Irish Celts* 155: '... no one had misnach enough to speak to us' (Wexford).

Mo bhrón! interj. Also as **mavrone**. My sorrow. 'Mo bhrón, they'll never win an All-Ireland' MJD (w. Cork); James Joyce, *Ulysses* 200: 'And we to be there, mavrone'

Mo chorp 'on diabhal interj. Also as **ma-horp-an-duoul, chorp an diouol.**' Liter-ally, my body to the devil! 'Marilyn Monroe! Oh, mo chorp 'on diabhal!' JL (w. Cork); Michael Banim, *Crohoor of the Billhook* 1, 46: 'ma-horp-an-duoul, you'll pay for all this together' (Kilkenny): Wm. Carleton, *Phelim O'Toole's Courtship* 2, 220: 'Chorp an diouol' (Tyrone).

Mo chroí interj. In form **machree**. My heart. A term of endearment. Gerald Griffin, *The Collegians* 134: 'Ma chree, ma lanuv': my heart, my child' (Limerick); Samuel Lover, *Legends and Stories of Ireland* 1,102: ' But, jew'l machree, they soon run back into his room'; Patk. Kennedy, *The Banks of the Boro* 48: ' but girls, machree, he'll be living for ever' (Wexford); *Lays and Legends of the North of Ireland* 1, 102: 'Och, Barney, machree! it's meself that was fooled'; Lord Tennyson, *To-morrow*: 'Och, Molly, we thought, machree, ye would start back agin into life'; James Joyce, *Ulysses* 286: 'Ben machree, said Mr Dedalus ...' (Gen.).

Mo chumha interj. My sorrow! As **mo chuma** in Patk. Kennedy, *Legendary Fictions of the Irish Celts* 237.

Mo ghoirm thú! interj. phr. 'The phrase means bravo!' *An Cho* (w. Mayo).

Mo ghraidhin croí tú interj. Also as **ma grine chree bu**. My heart's joy, you! An expression of either heartfelt congratulations or sympathy. Gerald Griffin, *The Collegians* 51: 'ma grine chree bu'. 'Bu' is an obvious misprint for *tú* (Limerick).

Mo ghrása phr. My own love. Used lightly to mean 'this fellow here'. 'Who would I see but mo ghrása ' PB (s. Tipperary).

Mo leanbh interj. In form **ma lanuv**. My child. Gerald Griffin, *The Collegians* 134: 'Ma chree, ma lanuv' (Limerick).

Mo léir interj. Alas! Woe is me! JL (w. Cork); DOC (Limerick).

Mo leon gamhain tú phr. My lion of a calf, you! 'An expression of admiration' Ham (e. Clare).

Mo nuar interj. As **monar**. O dear! NB (w. Limerick).

Modartha As **moidered, moithered**. Confused, bothered, annoyed. 'I'm moithered by you. Get out and leave me alone' JC (w. Cork); MacC (Dublin); MC (e. Mayo); PC (n. Clare). [Medieval *Annals of Loch Cé* and *Annals of Ulster* have *modarda*.]

Mogall n. 1. 'A husk. A grain of oats with the husk attached' *IG* (Kilkenny); PB (s. Tipperary). 2. The mesh of a net. 'We form a verb out of the word too: in thatching a rick of hay or a stack of oats, when the rushes were in place a man had to form intertwining loops of the súgán or straw rope to secure them. That was **mogalling**' *An Cho* (w. Mayo). 3. 'A cluster; a rush in football. "Mogall it, boys, mogall it, their supporters cried"' S Ua G (s. Tipperary).

Mogallach adj. Soft, kind, pleasant. 'A fine mogallach woman' *CBD* (n. Kerry).

Mogán n. 'A footless stocking' Del (Antrim). See *máirtín*.

Mogóirí n. pl. In forms **magories, mugoreens**. Wild rose hips, fruit of the sweetbriar, *rosa rubiginosa*. Children's rhyme: 'I'll tell you a story about Johnny Magorie/ He went to a wood and shot a tory' PON (n. Co. Dublin); W. B. Yeats, *Fairy and Folk Tales of the Irish Peasantry* 281 (1888): 'She got nuts and mugoreens.'

Móidín n. In forms **votcheen, votyeen, vokeen**. A devotee; a devout, pious person. Peadar O'Donnell, *Islanders* 125: 'Religion does all very well for Terry Mulvaney to thrown in, when he comes across a votcheen like you' (Donegal); W. H. Floredice, *Derryreel* 34: 'With the appearance of a votyeen (note: a Devotee, a Religieuse) upon her' (Ulster); 'Vokeen: A person who makes a display of "piosity"' MF (Westmeath).

Moiltín n. 'A ram' *CBE* 104 (Leitrim).

Móinéar n. 'A meadow' MJD (w. Cork); *CBE* 34 S (Galway).

Móineog n. Also as **moonogue**. 1. The red whortleberry, *Vacinium Vitis Idaea*: *EDD* (Antrim). 2. 'The bogberry, *empetrum nigrum*: *IG* (Meath); Con (Louth).

Moing n. 'An overgrown swamp' NB (w. Limerick); PB (s. Tipperary).

Moingeán n. 'A wet, marshy field' *CBD* (n. Kerry).

Móinín n. Also in form **moneen**. 1. 'A small bog meadow' McK (Leitrim); 'A small meadow' NB (w. Limerick); A meadow beside a dwelling-house' PLH (n. Roscommon). 2. 'A little bog or turf bank'; Gerald Griffin, *The Collegians* 81: 'Oyeh, if you'll never fut a moneen till then'. [To foot turf is to stand sods on the turf-bank in such a way as to allow the wind to blow through the little clamps to facilitate the drying process.]

Móinteán n. 'Bogland, moor' MS (e. Limerick); NM (w. Cork); *CBD* (n. Kerry); PB (s. Tipperary).

Móirí n. 'A grandmother' Con (Louth).

Moltachán n. A wether. Figuratively, 'a strong, simple-minded boy' PB (s. Tipperary).

Mongán n. In form **mangan**. 1. 'A swamp' JM (s. Kilkenny). 2. As **mongaun**. 'A quantity, a stone or two. "He carried home a fine mongán of potatoes on his back"' *CBE* 266 (mid-Tipperary). [2. Possibly connected with *mong*, ropes, cordage, to carry loads. But cf. *mang*, a bag.]

Mór a theastaíonn interj. 'Means "it's greatly he needs". It is always a sarcastic phrase. "Did you hear he's going to buy a Mercedes? Mór a theastaíonn Mercedes!" Or she would accept no perfume except *Joy*. "Oh then, mór a theastaíonn!" There's an echo in the background of "Far from *Joy* she was reared!" ' *An Cho* (w. Mayo).

Mór adj. Also as **moor**. Big. Frequently used of people, e.g. Paddy Mór. John Durant

Breval, *The Play is the Plot:* 'I was Maghloghan Moor's joy.'

Mór le phr. As direct translation **great with**, **friendly with.** James Joyce, *The Dead:* '"I suppose you were in love with this Michael Furey, Greta", he said. "I was great with him at that time", she said.'

Mórdháil n. 'Pride, boastfulness' *IG* (Kilkenny); *Sguab* (Cork).

Mórdhálach adj. 'Proud; living above one's means so that people will think you rich' *IG* (Kilkenny).

Mórtas n. Pride. 'They have no mórtas any more. It doesn't matter a traneen to them to be picked to play for their county' PC (n. Clare).

Mothall n. Also in form **musall.** A mop of hair. 'You'd want to take a shears, not a scissors, to that mothall of yours' MS (e. Limerick); H (n. Clare); JL (w. Cork); PB (s. Tipperary); 'a musall of hair' *IG* (Kilkenny).

Mothaolach adj. Innocent, trusting. 'He's too mothaolach to be wholesome' JPL (w.Cork).

Mothar n. 1. 'A small, sheltered field' H (n. Clare). 2. 'A high ocean swell' RBB (w. Waterford). 3. 'A thicket, dense undergrowth' MJD (w. Cork).

Muc n. Pig. As **muck,** plural **mucke** in John Michelburne, *Ireland Preserved;* and in Wm. Carleton, *Phil Purcel, the Pig-Driver* 1, 416.

Mucaire n. 'A slovenly worker' MC (e. Mayo).

Mucairis n. 1. The fastenings by which a basket is held on the back JPL (w. Cork); *CBD* (n. Kerry). 2. 'A cloth placed on the head by a person carrying a bucket etc.' *CBD* (n. Kerry).

Múchadh n. Literally, smothering, suffocation. Asthma. 'They say that people with the múchadh live long' MJD (w. Cork); MS (e. Limerick); OCn (Laois).

Múchtálaí n. 'A person with respitory troubles' *CBE* 266 (mid-Tipperary).

Múdabhall n. As **moodavowl, moodavow.** 'A person who listens attentively but who says nothing' MP (mid-Tipperary); *CBE* 266 (mid-Tipperary). [Irish?]

Muilleoir n. 'A miller' *IG* (Cavan).

Muintir n. People, relatives, family. In phrase, **Muintir na Tíre,** an organisation of country people.

Muintireach adj. Friendly. In form **meentrach** in Patk. Kennedy, *Legendary Fictions of the Irish Celts* 37: 'The king and queen were more meentrach to Jack to-day.' Glossed 'loving' (Wexford).

Muirbheach n In form **murrough.** An extensive beach; sandy soil adjacent to the sea. 'Many's the snipe I've shot on thon murrough' H (n. Donegal).

Muirc mairc phr. A state of confusion. 'He left everything muirc mairc after him' S Ua G (s. Tipperary).

Muire n., interj. In forms **viry, wirra, wisha, wurrah, musha, vuya, mwirra.** The personal name confined to the Blessed Virgin Mary. Anon., *The Pretender's Exercise:* 'Viry'; Gerald Griffin, *The Collegians* 50: 'Oh wirra, Eily!' As **wisha** ibid. 49: 'Wisha, but you're a droll man' (Limerick); Wm. Carleton,*Tubber Derg* 2, 391: 'Wurrah dheelish'. As **musha** ibid. 391: Musha, ye ate no breakfast, maybe?; Seumus MacManus,*The Bold Blades of Donegal* 106: 'Oh, wirra, wirra!' As **vuya** in Patk. Kennedy, *Legends of Mount Leinster* 66: 'Oh, vuya, vuya, how will I ever show my face again?' (Wexford); Eric Cross, *The Tailor and Ansty* 184: 'Mwirra, no.' An exclamation of grief: **A Mhuire is trua,** O Mary it is a pity, in form **Weirasthru!** in Samuel Lover, *Molly Carew* 21: **Dia is Muire dhuit,** 'God and Mary to you!', is a common salutation.

Muirealach n. The bent grass, *psamma arenaria.* Dermot O'Byrne, *Children of the*

Hills 111: 'A great waste of dunes lay before me ... spiky grass and patches of muirealach sprouting through a desert of sand.'

Múirín n. Also as **mooryeen**. 'Turf dust. "The turf is no good. Look at it crumbling into mooryeen"' TOM (s. Tipperary). 'Black, dry dust on a turf-bank' *CBE* 266 (mid-Tipperary).

Múirnín n. In phrase **a mhúirnín**, my little darling. In forms **avourneen, mavourneen**. Seumus MacManus, *Bold Blades of Donegal* 275: 'We heard his low voice, 'Mother?' 'Aye, a mhúirnín' she answered'. ibid. 333: 'For your honour and glory, avourneen'; 19th c. song: 'Come back to Erin, mavourneen, mavourneen'; James Joyce, *Ulysses* 293: 'Barney mavourneen's be it, says I.' Pejorative – 'She's a real múirnín' MF (Westmeath).

Múis n. Displeasure, dissatisfaction. 'There is some múis on him, and for the life of me I don't know why' G (s. Kilkenny).

Muisiriún n. In form **musharoon**. 'Mushroom' JPL (w. Cork). **Muisiriún síóg**, fairy mushroom *IG* (Kilkenny). Mrs S. C. Hall, *Tales of Irish Life and Character* 51: 'Musharoon gentry': upstarts (s. Leinster).

Múitseálaí n. As **moochawly**. 'A fumbling workman' *CBE* 266 (mid-Tipperary). [Cf. English and Scottish dialect *mooch*.]

Mulchán n. As **mulaghane**. Dried, baked curds. Richard Head, *Hic et Ubique:* '... de cow dat make de buttermilk ... for dy child and my shelf, and de mulaghane...'

Mullach n. 'Height, elevated ground' PC (n. Clare); 'It can take a while to reach the mullach of the Reek' Kiv (Sligo).

Mullachán n. 'A sturdy lump of a youngster' FF (Cavan); G (n.w. Donegal); *CBE* 104 (Leitrim).

Mullán n. 'A high field' *Pe* (Wexford).

Múnlach n. Liquid manure, sullage, putrid water. 'They sell slops for porter in that pub. Múnlach' JM (w.Cork). In form **múinleach** MF (Westmeath). As **moodick, moonluck, mooduck** *CBE* 98 (Kilkenny).

Muraichín. 'Hard, strenuous work. "We had great hard muraichín at it"' *CBD* (n. Kerry).

Murchadh n. Male personal name. In phrase **He saw Murchadh** – he has seen hard times. From Murchadh na dTóiteán, Murchadh of the Burnings, the notorious Earl of Inchiquin, a terrorist of Cromwell's time: NB (w. Limerick). Also in phrase 'there was great **Murchadh mór** there': great weeping and keening: NB (w. Limerick). In phrase **You'll get Murchadh** – you'll be severely dealt with: *IG* (Kilkenny).

Múrlach n. As **mórlach, múlach**. 'Mud, mire, liquid manure' *IG* (Kilkenny); 'Don't fall in the mórlach' JJH (w Waterford). Variants of *múnlach*.

Murlas n. Mackerel. 'You could catch the murlas with a bent pin, they were so plentiful' S (n.w. Donegal).

Murlóg n. 'A small, strong man' G (n.w. Donegal).

Murúch n. A mermaid. In form **merra** Kiv (Sligo). Also in form **merrow** in W.B. Yeats, *Fairy and Folktales*; Emily Lawless, *Grania* 142: 'My grandfather saw one once on the head of a merrow' (Mayo).

Músaí n. 'A sullen, silent person; one who never jokes or says a pleasant word' *IG* (Kilkenny).

Mustar n. 1. A sulk; ill-humour. 'He has a mustar on him' *IG*. (Kilkenny). 2. Pride, haughtiness. 'They'd sicken you, the mustar of them' *CBD* (n. Kerry).

Mustarach adj. 1. (Of weather) Stormy, blustery, showery' *IG* (Kilkenny). 2. Ill-humoured, sour *IG* (Kilkenny). 3. 'Boastful, conceited' *CBD* (n. Kerry); DOH (e. Limerick).

Múta máta n. 'A useless workman, untidy and slow' MJD (w. Cork); BOD (s.w. Cork). See **mútamálaí**.

Mútamálaí n. 'An awkward man; one who invariably botches a job' NB (w. Limerick).

Mútóg n. 'A home-made muzzle which prevents a young calf from swallowing straw or such foods as are detrimental to the young digestive organs' *An Cho* (w. Mayo).

N

Ná bac leis interj. Also in forms **nabocklish, nawbocklish, naboclish**. Don't bother with it; leave it alone. 'Ná bac leis: let it be' H (n. Clare); John Boyce, *Mary Lee or The Yank in Ireland* 282: 'But nabocklish I'll be even with ye yet' (Donegal); Michael Banim, *The Croppy* 1, 144: 'If he doesn't win you at the first offer, nawbocklish' (Kilkenny); Charles James Lever, *Charles O'Malley:* 'Arrest him – nabocklish – catch a weasel asleep' (Connacht); Patk. Kennedy, *The Banks of the Boro* 129: 'But, naboclish, we will find ourselves in the wrong box, maybe' (Wexford).

Nádúir n. Also as **nádúracht, nawdhoo**. Natural feeling, kindliness. 'There is not a bit of nádúir in that mare. She'd kick the foal to death if I left him with her' MJD (w. Cork); 'He has a great nádúir for you – he's very fond of you' MP (mid-Tipperary); 'She has a bit of a nawdhoo for him' OCn (Laois); 'The children have no nádúracht in them' CBD (n. Kerry).

Náire n. Shame. 'Stop saucering your tea! You'll bring náire down on us' JC (w. Cork).

Náirithe adv. Shamed, embarrassed. 'You bring me a present and I have nothing to give you. You have me náirithe!' MJD (w. Cork); H (n. Clare).

Nár laga Dia thú! interj. phr. May God not weaken you. 'A blessing as a reward for a service such as a lift in a car, opening a difficult bottle or door, tidying up a room' An Cho (w. Mayo).

Nára slán comórtas phr. 'There's no comparison' CBD (n. Kerry).

Nasc n., interj. Also as **naisc, nask**. 1. 'A cow-tying, or chain which ties round the horns. A *crobh nasc* is a fetter tied on the horn and foreleg to prevent a cow from going over fences' IG (Kilkenny); 'A nask is a fetter put on a cow' PJG (mid-Donegal). 2. 'Naisc! is said to cattle when driving them into their milking shed' PB (s. Tipperary).

Nathán n. Aphorism, proverb, pun, wisecrack. 'Usually in plural, **natháns**' H (n. Clare).

Nathántaíocht n. Use of punning, proverbs etc. 'I got tired of his nathántaíocht' H (n. Clare).

Néalla tóirní phr. Clouds of thunder. 'In phrase "You'll get néalla tóirní": you're in big trouble' Mac C (Monaghan).

Neamhspleách adj. 'Independent, unabashed. "He won't take charity. He's too neamhspleách' TOM (s. Tipperary); 'I am neamhspleách to them' IG (Kilkenny).

Neamp n. 1. 'A nip given with the fingers' CBE 104 (Leitrim). 2. Scissors cut. 'He cut a neamp out of his hair' MF (Westmeath).

Neantóg n. 1. A nettle. In Patk. Kennedy, *Legendary Fictions of the Irish Celts* 228: '... he pulled a neantog' (Wexford). 2. Also used to describe a touchy person' An Cho (w. Mayo); 'She's a right neantóg, that one' G (s. Kilkenny).

Ní fheadar phr. I don't know JL (w. Cork). **Ní fheadar an domhan**. I don't know (in) the world: in the least: CBD (n. Kerry).

Ní nach ionadh phr. 'It is not surprising' CBD (n. Kerry).

Níl a fhios agam phr. I don't know. As **niel eshighum** in Wm. Carleton, *The Poor Scholar* 2, 264. (Tyrone).

Níl sé istigh phr. In form **neen-sha-stigh**. He's not inside. Michael Banim, *Crohoor of the Billhook* 1, 214. Glossed by Banim as 'Not at home' (Kilkenny).

Níochán n. In form **nitchin**. A washing. 'It's a poor nitchin that hasn't a man's shirt in it' OC (Monaghan).

Niuc n. 'A rogue' OC (Monaghan).

Nóinín n. The daisy, *bellis perinnis*: MG (n.w. Donegal); MS (e. Limerick); Ham (e. Clare); *CBD* (n. Kerry).

Nuachas interj. Welcome! RBB (w. Waterford).

Nuaíocht n. 'News, novelty, curiosity. "You took your nuaíocht out of it" you have ceased to be curious or interested about it' *IG* (Monaghan).

Núdaí nádaí n. Also as **noodynaady, niúdar neádar**. 'A listless, indecisive person' MS (e. Limerick); *An Cho* (w. Mayo); James Joyce, *Finnegans Wake* 253: 'noodynaady'; 'He can't make his mind about a blessed thing. He's a real niúdar neádar' G (s. Kilkenny).

O

Ó a Dhia interj. O God! *IG* (Kilkenny).

Ó b'annamh liom phr. As seldom happened to me. 'O b'annamh liom to have the price of it' *IG* (Kilkenny).

Ócáid n. 1. 'A foolish or awkward person' *CBD* (Kerry). 2. A worn implement. 'Tis a right ócáid' ibid.

Och interj. 1. An exclamation of sorrow, regret, dissatisfaction or surprise. John Boyce, *Shandy Maguire* 11: 'Och, augh, weans dear, the ould times was the good times.' (Donegal). 2. In combinations och-anee-o, an exclamation of woe. Seumas Mac Manus, *A Lad of the O'Friels* 86: 'Och-anee-o, he sighed, isn't it the sorraful, sorraful pity' (Donegal).

Ochón v., interj. Also in forms ahone, ohone, o hone, ochone, oh hone, oconee. 1. To bewail, lament. Seumas MacManus, *In Chimney Corners* 190: 'And both of them keening and ochoning, one louder nor another' (Donegal). 2. Anon., *Sir John Oldcastle:* ' Ahone, ahone, ahone ...'; John Dunton, *Report of a Sermon:* ' ... deat's all-dewoureing mout, ohone ...'; ibid.: 'ochone, deare Cristians ...'; Anon.,*The Irish Hudibras:* 'O Hone!'; Thomas Sheridan, *The Brave Irishman:* 'Oh hone, my dear ...'; Seumas MacManus, *In Chimney Corners* 190: 'It's the sore pity of me this morning! Ochon! Ochon!' (Donegal); Samuel Lover, *Molloy Carew* 21: 'Och hone! Weirasthru!' (see *Muire*); W. B. Yeats, *The Countess Cathleen* 45: 'Ochone! the treasure room is broken in. The door stands open and the gold is gone'; James Joyce, *Finnegans Wake* 3: 'Oconee'.

Ocras n. Hunger. 'The style of them, my dear! But it wasn't long ago at all that they had nothing but the ocras' JS (e. Kerry); MS (e. Limerick).

Odhrán n. The cow-parsnip, *heracleum sphandylium*: PJG (mid-Donegal).

Óg adj. In form oge. Young. Wm. Carleton, Shane Fadh's Wedding 1, 52: 'Brine oge'; Somerville and Ross, *The House of Fahy*, 135: 'I assailed the (yacht) Eileen Oge, such being her inappropriate name, with desolate cries...' (w. Cork).

Óganách n. Also in form augenagh. 1. 'A young person' *IG* (Kilkenny). 2. 'A trickster' *IG* (Cavan); John Boyce, *Shandy Maguire* 89: '"Lave the road an' ... let your betters pass." "When I see them, my augenagh"' (Donegal).

Oíche go maidin phr. Translated literally as a night till morning. 'I hear ye had an oíche go maidin at the wake' MJD (w. Cork.); M. J. Mulloy, *The Wood of the Whispering* 191: 'We'll have a night till morning'.

Oíche Shamhna n. 'Hallow E'en' *IG* (Kilkenny).

Oighreach n. Also as irock. ' Redness or soreness of skin from cold or friction; chaffing or windgall' MS (e. Limerick); MG (n.w. Donegal); 'The east wind would give you irock' PON (n. Co. Dublin).

Oinniún n. Also in form innion. Onion. 'The Spanish oinniúns are a terror on the eyes' MS (e. Limerick); 'The innions make the stew' MW (s. Wexford; Gen.).

Óinseach n. Also in forms ownshuck, oonshuk, oonshugh. 1. A foolish woman. Michael Banim, *The Croppy* 1, 138: 'I done for that ownshuck' (Kilkenny); 'She's an oonshuk' *CBE* 98 (Kilkenny); Charles Kickham, *Knocknagow* 61: 'Don't be makin' an oonshugh uv yourself' (Tipperary). 2. 'A girl of immoral habits' PJG (mid-Donegal); 'A girl who goes astray' *IG* (Meath); Diminutive, **óinsín** *IG* (Kilkenny); JM (w. Cork); PB (s. Tipperary).

Oireachtas n. The Legislature.

Olagón n. 'A wail' MS (e. Limerick); 'You should hear the olagóns of her when she fell off the horse'. Hence **olagóning**, wailing.

Olltach n. 'A person who works charms or witchcraft' *IG* (Kilkenny).

Orc n. 'A small hound' NB (w. Limerick).

Orm prep. pro. In translated form, **on me**. James Stephens,*The Crock of Gold* 71: 'and then, him to be killed on me'.

Ortha n. In form **orragh**. A charm, incantation. 'When talking to an old farmer near Drumfad about the Fanad stone and its sup-erstitions he said, "there's many known about these ould orraghs and pishlags, but not near as many as there used" H (n. Donegal).

Os comhair phr. In front of. *Os* = over; a confusion regarding *comhair*, used in the prep. phrase *os comhair*, and *cóir* n., right, equity, with identical pronunciation, gave **overright**. In Gerald Griffin,*The Collegians* 49. *Overright* is still in general use, for *opposite*. 'He was sitting overright me; he saw me, all right' G (s. Kilkenny).

Osna n. A sigh. 'God save us, what caused that osna?' PD (s. Carlow).

Ótais n. An obese person. 'She must weigh half a ton. There must be some weakness there for her to become such an ótais' PD (s. Carlow).

P

Púca poill n. 'The toadstool' MS (e. Limerick); MJD (w. Cork).

Pacairlín n. A little packful. 'He's got a nice pacairlín of spuds' NB (w. Limerick).

Padalán n. 'A big-footed person' McK (Leitrim).

Padharcán n. 'The primrose' IG (Kilkenny).

Padhsán n. 1. 'A delicate person, usually complaining' NB (w. Limerick); CBD (n. Kerry); MP (mid-Tipperary). Diminutive, padhsáinín CBD (n. Kerry). 2. 'A pheasant' KB (e. Limerick).

Paic n. A rascal, a go-boy. 'He's a right paic' MF (Westmeath).

Páideog n. 1. 'A rushlight' MS (e. Limerick). 2. 'A fat baby' NB (w. Limerick). 3. 'A good-looking young girl' JPL (w. Cork).

Paidir capaill phr. Literally, the prayer of a horse. Said to one constantly harping on the same string. 'He complained all day about the way he was treated, making a paidir capaill out of it' MC (w. Clare). Also in translated form horse's prayer: 'Ara stop making a horse's prayer out of it' C (e. Limerick).

Paidrín n. or Paidrín páirteach In form padareen or padareen partauch; paudereen. The Rosary. John Boyce, Shandy Maguire 313: 'We hadn't the beads to say the padareen partauch' (Donegal); Wm. Carleton, Phelim O'Toole's Courtship 1, 210: 'I could ... have her thumpin' her breast an' countin her Padareens in no time'; Carleton, The Battle of the Factions 2,122: 'paudereen' (Tyrone).

Páintheach n. al. pánach. 'A plump person, or animal' JC (w. Cork); 'A fat hare' PB (s. Tipperary); 'A pánach' NB (w. Limerick).

Páirc n. 'A field' MS (e. Limerick). Diminutive, páircín MF Westmeath). Hence páirc mhór, big field, in form parkwore JB (s. Armagh & n. Louth).

Páiste n. A child. In form pastiah. Wm. Carleton, Felim O'Toole's Courtship 2, 189: 'It's not that you ought to be thinkin' of but the dismal poor house we have, wid not the laaugh or schreech of a pastiagh in it from year's end to year's end' (Tyrone). Diminutive, páistín, in forms paisdin, pashteen. In phrase a pháisdín, a term of address or endearment. Seumas MacManus, Bold Blades of Donegal 10: 'That's what ye could, a phaisdin ...'; W. B. Yeats's pashteen finn is páistín fionn, fair-haired little child. Páiste in West Muskerry means a lovechild. Plural, páistí. In Wm. Carleton, Tubber Derg 2,380: mo pháistí bochta, my poor children, as my pastchee boght (Tyrone)

Páit n. A simpleton. 'He was only an oul páit but he made a lot of money in the construction business and was wise enough to keep it' F (Mayo).

Palachán n. A large amount. 'He got a fine palachán of money from the uncle's will' Mas (s. Tipperary).

Paltóg n. In forms polthog, polthogue, palthogue. 1. 'A blow, thump, wallop' OCn (Laois); Lays and Legends of the North of Ireland 8: 'The peats flew through the house, and whack came palthogue on the farmer's back'; Seumas MacManus, Bold Blades of Donegal 2: 'I reached a polthogue that took the fellow between the two eyes and toppled him'; ibid. A Lad of the O'Friels 148: 'after being struck a polthog fit to kill a bull'; PON (n. Dublin). 2. 'An inconveniently large stone' An Cho (w. Mayo). 3. 'A big word, a "jaw-breaker"' ibid. 4. A heavy shower of rain. Jane Barlow, Bogland Studies 19: 'Wid the storms an' the mists an' the

148 *Pánaí*

polthogues o' rain'. 5. Hence, to rain heavily. Barlow, *Irish Idylls* 78: 'Polthoguin' fit to drownd a water-rat' (Connacht). [Cf. English dialect *polt, pelt,* strike *EDD*]

Pánaí n., adj. Also as **pawny**. 1. 'A fat, heavy child; a big lazy chicken' MF (Westmeath). 2. 'Large-sized, especially of rabbits and rats' PLH (n. Roscommon).

Pantar n. Diminutive, **pantairín**. A plump child. A term of affection for same. 'He's mama's little pantairín, he's mama's boyeen bán – a mother's lullaby' JC (w.Cork).

Párdóg n. 'A three-legged pot' PON (n. Dublin).

Parúil n. 'Injunction, prohibition. "She put a parúil on me not to do it' MC (e. Mayo).

Pasáil n., v. As **poss, possauling**. 1. (Act of) trampling; to trample. 'Such a possauling the cows gave the cornfield' JL (w. Cork); 'The cows possed the corn in the high field' MS (e. Limerick). 2. 'To poss: to beat clothes in water to cleanse them' LB (s.w. Dublin); *IG* (Kilkenny). [< English *poss. Piers Plowman* (prologue): ' A cat of a coorte ... pleyde with hem perilouslych and possed hem aboute' Cf. also French *pousser.*]

Pat-shúil n. 'A half-shut eye' *IG* (Kilkenny). [Irish, *pat,* moderately, used in compounds.]

Patachán n. 'A plump little fellow – referring to a child' MC (e. Mayo).

Pataire n. 'A plump baby' R (s. Galway).

Patalachán n. 'A child who has reached the age of walking and mischief' MJD (w. Cork).

Patallóg n. 'A child' *CBD* (n. Kerry); OCn (Laois).

Patalong n. In form **potthalowng**. *EASI* 305: 'An awkward unfortunate mishap, not very serious, but coming just at the wrong time. The Irish is patalong but I do not find it in the dictionaries' (Munster). [Cf. *matalang, batalang,* accident, disaster *Dinn*]

Path n. Also as **pah**. A child's word for a sore or a hurt. 'The word is used even in English, as "the fire would make a pah on you"' *Dinn* (Donegal).

Péac n. 'The sprouting germ of a vegetable' MC (w. Clare); *IG* (Kilkenny).

Peáice n. 'Bread made from yellow meal (maize) and water' *CBD* (n. Kerry).

Pealltóg n. Also in form **polths**. A piece of rough cloth. 'Clothes made from old flour bags or the like in the bad times, they used to call them pealltógs' FF (Cavan); Mac C (Monaghan); 'With all the money she has, you'd think she wouldn't be dressing in old polths' J (s. e. Wexford).

Peasán n. As **pessan**. A paunch. Hence, 'a small, paunchy man' OC (Monaghan)

Peata n. Pet. 'He turned out to be an old woman's peata, useless for anything that resembles work' R (n. Clare); C (Limerick). [The English *pet* is from the Old Irish *peta, al. petta,* a tame or domesticated animal. See *Revue Celtique* XLIV.]

Peataireacht n. Petulant, childish behaviour. Said to a child: 'Stop your peataireacht and eat your dinner' H (n. Clare); MJD (w. Cork).

Peatóg n. 'A ball of butter' NB (w. Limerick).

Peidhleacán n. 1. The butterfly. 2. An effeminate man MJD (w. Cork). 3. A vain woman. 'She don't do a tap of work, not even to make her husband's dinner. All she is is a peidhleacán' R (n. Clare).

Peilic n. 'A basket used for carrying potatoes' Con (Louth).

Péist na gcluas n. 'The earwig' *CBD* (n. Kerry).

Péisteog n. 'A puny person, literally a small worm' MC (e. Mayo).

Piachán n. Also as **peehawn**. 1. Hoarseness. 'Traditionally the piachán is about the third (and last) excuse for not being able to sing, before one *does* eventually sing, at a party' *An Cho* (w. Mayo); 'I still have a peehawn in my voice from the cold I got' J (s. e. Wexford); Mac C (Monaghan). 2. 'An old woman with a "spidery" voice' Kiv (Sligo).

Pianán n. 'A well-fed person' *CBD* (n. Kerry).

Piarda n. 'A big, fat person or animal. You could say, she's the divil of a piarda of a woman' MJD (w. Cork).

Pic adv. In phrase 'We beat them pic': we beat them hollow K (n. Kerry). [*Pic*: very much, exceeding, plentiful *Dinn*.]

Píce n. Pike, spear. As **pheeka** in Wm. Carleton, *Fardorougha the Miser* 380: 'be dha pheeka laght' (bíodh do phíce leat): have your pike with you (Tyrone).

Piceog n. 'An inquisitive person' McK (Leitrim).

Pigín n. Piggin. 'A wooden milking pail' *Pe* (Wexford).

Pílí n. 'A large specimen. It usually refers to a living thing, and, in usage, is reserved for something long and thin – freakish and overgrown ... the word cannot be used without the proper Irish idiom. You don't say "His daughter is a pílí." You say "He has a pílí of a daughter"' *An Cho* (w. Mayo).

Pilibín n. *al.* pilibín míog. Also as **philip-a-week**, **phillibeen**, **pilibeen**. 1. The green plover, lapwing, *Vanellus vanellus* MS (e. Limerick); 'There's not as much fat as her as you'd find on the pilibín míog' JL (w. Cork); 'Scarce now, the philip-a-week' LB (s. w. Co. Dublin); Charles Kickham, *Knocknagow* 247: 'I'm king of Munster when I'm in the bog, and the phillibeens whistling about me' (Tipperary); Brian O'Nolan, *At Swim-Two-Birds* 14: 'the pilibeen'. 2. 'A child's penis' Dee (Waterford); JPL (w. Cork).

Pililiú interj. Also in form **pililoo**. An exclamation of surprise or sorrow. Gerald Griffin, *The Collegians* 33: 'Dan made a pililoo ... over her'.

Pilirín n. 'A small cape in the shape of a heart at the back, the apex reaching to the middle of the back, extending over both shoulders, and buttoned in the front' *IG* (Meath). [Cf. '*Peall*: a veil, covering *Dinn* < English *pall*.]

Pincín n. In form **pinkeen**. 1. The minnow, *Leuciscus phoxinus*. Jane Barlow, *Irish Idylls* 169: 'Fishing for pinkeens along the river' (Connacht). 2. Figuratively, a small, contemptible person. Samuel Lover, *Legends and Stories of Ireland* 1,43: 'I'll turn you into a pinkeen'; Crofton Croker, *Fairy Legends and Traditions* 199: 'What matter what she says, you pinkeen' (Munster); Emily Lawless, *Grania* 2, 89: 'Just a poor little pinkeen of a fellow, not up to my shoulder' (Mayo). [< English *pink* + Irish diminutive suffix, *ín*.]

Píobán n. The windpipe *NMAJ* (s. w. Clare); *CBD* (n. Kerry).

Pioc n. 'An illness of the throat in chickens. The word is onomatopoeic. 'Used of a person: "he would give you the pioc" = he would annoy you. He was piocing and coughing' H (n. Clare); *IG* (Kilkenny).

Píollardaí n. 'A sporting type; inclined to roam' *CBD* (n. Kerry).

Píopán n. 'A spout. Also known as **pípín**' *CBE* 266 (mid-Tipperary).

Píosán n. 'A sickly person' MS (e. Limerick).

Píothán n. 'The perriwinkle' RBB (w. Waterford). In form **paycaun** D (s. e. Wexford); **peekaun** By (s. e. Wexford).

Pis mionnáin 'The wild vetch' MS (e. Limerick).

Pis n. Vulva JL (w. Cork); R (s. Galway); PC (n. Clare).

Piscín n. Also as **pishkeen**. 'A kitten' JL (w. Cork); RBB (w. Waterford); PC (n. Clare). Also in forms **pusheen** J (s. e. Wexford); **pisín** G (n.w. Donegal); **pushkeen** *CBE* 266 (mid-Tipperary).

Pisín interj. 'Said when calling a cat' McK (Leitrim).

Pislín n. A dribble: 'water escaping from the mouth as with an infant' *IG* (Monaghan); *An Cho* (w. Mayo).

Pisreog n. *al.* piseog; pistreog. As **pishogue, pisthrogue, pishrogue, pistra, pishtrug.** 1. Superstitious practices. Wm. Carleton, *Phelim O'Toole's Courtship* 2, 202: 'Clear out, both of ye, till I begin my pishtrogues wid the sick child' (Tyrone); Jane Barlow, *Lisconnel*: 'A result which the neighbours were occasionally disposed to view with mistrust, as probably wrought through the agency of 'some quare old pishtrogues' (Connacht); Patk. Kennedy, *Evenings in the Duffrey*, 357: 'He threw pishrogues on our eyes' (Wexford). 2. Superstitions. Crofton Croker, *Fairy Legends and Traditions*: 'He had no right to bring his auld Irish pishogues to Rome' (s. Munster); 'As pishtrug in Cavan' MJM; 'Only oul' pistras' JB (s. Armagh, n. Louth.).

Piteog n. Also as **pittiogue.** An effeminate man. 'A man who prys into things, in the household or elsewhere, that are supposedly or understood to belong entirely to the sphere of woman' Tr (Donegal); *An Cho* (w. Mayo). Wm. Carleton, *Tubber Derg:* 2, 392: 'pittiogue'. Carleton's gloss: 'Untranslatable – but means a womanly man – a poor effeminate creature' (Tyrone).

Pitire n. 'An extremely mean person' RBB (w. Waterford).

Plab n. 'A piece of mud or mortar; anything soft' *IG* (Kilkenny). Diminutive, **plaibín** – 'A small quantity of mortar' *IG* (Kilkenny).

Plaic n. Also as **pleáic.** 1. The buttocks. 'What some of them hooligans need is an ash plant across the plaic, good and strong, and often' JL (w. Cork). 2. 'Common in nicknames for fleshy people e. g. Feilimidh plaic' Mac C (Monaghan). 3 'A mouthful' *IG* (Kilkenny); PJG (mid-Donegal). 'I've heard pleáic for the buttocks in west Waterford' RBB.

Plaicide n. The top of the head. 'There's very little thatch on his plaicide' MJD (w. Cork).

Plaide n. In form **plaid.** A piece of woolen stuff or a dress of a check or tartan pattern' (Gen. Ulster).

Plámás n. Flattery, cajolery (Gen.).

Plámasach adj. Flattering. 'You'd get plenty of soft talk from him. He's very plámásach' H (n. Clare).

Plámásaí n., adj. Also as **plásaí, plausy.** 'Cajoler, flatterer. "A real old plámásaí"' H (n. Clare); 'It was "Yes, Father, no, Father, wonderful sermon, Father". Oh, but she's some plásaí, that one, I tell you' PON (n. Co. Dublin); MF (Westmeath); 'He's the greatest plausy you'd meet in a day's walk' LB (s. w. Dublin); MW (s. Wexford); 'Cajoling, flattering' PLH (n. Roscommon).

Plancadh n. 'A beating, a trouncing, especially with a stick' *IG* (Kilkenny.)

Plaosc n. 'The skull' *CBD* (n. Kerry).

Plás n. 'A place where turf is spread' *CBE* 34 S (Galway).

Plásóg n. 'A sheltered little field where a man would bring his ewes or his mare to foal in' JL (w. Cork).

Plátóg n. A good smack. 'He gave her a big plátóg of a kiss' *CBD* (n. Kerry).

Pleabhait n. A simpleton. 'What sort of a pleabhait of a fool are you?' JL (w. Cork).

Pleabhtar n. A fool. 'I don't know what kind of a pleabhtar would do the likes of that' RBB (w. Waterford).

Pleib n. 'A foolish person' *CBE* 34 S (Galway).

Pleibide n. A foolish person. 'A senseless person' *CBE* 34 S (Galway). See *leibide.*

Pleibiste n. 'A big, soft person' MS (e. Limerick); PB (s. Tipperary).

Pléicín n. 1. 'A ragged garment' *Pe* (Wexford). 2. 'A bandage' D (Kildare). 3. 'A headshawl' *IG* (Meath); FF (Cavan).

Pleidhce n. Also as **pleidhc**. A simpleton, fool. 'Look at your man, making a pleidhce of himself as usual' PC (n. Clare); 'In form pleidhc' *CBD* (n. Kerry); 'Often used instead of Christian name for such a person (male)' e.g. Pleidhc Murphy' H (n. Clare). See *leidhce*.

Pléiseam n. Foolery, nonsense. In forms **plaisham, plasham**. Stress on second syllable. 1. A fool. Patrick MacGill, *Glenmornan* 35: 'She's a plaisham, God help her' (Donegal). 2. Used imprecatively: Peadar O'Donnell, *Islanders* 133: 'Plasham on you' (Donegal). [Cf. Tudor *play sham*.]

Pleispín n. Also as **pleesbeen**. 'A pleispín is a small person' NB (w. Limerick); George Fitzmaurice, *The Pie-Dish* (Kerry): 'Don't be giving me talk, you little pleesbeen ...'

Pleist n. A thump, a flop. 'He got one terrible pleist when he fell off the roof' G (s. Kilkenny); NB (w. Limerick).

Plimp n. 'A sudden fall, a crash. "He came off the horse of a plimp"' R (s. Galway).

Plispín n. A worthless person, a ne'er-do-well. 'You don't tell me he gave that plispín a job?' G (s. Kilkenny); *Sguab* (Cork); NB (w. Limerick).See *pleispín*.

Plobaire n. 1. 'A person who talks without making much sense, or a person who talks indistinctly' H (n. Clare). 2. 'A child with plump cheeks who cries easily' H (n. Clare); *CBD* (Kerry). 3. 'A man with a big paunch' PB (s. Tipperary). See *plobar*.

Plobaire n. As **plob**. 'One who speaks indistinctly, as a soft, or foolish person might' H (n. Clare); Hence **plabbery**, indistinct 'soft' talk. James Joyce, *Ulysses* 664: '... and make a declaration with his plabbery kind of manner to her like he did to me ...'

Plobán n. 'A small hole – such as the track of a beast's hoof – filled with water' *IG* (Monaghan).

Plobar n. In form **plubber**. Incoherent, excessive talking. Hence **to plubber**. Hence **plubbering**. Dermot O'Byrne, *Children of the Hills* 41: 'Ye have me heart-scalded altogether with your plubbering of fairies' (Donegal). See *plobaire*.

Plodán n. 'A pool of standing water' *IG* (Meath; n. Dublin).

Plóid n. Torture. An imprecation. Peadar O'Donnell, *Islanders* 132: 'Ploid on you, Manus, but yer clean gone' (Donegal).

Plubóg n. A plump person. 'They tell me that them Arabs like fine plubógs of women' JL (w. Cork).

Pluc n. Also in form **pluck**. The cheek. Look at the pluc of him (in reference to a well-fed, fat-cheeked child' MF (Westmeath); McK (Leitrim); *Pe* (Wexford); *CBD* (n. Kerry); James Joyce, *Ulysses* 344: 'Cissy Caffrey bent over him to tease his fat little plucks and the dainty dimple on his chin.'

Plucamas n. Mumps. 'She has the plucamas' NB (w. Limerick); MC (w. Clare); JL (w. Cork); PB (s. Tipperary).

Plúch v. As **plook**. To throng, fill completely. Hence **plookin**. 'The bags are plookin full' MH (Meath).

Plúchadh n. (Act of) choking. Hence **plughering**: 'coughing in a choking manner' Mac C (Monaghan).

Pludach n. 'Mud, slush' *Pe* (Wexford); LB (s. w. Dublin).

Plúrach n. '(Of potatoes) Floury' *GC* (Laois).

Plúróg n. 1. 'A young, soft, beautiful woman' JPL (w. Cork). 2. 'A floury potato' RBB (Waterford).

Poc n. In form **puck**. 1. 'A stroke in the game of hurling.' Hence **puck** in ice-hockey. 2. A blow with the fist. 'A puck in the gob would quieten him' Smy (n. Clare). Hence **puckers**, boxers in James Joyce, *Ulysses* 250: 'He stood looking in at the two puckers stripped to their pelts ...' 3. Diminutive, **poicín**, a football, as **puckeen**

in Patk. Kennedy, *Legendary Fictions of the Irish Celts* 155: '... three old gentlemen began to kick a puckeen' (Wexford). **4.** 'A small sack, bag or basket, when full. "You'd think it was going to America she was going she had so many pucks and parcels"' LB (s.w. Dublin). Diminutive, pocán, also as puckawn. Phrase 'the shaking of the pocán' – the last child in a family: translation of *craitheadh an phocáin* MG (n.w. Donegal). **5.** A male goat, puck goat. Jonathan Swift, *A Dialogue in Hybernian Stile:* '... our cows will never keep a drop of milk without a puckawn' (Gen.). **6.** 'A proud, haughty, well-fed fellow' *IG* (Monaghan); 'A well-fed specimen. An over-fed pup could be called a pocán (and would, if he had also misbehaved by taking milady's nylons for a game of snakes and ladders). So also could a fat little watch-and-chain man (and probably would if he had terminated a football game in his field, or refused a subscription for a popular cause' *An Cho* (w. Mayo). **7.** 'A pocán is a hinge' NB (w. Limerick).

Podhailis n. 'A filthy woman. A woman who was washed when she was born but not since. Have I ever heard a man called a podhailis? No, airiú' JL (w. Cork).

Póg n. Also in forms **poge, pogue, poage.** A kiss. (Gen.). Anon., *Purgatorium Hibernicum:* 'An gave the one litle poge for old acquaintance'; *Lays and Legends of the North of Ireland* 9: 'The Masons were well mulvathed with many a pogue from the cruiskeen lawn'; *Poole* (s. e. Wexford): 'Each bye gae a poage.'

Poicéad n. 'A dam across a stream' *CBD* (n. Kerry).

Póicín n. 'A tiny house, without much light' NB (w. Limerick); *CBD* (n. Kerry).

Póirín n. **1.** 'A small potato' *An Cho* (w. Mayo); *EASI* 304: 'Poreens: Very small potatoes – mere crachauns – any small things such as marbles etc. As porrans in Ulster.' As **póitín** MF (Westmeath). **2.** As **porrian** – 'A small seed potato' JB (s. Armagh & n. Louth). As **poriceen** Mac C (Monaghan). **3.** As **porran:** 'A puny person. "He's a wee porran of a man"' O'K (Tyrone).

Póirse n. 'A narrow road or lane going to a farmhouse' JM (w. Cork); 'A narrow dirt road' MC (e. Mayo).

Póirseáil n. (Act of) rummaging, searching, groping. 'What póirseáil have you back there?' JL (w. Cork). Hence **póirseáling.** 'She spends the day póirseáling in the hay looking for eggs' JL (w. Cork); BOD (s. w. Cork).

Poirtleog n. 'An armful of rushes' Con (Louth).

Poitín n. Also in forms **poteen, potheen, potsheen, pukeen. 1.** Illicit whiskey. J. M. Synge, *The Playboy of the Western World* 84: 'The peelers is fearing him, and if you'd that lad in the house there isn't one of them would come smelling around if the dogs itself were lapping poteen from the dungpit in the yard'; Jane Barlow, *Irish Idylls* 107: 'He employed her in conveying jars of potheen from a certain wholly illicit still' (Connacht); Jonah Barrington, *Personal Sketches:* 'Heigh for the potsheen, and contraband' (Leinster). In compound **potsheen-twang.** A lie. Jonah Barrington, ibid.: 'Nature had not given him enough of what they call the 'potsheen-twang'; *Patterson* (Antrim): 'A double potsheen twang, a hell of a lie'. **2.** As **pukeen.** 'A small pot. Applied humourously to a little plump child' MF (Westmeath).

Poll dóite n. phr. Literally, burnt hole. 'A useless person' *CBE* 104 (Leitrim).

Pollán n. 'A hole' McK (Leitrim).

Pollóg n. 'A store of money' PB (s. Tipperary); DOH (e. Limerick).

Pór n. 'The seed of the dock plant' *IG* (Cavan); Con (Meath).

Portán n. Also as **partaun. 1.** 'Wet sod; grassy top of turf bank' *IG* (Cavan). **2.** The crab. John Boyce, *Mary Lee or The Yank in Ireland* 20: 'Bade him get up and not lie there like a partaun' (Donegal).

Postachán n. Also as **pustaghaun, pustogue. 1.** 'A place-hunter' C (Limerick). **2.** *EASI* 309: 'A pustaghaun: a puffed-up, conceited fellow. The corresponding word applied to a girl is pusthoge' (Wexford).

Potach n. 'Surly-looking; e. g. she has a potach head on her' MF (Westmeath).

Potaimín n. Perspiration on the forehead. 'It would rise potaimín on you' CBD (n. Kerry).

Pótaire n. 'A drunkard' NB (w. Limerick).

Potharnáil n. 'A persistent cough' IG (Kilkenny).

Potharnálaí n. 'A person who has a persistent cough' IG (Kilkenny).

Prabás n. 'A fat person. A term of contempt' McK (Leitrim).

Prabhait n. al. **prabhtún**. Pulp. 'The spuds are in prabhait by you' JL (w. Cork); 'He made prabhtún of it' BMacM (Kerry); CBD (n. Kerry).

Prácás n. Also in form **praughas**. 1. 'A disorderly, dirty heap of things, a mess; also a reviling epithet applied to a person' H (n. Clare). 2. 'Inferior corn' G (n.w. Donegal). 3. 'A praughas is a stew. Also a meal the materials for which are hurriedly got together' BASJ (Cavan, Leitrim).

Práib n. Also as **prawb**. Diminutive, **prabeen, prawpeen**. 1. Sticky mud. "The place is in prawb" CBE 266 (mid-Tipperary). 2. 'A paste of any kind; a mess of oatmeal; fresh cow dung' G (n.w. Donegal); Wm. Carleton, *Phelim O'Toole's Courtship* 2, 200: 'You've thramped upon Dunroe's hungry grass and only for somethin' it's a prabeen you'd be afore you'd see home'; Carleton, *The Brothers*, 155: 'She hadn't ris from the table when she was in a prabeen' (Tyrone); 'The field around the stream is in prawpeen from the cows' PD (s. Carlow). 3. Hence, **prawbin**, making dirty; **práibeálaí**, as **prawbawly**, a person who dirties things, or makes a mess. Stop, you prawbawly, and don't be prawbin the bread with your dirty fingers: CBE 266 (mid-Tipperary).

Práicín n. As **prawkeen**. EASI 307: 'Raw oatmeal and milk' (quoting P. J. McCall, South Leinster).

Práinn n. Urgent need. Hence **práinneach**, as **praunyuk**. 'I'm praunyuk for a drink means, I'm in urgent need of one' D (s. e. Wexford).

Práisc n. al. **práis, prawsh**. 'Dirt, filth. "The place is in práisc by ye"' JL (w. Cork); 'Práis, or prawsh, a mess' TOM (s. Tipperary).

Práiscín n. Also in forms **praskeen, prauskeen, bráiscín, brasken**. 'An apron' PC (n. Clare), OCn (Laois).; 'Práiscín is an apron made from a bag, and used when sowing potatoes' CBE 47 S (Galway); Mrs S. C. Hall, *Tales of Irish Life and Character* 161: ' She wiped the aforesaid table with the corner of her praskeen ...' (s. Leinster); William Carleton, *The Poor Scholar* 2, 276: '... lave soap and a prashkeen afore you go to milk, till I bathe the dacent boy's feet' (Tyrone); Michael Banim, *The Croppy* 2, 268: '... throw off the prauskeen'. Glossed as 'rough apron' (Kilkenny). 'Ten shillings a quarter, a pair of brogues and a praskeen was the common wage of a farmer's girl' H (n. Donegal); MF (Westmeath); IG (Cavan). al. **bráiscín** IG (Monaghan). In form **braskan** JB (s. Armagh & n. Louth).

Praiseach bhuí n. Also in form **presaugh**. Charlock, *Sinapis arvensis*. William Carleton, *Val McClutchy* 18: 'I'll forgive till the fulsome presaugh grows on his hearth' (Tyrone).

Praiseach n. 1. 'Thin porridge, gruel' MJD (w. Cork); JS (e. Kerry) 2. Used in phrase 'to make praiseach of something' = to make a mess of it (Gen. Munster).

Praisteal n. 'Potatoes cooked under smouldering turf fire' MG (n.w. Donegal).

Pramsa n. 'Roasted wheat, ate with butter years ago' JL (w. Cork).

Práp n. Diminutive, **práipín**. A mess. 'The potatoes are over-cooked; they are in práp' MS (e. Limerick); IG (Kilkenny); 'He made práipín of the stew' AOL (mid-Waterford).

Práta n. Potato. In forms **pratie; praita** Pe (Wexford); **pratey, preties, praties** in James Joyce, *Finnegans Wake* 515, 31, 56;

paytee J (s. e. Wexford); Mrs S. C. Hall, *Tales of Irish Life and Character* 17: 'Mother, hould your whisht and mind the paytees' (s. Leinster).

Preab n. Also as **prab**. 1. A jump, a start. 'That fair knocked a prab out of you' J (s. e. Wexford). 2. 'A spadeful of earth. "He dug a preab"' MC (e. Mayo).

Préacán n. 'A gap in a field' NB (w. Limerick).

Préachán n. Also in form **praychaun**. A crow, rook. 1. Figuratively, a stingy person. "A hungry praychaun of a fellow" *CBE* 266 (mid-Tipperary). 2. Figuratively, 'a person with a bad singing voice' PD (s. Carlow).

Preib n. 'The foot-rest on a spade' MF (Westmeath).

Preiceall n. Also as **preckal**. 1. 'A double chin' *CBE* 266 (mid-Tipperary). 2. 'The gills of a cock' JPL (w. Cork); RBB (mid-Waterford). 3. 'A discontented appearance: "He has a preckal on him all day"' *CBE* 266 (mid-Tipperary). See *sprochall*. [< Latin *spiraculum*.]

Preicleachán n. As **precklachaun**. 'A sour, discontented person' *CBE* 266 (mid-Tipperary).

Preith interj. 'A call to a horse to entice him to come to you' F (Mayo).

Prioca n. 'A short stick' FF (Monaghan).

Príompa n. Rump. 'Nice long legs and a fine príompa. I wouldn't say no to her at all' JL (w. Cork).

Priompallán n. 1. The dung beetle. 'A beetle that flies; a man who acts socially beyond his station, flies too high and is destined to fall' H (n. Clare); RBB (Waterford). 2. 'The bumble bee' *IG* (Kilkenny).

Priosla n. 'Drivel at the mouth or nose' RBB (s. Kilkenny).

Prioslaí n. Also as **prisslee**. 1. 'A dribbler; an ugly, dirty person' *CBD* (n. Kerry). 2. Dribbles. 'His chin and vest were covered with prisslees' *CBE* 266 (mid-Tipperary). 3. 'Also the name used around here for the smaller fibres of the potato root. "The prisslees are gone across the furrows and you'll injure the praties if you earth them"' *CBE* 266 (mid-Tipperary).

Prioslálaí n. As **prisslawlee**. 'A dribbler' *CBE* 266 (mid-Tipperary).

Prisbíní n. In form **prisbeens**. 'Small turnips' G (s. Kilkenny).

Pritil n. 'The iron punch with which the blacksmith makes the holes in the shoes' *IG* (Monaghan); FF (Cavan).

Proc n. *al.* **procaire**. 'A worn spade' NB (w. Limerick).

Prochaidh n. 'A dug-out from which people procure coal' *CBE* 104 (Leitrim).

Prochóg n. 1. 'A secret place, in which things were stored. Things were hidden there, such as eggs, which the farmer's wife sold for pin-money' Kiv (Sligo). 2. 'A feast of eggs eaten out in the open on Easter Sunday.' So named from the search for these hidden eggs by children prior to the feast. 3. 'A hovel' JL (w. Cork). 4. 'A handsel of money. "They got a fine prochóg of money out of the accident"' MC (e. Mayo).

Progaí interj. 'Name used in calling a cow. Repeated' MF (Westmeath).

Pronnóg n. A fragment. 'He made pronnógs of the car against the ditch' Dee (w. Waterford).

Pruch n. 'A little delapidated house. 'Why don't you knock down that little pruch of a byre and build a proper one?' O'K (Tyrone); MF (Westmeath).

Prúisneog n. 'A surly-looking fellow who would hardly salute you' NB (w. Limerick).

Prúntach n. 'A fat person; but that's only half the story. The prúntach is so fat and bulky that she (note! *–she*) deserves a page to herself ... the very sound of the word suggests excess avoirdupois impinging (by the law of gravity) upon a soft or delicate mass of matter. Add to this the adhesion of the messy mass to folds upon folds of heavy woolen or serge material, and here you have the quintessence of prúntach-hood indeed ...You are driving to town and on the rear seat of the car you have left the special apple-pie which your mother sends to her daughter-in-law. Thomas's wife wants a lift; she sits in, says "Thanks be to God" and – then you remember! The prúntach!' *An Cho* (w. Mayo). [Cf. *Prútach*: anything big *Dinn*]

Pú pá n. A mess, a faux pas. 'He made a right pú pá of that job' NB (w. Limerick).

Púca n. Also in forms **pooka, phooka**. Hobgoblin, puck. Seumus MacManus, *Bold Blades of Donegal* 119: 'The púca is the one only evil spirit to be met with in Ireland. He is of a shadowy, dark, indefinite form, set low as if he went on all fours .... Always it is on his back ... that he tries to carry off his unfortunate victim. And woe to him that takes the púca's ride'; *Lays and Legends of the North of Ireland* 22: 'On went the phooka with nivir a halt, Through bog an' rough heather an' on by Lough Salt'; Crofton Croker, *Fairy Legends and Traditions* 139: 'The peasantry usually ascribe accidental falls to the agency of the Phooka' (Munster); Seumas MacManus, *The Bend in the Road*, intro. viii: '... in whose valleys and woods all sorts of goblins, pookas and even the terrible each uisge, (water horse) are all making their last stand against the vain, unholy, scepticism of the age' (Donegal); James Joyce, *Finnegans Wake* 102: '... with pawns, prelates and pookas ...' (Gen.). Hence **Phooka Rey** The head, or king of the fairies, in W. H. Floredice, *Memories of a Month among the Mere Irish* 97: 'The Head of the Fairies in Rooskey – the Phooka Rey – brought an old goat to the fair.' [*rey* < *rí*, king.] 3. 'A snail' JB (s. Armagh & n. Louth).

Púcadán n. 'A scarecrow' ER (Louth).

Púcaí n. 'Black clouds. "I wouldn't go far to-day without a raincoat. Look at the púcaí"' RBB (w. Waterford).

Púcán n. Also as **pookawn, pookhaun**. A fishing smack; an open boat with mainsail and jib DC (Galway); Jane Barlow, *Kerrigan's Quality* 110: 'I do be tellin' him

'tis as good as biddin' the say wather rise up and do disthruction on him to go proddin' an oar into it out of any such quare little pookawn'; ibid. *Strangers at Lisconnel* 170: 'Wid the coffin just skimmin' and swimmin' away down the sthrame ahead of them, as aisy and plisant as if it was a bit of a pookawn' (Ulster); Emily Lawless, *Grania* 2, 103: 'There is the bay, very near indeed, with, perhaps, a pookhaun or a hooker upon it' (Mayo).

Púcóg n. 'A covering for the eyes of thieving animals' MF (Westmeath). See *púicín*.

Púdarlach n. 'A spoiled child' RBB (w. Waterford).

Púicín n. 'A blindfold; a tin shade put over a thieving cow's eyes' NB (w. Limerick). Hence **pookey-bonnet**: 'A 'coal-scuttle bonnet, almost hiding the face. Worn by a few old women until 1900 or later' LB (s.w. Dublin). See *púcóg*.

Puililiú interj. As **whillalyoo, fuililallo, who-la-loo, puililillew, pillilew, philliloo, phillelew**. Exclamation of surprise or feigned surprise. 'Puililiú' GC (Laois). As 'fuililallo' in Richard Head, *Hic et Ubique*. As 'who-la-loo' in John Michelburne, *Ireland Preserved*. As 'puililillew' in Anon., *A Dialogue between Teigue and Dermot*. In form 'pillilew' in Somerville and Ross, *Oh Love!, Oh Fire!* 164. Samuel Lover, *Legends and Stories of Ireland* 1, 189: 'There was no use in life in settin' up a phillelew'; Crofton Croker, *Fairy Legends and Traditions* 26: 'He'd snap at and bite and there was the philliloo' (Munster).

Púirín n. 'A hole in the wall for sheep' CBE 34 S (Galway); 'A hole in the henhouse wall. "Close the púirín or the fox may get in"' MC (e. Mayo).

Puirtleog n. 'A bunch of rushes' CBE 104 (Leitrim); FF (Cavan).

Puisín n. Also as **pusheen**. 1. Pussy-cat, kitten. George Fitzmaurice, *The King of the Barna Men*: '... 'tisn't himself is up in the room at all, but the pusheen' (Kerry). 2. 'A baby rabbit. "The little puisíns were out eating"' OCn (Laois).

Púiste n. 'A fat person' *IG* (Kilkenny).

Puiteach n. Boggy ground, mud, mire. 'The place is in a puiteach' MF (Westmeath); SF (mid-Wexford); 'Making a mess of anything can be called making puiteach of it' *An Cho* (w. Mayo).

Punann n. 1. 'A sheaf' JL (w. Cork). 2. A shapely woman. 'Oh my God, look at that for a punann' – a farmer in a Cappoquin, Co. Waterford, public house, decribing Marilyn Monroe. Overheard by editor.

Puncán n. 'A hummock' MF (Westmeath).

Puntam n. 'A busy little womaneen' JL (w. Cork). [< English *bantam*]

Puntán n. A sum of money. 'He had a nice little puntán of money' *CBD* (n. Kerry).

Púr n. A stream of smoke. 'The two Yanks were there, one on each hob; and the next thing the dog chased the cat across the hearth, and knocked the tea-pot into the fire, and up goes the púr of smoke ... the Yanks were destroyed' *An Cho* (w. Mayo).

Púróg n. 'A small stone' RBB (w. Waterford); MJD (w. Cork).

Pus n. Also in form **puss**. 1. The mouth. 'I said it up to his pus' G (s. Kilkenny). 2. A sulky expression, pout. Seumus MacManus, *In Chimney Corners* 172: 'Away the master goes with his mouth in a puss' (Donegal). Hence **pussing**, sulking, crying (Gen.); **pusachán**, also in form **pustakawn**: 'A baby who cries incessantly' OCn (Laois); H (n. Clare); LB (s. w. Dublin). **Puss-music**, jigging or lilting. Eric Cross, *The Tailor and Ansty* 44: 'Sometimes there was not even fiddle and flute. Then they would dance to puss-music, music made by the mouth alone,

without any instrument'. **Pus mhadadh**, literally, mouth of a dog. 'A person with a receding chin' H (n. Clare). **Pussful** in James Joyce, *Ulysses* 200: '... the way we do have our tongues out a yard long like the droughty clerics do be fainting for a pussful'.

Pusachán n. 'A special kind of currant bun which was always associated with fair days and pattern days in Louisburgh. It was really a miniature loaf-of the same texture, shape and, presumably recipe – and was sold at the unbelievably low price of one penny. The perfect reward for a child who did an errand was "a penny for a pusachán"' *An Cho* (w. Mayo).

Puslaide n. 'A sore on the lip' *IG* (Kilkenny); 'A cold sore' PD (s. Carlow)

Pústóg n. 'An untidy woman' NB (w. Limerick).

Putachán n. 'A fat and lazy person' *CBE* 34 S (Galway).

Putalóg n. 'A plump woman' RBB (w. Waterford). [*Díolaim Dhéiseach* has *putalóg*: a fat chicken.]

Puth n. As **pwih**. 'A forced breath when an animal is ill or too full' Mac C (Monaghan).

Puthamálaí n. As **puhamawlee**. 'A broken-winded, puffing person: "He's gone in a puhamawlee"' *CBE* 266 (mid-Tipperary).

Puthlachán n. In form **puhlachaun**. 'A well-rounded little girl' *CBE* 266 (mid-Tipperary).

Putóg n. 1. 'A pudding' *CBE* 34 S (Galway). 2. 'A row-lock' Del (Antrim). Plural **putóga**. 'Guts, intestines' NB (w. Limerick).

R

Rab n. 'A pet animal, an animal you'd rear without its mother. Most of the children going nowadays would let a rab die of hunger before they'd look after it' JL (w. Cork). [In *Cnósach Focal o Bhaile Bhúirne*, 'rab' is glossed as a pet lamb or kid; a pet banbh, however, is 'peata.' JL did not make this distinction.]

Rábach adj. Generous, good-natured. 'A rábach poor devil' PB (s. Tipperary).

Rábaire n. 'A strong, active person, tall or small' NB (w. Limerick).

Rabh n. 'A saw' MJD (w. Cork).

Rabhcán n. Also as rookaun. 1. 'A simple song; a song made up about some local happening or about some local person, or the like' JPL (w. Cork). 2. *EASI* 315: 'Rookaun: Great noisy merriment. Also a drinking bout' (Limerick).

Rabhdlamán n. In form rowdlamaun. An irresponsible oaf. 'He's some rowdlamaun. He took the engine apart and now he can't put it together again' Dee (w. Waterford).

Rabhlamán n. A small, plump person. 'A little barrel of a woman like myself' JC (w. Cork).

Rablach n. 1. 'A rabble. Thon rablach caused all the trouble at the match' PJG (mid-Donegal). 2. 'A throng of people, not necessarily a rabble' H (n. Donegal). See *brablach*.

Rabúnaí n. 'A tall athletic man' *IG* (Kilkenny).

Rác v. As rawk. To steal. 'Many's the day I spent with him rawking apples' NB (w. Limerick).

Racadán n. 'A hard man; a brawler' Mac C (Monaghan).

Rácálaí n. 'A restless person' MS (e. Limerick).

Racán n. Uproar, brawl, riot. In form rackhan in Wm. Carleton, *The Party Fight and Funeral* 1, 182 (Tyrone).

Racht n. In form rockt. 'A violent fit or outburst. "He got a rockt of coughing"' *CBE* 266 (mid-Tipperary).

Radaire n. As roddera. 1. 'A fun-maker' *CBE* 266 (mid-Tipperary). 2. 'A blow struck to send a moving hurling ball flying faster' DOC (Limerick).

Radalach n. 1. 'Mud, slime' RBB (n. Waterford). 2. 'A lanky, untidy person' RBB (n. Waterford); PC (n. Clare). 3. 'Useless matter. "What hay we have is only radalach"' *CBE* 266 (mid-Tipperary).

Rae n. 'A little rae of a woman' PD (Carlow). [Cf. *réad:* something small *Dinn.*]

Raga n. 'A harmless kind of playboy or rake; a man who harms nobody but himself' RBB (w. Waterford).

Ragaire n. 'A young person who says up late' *IG* (Meath).

Ragaireacht n. '(Act of) staying up late' *IG* (Meath).

Ragarnáil n. 'Noise, especially boisterous talk' NB (w. Limerick).

Ragarnálaí n. 'A noisy person who usually talks nonsense' NB (w. Limerick).

Ráibéis n. As rawbaysh. 'A fistful of hay' MW (s. Wexford).

Raic n. 1. 'A quarrel, trouble' PC (n. Clare). 2. 'Noise in a crowd' H (n. Clare).

Raideog n. Bog myrtle, *Myrica gale*: PJG (mid-Donegal).

Raidhse n. A sufficiency. 'Have you enough?' 'Yes. thanks; raidhse' MS (e. Limerick); MJD (w. Cork). See *reimhirse*.

Ráig n. 1. "A fit of temper: "The ráig of the drink was on him"' *CBE* 266 (mid-Tipperary); 'A sudden outbreak, fierce while it lasts, but with the latent hope that it will soon finish. We think especially of two kinds – a ráig or temper and a ráig of rain' *An Cho* (w. Mayo). 2. 'Sport; a spree' *IG* (Kilkenny); 'They went off on a right ráig after the game' AOL (mid. Waterford).

Raillimín n. Also **ralameen**. A weakling. 'A thin, puny raillimín of an animal' MC (e. Mayo); 'How much are you looking for the ralameen of a calf?' R (s. Galway)

Railliúnach n. In form **rallianach**. A loutish fellow. Seumus MacManus, *Bold Blades of Donegal*, 24: 'Pat's a rallianach of a fellow ... too hasty in temper.'

Ráiméis n. Also in forms **rámás, rámáis, rhaumaush**. Nonsensical talk. 'That priest talks a lot of oul' ráiméis' JL (w. Cork); James Joyce, *Ulysses* 324: 'Raimeis, says the citizen'; 'You never hear anything sensible from him, only rámás' S (s. e. Wexford); 'That's all rámáis' PW (s. e. Wexford); Michael Banim, *The Croppy* 3, 79: '... when you and I forged the rhaumaush of a story about my gettin' her from the fairies...' (Kilkenny). Hence **ramshin'**. Mrs S. C. Hall, *The Maid of Bannow*: 'He was ramshin' with the fever, poor sowl' (s. Wexford).

Raingealtach n. 'A tall, ungainly person. A raingealtach can be male or female' *An Cho* (w. Mayo).

Raispín n. 1. 'A miser' MS (e. Limerick); DOC (Limerick). 2. 'A troublemaker' RBB (s. Kilkenny). 3. 'A wizened person' *CBD* (n. Kerry). 4. 'A young brat' JL (w. Cork).

Ráistín n. As **raushteen**. 1. 'A small, square-mouthed shovel, used for chopping boiled turnips etc. for pigs or cattle' *CBE* 266 (mid-Tipperary); 'an old worn-out shovel' MS (e. Limerick). 2. 'Anything that has outlived its usefulness' PB (s. Tipperary).

Ráithín n. Also as **raaheen**. 1. 'A swathe of new-mown hay' MC (w. Clare); *CBD* (n. Kerry). 2. 'A little wall of sods of turf built up to dry' *CBE* 266 (mid-Tipperary). 3. 'A fairy fort: that's a raaheen' JV (e. Wicklow).

Raithneach n. Also in forms **ringagh, raanyuck**. 1. Ferns, bracken JL (w. Cork); NB (w. Limerick); LOS (Clare); 'Bracken we call ringagh' OC (Monaghan). 2. A trampled, bruised mass. 'The tinkers' horses got into the cornfield and made raithneach of it' JL (w. Cork); 'The cattle made raanyuck of the cornfield' D (s. e. Wexford).

Ramaire n. 'A tall, long-legged fellow' *IG* (Kilkenny).

Ramallae n. 1. 'Slime on fish' RBB (w. Waterford). 2. **Ramallae seilide**, in form **ramallae shelliky**: 'the slime left by a snail' MW (s. Wexford).

Ramsach n. Also as **romsagh**. 'A row, bustle, tumult. "There was some ramsach at the meeting last night"' SOG (s. Tipperary); 'They came there for the romsagh, not to dance. That was plain' PD (s. Carlow).

Ramsáil n. (Act of) searching. 'What ramsáil have you? You won't find the bridle under the stairs' JL (w. Cork).

Ránaí n. Also in forms **ráinne, rawnyeh, rawny**. 1. 'A thin, lank person or animal' OC (Monaghan); 'A little rawnyeh of a cat' Kiv (Sligo); 'Ráinne: a thin, gaunt beast' MF (Westmeath); As 'rawnyeh' LB (s.w. Dublin); James Joyce, *Finnegans Wake* 437: 'rawny'. 2. 'Ránaí: an imbecile' *CBE* 104 (Leitrim).

Rangás n. Also in form **roungaws**. 1. High jinks, fun. 'For a man well past his prime, he's a divil for the rangás' JM (w. Cork). 2. 'Straying around after being intoxicated, or after some upset. "He's on the roungaws for the past week after all the liquor he drank"' *CBE* 266 (mid-Tipperary).

Rann n. 1. A quatrain, verse or stanza. Wm. Carleton, *Phelim O'Toole's Courtship* 2,194: '... let me go on wid me rann ...' (Tyrone); Seumus MacManus, *Bold Blades of Donegal*, 202: 'The Divil posed him with old pagan ranns, tryin' for to trip him'; James Joyce, *Ulysses* 310: '... it bears a striking resemblance ... to the ranns of ancient Celtic bards.' 2. An angry speech. 'He put a rann out of him' *IG* (Kilkenny).

Raonán n. Also as **raynaun**, *al.* **raoinín**, in form **rayneen**. 'A mark made with a spade or plough in a tillage field, as a guide for sowing a row of cabbage, etc., straight' *IG* (Kilkenny); 'A rayneen is a little drill or channel in the ground for root, onion or cabbage seed' *CBE* 266 (mid-Tipperary).

Rapla húta n. Bustle, commotion. 'Man dear, there was rapla húta at the election meeting' G (n.w. Donegal).

Rásaí n. A rambling woman, a gypsy. In forms **rossie**, **raucie**. 'A rossie is a girl with a certain reputation, not a prostitute, but an enthusiastic amateur' SS (Dublin city); James Joyce, *Ulysses* 363: 'If they could run like rossies she could sit ...' Also in *Finnegans Wake* 285; 'A raucie is a gad-about girl' PON (n. Dublin).

Rásta n. 'A woman who has nothing better to do than go from house to house telling stories about the neighbours' JC (w. Cork).

Rata bata n. 'Great fuss or noise' *IG* (Kilkenny).

Rata n. 1. 'A young hare. You'd hear "as mad as a rata"' JL (w. Cork). 2. 'An unruly child' DOC (Limerick).

Ráth n. Also in form **rath**. Earthen ring-fort, home of the fairies (Gen.); Seumas MacManus, *The Bend of the Road*, intro. viii: 'Sportive, mortal-loving fairies ... hold midnight dances on green raths' (Donegal).

Rath n. Luck *IG* (Kilkenny); 'There's no rath on the spuds this year, with the wet Spring' JC (w. Cork).

Rathalach n. 1. 'A big brawny person – usually fat' NB (w. Limerick). 2. 'Tangled straw, thread, etc' *IG* (Kilkenny).

Ré n. Also as **ray**. 1. 'A stretch of moorland' JC (w. Cork). 2. 'A piece of level ground. "And they kept the flag floating in Tom Daniel's ray"' *The Terrors:* a Clare hurling song Smy (n. Clare). 2. In tillage, a row. 'I have heard ray commonly in the English of south Kilkenny as a unit of measurement of crops, e.g. a ray of potatoes' RBB; 'A term used for a row of loads of dung in the garden or tillage field. "Leave eleven drills to the ray", or "Leave ten yards between every load in the ray"' *CBE* 266 (mid-Tipperary).

Reachaire n. *al.* **reathaire**. In form **rahery**. A small pony. Wm. Carleton, *Shane Fadh's Wedding* 2, 60: '... some on horses, some on mules, others on raheries and asses.' Carleton's gloss: 'a small, shaggy pony, so called from being found in great numbers on the Island of that name' (Rathlin, off the coast of Antrim); 'A Cushendall pony' *Dinn*.

Reathach n. 'A wild, half-civilized person' NB (w. Limerick).

Réice n. 'A rake, a rover, a wild divil' JL (w. Cork); RBB (w. Waterford).

Reimhirse n., adj. 1. Plenty. 'We had a great reimhirse after killing the pig' *CBD* (n. Kerry). 2. A rarity. 'Fresh meat was a great reimhirse to us' ibid. 3. Generous. 'She was a reimhirse woman' ibid. Same word as *raidhse* above.

Réiteach n. As **raytshuch**, **raythers**. 1. 'Position of ease at work; e.g. pull out the churn to the middle of the floor where you'll be in raytshuch, i.e. where you can work with greater ease' MF (Westmeath). 2. Solution, settlement. Hence phrase **making raythers**, effecting a settlement *BASJ* (Cavan).

Réiteog n. 'A "pull through", to clean a gun' H (n. Clare). See *réiteoir*.

Réiteoir n. 1. 'Conciliator, peacemaker' *BASJ* (Cavan). 2. 'A cleaner for a pipe' MS (e. Limerick); *CBE* 98 (Kilkenny); *CBD* (n. Kerry).

Réitigh v. Arrange, put in order. In translated form, **ready**. M.J. Mulloy, *The King of Friday's Men* 43: ' Ready the bed' 'Ready the table, let ye' JC (w. Cork).

Reo n. 'A frosty fog' *IG* (Kilkenny).

Reo v. As **row**. To freeze. 'The east wind would row the arse off you' PD (s. Carlow).

Rí-rá n. Also in forms **ree-raw, reeraw**. 1. Hubbub, uproar. 'Such rí-rá you never saw, everyone talking at once, and the chairman unable to control things' Smy (n. Clare); James Joyce, *Finnegans Wake* 111: 'ree-raw' (Gen.). 2. In phrase **in** or **on the ree raw**: 'drunk and disorderly' PJG (mid-Donegal). Often coupled with **ruaille-buaille**, hubbub, tumult. As **ree raw and roola boola** PD (s. Carlow).

Rí-rá-reaidilí n. 'Nonsensical talk' JJH (w. Waterford).

Riabh n. A stripe. Hence **rife**. *EASI* 315: 'A scythe sharpener, a narrow piece of board punctured all over and covered with grease on which fine sand is sprinkled. Used before the present emery sharpener was known' (Carlow)

Riabhach n., adj. Brindled. 'Did you milk the riabhach? JC (w. Cork); 'A riabhach cow' NB (w. Limerick); *CBD* (n. Kerry). In phrase **riabhach days** MP (mid Tipperary): 'The days of the brindled cow, i.e., the closing days of March or the opening days of April ... the legend is that the brindled cow complained at the dawn of April of the harshness of March, whereupon March borrowed a few days from April, and these were so wet and stormy that the brindled cow was drowned; hence March has a day more than April, and the borrowed days are called laetheanta na riaibhche' – the days of the brindled cow' *Dinn*.

Riabhóg n. The pippit, *anthus* McK (Leitrim); NB (w. Limerick).

Riasc n. 'Waste or swampy ground where only rushes grow' G (n.w. Donegal); *Pe* (Wexford); H (n. Clare); *CBE* 47 S (Galway): 'The cows are in the riasc.'

Ribe n. A single hair. As **rib**: 'He hadn't a rib, he was bald' LB (s.w. Dublin).

Ricil n. As **rickle**. 'A small stack of turf' Mac C (Monaghan); SH (Derry); TB (Cavan).

Righin adj. 1. Tough. 'That meat is very righin' JPL (w. Cork). 2. Stubborn. 'He can be as righin as a mule' RBB (w. Waterford).

Righneálaí n. 'A dawdler; a slow worker' H (n. Clare); MS (e. Limerick).

Ríobal n. 1. 'Mud, mire' NB (w. Limerick). 2. 'Piece of clothing hanging down behind; raggle-tail' DOH (e. Limerick).

Rith searraigh phr. Literally, the run of a foal. 'An impetuous rush, a reckless manner, an unsustained effort' *Dinn*; 'He do be ever going round in a rith searraigh, falling over himself and getting in everybody's way' JL (w. Cork).

Rithe seama phr. 'Nonsensical talk, ráiméis' JL (w. Cork); *Cnósach Focal o Bhaile Bhúirne* has **rotha seama** 'a person who talks ráiméis.'

Ritheán n. 'A noose or coil' McK (Leitrim). See *rothán*.

Roc n. 'A furrow hollowed out by the streams of winter but dry in summer' FF (Louth).

Rochall n. ' A spancel on a horse's front legs' *CBD* (n. Kerry). Same word as *urchall*.

Rógaire n. Also as **roghara**. A rogue. 'You're an almighty rógaire, I'm thinking' Smy (n. Clare); JL (w. Cork); JJH (w. Waterford); Wm. Carleton, *Phelim O'Toole's Courtship* 2, 193: '... a roghara ruah'. Glossed by Carleton as 'you red rogue' (Tyrone).

Rogha n. Choice. Sweetheart. As **ro** in Anon. *Purgatorium Hibernicum*: 'Ful Dee, ro, dou unlucky jade ...' For *Ful Dee* see *Fuil Dé*.

Róidín n. Little road. As **rodden** *EASI* 314. (Ulster)

Roilleán n. 'A tall, awkward fellow' OC (Monagahan).

Roilleog n. Darnel. 'A mountain plant, something like heather, about a foot high. Perhaps the same as the darnel mentioned in Matthew13:24 seq.' *An Cho* (w. Mayo).

Roisín n. In form **risheen**. 'A light meal, a snack' J (s. e. Wexford); 'the tea you would get in the field' *CBE* 34 S (Galway).

Róistín n. 'A grid iron' *CBE* 34 S (Galway); RBB (w. Waterford).

Rómánsaíocht n. Romancing, in the sense of talking nonsense. 'What rómánsaíocht have you? That we'd be better off with a new government, is it?' JL (w. Cork).

Rón n. The seal. Plural **róns** JJH (w. Waterford).

Ropach n. In form **ripock**. 'A row or fight; excitement, great noise. "Such ripock as was there"' *CBE* 266 (mid-Tipperary).

Ropaire n. *al.* **rapaire**. **1.** In forms **rapparee, raparee**. A cut-purse, robber or thief; a highwayman. John Michelburne, *Ireland Preserved:* 'We be dose, de rebels call rapparees'; William Carleton, *Willy Reilly* 75: 'This red raparee'; James Joyce, *Ulysses* 293: 'Doing the rapparee and Rory of the hill.' **2.** In abbreviated form **rap**, in phrase 'I don't give a rap'. 'A counterfeit coin of about half a farthing passing current for a halfpenny in 18th century Ireland: 'is gan agam de stór Fodla ach aon ropaire amháin', while I have of Ireland's treasure but a single ropaire' *Dinn*. **Rap** was first seen in print in Swift's *Drapier Letters*, 1724.

Roplachán n. 'A young, care-free man' DOC (Limerick).

Rothán n. **1.** 'A hank of fish, berries, mushrooms etc. threaded together on string or on a stem of grass' RBB (Waterford). **2.** 'A volume of angry words or imprecations' *IG* (Kilkenny). **3.** 'An endless succession of houses, trees etc.' *IG* (Kilkenny).

Rua adj. Red-haired. As **ruadh**. J. M. Synge, *The Well of the Saints* 36: 'That should be Patch Ruadh, with the gamey eyes in him, and the fiery hair'; Brian Friel, *Translations*

18: 'Nellie Ruadh's baby was to be christened this morning.'

Ruagán n. **1.** 'A bitterly cold wind' S (n.w. Donegal). **2.** 'A fit of anger' MH (Tyrone).

Ruaig n. A rout. 'But you have to use the word in the right phrase. And the right phrase here is, as in so many cases, a direct translation from Irish. So if cattle walk into your front lawn, or if children peer in through your window, you don't just ruaig them, you put the ruaig on them' *An Cho* (w. Mayo).

Ruaille buaille n. In forms **roola boola, rooly booly**. 'Ructions, commotion.' 'Such rooly booly as they had' *CBE* 266 (mid-Tipperary); 'You never saw such rooly booly' PD (s. Carlow). See *rí rá*.

Ruaille n. **1.** 'A tall fellow' *IG* (Kilkenny). **2.** 'A slovenly woman' FF (Monaghan). Diminutive, **ruaillín** *IG* (Meath).

Ruailleach n. Also as **roolach, roolyeh**. A slattern. Michael Banim, *The Croppy* 1, 190: 'Och, presarve us from such slaughterin' roolachs!' (Kilkenny). *al.* **ruaille**, as **roolyeh**: 'A slovenly person; chiefly said of women' LB (s.w. Dublin).

Ruaim n. 'The alder tree' JPL (w.Cork).

Ruaisc n. 'A tall man' *IG* (Kilkenny).

Ruamáile n. 'Scum on stagnant water' *CBD* (n. Kerry).

Ruathar n. Also as **roohor**. **1.** A rush, sudden attack. 'The bull gave a ruathar at me; thank God I had the dog with me' JPL (w. Cork). **2.** 'An attack of illness. "Tis the roohor of death that's on him"' *CBE* 266 (mid-Tipperary).

Ruathar péiste comp. n. 'A charm to cure stomach pains in calves' MC (w. Clare). See *snaidhm na péiste*.

Rúbóg n. A heavy blow. 'A rúbóg in th' ear *CBD* (n. Kerry).

Rúcach n. **1.** 'A big, stupid man' JPL (w. Cork). **2.** 'A summer visitor to Kilkee, Co.

Clare'. Plural **rúcaigh**. 'The natives are called *báirnigh* as opposed to *rúcaigh*' *Dinn*.

Rúcán n. A big, rough man. 'There was a time when all they let into the polis were big ignorant rúcáns' RBB (s. Kilkenny). *al.* **rúcánaí** PB (s. Tipperary).

Rud salach n. phr. In form **rud sloch**. Dirty thing. 'Said to a child who had dirtied his clothes while splashing in mud, for example. "Oh, rud sloch!"' PD (s. Carlow); *CBE* 266 (mid-Tipperary).

Ruibh n. 'Real venom. "She had the ruibh in her because I didn't do as she asked"' MC (e. Mayo).

Rúisc n. 'A loud report' *CBE* 266 (mid-Tipperary); 'A loud fart' JL (w. Cork); PC (n. Clare).

Rúisceán n. 'A clumsy fellow' OC (Monaghan).

Rúiteach n. 1. Uproar. 'If a teacher leaves a classroom for a long period, rúiteach is an odds-on probability. It occasionally raises its ugly head at committee meetings. And there is also the domestic variety; a boy, say, has stayed too long in town while the family are tying oats. Arriving at the field at sundown, he is met by a young Job's comforter:

'Where were you? There's rúiteach!"' *An Cho* (w. Mayo). 2. 'Fast movement, especially of animals. "The bullock made a rúiteach down the field"' MC (e. Mayo).

Rúitín n. A cleft hoof. 'There was a stone between the cow's rúitíns' NB (w. Limerick).

Ruóg n. 'A waxed cord' PB (s. Tipperary); 'A cobbler's waxed thread' *CBE* 266 (mid-Tipperary); 'A stout cord made of plaited flax' *IG* (Meath); 'A piece of cord plaited with the hand' *IG* (Monaghan).

Rúpach n. 'A slovenly woman' *IG* (Kilkenny).

Rúpáil n. 'Fast, unmethodical work' MC (e. Mayo).

Rúscadh n. 'Poking, stirring, shaking. 'We got a bad rúscadh in the ferry, the storm was so bad' JM (w. Cork). Hence **rúisc**. 'Rúisc the calves' feed well' FF (Cavan); *IG* (Meath).

Rúscán n. In form **ruscaan**. A vessel made of bark. John Michelburne, *Ireland Preserved*: '... eat dy fill of pease, bread, and ruscaan butter'.

Rútálaí n. 'A fumbler. A clumsy fellow' H (n. Clare).

S

Sabhaircín n. In form **sharakeen** *BASJ* (Cavan). The primrose, *primula vulgaris.*

Sacán n. The fieldfare, *turdus pilaris* JL (w. Cork); NB (w. Limerick).

Sadalachán n. A low-sized, heavily-built person or animal. 'That sadalachán of a cob is as good as any pair of horses' MJD (w. Cork).

Sagart n. Also as **sogarth, soggarth.** Priest. James Joyce, *Finnegans Wake* 485: 'Sagart can self laud nilobstant ...'; Wm. Carleton, *Going to Maynooth* 2, 99: 'When old Denis got the young sogarth fairly in motion ...' (Tyrone); Michael Banim, *The Croppy* 1, 40: 'Nanny the soggarth put upon me' – Nanny the priest baptised me. (Kilkenny); James Joyce, *Ulysses* 295: 'Soggarth Eoghan O'Growney...'

Saidhbhín n. 'A leek' *IG* (Kilkenny).

Sail chuach n. In form **sal cook**. 1. The violet, *viola* SOB (s. Tipperary); AOL (mid-Waterford). In translated form, **cuckoo spit**. [*sail*, impurity]. (Gen.). 2. *EASI* 243: 'Also the name of a small frothy spittle-like substance, found on leaves of plants in summer, with a little greenish insect in the middle of it' (Limerick).

Sail éille n. As **shillelagh, shillela**. A cudgel used in faction fighting in the 18th and 19th centuries. [*Sail*, cudgel; *éille*, genitive of *iall*, thong, by which it was wrapped around the wrist. The word has nothing to do with the oak woods of Shillelagh, Co. Wicklow.] Thomas Sheridan, *The Brave Irishman*: 'By my shoul, if I take my shillela to you, I'll make you skip like a dead salmon'; M.J. Mulloy, *The King of Friday's Men* 19: 'The men 'll be stiffened ... after the shillelagh fighting at the Pattern'.

Sail ghreadadh n. In form **salgraddy**. A beating. "I gave him a salgraddy out the door"' AG (s. Tipperary). [*sail*, a cudgel; *greadadh* = a beating]

Sáil i bhfad siar phr. Literally, sole-far-back. As **saulavotcheer** in *EASI* 316. 'A person having lark-heels.' This is a person down-at-heel (Limerick).

Sail n. In form **sal**. 1. 'A plank or butt of a tree across a stream.' "You can cross the trench on a sal."' *CBE* 266 (mid-Tipperary). 2. 'A heavy, useless woman. "She's only an oul sal"' *CBE* 266 (mid-Tipperary).

Sáile n. A condiment, dip, or kitchen, used with potatoes. 'My mother made sáile from melted butter, salt, and the garlic you'd find growing wild' JC (w. Cork).

Saileachán n. The willow tree. In forms **sonaghan** and **sollaghan** in the compounds **sonaghan-stick** and **sollaghan-stick**: 'willow sticks peeled in rings, formerly carried by those who offered their services at the hiring market in Drogheda' PON (n. Dublin).

Sáiliní n. pl. 'Pieces on the heels of stockings' *IG* (Cavan).

Saileog n. In form **thillog**. 'The willow tree' Q (Donegal).

Sailm na marbh phr. In form **sallin-na-morra**. Psalms of the dead. Michael Banim, *Crohoor of the Billhook* 1, 221: 'The sallin-na-morra, or death prayers, was a celebrated chant, pathetico-ludicrous ...' (Kilkenny).

Sáiteán n. As **sawthawn**. 'A stud, in creel-making' PLH (n. Roscommon).

Salach adj. Also in form **sallagh**. Dirty. Used with Christian name in derogatory sentences – 'Mickey salach' FF (Cavan);

MF (Westmeath); *IG* (n. Co. Dublin);
Dermot O'Byrne, *Children of the Hills* 53:
'To have taken up with a strapach salach the
like of thon' (Donegal); Wm. Carleton, *The
Station* 1, 155: '... and bore so indifferent a
character in the country for cleanliness, that
very few would undertake to eat her butter.
Indeed she was called Katty Sallagh on this
account ...'

Salacha n. pl. Willows. In forms **slochs,
sloughs.** 'Slochs are wet places where sallies
thrive' JPL (w. Cork); J. M. Synge, *The
Well of the Saints* 75: 'There's the little path
going up through the sloughs ...'

Sálóg n. Also as **saulogue.** *al.* **sáilín,** in form
sauleen. 1. 'The remnants of pipe tobacco
at the bottom of the pipe, which is placed
on top of a new pipeful, as it lights easier
than the fresh filling' MS (e. Limerick); PB
(s. Tipperary). As **sáilín,** in form **sauleen**
IG (Kilkenny). 2. 'Some measure added to
an item such as corn or potatoes being sold.
"You ought to give us a little saulogue with
it"' *CBE* 266 (mid-Tipperary).

Samhailt n. In forms **sowlth, soulth, soult.**
1. Phantom, spectre. Gerald Griffin, *The
Collegians* 196: 'The sowlth was seen upon
the Black Lake' 'A formless luminous
apparition'; *EASI* 331, quoting W. B. Yeats.
James Joyce, *Ulysses* 409: '... and himself
after me the like of a soulth'. 2.
Figuratively, 'a man who has grown thin
and wasted from illness. "He's gone in a
soult"' *CBE* 266 (mid-Tipperary).

Samhain n. 1. Pagan feast coinciding with
All Hallows, November 1. As **sowan** in
James Joyce, *Finnegans Wake* 356. 2. As
sowins; sowins. 'A porridge or gruel of
soured oat-mash traditionally eaten on
Hallow E'en' O'K (Tyrone); 'The husks
of grain after first crushing are mixed
with flour and oatmeal and put in a tub;
boiling water is then poured on, the
contents stirred and covered for five or six
days until soured; then strained with a sieve,
the water drawn off, residue stirred and
boiled and eaten as porridge' Tr (Donegal);
Jonathan Swift, *A Dialogue in Hybernian
Stile:* 'Why, sometimes sowins and
sometimes stirabout.

Samhaineachán n. As **sonaghan.** *EASI*
330: 'A kind of trout that appears in certain
lakes in November ... "November-fellow"'
(Ulster).

Samhaisc n. 1. 'A four-year-old beast' MJD
(w. Cork). 2. An adolescent boy. 'He's a fine
samhaisc of a garsún, with nothing on his
mind but women' JL (w. Cork).

Sámhán n. Also as **sauvaun.** A short sleep; a
nap. Michael Banim, *The Croppy* 1, 95: 'I
was in a raal sauvaun of a sleep. Glossed by
Banim as 'comfortable drowsiness.' (Kilkenny); 'Whatever about apples, a sámhán a
day keeps the doctor away from an old man'
JL (w. Cork). 'There's a sámhán on her' NB
(w. Limerick); MS (e. Limerick); *CBD* (n.
Kerry); PB (s. Tipperary). Hence **sámhán-
ing,** 'taking life easy without fuss or hurry'
CBD (n. Kerry).

Sámhas n. As **sawvas.** 'Pleasure, delight'
Mac C (Monaghan). 'A nap after a meal is
what I'd call sawvas' TB (Cavan).

Samhdaí n. 'A young, fresh looking, healthy
girl' S (n.w. Donegal).

Samhradh n. Summer. In phrase **Lá
Samhraidh,** a summer's day. 'Nice day.'
'Yes, thank God, a real Lá Samhraidh' LOS
(w. Clare).

Sánas n. A lull in a rain storm. 'Stay inside,
let ye, until a sánas comes' MJD (w. Cork).

Santach adj. Greedy; intensely eager. 'They'll
never win anything; they are not santach
enough' RBB (w. Waterford); H (n. Clare).

Saoiste n. 1. A hassock of plaited straw or
rushes. Diminutive, **saoisteóg** JL (w. Cork).
Also as **siostóg.** Seumus MacManus, *The
Bend of the Road:* 'The second seat of
honour ... which was a stump of a tree with
a siostog of plaited straw on it, by way of
luxury, was yet vacant' (Donegal). 2. 'A lazy
man, or animal, who spends his day
stretched out, is called a saoiste' PB (s.
Tipperary).

Saoistín n. 'A small, fat woman' JJH (w.
Waterford).

Saothar n. Stress, effort. 'Look at the saothar that's on him' NB (w. Limerick); *CBD* (n. Kerry); JM (w. Cork).

Sasanach n. In form **Sassenah**. Englishman. Wm. Carleton, *Phelim O'Toole's Courtship* 2, 188: '... his grandfather ... won it from the Sassenah ...' (Tyrone).

Sásta adv. Also in forms **sastee**, **sausty**. Content, happy. 'A tidy little womaneen sásta' *CBD* (n. Kerry); 'I'm grand and sastee, thanks' J (s. e. Wexford); Patk. Kennedy, *Legendary Fictions of the Irish Celts* 128: '... lying snug and sausty before the fire' (Wexford).

Scabhaire n. 'A brat who has too much talk' NB (w. Limerick).

Scabhat n. 'A narrow laneway or alley' AOL (mid-Waterford).

Scablálaí n. 'An untidy workman' *CBD* (n. Kerry).

Scabóg n. 'A tall person' *CBE* 34 S (Galway).

Scadán caoch n. Lady Morgan, *The Wild Irish Girl* 84: 'To supply the want of this, by them highly esteemed luxury, (fresh milk) they cut an onion into a bowl of water, into which they dip their potatoes ... This they call a scadán caoch, or blind herring' (Leinster).

Scadán n. In forms **skodaun**, **scaddan**, **scaddin**. 1. Herring. Dermot O'Byrne, *Children of the Hills*, 109: 'Sure the scaddan'll not be in it for a couple of weeks' (Donegal). 'The scaddin aren't as plentiful nowadays as they used to be' JB (s. Armagh & n. Louth). 2. Figuratively, 'a thin person. "He's gone in a skodaun, the poor devil"' *CBE* 266 (mid-Tipperary).

Scadhrach adj. In form **skyrky**. 'Blatant, full of go. "She's very skyrky in herself"' *CBE* 266 (mid-Tipperary).

Scafaire n. 'A strong, vigorous man' DOH (e. Limerick); *Sguab* (w. Cork); *IG* (Meath).

Scaifte n. A crowd. 'She had a big scaifte of children' MG (n. w. Donegal).

Scailmín n. 'A crowd of men, women and children working together in a field' *IG* (Kilkenny).

Scailp n. 1. Also as **scalp**, **scolp**, **scalpeen**. *EASI* 316: 'A rude cabin, usually roofed with scalps or grassy sods, whence the name. In the famine times – 1847 and after – a scalp was often erected for any poor wanderer who got stricken down with typhus fever: and in that the people tended him cautiously till he recovered or died.' (Munster). 2. A rocky place overgrown with thorn, briars etc. JJH (w. Waterford). As **scalpy**. Usually associated with fairies in Donegal. Peadar O'Donnell *Adrigoole* 249: 'Passing a scalpy she feared a hand would seize her ... She tip-toed past the gentle bush'. 2. 'A cold, miserable little house' DOH (e. Limerick); MC (w. Clare); *CBD* (n. Kerry).

Scailpín n. 'A salted mackerel' NM (w. Cork) 'A kipper' JC (w. Cork).

Scailtín n. In form **scalteen**. 1. Alcoholic beverage. George A. Little, *Malachy Horan Remembers:* 'They always had scalteen ready at the Jobstown Inn. Men, in weather like this, out from morning till night without a bit, would be coming in with the mark of the mountain on them. Scalteen would make a corpse walk. It would put the life back in them, but make them drunk too. It was taken red hot. Thay made it from half a pint of whiskey, half a pound of butter, and six eggs. You should try it some time, but when you have it down go to bed while you are still able.' 2. 'Gruel for a cold' *CBE* 34 S (Galway).

Scaimh n. Also in form **skov**. 'A snarl' NB (e. Limerick); 'I saw the dog making for me with a scaimh on him' PC (n. Clare); 'A snarly appearance. "He has an old scov on him"' *CBE* 266 (mid-Tipperary). Hence 'Don't be scovin' at me' ibid.

Scaimheachán n. In form **skovachaun**. 'One who has a snarly appearance' *CBE* 266 (mid-Tipperary).

Scaipeach adv. Wasteful, free-spending. 'He is very scaipeach with his money' H (n. Clare).

Scairbhín n. The last fortnight in April and the first in May, when rough weather may be expected. Often called scairbhín na gcuach (the cuckoos' rough weather) JL (w. Cork); *CBD* (n. Kerry).

Scaird n. In form **skoord**. 'A squirt, splash. Mainly used in reference to an animal's anal discharge. "The cow nearly hit me with a big skoord"' *CBE* 266 (mid-Tipperary).

Scairt n. Also as **skort, scorth, scort**. 1. A shout, a loud laugh. Dermot O'Byrne, *Children of the Hills* 56: 'He'd be left in the latter end with the skin cracked on his four bones with the scairts of laughter they'd take out of him' (Donegal); MS (e. Limerick); H (n. Clare); PB (s. Tipperary). Hence,' they were scortin' out laughing' *CBE* 266 (mid-Tipperary); JF (Limerick). 2. The diaphragm. 'In a local cure carried out by a blacksmith the words used were: D'ucht a bheith socair is do scairt a bheith réidh, in ainm an athar agus an Mhic agus an Spioraid Naoimh.' (That your chest might be settled and your diaphragm at ease, in the name of the Father, the Son and the Holy Spirit) H (n. Clare). 3. A covert, thicket. 'The rabbit was lying in a scairt' NB (w. Limerick); PB (s. Tipperary); George Fitzmaurice, *The Pie-Dish* (Kerry): '... my legs all scrope from scorths of briars ...' Diminutive, **scairtín**, also as **scarteen** *CBD* (n. Kerry); JS (e. Limerick).

Scalladh dubhach phr. In form **skollaka dhook**. 'A sorrowful scolding. "I'll tell you, he got a skollaka dhook"' *CBE* 266 (mid-Tipperary).

Scalladh croí n. phr. 'It was a scalladh croí to the poor woman, after all her work, to see her tramp of a son going to jail' PC (s. Wexford); *CBD* (n. Kerry).

Scalltán n. In forms **scalltóg, scaldie, scalder**. 'A fledgeling; a young hedgerow bird before it leaves the nest. Also applied to any small, delicate-looking person or animal' O'K (Tyrone. Gen. Ulster); *EASI* 316: 'scalder' (Munster.) [< old Norse, *skalli*, a bakdhead.]

Scamh n. 'A narrow, thin face with an unhealthy complexion. "Look at the scamh of him"' *CBD* (n. Kerry).

Scamhachán n. 'A little boy' McK (Leitrim).

Scannán n. 'The filament around the entrails of animals' *IG* (Kilkenny).

Scanróir n. 1. 'A person who never seems to stop working; always on the move, always in a hurry' DOC (Limerick). 2. 'A miser; one troubled by the world' BOD (s.w. Cork).

Scaob n. 'A lump of clay' MS (e. Limerick).

Scaoidín n. 'A small potato' MG (n.w. Donegal).

Scaoil a' bheilt phr. In form **skeelavelt**. Literally, loosen the belt. 'A carelessly dressed person, a streel. "She's going round in a skeelavelt"' *CBE* 266 (mid-Tipperary).

Scaoinse n 'A tall, gangly person' JL (w. Cork); 'A tall girl' *IG* (Kilkenny).

Scaothaire n. 1. 'A man who is always boasting' JPL (w. Cork). 2. 'A person who squanders his money' *CBD* (n. Kerry).

Scata n. 'A crowd' *Pe* (Wexford).

Scáth n. In forms **scaw, scah**. 1. Shadow, shade. 'Stay on my scaw, means stay close to me' PD (s. Carlow). 2. Pretext. 'He came on the scáth of being a friend of mine, although I hardly knew him' AOL (mid-Waterford). 3. Bashfulness, modesty. 'He has no scah in him: said of one who would perhaps say something immodest or tactless in certain company' Tr (Donegal).

Scathamh n. As **skohav**. 'A short space of time. "Stay for another little skohav"' *CBE* 266 (mid-Tipperary).

Scáthlán n. As **scallan**. Open shelter. A shed such as was used for Mass in Penal times. Seumus MacManus, *Bold Blades of Donegal* 220: 'Instead of going to Mass at Frosses that day, we attended in the Ardaghey corner of the parish, where they had only a scallan ... the three-walled, thatched shed that was of size enough to shield from the weather the priest and the altar-table.'

Sceach n. Also in forms **sciog, skiog**. 1. Whitethorn, hawthorn. 'Put a sceach in the ditch' G (s. Kilkenny; Gen.); Seumus MacManus, *The Bend of the Road* 264: 'Their late musician (who had hung his instrument on the skiog before he dashed away; a story of fairies revelling to entrancing music under a skiog bush' (Donegal); Seumus MacManus, *A Lad of the O'Friels* 77: 'It was a sciog bush – a fairy thorn' (Donegal). 2. Figuratively, a prickly, quarrelsome person. 'He has a hard time with that sceach of a woman' AOL (mid-Waterford).

Sceachaill n. A lump, tumour. 'I don't like the look of that sceachaill the cow has on her udder' JL (w. Cork).

Sceachóid n. 1. 'The haw, or berry of the whitethorn' JM (w. Cork); RBB (s. Kilkenny). *al.* sceachóir PD (Carlow); *IG* (Kilkenny). 2. 'The blossom of the whitethorn' D (s. e. Wexford).

Sceachóirí muc n. pl. 'The berries of the sweetbriar' *IG* (Kilkenny).

Scead n. In form **shkad**. 1. 'A blaze on a horse's forehead. "Who owns the mare with the shkad?"' *CBE* 266 (mid-Tipperary). 2. A whiteish cast in a person's eye. "The shkad eye of the Ryans"' *CBE* 266 (mid-Tipperary). See *sceadshúil.*

Sceadshúil n. In form **shkadhool**. 'A squinting or crooked eye' *IG* (Kilkenny); 'The shkadhool runs in certain families, they say' PD (s. Carlow).

Scéal n. Also as **shkale, skeal**. A story; news. 'Any scéal at all?' *CBD* (n. Kerry); *Sguab* (Cork); NB (w. Limerick); 'Have you any shkale' *CBE* 266 (mid-Tipperary); 'Any scéal at all from town?' 'Divil the scéal' MS (e. Limerick); Anon., *The Irish Hudibras:* '... ygo vidout My skeal, vid finger in my mout ...'

Scéalaí n. Storyteller. As **scéaluidhe** in Patk. Kennedy, *Legendary Fictions of the Irish Celts* 4: 'good scéaluidhes' (Wexford).

Scealbóg n. 1. 'A splinter' Smy (n. Clare). 2. 'A strip of cloth used as a bandage' MS (e. Limerick); 'A shred, a bit of rag' *Sguab* (w. Cork); MS (e. Limerick).

Scealpaire n. Also as **skelper**. 1. 'A pilferer, a grabber' PB (s. Tipperary). 2. A ravenous eater; one who snaps up food at the table. M.J. Mulloy, *The King of Friday's Men* 21: 'I'll have five hundred great skelpers against us'.

Scéaltach adj. Literally, storied. 'Chatty, friendly' *IG* (Kilkenny).

Sceamh n. In form **sgah**. Deposit on surface, scum. 'Give me a glass without that skah on it' PJG (mid-Donegal).

Sceamhaoil n. The barking of a dog. Hence **sceamhaoiling**. 'What sceamhaoiling had the dog all night?' JL (w. Cork).

Sceamhlachán n. Yelper, howler. 'What the divil is wrong with that sceamhlachán of a dog?' MJD (w. Cork).

Scearc interj. 'What you would say to hunt out the hens' *CBE* 34 S (Galway).

Scearrach n. 'Soft excrement of a bird or animal' H (n. Clare). See *sciorrach.*

Sceartán n. *al.* **sciortán**. 'A tick found on animals' MC (w. Clare); NB (w. Limerick); MC (e. Mayo).

Sceatharach n. A ramshackle, delapidated object. 'A job not well done, for example a badly-made hay-stack' NB (w. Limerick); 'He leaves the house in a sceatharach behind him' MJD (w. Cork).

Sceidhtear n. In form **shkiter**. 'A wayward woman' MS (e. Limerick); 'A wayward person' *CBE* 266 (mid-Tipperary).

Sceidín n. 'The milk-and-water drink so popular during the hay-making season. In this sense it is used as a disparaging name for weak tea' *An Cho* (w. Mayo).

Sceilimis n. Also as **skelemish**. 'Fright, terror; fearful commotion' NB (w. Limerick); *CBE* 266 (mid-Tipperary).

Sceilp n. Also in form **skelp**. Slap, cut of whip or stick. In form **skelp**. Somerville and Ross, *Lisheen Races, Second-hand* 79: 'Skelp her, ye big brute!, says I. What

good's in ye that aren't able to skelp her ...
Leigh Kelvey was sufficiently moved to ask
me if skelp was a local term'. [Cf. dialect
English *skelp*, 15th c.]

Sceilpéir n. In form **shkelper**. 1. 'A rogue, a
fellow that would steal the eye out of your
head JL (w. Cork). 2. 'A tall, loose-jointed
fellow' *CBE* 266 (mid-Tipperary).

Sceilteannóg n. 'Green scum seen on
stagnant water' *IG* (Cavan).

Scéiméir n. 'A schemer' LOS (w. Clare).

Scéimhiúil n. In form **scamool**. 'Good-
looking' McK (Leitrim).

Sceimhle n. Terror. 'Anyone who'd put an
old person through a night of sceimhle
should be hung' JC (w. Cork).

Sceo n. 'A thin covering, like you'd see sugar
on a cake.' 'There's a sceo of snow on the
ground' JC (w. Cork).

Sceochaíl n. Loud, strident talk. Hence
sceoching. 'Listen to the sceoching out of
him' H (n. Clare).

Sceoidín n. 'A wee man of no account' PJG
(mid-Donegal).

Sceolbhach n. The neck and throat. 'Once
the badger caught him around the sceolbhach that was the end of it' JL (w. Cork).

Sceon n. Also as **scéin**, **skone**. Terror, fright.
'There was sceon in his eyes' NB (w.
Limerick); JL (w. Cork); 'He put the scéin
of God in me' PC (n. Clare). Hence, 'he
skoned hell out of me' *BASJ* (Cavan).

Scian n. As **skeene**, **skein**. A knife. Anon.,
The Welsh Embassador: '... I shall trust my
skeene into dy rotten guts ...'; John
Michelburne, *Ireland Preserved*: 'Pulls out a
skein out of his pocket.'

Scian trá n. 'A knife used to prize limpets off
rocks' BC (s. Wexford).

Sciath n. Also as **sciach**, **skeuch**. Diminutive, **sciathóg**, **skeeoge**. A shallow, shield-

shaped basket. 'A sciach is a flat, oval vessel
of willow rods for straining potatoes' AG (s.
Tipperary); Seumus MacManus, *Bold Blades
of Donegal* 312: 'I took in a sciath of turf,
and Uncle Donal built a nice fine fire'.
Traditional phrase: 'Ghabh Brighid soir is a
sciath léi' – St. Brigid has gone east with
her shield-shaped basket MG (n.w.
Donegal); MS (e. Limerick); 'I'm going out
for a sciathóg of spuds' JC (w. Cork). Glossed as 'a basket to wash potatoes' in Gerald
Griffin, *The Collegians* 94 (Limerick).
Michael Banim, *The Croppy* 3, 74: '... then
ye may burn the skeuchs an' spill out the
murphies on silver dishes ...' (Kilkenny);
Patk. Kennedy, *Legendary Fictions of the
Irish Celts* 148: '... a poor woman was straining her supper in a skeeoge' (Wexford); *GC*
(Laois, n. Kilkenny).

Sciathán n. As **sciachán**. An extension. 'A
clamping of turf over the level of the creel'
NB (w. Limerick).

Scib n. 1. 'A small basket, made from sally
rods, for bringing in turf' *CBE* 34 S
(Galway). 2. A basketful. 'Bring me in a scib
of turf' OCn (Laois). 3. 'A mean woman'
NB (w. Limerick).

Scib n. Also in forms **skib**, **sciob**, **shkib**. 'An
airy scib of a girl with little sense' JL (w.
Cork); 'A female of little character' TOM
(s. Tipperary); 'A sciob of a girleen with
nothing on her mind but dances' PB (s.
Tipperary); 'A bold, flirtatious girl, a shkib'
SOB (s. Tipperary).

Scibirlíní n. pl. In form **scibirleens**.
Pendulous breasts PD (s. Carlow); G (s.
Kilkenny).

Scidín n. Also in forms **sciadin**, **skiddin**. 1.
A small potato. Seumus MacManus, *The
Bend of the Road* 47: 'He happened to throw
up five or six sciadins of praties in the mud'
(Donegal); Patrick MacGill, *Glenmornan* 42:
'Scaddan and skiddins' (Donegal). 2. A
trifle, a worthless present. 'Just look at the
skiddin he bought me for Christmas' S
(n.w. Donegal). [Cf. Latin *schedium*, a thing
made suddenly *Dinn.*]

Scileach n. 'A dash of water through a drink'
IG (Cavan).

Scimín n. 1. 'A plate used in mixing butter' 2. A saucer-shaped vessel for skimming milk. NB (w. Limerick).

Scinc n. In form **skink**. 'Watery tea or porridge' PD (s. Carlow); G (s. Kilkenny).

Scinceáil v. In form **skinkin'** 1. 'Pouring liquid from one vessel to another, to cool it' MG (n.w. Donegal). 2. 'Messing around, splashing in the kitchen sink, as children love to do' MG (n.w. Donegal).

Sciob v.; n. Also in form **skib**. 1. v. 'Snatch' *IG* (Kilkenny). 2. 'To skib or trim a hay stack by pulling away the hay sticking out' MG (n.w. Donegal); *Pe* (Wexford). 3. n. 'A game of throwing small coins to small boys who all struggle and wrestle to pick them up' *IG* (Meath, Monaghan).

Sciobaire n. 'A man of unprepossessing appearance; a ragged-looking man. The primary meaning may be pickpocket' *IG* (Kilkenny).

Sciodar n. Also in forms **scitter, scutter**. 1. 'Scour, diarrhoea' JC (w. Cork); R (n. Clare); OC (Monaghan). 2. 'Thick sour milk containing knobs of whey' NB (w. Limerick); PB (s. Tipperary); *CBD* (n. Kerry); 'The lawyers got the cream while their clients got the sciodar' JL (w. Cork). 3. 'Thin gruel' D (Kildare).

Sciollach n. Any matter flaked or crumbled. Hence, 'he made sciollach of the car against the ditch' MJD (w. Cork).

Sciollán n. Also as **skilyawn**. *al.* **sciollóg**. 'A slice of potato containing an 'eye' for planting' M (w. Cork); MS (e. Limerick); PB (s. Tipperary); 'At this writing (1923) Ireland is full of murderous weapons whereby men are blowing one another to bits, while the farmer hasn't a gun; the crows are laughing at him; in some cases they haven't left him a skilyawn and have eaten his corn' GC (Laois); 'I cut my hand cutting sciollógs' PD (s. Carlow).

Sciomáil vb. n. 'Prowling for food, as a dog or a pig; loafing or watching for drink, in the case of a man' *IG* (Kilkenny).

Sciomálaí n. 'A loafer; a dog, pig etc. which searches for food.' 'A mean sciomálaí' *IG* (Kilkenny).

Sciomradh vb. n. In form **shkimmering**. 'Act of cleaning, brightening. "She was shkimmering the house. She has the place shkimmered well" ' *CBE* 266 (mid-Tipperary).

Sciorr v. In form **skir**. 'To skim a stone over lake water' MG (n.w. Donegal).

Sciorrach adj. Slippery. 'Drive slow, the road can be very sciorrach in the frost' R (s. Galway). See *scearrach*.

Sciorrachán n. 'A slippery person, a sleeveen' R (s. Galway).

Sciothaire n. 'A giggler, titterer. "I thought I'd be put out of the chapel. I was sitting next to that sciothaire, Maidhcín, and he had me as bad as himself' MJD (w. Cork).

Sciuird n. Also in form **skew**. A rush, run, or race. 'He often gives a sciuird in to see us' JL (w. Cork); BOD (s.w. Cork). 'He gave a skew up to see us, but that's all it was. He only stayed a minute' J (Wexford).

Sciúnach n. 'A light covering. "The wee wain hadn't much more than a sciúnach to her back in the line of clothes' S (n.w. Donegal).

Sciúrtóg n. 'A coin of little value. "I haven't as much as a sciúrtóg with me" ' MC (e. Mayo).

Sclamhaire n. In form **sklaffer**. 'A lout' PJG (mid-Donegal).

Sclamhóg n. 'A wee bite. "Give the wain a sclamhóg of cake' MG (n.w. Donegal).

Scodalach n. 'A big, heavy glutton of a person' NB (w. Limerick); PB (s. Tipperary).

Scóig n. 'The neck of a bottle' *CBE* 104 (Leitrim).

Scóilín bró n. phr. As **skoleen bro**. 'A piece of bacon' PLH (n. Roscommon).

Scoiltín n. 'What they call a sceallán in the south. A seed potato with one eye, for planting' MG (n.w. Donegal).

Scoiteán n. In form **scothawn**. 'Anything cut, clipped etc. "A scothawn of a tail, mane"' OCn (Laois).

Scóitséir n. In form **scotcher**. 'A person fond of himself; a shaper, a boaster' RBB (s.Kilkenny).

Scoláire n. Scholar. In form **scholawra**. A term of endearment. 'Now, scholawra, what will you have?' W (e. Wicklow).

Scolb n. Also in form **scollop**. A rod for fastening down thatch. Seumus MacManus, *Bold Blades of Donegal* 89: 'We had taken the precaution to tie our end of the string to a scollop in the thatch'; Wm. Carleton, *Larry M'Farland's Wake* 1, 86: 'Larry spoke to his brother, who was a sober, industrious boy, that had laid down his scollops for the windy day.' Carleton misread the Irish proverb, **Ní hé lá na gaoithe lá na scolb.** In a footnote he has: 'In Irish the proverb is **Ha nahn la na guiha la na scuilpagh**: that is, the windy or stormy day is not that on which the scollops should be cut. The proverb inculcates preparation for future necessity.' What the proverb means is that the stormy day is no time to put scallops in place in a straw roof; it illustrates the futility of undertaking work too late.

Scológ n. In form **scullogue**. 1. 'A farmer's boy' G (s. Kilkenny); PD (Carlow); James Joyce, *Finnegans Wake* 398. 2. 'An officious, meddling old man' RBB (w. Waterford). 3. 'A scullion' MH (Tyrone). 4. 'A young seagull' Del (Antrim).

Scoltán n. 'Hallow E'en high jinks' *CBE* 98 (Kilkenny).

Sconsa n. Also **scunce**. 1. 'A sconsa is a sconce for candles' *IG* (Meath). 2. 'A rod fence which grows scollops, sally rods used in thatching. "Cut a few scollops from the scunce"' MC (e. Mayo). 3. 'An idle gossip. " Pay no heed to that oul scunce's talk"' Mac C (Monaghan); FF (Cavan).

Sconsa n. In form **skounsa**. 'A fence or drain' S Ua G (s. Tipperary).

Scoraíocht n. A friendly visit to a neighbour's house at night. Eric Cross, *The Tailor and Ansty* 45: 'There would never be a "Scoraíocht" without some grand fun and songs and stories' (w. Cork; Kerry).

Scoróg n. 'A straddle-peg from which the creels hang on either side' *An Cho* (w. Mayo).

Scót n. A narrow, windy gap or defile. 'I must take the lambs down from the scót. They'd perish from the cold there' JL (w. Cork).

Scoth n. The best of the flax; a fine shirt from such flax. *Poole* (s. e. Wexford): 'Fan ee-daff ee aar scoth' – when stripped in their shirts.

Scothóg n. 'A tassel-especially the ornamental tassel on the edge of a woolen scarf, a counterpane, or on a weaver's blanket' *An Cho* (w. Mayo).

Scrábach adj. 1. Untidy. 'He's a scrábach workman: he makes a bigger mess than he found' JL (w. Cork). 2. Broken, showery weather. 'It was a miserable, scrábach day in town' MS (e. Limerick); Ham (e. Clare); PB (s. Tipperary). See *scráib*.

Scrábálaí n. In form **skrawbauly**. 'A scraper or scratcher. One who pulls and drags at his work instead of working in a proper methodical manner' *CBE* 266 (mid-Tipperary).

Scrabha n. Also in form **skrou**. A sudden rush; an eager attempt. 'He made a skrou at her' NB (w. Limerick); 'He gave a skrou of the scythe at it' *CBE* 266 (mid-Tipperary); 'He has a skrou in him for the work' idem.

Scrabhadh vb.n. In form **skrouing**. Scraping. 'He was skrouin' the stirabout out of the pot' *CBE* 266 (mid-Tipperary).

Scráib n., v. In forms **scrawb, scrab**. 1. A scratch, scrape. 'Did the old lady give you that scrawb on your face?' PD (s. Carlow); 'I was cutting sceachs and they scrawbed the face off me' Dee (Waterford); (Gen.); 'The cat scrabbed my arm when I went to lift her' O'K (Tyrone). 2. 'A shower of rain. "There's a scrawb coming" ' NB (w. Limerick); MS (e. Limerick).

Scraidín n. In form **scradyeen, scradeen**. 1. A worthless little person or thing. 'He's only a scradyeen of a wee man' O'K (Tyrone); G (n.w. Donegal); Patk. Kennedy, *The Banks of the Boro* 104; 'Is there no particularly ugly, insignificant, miserly little scradeen in the room?' (Wexford). 2. 'The butt of a cigarette' OC (Monaghan).

Scraiste n. Also in form **scrashtee**. 1. 'A miser' NB (w. Limerick). 2. 'A lazy person' H (n. Clare). 3. 'A hooligan' RBB (s. Kilkenny). Anon., *The Pretender's Exercise*: 'scrashtee.'

Scraith n. Also in form **scraw**. 1. Strip of lea-sod pared off. 'They never had anything but an old bothán roofed with scraws' Dee (w. Waterford); *An Cho* (w. Mayo). Hence **scrawing**. 'I spent the evening scrawin' the back yard' O'K (Tyrone). 2. A layer. 'Said of rash or sore – the rash is in a scraith' MF (Westmeath).

Scraith chloch n. Rock lichen. 'The fungus that grows on rocks and is used to make a beautiful, natural dye of russet shade. The dye is used, especially, on homespun yarn. When the wool is spun it is tied in hanks and boiled in water with the scraith chloch. Articles made from this wool bear the name; especially we speak of "scraith chloch stockings" ' *An Cho* (w. Mayo).

Scraith ghliogair n. 'A quagmire, a scraith (q.v.) growing on surface of a boghole' MF (Westmeath); *CBE* 104 (Leitrim). See *scraith loinge*.

Scraith loinge n. In forms **scralung, scrawlung**. 'Quaking sod, surface of quagmire' H (n. Donegal). See *scraith ghliogair*.

Scrámóga n. In form **scramogues**. 'The last of the porridge in a pot' *CBE* 34 S (Galway).

Scrathán n. A shallow covering of green sod. 'They buried the informer up on Mullach an Ois under a scrathán' JL (w. Cork).

Scrathóg n. 1. 'A grassy sod of turf' MS (e. Limerick). 2. 'The bladder of an animal, used to make a football in days long gone' G (n.w. Donegal); *CBE* 104 (Leitrim). 3. 'Apple or potato peelings' S (n.w. Donegal). 4. 'A flat wicker basket, off which potatoes are eaten' Wm. Carleton, *Larry M' Farland's Wake* 1, 91 (footnote). (Tyrone).

Screaball n. Potato peelings – 'They never threw out the screaball in my young days. Screaball was food, and food was scarce' S (n.w. Donegal).

Screabh n. 'A crust, scab' *IG* (Cavan, Meath, Monaghan).

Scréach n. In forms **screagh, skreigh**. A yell, screech. 'She let some screagh out of her when I jumped from behind the door' O'K (Tyrone); R.S. Brooke, *The Story of Parson Annaly* 250: 'Sir Pether (a ghost) had vanished among the trees, laughing and skreighing' (Ulster). In phrase **screagh o' day**. Dawn, cock-crow. 'Hard working risers are often heard to proclaim that they are up and about since the screagh of day' O'K (Tyrone).

Scréachóg n. 'One who is always crying' *CBE* 34 S (Galway).

Screag n. 'A rock; a rocky eminence' PB (s. Tipperary).

Screag n. In form **scrag**. 'A hardened, wasted person. "He's gone in a scrag" ' *CBE* 266 (mid-Tipperary).

Screalbh n. A field full of small stones. 'That screalbh of a field is a whore to plough' JL (w. Cork).

Screamall n. In form **skrammel**. 'Weeds that grow in a drainage trench or elsewhere in water. "The well is covered in skrammel. The water can't run, in the way the dyke is all one skrammel" ' *CBE* 266 (mid-Tipperary).

Screatall n. 'A very small bit; a morsel. "He hasn't a screatall of sense"' *CBD* (n. Kerry).

Scríbín n. 1. 'A luck-penny given to a buyer at a fair' RBB (s. Tipperary). 2. 'A strip of hay etc, left uncut' *CBD* (n. Kerry). 3. Plural **scríbíní**. 'Scrapings from a pot, etc.' *CBE* 104 (Leitrim).

Scríd n. As **screed**. 'A rag, tatter' Ham (e. Clare); Del (Antrim); RBB (s. Kilkenny); 'I knew her when she hadn't a screed to her back' PD (s. Carlow).

Scriltheach n. 'An untidy person; of a very precise description, however. The essence of scriltheach-hood is frayed edges-of cuffs, of trouser-ends, and of hems on skirts or on coats. One (historical) quotation catches the idea: "Mary, why would a tidy girl like you marry that oul' scriltheach"' *An Cho* (w. Mayo).

Scríob n. Also as **scribe**. A furrow, mark or limit; a mark cut in a field to guide a ploughman MS (e. Limerick); J.M. Synge, *The Playboy of the Western World* 87: 'I've seen none the like of you the eleven long days I am walking the world, looking over a low ditch or a high ditch on my north or south, into stony, scattered fields, or scribes of bog where you'd see young, limber girls, and fine, prancing women making laughter with the men.'

Scríobadh an chrúiscín phr. The scrapings of the jug. 'The last born of a family' MJD (w. Cork).

Scrios lom ort interj. phr. Bare ruination on you. 'A common imprecation' *CBE* 104 (Leitrim).

Scrios n. Destruction. 'He did clean scrios at the card game. He must have won a fortune' AOL (mid-Waterford).

Scriosán n. 'A light summer dress. "You'll get your death at the shore in that scriosán. Take a coat with you."' S (n.w. Donegal).

Scroblach n. Rubbish; unwanted clothes etc. 'You might as well throw out that scroblach you have in the wardrobe. All they do is fed the moths' MG (n.w. Donegal).

Scrogall n. 'A long, thin neck' H (n. Clare); 'A bottle of stout by the scrogall, please': by the neck, no need for a glass' Smy (n. Clare); *CBE* 98 (Kilkenny); *JCHAS* (Cork); *CBD* (n. Kerry).

Scroglachán n. In form **scruglachaun**. 'A long-necked person' *CBE* 266 (mid-Tipperary). See *scrogall*.

Scrúdarsa n. 'The bits of butter found floating in buttermilk' FF (Monaghan).

Scuab n. 'A brush' McK (Leitrim); MS (e. Limerick).

Scuaibín n. 1. Diminutive of **scuab** (q.v.) 2. 'The final game at a card party, when the pool as well as the stakes are played for' *BASJ* (Cavan). 3. Hence **scuaibín man**: 'A trick-of-the-loop, a card sharper or professional gambler' *IG* (Kilkenny). 4. Hence **scuaibín house**: 'a gambling house' *IG* (Kilkenny). 5. A minor altercation. 'There was some scuaibín between them after the ball was cleared' *CBD* (n. Kerry).

Scúille n. 'A farmhouse kitchenmaid' FF (Louth). [< English *scullion*.]

Scuinn n. Diarrhoea. 'He took the ditch from the scuinn like there was a bull after him' JPL (w. Cork).

Scut interj. 'What you would say to hunt out the cat' *CBE* 34 S (Galway). *al.* **scuit** RBB (s. Kilkenny); JC (w. Cork); PD (s. Carlow).

Sé do bheatha interj. Welcome *IG* (Kilkenny). In Wm. Carleton, *Tubber Derg* 2, 380 as **she dha veha**.

Sea go deimhin interj. Yes indeed. As **sha gu dheine** in Patk. Kennedy, *Legendary Fictions of the Irish Celts*, 71 (Wexford).

Sea interj. Also in form **sha**. Yes! Indeed! James Joyce, *Grace* 173: 'Sha,'s nothing, said Mr Kernan.'

Seabhac n. Hawk. 'A thin, cadaverous fellow' *IG* (Kilkenny).

Seach n. Also as **shuch**. 'A smoke of pipe tobacco. In my young days the master would often leave the room an go out for a seach' MS (e. Limerick); 'He was having a shuch by the fire' PD (s. Carlow).

Seachain interj. Beware! Mind yourself! LOS (w. Clare); JM (w. Cork).

Seachrán n. Also in forms **saughran, shuckerawn, shaughraun**. In phrases. William Carleton, *The Poor Scholar* 2, 301: 'What's a shaughran wid you'. **To be on the seachrán**: 'to be "on the road", begging' Tr (Donegal); 'to be left in the lurch: to find that one's lover married someone else' NB (w. Limerick); 'to be behaving in a dissolute fashion' RBB (s. Kilkenny); James Joyce, *Ulysses* 136: 'We'll paralyse Europe as Ignatius Gallaher used to say when he was on the shaughraun ...' **To have a seachrán on one**, to be somewhat mad' Tr (Donegal). **Shuckerawn clothes** – glossed by Michael Banim in *The Croppy* 1, 211 as 'meanly-contrived' (Kilkenny).

Sead n. In form **shaad**. A louse. John Michelburne, *Ireland Preserved*: '... and he did call her a feisting, farting, stinking shaad.'

Seafaid n. In form **shaffid**. 'A yearling heifer' S Ua G (s. Tipperary).

Seafóid n., interj. Nonsense. 'What sort of seafóid is that you have?' JL (w. Cork); 'Beside its general use it is also applied to the childish ramblings which sometimes accompany old age. Used as an interjection after somebody's contribution at a public meeting the term is almost equivalent to withdrawal of ambassadors!' *An Cho* (w. Mayo).

Seáilín n. 'A little shawl' CBE 104 (Leitrim).

Seal n. In form **shall**. While, spell. 'I spent a shall in Manchester' Mac C (Monaghan); 'I'm going out for a shall' TB (Cavan).

Scalaí n. 'A contrary person' Mac C (Monaghan).

Sealbhán n. 'A crowd of people, gathered for a fair, a sports day or the like' G (n.w. Donegal); 'A flock of sheep' Del (Antrim).

Seamhrach adj. 'Neat, tidy' CBD (n. Kerry).

Seamróg n. Shamrock, *trifolium repens. al.* **seamaróg** DOH (e. Limerick). As **shamrokes** in Ben Jonson, *The Irish Masque*: 'I vill giue tee leaue to cram my mout phit shamrokes and butter ...'

Séan agus sonas phr. In form **shey-an agus sonus**. Literally, prosperity and happiness. Michael Banim, *Crohoor of the Billhook* 1, 16: '"Go dthoga diuyh ... shey-an agus sonus duiv", bespoke his mendicant profession'; *recte* 'Go dtuga Dia séan agus sonas daoibh': may God grant you prosperity and happiness (Kilkenny).

Seán dearg n. phr. Literally, Red Seán. 'Brown binder twine, used for tying hay' MC (w. Clare).

Sean nós n. phr. Also as **shanaos**. Literally, old custom. Method of traditional singing (Gen.). Lady Morgan, *The Wild Irish Girl*, 191: 'A nurse hums old cronans or amuses me with what she calls a little shanaos'.

Seán Saor n. 'The travelling salesman who erected his stall on fair days' H (n. Clare); BOD (s. w. Cork).

Seanachal n. In form **shanahal**. In term **shanahal flag**: 'the flag that serves as a window ledge' CBE 98 (Kilkenny).

Seanachogaint n. Literally, old chewing. (Act of) complaining. 'Stop your seanachogaint' CBD (n. Kerry).

Seanad n. The Senate. James Joyce, *Finnegans Wake* 372.

Séanas n. 'A gap between the upper front teeth' JC (w. Cork); MF (Westmeath). Diminutive, **séanaisín** NB (w. Limerick). See *fánas*.

Seanbhean n. 1. 'An old woman. "A poor seanbhean came to the door a while ago"' G (s. Kilkenny). 2. 'A young girl who is too grown up in her ways' CBD (n. Kerry); 'A girl who is old-fashioned in dress and manner' NB (w. Limerick).

Seanchaí n. Also in forms **shanachie, shanachy, senachy**. Teller of traditional stories; one versed in folklore and genealogy. Seumus MacManus, *The Bend of the Road* 53: 'We would, in the wildest night in winter, travel far and fare ill to hear a story of Dan – the great Dan – from the most indifferent shanachy'; Seumas MacManus, *Bold Blades of Donegal* 328: 'We sat on our hunkers drinking it from the shanachie ... trolling out his story'; ibid. 166: 'Our intense desire to own a handball it was that drove us to introduce the Devil to the card game ... not any frivolous wish to give the countryside's shanachies an exciting subject for a generation after' (Donegal); Lady Morgan,*The Wild Irish Girl* 192: 'Senachy was the name of the antiquary retained in every noble family to preserve its exploits etc.' (Leinster).

Seanchas n. Also in forms **shanagh, seanach, shanachus, seanahas**. Talk, conversation, storytelling. 'That's enough of the seanchas, childer; time for bed' Dee (w. Waterford); Michael Banim, *Crohoor of the Billhook* 1,15: 'their appetite for shanachus, a word expressive of reverend gossip, when entered into by a pleasant conversational party ...' (Kilkenny); 'A friendly exchange of yarns about times past. To shanagh means to talk or chat' O'K (Tyrone); Seumus MacManus, *A Lad of the O'Friels*, 306: 'Sit ye down till we have a seanach.' (Donegal); John Boyce, *Mary Lee, or The Yank in Ireland* 26: 'He's fond of a seanahas' (Donegal).

Seandraoi n. Literally, old druid. 'A young lad with all the airs of a wise old man' MS (e. Limerick); NB (w. Limerick); 'An old man, or one who feigns age to escape work' CBD (n. Kerry); 'A young man in delicate health' *IG* (Kilkenny).

Seanduine n. As **shandanagh**. Old person. George Fitzmaurice, *The Pie-Dish*: 'It's roused entirely the old grey shandanagh is in himself' (Kerry).

Seanduine n. Old person. 1. An old man. 'What interest would she have in a seanduine like you?' JL (w. Cork). 2. 'A young person who is too precocious' NB (w. Limerick); 'A very conservative young man' ibid.

Seangán n. Also as **shingawn, shangan, shingan**. 1. 'An ant. 'Get up out of that before the seangáns eat you alive'' JC (w. Cork); 'The shangans are amazing creatures' PJG (mid-Donegal); 'The shingans are building away there' PON (n. Co. Dublin). 2. Figuratively, a weak person. 'I know him well; a miserable seangán of a man' MJD (w. Cork); Wm. Carleton, *Ned M'Keown* 1, 11: 'Get out, you shingaun'. Carleton's misleading gloss is 'fairy-like, or connected with the fairies' (Tyrone). Michael Banim, *Crohoor of the Billhook* 1, 22: 'What's that you say there, you shingawn you?' Glossed, erroneously, by Banim as 'a diminutive being'.

Seanóg n. 'A black, hooded cloak worn by women' JW (s. Tipperary).

Séantóir n. 'A pervert' MF (Mayo).

Searbhán n. 1. A bitter, sarcastic person. 'He's a nasty oul' searbhán, and he wouldn't have a good word to say about his own mother' PD (Carlow). 2. 'The dandelion' PB (s. Tipperary).

Searbhas n. In form **sharoos**. 1. Bitterness, sarcasm. 'That's enough of your sharoos. Keep a civil tongue in your head' JC (w. Cork). Hence **sharoosach**, sarcastic. 'She's a sharoosach old strap' RBB (s. Kilkenny). 2. To be annoyed by somebody's behaviour. 'That one sharooses me with her airs and graces'; 'I was never as sharoosed in all my born life' J (s. e. Wexford).

Searrach n. 'A foal' JL (w. Cork); MC (e. Mayo). [See *rith searraigh*.]

Seas n. 1. 'A bench in a hayrick caused by cutting away portion of it' MF (Westmeath). 2. 'A heap of straw' *IG* (Cavan).

Seasamh n. (Act of) standing. Phrase 'He fell out of his standing', direct translation of *thit sé as a sheasamh* – he collapsed W (e. Wicklow); PD (Carlow); FM (s. Wexford).

Seascaire croí n. In form **shasagh cree**. Heart's-ease, *Prunella vulgaris* H (n. Donegal).

Seatach n. 'An urchin; an illegitimate child' *IG* (Kilkenny). [Cf. *siota*: 'a pet, a chit, an ill-bred child' *Dinn.*]

Seibineach n. Also **shebanock**. 1. 'A big fat cat' JC (w. Cork). 2. 'A woman of imposing stature' H (n. Clare). 3. 'A big strong man: "A seibineach of a man"' *An Cho* (w. Mayo); 'A strong bouncing person or animal. "He killed a great big shebanock of a rabbit"' *CBE* 266 (mid-Tipperary).

Séideán n. (Act of) panting. 'There was a séideán in him: he was panting' *CBE* 104 (Leitrim).

Séideog n. 'A puff of breath, wind' *CBE* 104 (Leitrim).

Seift n. Also in form **sheft**. A plan, strategy. Hence **shefting**. 'If you haven't the proper tools to do a job, you have to resort to shefting, devising some strategy' Mas (s. Tipperary). 'What shefting have you? said to a person too slow to pay up' MP (mid-Tipperary).

Seilmide n. Snail, slug. 'Seilmide, seilmide, put out your horn. A children's saying' H (n. Clare). In form **sheliky pooky** FM (Wexford). **Shellachy-booka-baaka**-ER (Louth).

Seirgtheach n. 'A wasted, withered person. "The poor old seirgtheach would be as well off in St. Mullins graveyard"' PD (Carlow).

Seisceann n. In forms **sheskin, shaskeen, shaskin**. (Ulster). Sedgy bog, marsh, swamp.

Seisreach n. 'A pair of plough horses' *CBD* (n. Kerry).

Séithleach n. 'A tall, useless, lazy wretch' JL (w. Cork).

Seo amach linn phr. Let's go out! 'Said when about to leave a public house' *CBD* (s. Kerry).

Seó bóthair n. phr. Literally, road show. A spectacle. 'Stop making a seó bóthair of yourself' JL (w. Cork); PB (s. Tipperary).

Seo interj. Here! Peadar O'Donnell, *Adrigoole* 127: 'Seo, this oul' chat won't put up a fence'. In phrase **Seo well**, all right. Peadar O'Donnell, *The Knife* 141: 'Will you shut yer mouth? ... Seo well, I won't say a word' (Donegal).

Seoch n. In forms **shough, sheugh, sheuch, shaugh**. 1. A gripe, ditch, drain on roadside. Wm. Carleton, *Shane Fhad's Wedding* 2, 62: '... sometimes one in crossing a stile or ditch would drop into the shough' (Tyrone); Seumas MacManus, *A Lad of the O'Friels* 54: 'I had much ado to leap the sheuchs' (Donegal). 2. In phrase **in the sheugh**, ruined. 'If I hadn't wrocht it carefully, it 'ud be in the sheugh' H (n. Donegal); 'A Donegal body has no need to look in a dry shaugh for her answer – good at repartee' ibid.

Seoinín n. In form **shoneen**. Literally, Little John (Bull). A derisory name for an Irishman who apes English ways. James Joyce, *Ivy Day in the Committee Room* 135: 'Hasn't the working man as good a right to be in the Corporation as anyone else – ay, and a better right than those shoneens that are always hat in hand before any fellow with a handle to his name?'

Seoirseáil n. Hustle, bustle. 'What's the seoirseáil in aid of?' NB (w. Limerick). Hence, **seoirseáiling**. 'She was seoirseáiling around in the wet' ibid.

Seolta adj. In phrase **go seolta** 'At ease, proceeding smoothly. "Things are go seolta, thank God"' MC (e. Mayo).

Seordán n. 1. 'A wheeze in the bronchial tubes' MS (e. Limerick); *CBE* 266 (mid-Tipperary). 2. 'A whistling of the wind in a chimney. "There's a seordán in the chimney to-night"' *CBD* (n. Kerry); PB (s. Tipperary).

Sí gaoithe n. In form **shee gwee**. Literally, fairies of the wind. A whirlwind, thought to be caused by fairies on the move. 'The tinker went out of the yard like the shee gwee, and the little dog after him' J (s. e. Wexford); MS (e. Limerick); JL (w. Cork).

Sí n. Also spelled **sidhe, sidh, siodh**. The fairy host; the people of the sí, or fairy mound JL (w. Cork. Gen. Munster).

Siamsáil v. Wailing. 'It is often the repeating wail of a child that has been chastised or disappointed. The siamsáil actually outlives the sorrow and has to continue, even in scarcity of breath, as if to advertise the injustice that has been done' *An Cho* (w. Mayo).

Siansach n. 'A ringing sound. "The horse knocked siansach out of the road"' MJD (w. Cork).

Síbín n. In form **shebeen**. A place where drink is sold without a licence. J. M. Synge, *The Playboy of the Western World* 91: 'It'd be a crazy pot-boy'd lodge him in the shebeen where he works by day ...'; Somerville and Ross, *The Last Day Of Shraft* 253: 'In a blinding flash of insight I realised that my brother-in-law and I had been taken red-handed in a shebeen, that is to say, a house where drink is illicitly sold without a licence' (w. Cork); James Joyce, *Ulysses* 312: 'Blind to the world up in a shebeen in Bride street ...'

Sifín n. In forms **sheefin, shifeen, shiffin**. Stem of corn, hay, straw, rush. In phrases **sifín siúil**, the travelling straw, **oíche na sifín**, the night of the straws, **lá na sifín**, the day of the straws. In Donegal folklore. 'Dan O'Connell boasted that he could raise Ireland in one day or send a message from end to end in twenty four hours. On that night (oíche) from various headquarters, a man went forth from a house with a straw (sifín) to the next house. He of that house had immediately to pull a straw from his thatch and start off to the next house, and so on; each man going to the nearest house to his own. Thus word was passed all round Ireland in one night' Tr (Donegal). Phrase, **to lean on a shiffin**: 'to depend on somebody, or something, untrustworthy' JV (e. Wicklow).

Síle an phíce n. Also as **sheelafeeka**. The earwig. 'The place is crawling with sheelafeekas' *CBE* 266 (mid-Tipperary).

Síle n. Also as **sheelah**. 'An effeminate man' G (n.w. Donegal); 'A man too fond of female society, a mollycoddle' Q (Donegal); 'He's around the house in an old sheelah' *CBE* 266 (mid-Tipperary); '*EASI* 320:

'Used in the South as a reproachful name for a boy or a man inclined to do work or interest himself in affairs properly belonging to women.'

Síle na gCíoch n. phr. In forms **Sheila na Gig, Sheelin-a-gig**. An obscene stone fertility fetish, representing a woman displaying her breasts and vulva. Michael Banim, *Crohoor of the Billhook* 1,188: 'Strike up Andrew Carey, or Sheelin-a-gig, or something that's hearty.' Here, the name of a dance tune.

Silte adj. 'Inefficient, careless. "That work is as silte as I've ever come across"' MW (s. Wexford).

Silte *al.* **silteach**. Drooped; looking weak; enfeebled, unwell. 'He's silte, the poor man' PB (s. Tipperary); 'I'm feeling silteach' Mas (s. Tipperary).

Simide n. A layabout. 'Not a stroke of work does he do, that simide' JL (w. Cork).

Simidín 'A small stack of corn, especially a field stack. "All he made was one simidín that day"' MC (e. Mayo).

Sin é phr. 'That's it' H (n. Clare).

Sin scéal eile phr. 'That's another story' H (n. Clare).

Singirlín n. 1. As **shingerleens**. *EASI* 321: 'Small bits of finery; ornamental tags and ends-of ribbons, bow-knots, tassels etc. – hanging on dress, curtains, furniture etc.'. 2. 'An icicle' MS (e. Limerick). 3. 'The flowers of the fuchsia' JC (w. Cork).

Sinn Féin n. phr. Ourselves. A nationalist political party inspired by the writings of Arthur Griffith from 1899 onwards. Latterly the political wing of the IRA. In James Joyce's *Ulysses* 163, the term is used loosely by Bloom when he means the IRB. This was commonly done by the British Army of the day. Ibid. 304: Sinn Fein amhain, *recte* Sinn Féin amháin, ourselves alone.

Síob n. In form **sheeve**. 'Light rain' *Pe* (Wexford).

Síobadh sneachta n. In form **sheebow**. A blizzard. W. F. Marshall, *Sarah Ann*: 'But I'm for tacklin' Sarah Ann/ No matter if the snow/ Is everywhere sheebowin'/ When the morra comes I'll go'; O'K (Tyrone).

Siobhán fhada n. The heron, *ardea cinerea* CBD (n. Kerry). *al.* **Siobhán na bPortach** SOM (w. Cork), in form **Joanie the Bog** MJD (w. Cork).

Siocán n. Also as **shuckaun**. 1. 'Light frost' MF (Westmeath). 2. 'A cold, aloof person' NB (w. Limerick). 3. The fieldfare, *Turdus pilaris*: NB (w. Limerick); CBE 266 (mid-Tipperary). 4. A weak person. '"He's like a dying siocán – in a very weak state from illness' SOM (w. Cork).

Síofra n. 1. 'A fairy; a changeling' RBB (w. Waterford); PC (n. Clare) 2. 'A small, light person' DOC (Limerick). 3. 'A deceitful, or churlish person. "I wouldn't trust that síobhra an inch"' MS (e. Limerick); CBD (n. Kerry). 4. 'A pale, wan person' DOH (e. Limerick).

Síog n. Also in form **sheeg, shig**. 1. A stripe, streak. 'She have black hair one day, and blonde sheegs through it the next' Dee (w. Waterford); 'A dark streak down a horse's backbone; a good sign of a horse' JL (w. Cork). 2. 'A large quadrangular block of hay' DOH (e. Limerick); 'A pile of hay, corn, or flax, thatched and roped down for the winter; a long, rectangular arrangement of hay-bales built in a field' O'K (Tyrone); MS (e. Limerick.) 3. Hence 'to shig: to stack bales or sheaves' O'K (Tyrone); 'He's only cuttin' the corn when he should be shiggin' it' G (n.w. Donegal).

Síog n. Also in forms **sheeog, sheehogue**. 1. A fairy. Michael Banim, *The Croppy* 1, 230: 'D'ye think, ye sheeogs o' the Divil, that it's a bosthoon ye have to talk to?' (Kilkenny); Percy French, *To E.R.*: 'For once you heard the fairy bells and saw the little sheehogues play'. 2. 'A good-for-nothing boy fond of sitting at the fire' MF (Westmeath). 3. 'A small effeminate-looking man' FM (s. Wexford). 4. 'A term of endearment for a sprightly, mischievous girl' *An Cho* (w. Mayo).

Síogaí n. Also in forms **sheegie, shiggy**. 1. An elf. Michael Harkin, *Inisowen: its History*, 178: ' It was the doings of the sheegie' (Donegal). 2. In combinations **sheegie-thimble, shiggy-thimble**, the foxglove H; Q (n. Donegal).

Siogán n. 'A line of sods of turf thrown loosely together' MC (w. Clare).

Siolla n. 'A glint of sunlight; a bright spell between showers' PB (s. Tipperary).

Siolla n. Also in form **shulla**. 1. A puff of wind. 'Give the fire a siolla of the bellows' C (e. Limerick). 2. 'A jot or tittle; a short period of time. "Make a shulla": hurry up' MP (mid-Tipperary); '"Stay another shulla"; "Give me a little shulla": court me for a little while' CBE 266 (mid-Tipperary). 3. A push. 'Give him a shulla over the wall' Mas (s. Tipperary)

Síománach n. *al.* **síomán**. 'A loiterer; a dead-and-alive creature' NB (w. Limerick).

Síorraí adj. In form **sheery**. Eternal. In phrase **murder sheery**! Mac C (Monaghan); TB (Cavan).

Síos interj. In form **chise**. Down! Michael Banim, *Crohoor of the Billhook* 1, 234: '"Chise! Chise!" roared out a number of stentorian voices ...' (Kilkenny).

Sioscadh n. 'Whispering, especially of that subdued kind that we associate with plotting, or with anxiety, or with reverence. Women at the back of a church are prone to sioscadh' *An Cho* (w. Mayo).

Siota n. 'The covered foreward part of a fishing boat under which sleeping accomodation was provided' RBB (w. Waterford).

Siotalach n. In form **shutaloch**. 'A soft, fat young animal such as a rabbit or a pup' CBE 266 (mid-Tipperary).

Síreagán n. 'One who is too well off' NB (w. Limerick).

Siúd ort interj. In forms **sha-dhurth, shud-orth**. A toast: 'here's to your health!'

Michael Banim, *Crohoor of the Billhook* 1, 180: '... room was made for Shea; and "shadhurth, a bouchal" addressed to him ...' (Kilkenny); Wm. Carleton, *Phelim O'Toole's Courtship* 2, 227: 'Talkin's druthy work. Shudorth a rogarah! an' a pleasant honeymoon to us!' Carleton's gloss: 'this is to you, you rogue' (Tyrone).

Siúlóir n. In forms **shooler, shuler**. 'A wanderer, tramp, one who roves. Often applied in a derogatory way to itinerant families' O'K (Tyrone); PLH (n. Roscommon); *The Shooler's Child*: title of play by Seamus O'Kelly. Hence **shoolin**. Michael Banim, *Crohoor of the Billhook* 1, 90: 'I gave over the shoolin' life' (Kilkenny).

Siúnán n. As **shoonaun**. *EASI* 321: 'A deep, circular basket, made of twisted rushes or straw, and lined with calico; it had a cover and was used for holding linen, clothes etc.' (Limerick and Cork); GC (Laois, n. Kilkenny).

Siúnsa n. 'A smart belt of a stick' MJD (w. Cork).

Slab n. In form **slob**. Mud, slush. 'I tripped, and went up to my arse in slob' D (s. e. Wexford); RBB (Waterford). Hence **slobs**, alluvial lands at the sea's edge, such as the Wexford harbour slobs. [Old Irish *slab*, mud.]

Slabaire n. 'A person who is careless about his dress, his food, or his work' DOC (Limerick).

Slabar n., v. 1. Mud, gunge. 'He fell coming home from the pub and you should see the slabar on his new suit' JM (w. Cork); Seamus Heaney, *Death of a Naturalist* 15: 'But best of all was the warm thick slobber/ Of frogspawn that grew like clotted water/ In the shade of the banks ...' (Derry). 2. To spill a drink or food in a clumsy manner. 'He slobbered the drink all over the table' J (s.e. Wexford); G (s. Kilkenny); J.M. Synge, *The Well of the Saints* 24: 'If it is can't you open the big slobbering mouth you have and say what way it'll be done ...'; Seamus Heaney, *Death of a Naturalist* 21: 'Something slobbered curtly, close, / Smudging the silence ...' (Derry). See *slab*.

Slabrachán n. As **slobrachaun**. 'A slobberer; a person who eats or works in a sloppy fashion' PD (Carlow); *CBE* 98 (Kilkenny).

Slac inter. 'Said when hunting out the ducks' *CBE* 34 S (Galway).

Slacht n. 'Tidiness, neatness; engaging appearance or manners. "There's no slacht in her" would be said of a young woman who was not pretty, or of a woman who was slovenly or a bad housekeeper' *IG* (Kilkenny; JL (w. Cork); H (n. Clare); OCn (Laois); MC (e. Mayo).

Slachtmhar adj. Tidy. 'He's a slachtmhar person' MS (e. Limerick); JM (w. Cork); OCn (Laois); *CBE* 47 S (Galway).

Slaim n. 'A pancake' McK (Leitrim).

Sláimín n. 'A slovenly, untidy woman' *IG* (Kilkenny).

Sláinte interj. Health! A toast. James Joyce, *Ulysses* 53: 'There was a fellow I once knew in Barcelona, queer fellow, used to call it his postprandial. Well: sláinte!' As **slaunty** in *Finnegans Wake* 311. **Sláinte mhilis** interj., sweet health!, as **slaw the Mellish** in Michael Banim, *Crohoor of the Billhook* 1, 271: '"Slaw the Mellish", said Andy, smacking his lips' (Kilkenny).

Slám n. 1. 'A pancake' H (n. Clare). 2. A handful. 'Seán took a slám of flour out of the sack' ibid. 'You could get a slám of money ... a picturesque way of referring to a legacy: "They got a great slám of money when the uncle died"' *An Cho* (w. Mayo).

Slám n. Dirt, slime. Hence **to slám**, to daub *Pe* (Wexford).

Slamairce n. 1. A soft mass. 'The spuds are in slamairce by you' JC (w. Cork). 2. 'An untidy woman' JL (w. Cork). [Cf. dialect English *slammerkin*, a fat, slovenly woman. George Brittaine, *Irishmen and Irishwomen*: 'She felt in good humour with all the human race, even with Kitty Moore, the slammerkin housewife'.]

Slámóg n. 'An untidy girl' MP (mid-Tipperary); MC (e. Mayo).

Slámóg n. 'An untidy woman' DOC (Limerick); 'She's only a slámóg of a straoil' JL (w. Cork); PB (s. Tipperary).

Slán interj. Farewell! **Slán leat**, said to departing person, as **slane lets** in Anon., *Captain Thomas Stuckley*. **Slán agat**, said by departing person, as **slane haggat** in *Captain Thomas Stuckley*.

Slánlus n. Literally, health herb. 1. The water plaintain, *Alisma plantago*. 2. Floating pond-weed, *Potamogeton natans*. 3. Ripple grass, ribwort: *Plantago lanceolata* and *Plantago major* G (n.w. Donegal); MF (Westmeath); Lys (Kerry); NB (w. Limerick); *BASJ* (Cavan).

Slaodaí n. In form **sloody**. 'A lazy, good-for nothing person. "Get up out of that, you sloody"' MG (n.w. Donegal).

Slaoiste n. In form **sleeshta**. 'A useless person who never did a stroke of work in his life' TB (Cavan).

Slat mhara n. In form **slock-marra**. The stem of *Laminaria bulbosa*. 'They form a useful cudgel. When the bailiffs went out to Tory Island for taxes "the wimmen bate them out of it with slock-marra"' H (n. Donegal).

Sláthach n. Slime in water. Hence **slawhagh**, 'muddy, dirty' MF (Westmeath).

Sleabhac n. Also as **sleabhcán, sloukane, sloke, sluke, slouk**. *EASI* 328: 'A sea plant of the family of laver (*Porphyra laciniata*) found growing on the rocks round the coast, which is esteemed a table delicacy; dark-coloured, almost black; often pickled and eaten with pepper vinegar etc. Seen in all the Dublin fish shops. The name ... is now known all over the Three Kingdoms, is anglicised from Irish *sleabhac, sleabhcán*.'

Sleabhcán n. 1. In form **schlooker**. 'A worthless, untrustworthy person' S Ua G (s. Tipperary). 2. 'A cow's horn' *CBE* 104 (Leitrim).

Sleamhnán n. 'A sty in the eye' MC (e. Mayo); 'The old people used to cure the sleamhnán with a poultice made of bread and cat's piss' PC (n. Clare).

Sleamhnánaí n. 'A slippery customer, a sloucher' H (n. Clare); 'A sly fellow who usually goes alone' NB (w. Limerick).

Sleán n. Also in form **slane**. 'A spade for cutting turf' Ham (e. Clare); JM (w. Cork); *CBE* 104 (Leitrim); Stephen Gwynn, *The Glade in the Forest* 207: 'They brought me a spade and a slane for cutting turf'; JB (s. Armagh & n. Louth); TOM (s. Tipperary).

Sleis n. Variant of **slios**. Slope. 'A person who walks with a lean to one side, indicating stubborness or belligerence. "He has a sleis on him"' Ju (Sligo).

Sléisín n. 'A method of wrestling whereby the leg is put over the hip of the opponent, with a sudden pull downward' *IG* (Meath).

Slíbhín n. In forms **sleeveen, sleevin**. A sly person. 'A real sleeveen, that one' MW (s. Wexford); Flann O'Brien, *The Dalkey Archive* 146: 'What are you doing hiding here, you long-faced sleeveen?'; Samuel Lover, *Legends and Stories of Ireland* 2, 180: 'How the man was chated by a sleeven vagabond.'

Slibire n. In form **slibidge**. 'A bedraggled person or animal. 'What did you get? I only got one old slibidge of a rabbit' OCn (Laois).

Slige n. In form **shlig**. 'A thin splinter of stone' *CBE* 266 (mid-Tipperary).

Sligín n. In form **sliggin**. 1. A little shell 2. 'A thin, flat stone, ideal for skimming over water' D (Kildare).

Slincín n. 'A stillborn child or animal' TdeB (Galway). [Cf. *Slink:* an abortive or premature calf or other animal' *OED*.]

Slinneánaí n. 'A tall, narrow, good-for-nothing type of fellow' Ham (e. Clare).

Slinneánaí n. In form **shlingauny**. 'A lazy lounger, one who has a shoulder of laziness in his appearance' *CBE* 266 (mid-Tipperary).

Slinnín n. 'A small piece of slate. This word is used in the neighbourhood of the slate quarries, Walsh Mountains, Kilkenny' *IG*

Slíocaithe pp. In form **shluckt**. Polished, sleek. 'Wait until I have myself shluckt' *CBE* 266 (mid-Tipperary).

Sliocht n. Mark, trace, track. Phrase **tá a shliocht air**, translated as **sign's on it**. 'He worked hard, and sign's on it; he's well off now' PD (s. Carlow); (Gen.). [Cf. *dá chomhartha sin*.]

Slíodóir n. Also as **sleedar**. 'A sneaking, skulking person' PC (n. Clare); 'A proper sleedar of a young fellow' MW (s. Wexford).

Slíomadóir n. 'A cunning, tricky person' *CBE* S 34 (Galway).

Sliopach n. In form **slippaugh** Numbness. John Boyce, *Shandy Maguire* 201: 'That divlish Haybrew (Hebrew language) pit a sort av a slippaugh on my tongue that I'll niver get rid av' (Donegal).

Sliosta adj. Fair, courteous. Hence to **sleuster**, to flatter, cajole H (n. Donegal).

Sliotar n. *al.* **sliodar**. A hurling ball (Gen.); 'A puck of the sliodar' NB (w. Limerick).

Sliseach n. 'A person with big feet' PB (s. Tipperary).

Sliseog n. 1. A sliver of wood; 'a piece of stick that goes up under the nail' *CBE* 34 S (Galway). 2. 'A slip of a girl' McK (Leitrim); *IG* (Cavan); *CBE* 34 S (Galway).

Sliúcaire n. In form **shlooker**. 1. 'A slinker, a sly-boots' PD (s. Carlow); 'A man who listens behind ditches to the conversation of his neighbours' PB (s. Tipperary). 2. 'One who shirks work' *CBE* 266 (mid-Tipperary).

Sliúch n. 'A sly person' MP (mid-Tipperary).

Sliúdar v. 'To cajole' MF (Westmeath); 'That fellow would sliúdar a farmer out of his bank balance' FF (Meath).

Sliústar n. In form **slewster**. A passionate kiss. Wm. Carleton, *The Geography of an Irish Oath*, 15: '"Give me a slewsther, agrah – a sweet one now!" He then laid his mouth

to hers'. Carleton's gloss: 'A kiss of fondness'.

Sloc n. 'A hole, pit, hollow' NB (w. Limerick).

Slóchtán n. The sow-thistle, *Sorchus arvensis*: *CBE* 34 S (Galway).

Slod n. 'A pool of stagnant water' G (n.w. Donegal); Diminutive, **slodán** S (n.w. Donegal)

Slog n., v. In form **slug**. 1. A draft, swig of liquid. 'Here, take a slug of this, it will straighten you out' O'K (Tyrone). 2. Hence, to swallow. 'He said he wasn't hungry, but he fairly slugged down his dinner' Smy (n. Clare); Seamus Heaney, *Death of a Naturalist* 21: 'My mother took first turn, set up rhythms that slugged and thumped for hours ...'

Sloga n. A pothole; a rut in a road. 'You could drown a litter of pups in the slogas of the road' MJD (w. Cork).

Slogaire n. Also as **sluggara**. 1. 'A quagmire; a hole in the surface of a bog' MC (w. Clare); 'Quicksand' *CBE* 266 (mid-Tipperary). 2. 'A glutton, especially in drink. "That slogaire drank every drop in the bottle"' MC (e. Mayo).

Slogóg n. 'A big draft, swig' RBB (Waterford).

Slograch n. As **slogra** 'The hole through which a field drain enters a subterranean drain' MS (e. Limerick).

Slotaire n. 'An untidy person' *IG* (Cavan). [< English *slut*]

Slua n. As **slew**. Multitude, host, army. Seumus MacManus, *Bold Blades of Donegal* 33: 'mercilessly cutting down slews of Turks who had escaped annihilation in the first onset'; 'A gang of youngsters' SOM (n. Co. Dublin).

Slúisteoireacht n. Also as **slewsthering**. (Act of) lounging, idling. William Carleton, *Shane Fadh's Wedding* 1, 62: 'There was nothing but shaking hands and kissing and all kinds of slewsthering'; 'He spends the days in bed and the nights at the dances slewsterin' around after women' PJG (mid-Donegal).

Slután n. Snap apple. 'A children's game for Hallow E'en' RBB (w. Waterford).

Smacht n. Control, authority, discipline. 'Mind now! I'll put smacht on you' BOD (s.w. Cork).

Smailc n. Also as **smalick**. 1. A blow. 'A few good smailcs I got in my time from the master' PC (n. Clare). Hence to smalick, to beat, thrash. 'I'll smalick that young hallion who keeps ringing my door-bell at night' O'K (Tyrone). 2. 'To smailc, to eat avariciously' *An Cho* (w. Mayo).

Smalcaire n. Also in forms **smalkera**, **smalcra**. 'A home made wooden spoon used for eating Easter eggs at Clúideog' (q.v.) OC (Monaghan); *EASI* 328: 'Smalkera, a rude, home-made wooden spoon'; 'Smalcra' JB (s. Armagh & n. Louth).

Smeach n. Also as **smock**. 1. 'A blow or puck in the game of hurling' Smy (n. Clare). 2. Movement. 'We found him on the road with the bike on top of him. There wasn't a smeach out of him. Drunk as a maggot' PD (s. Carlow); 'Smeach, a jerk' NB (w. Limerick); 'Smock' PON (n. Dublin).

Smeachán n. 1. Also in form **smathan**, **smahan**. Taste, nip, small amount of drink. James Joyce, *Counterparts* 107: 'We'll have just one little smahan more and then we'll be off'; Flann O'Brien, *The Dalkey Archive* 127: 'Does he take e'r a smahan of Jameson or Tullamore?' 2. 'Smeachán: a kiss' MS (e. Limerick). [< English, *smack*]

Smeadar n. 1. A mess of soft food, such as porridge. "There was smeadar all over the floor"' MC (e. Mayo). 2. Hence, to smear. 'When he got him on the ground he smeadered his face with mud' H (n. Clare). 3. A blow. 'I gave him a smeadar on the pus' H (n. Clare). As **smadder** in Walter Macken, *Mungo's Mansion* 3. *al.* **smeádar**. 'A heavy blow. "We hit him a smeádar"'

CBD (n. Kerry); *IG* (Carlow). Hence **smeádared** FM (s. Wexford); PD (s. Carlow); G (s. Kilkenny).

Smearach adj. 'Greasy-faced' *IG* (Kilkenny).

Smearachán n. 1. 'A greasy-faced, swarthy woman' *IG* (Kilkenny); 'A no-good, grimy-faced person' MC (e. Mayo). 2. 'A person who always plays up to what he thinks are his betters, the clergy and the like' PD (Carlow). 3. 'A miserable person' *CBE* 34 S (Galway).

Sméarálaí n. 'Smearer, messy worker' NB (w. Limerick).

Smidiríní n. In form **smithereens**. Seamus Heaney, *Wintering Out* 75: 'Trout were flipping the sky/Into smithereens' (Gen.).

Smig n. 1. 'Chin, especially a pointed chin' H (n. Clare); *An Cho* (w. Mayo). 2. 'Beard on chin' MF (Westmeath). 3. 'A goat's beard' MF (Westmeath). Diminutive, **smigín**. 'One delighful use of the word smigín, little chin, is when it is applied to help, a chin-hold, given to a non-swimmer by an adept: "Give me a smigín" is the gentle request' *An Cho* (w. Mayo).

Smig mhadadh n. Literally, chin of a dog. 'A receding chin' H (n. Clare). See *pus mhadadh*.

Smionagar n. In form **smindhers**. Smithereens. Seumus MacManus, *Bold Blades of Donegal* 297: 'The utorious scamp o' mine has my heart in smindhers.'

Smior n. 'A thin, worn person' NB (w. Limerick).

Smíst n. 1. 'A fool' NB (w. Limerick). 2. 'A big, lazy person' JL (w. Cork).

Smuais n. In form **smoosh**. Marrow. 'From this comes the meaning attached to it here – spirit, life, pride. "There's no smoosh in her at all"' *CBE* 266 (mid-Tipperary).

Smuaiseáil n. In form **smooshin**. (Act of) sniffing. 'Nosing, and not enclined to eat. The pigs are only smooshin' *CBE* 266 (mid-Tipperary).

Smuaiseálaí n. In form **smooshauly**. 1.
'One who trifles with his work' *CBE* 266
(mid-Tipperary). 2. 'A groper' ibid.

Smuasachán n. 'A silent, dour, unpleasant
fellow' H (n. Clare); 'A sniveller' RBB
(Waterford).

Smuasaíl n. Snivelling, unpleasantness. 'Give
over that smuasaíl and do the job' H (n.
Clare); RBB (w. Waterford).

Smuc interj. 'What you would say to hunt
out the pigs' *CBE* 34 S (Galway).

Smugach adj. 'Bold, conceited, sure of
oneself. 'I can't stand somebody that
smugach' DOC (Limerick). [< English
smug]

Smugachán n. 'A conceited person, sure of
himself' DOC (Limerick). See *smugach*.

Smugairle n. Snot, sniffle. Plural, **smug-
airlí**. Hence **smugairling**. 'Stop that smugairling and blow your nose' H (n. Clare).

Smuilc n. 1. A surly expression. 'I'll knock
that smuilc off you' JPL (w. Cork); H (n.
Clare). *al.* **smulc** PB (s. Tipperary). 2. 'A
pug-nose' RBB (w. Waterford); s. Kilkenny);
JL (w. Cork).

Smuilceachán n. 'A surly looking person'
NB (w. Limerick). *al.* **smulcachán** PB (s.
Tipperary); DOC (Limerick).

Smúit n. In form **smidge**. Smudge. 'Don't
put a smidge on that new dress' TB
(Cavan); Mac C (Tyrone).

Smulcais n. Rubbish. 'The hay you'd find,
wet and trampled at the bottom of a rick;
useless for anything' JL (w. Cork).

Smúránaí n. 'A quiet, lazy, crafty person'
DOC (Limerick); 'A "cute hoor"' PC (n.
Clare).

Smúsach n. Pulp. 'He made smúsach of the
car against the gable of the house' JL (w.
Cork).

Smut n. 1. 'A frown, an angry expression
on a person's face' G (n.w. Donegal)

2. Phrase **Domhnach na smut**: 'The
Sunday of the frowning faces, the first
Sunday in Lent, from the discontented
appearance of the women who did not get a
man' Tr (Donegal). 3. 'A stump, a broken-
off bit: "Give me a smut of tobacco"' NB
(w. Limerick); PB (s. Tipperary). 4. 'A
small, cocked nose' LB (s.w. Dublin). Diminutive, **smután** n. 'A block or stump of
timber' JL (w. Cork); RBB (w. Waterford);
NB (w. Limerick); MC (w. Clare).

Snab n. Stub. 'A snab of a candle.' Diminutive, **snabóg** OCn (Laois). As **snoboge** in
EASI 329 (Carlow).

Snadaí n. Also as **snoddy**. 'A sneak' *IG*
(Cavan); '"Come out here you snoddy, and
fight like a man," says he to the Guard' FF
(Monaghan).

Snag n. 'A snort after crying' MF (Westmeath). Hence **snagging**.

Snágaí n. As **snawgey**. 'A lifeless person,
a slowcoach. "That oul' snawgey would take
a week to do a day's work"' J (s.e. Wexford).

Snagarnach n. 'A stammer, stutter. Hence
snoggering PJG (Donegal).

Snaidhmín na péiste n. Literally, knot of
the worm. 'A knotted cord charm for curing
calves with gripe' MS (e. Limerick). See
ruathar péiste.

Snámhaí n. Also as **snaawee**. 'A sneaky
person, a dawdler, a creeper' OCn (Laois);
Mac C (Monaghan). See *sníomhaí-snámhaí*.
'A thin, miserable-looking person' MG (n.w.
Donegal); George Fitzmaurice, *The King of
the Barna Men*: '... and the snawwees will be
quaking before the Champion of Carraweira
...' (Kerry).

Snámhán n. Also as **snawvaun, snauvaun**.
1. (Act of) 'walking gracefully as if floating
on air' DOC (Limerick); 'She thinks a lot of
herself. 'Look at the snawvaun of her across
the room' Smy (n. Clare). 2. *EASI* 329:
'From *snámh*, swim: moving slowly like a
person swimming'.

Snámhánaí n. As **snawvauny**. 'A crawler, a
person dragging in speech or movement.

"She's a tedious snawvaunee"' *CBE* 266 (mid-Tipperary).

Snamhóg n. Also in form **snawag**. 'The young female crab, especially at mating time when it casts its shell' H (n. Donegal). [Cf. *Snamhaim*, I peel, decorticate. The male crab is *tarbhán* (q.v.).

Snaoisín n. In form **sneeshin**. Snuff. W.H. Floredice, *Memories of a Month among the Mere Irish*: 'He ups with the goolden snuff box ... and throws the full of it in Mary's face.'

Snas n. Also as **snosh**. 1. Polish, good appearance. 'You put a good snas on the work = you finished it well' OC (Monaghan); MF (Westmeath); LB (s.w. Dublin). In form 'snosh' *Pe* (Wexford); *EASI* 329: 'Neatness in clothes' (Carlow). 2. 'A type of lichen that grows in a well' PB (s. Tipperary).

Snasta adj. Well-finished: 'He did a snasta job' MF (Westmeath).

Snáthaid an diabhail n. The crane fly. In translated form, **devil's needle** MW (s. Wexford).

Snáthaid n. As **snawd**. 'A peg used to hold scallops in thatch' O'K (Tyrone)

Snáthán n. A little drop. 'He couldn't be drunk. All he had was a snáthán' PC (n. Clare). See *smáthán*.

Sneách n. 1. 'A very dirty person' PD (s. Carlow). 2. A slow person. 'Someone you are waiting for to come forward with cooperation, and that the wait seems interminable' *An Cho* (w. Mayo).

Sneachta séideáin n. Also as **snachta shaidhaun**. 'Wind-blown snow' MS (e. Limerick); *EASI* 329: 'Dry, powdery snow blown about by the wind: snachta shaidhaun' (Munster).

Sneás n. 'A sly, safe fellow' DOH (e. Limerick).

Snibire n. In form **shnibbirra**. 'An uncivil little person' *CBE* 266 (mid-Tipperary).

Sniog n. A drop. 'That much money for an old cow that haven't a sniog of milk!' JC (w. Cork).

Sníomhaí- snámhaí n. In form **sneewee snawee**. 'A good-for-nothing, fawning person' OC (Monaghan). See *snámhaí*.

Snugadán n. A sneak, a crafty person. Dermot O'Byrne, *Children of the Hills* 85: 'Then me old snugadán goes to Aillin' (Donegal).

Soc n. Also in form **sock**. Projecting end, nose. 'The soc is the point projecting from a plough or an anvil' MC (e. Mayo); 'The sock is the metal point fitted to the cutting edge of a plough' O'K (Tyrone); Seamus Heaney, *Death of a Naturalist* 24: 'An expert. He would set the wing/ And fit the bright steel-pointed sock.'

Socadán n. 1. 'A person who can't mind his own business' JPL (w. Cork) 2. 'A tight-lipped person with a hungry appearance' H (n. Clare).

Socair adj. Tranquil, comfortable. In phrases 1. **socair and easy** *IG* (Meath). 2. **Go socair** 'in an easygoing manner, calmly, "The horse was going go socair down the road when suddenly he shied at something and took off"' MC (e. Mayo).

Sóclach adj. Prosperous, comfortable. 'They are good and sóclach now after all their misfortune' TB (Cavan); *IG* (Meath, Monaghan).

Sodar n. A trot. 'I took the colt down the field at a nice easy sodar' MS (e. Limerick). 'There was a great sodar on him, he was in a great hurry' H (n. Clare). Hence **sodaring**, trotting *CBE* 98 (Kilkenny).

Sodóg n. 1. 'A soda cake, a thick pancake, especially one baked under the embers' McK (Leitrim); PD (s. Carlow); MC (Meath, Louth). 2. A buxom young woman. 'Well, isn't she the fine little sodóg' G (Kilkenny).

Solas n. Light. In phrase, **a sholais mo shúl agus mo chroí** in Wm. Carleton, *Tubber Derg* 2, 375, in form **A suilis mahuil agus**

machree (Light of my eyes and my heart). Also in Carleton, *Shane Fadh's Wedding* 2, 77 as a **suilish macree**, glossed by Carleton as 'light of my heart'.

Soláthar v. In form **slawher**. 'Gathering provision. "The ducks are going to slawher for themselves"' *CBE* 266 (mid-Tipperary).

Somachán n. As **summachaun**. 1. 'A soft innocent child' *EASI* 338 (Munster). 2. ibid. 'In Connaught it means a big, ignorant, puffed-up booby of a fellow'; *CBE* S 34 (Galway). 3. 'A small stack of hay' PLH (n. Roscommon).

Sonas n. In forms **sonce**, **sonce**. Happiness, luck, prosperity. 'Something of good size and value would be said to have some sonce with it' *Ballymena Observer* (Antrim).

Sonasach adj. In form **sonsy**. Happy, lucky, prosperous. William Carleton, *Shane Fadh's Wedding* vol 1, 82: 'sonsy Mary she was called'; 'Covering a multitude of applications, sonsy is a catch-all adjective denoting approval: nice, lucky, well-proportioned, neat, prosperous, healthy' O'K (Tyrone); LB (s.w. Dublin).

Sonc n. A nudge, push. 'I gave him a sonc in the ribs' H (n. Clare); *CBE* 266 (mid-Tipperary).

Sonuachar n. Also in form **sonuher**. A marriage partner. 'A toast to an unmarried person: Sláinte and sonuachar!' MS (e. Limerick); 'A toast to an unmarried person: Sonuachar to you!' H (n. Clare); Gerald Griffin, *The Collegians* 49: 'Sonuher to me, if I know.'

Sop n. 1. Wisp of hay, straw, etc. Somerville and Ross, *Great Uncle McCarthy* 11: 'Well, that's a fine raking horse in harness...and you'd drive him with a sop of hay in his mouth'; 'Toilets, is it? We had to make do with the wide open ré (q.v.) and a sop' JL (w. Cork); DOH (e. Limerick); PC (n. Clare); PB (s. Tipperary) AOL (Waterford); RBB (s. Kilkenny). Diminutive, **sopóg**, as **sopog**. 'A wisp of straw to stop the draught from entering under the door' Mac C (Monaghan). Diminutive, **soipín**, as **sippy**. 'A ball of rolled súgáns, hay or straw ropes,

used instead of a real ball in hurling and football' PC (n. Clare). 2. Straw bedding. J. M. Synge, *The Well of the Saints* 56: ' It was not, Molly Byrne, but lying down in a little rickety shed...across a sop of straw'; 'It's time to hit the sop' JM (w. Cork).

Sopachán n. A wispy person. 'A sopachán like him! A scarecrow!' AOL (mid Waterford).

Sopalach n. *al.* **sopaoileach**. 'Soft, rotten straw or sopalach' IG (Kilkenny); 'Sopaoileach is what farmers might call "long-manure", as distinct from the short variety which is so suitable for top-dressing in meadows. The word is a compounds of two words: *sop*, meaning wisp (of straw, hay etc.) and *aoileach*, manure' *An Cho* (w. Mayo).

Sopóg n. 'A torch made of straw, rushes, or bog-deal, used by poachers on the river below' PJG (mid-Donegal).

Sotal n. In form **suthal**. Arrogance. 'There's suthal for you' *CBE* 266 (mid-Tipperary).

Spac n. Also in form **spock**. 'A badly made hurley' MS (e. Limerick).

Spadach n. 1. Wet, heavy turf sods. 'White turf' McK (Leitrim). 2. 'Very light, bulky turf from the top of the bog' PLH (n. Roscommon). *al.* **spadalach** PB (s. Tipperary); JL (w. Cork). Also in form **spadar** 'heavy, wet turf placed at the back of the fire' MG (n.w. Donegal).

Spadal n. 'A small, long-handled spade used by ploughmen for keeping their ploughs clean' IG (Meath). Dimunitive, **spadaillín** MS (e. Limerick). [< Latin *spatula*.]

Spadalach n. In form **spodaloch**. 'An ungainly lump of a man' *CBE* 266 (mid-Tipperary).

Spadán n. 1. 'Ground dug for potatoes without any manure under the sod' McK (Leitrim). 2. 'Poor land' PB (s. Tipperary). 3. 'A four-sod ridge' PLH (n. Roscommon).

Spag n. 'A purse, a tobacco pouch' H (n. Donegal; PJG (mid-Donegal).

Spág n., v. Also as **spaag, spaug, spawg.** 1. Large foot. 'He came into the kitchen trailing his big dirty spágs all over the clean floor' O'K (Tyrone); Seumus MacManus, *Bold Blades of Donegal* 56: 'If we told him to put his big spaag a foot in the fire he'd do it'; James Joyce, *Ulysses* 130: 'Taking off his flat spaugs and the walk'; Flann O'Brien, *The Dalkey Archive*, 49: 'I recede portentously from the sea, the sergeant beamed, except for a fastidious little wade for the good of my spawgs'. 2. To walk. Peadar O'Donnell, *Adrigoole* 144: 'Ye'd think Neddie Brian himself 'ud have made her spág it' (Donegal). Hence **spagging**, walking Q (Donegal).

Spágadán n. 'A toddler' MC (e. Mayo).

Spágaide n. 'One who has big feet' *CBE* 34 S (Galway).

Spaid n. 'Wet turf' NB (w. Limerick). See *spadach, spadar*.

Spaidire n. Also in form **spadder.** 'An unsteady person, inattentive to his work' RBB (Waterford); 'He has no job because he's nothing but a spadder' G (n.w. Donegal).

Spailpín n. In forms **spawlpeen, spalpeen.** An itinerant or seasonal labourer. 1. Jonathan Swift, *A Dialogue in Hybernian Stile*: 'In short, he is no better than a spawlpeen ...'; Thomas Sheridan, *The Brave Irishman*: '... there ishn't one of these spalpeens that has a cabin upon the mountain ... that will be keeping a goon'; William Carleton, *Phelim O'Toole's Courtship* 2, 188: '... Tyrrell O'Toole, who won it from the Sassenach at the point of his reaping hook, during a descent made upon England by a body of spalpeens, in the month of August'. 2. 'An unkempt, coarse roughneck' O'K (Tyrone); James Joyce, *Finnegans Wake* 32: '... for the hungerlean spalpeens of Lucalizod ...'

Spairt n. Also as **spart, spairteach, spatcha.** 'A big, soft sod of turf' H (n. Clare); 'Spart is wet turf' PB (s. Tipperary); 'Spairteach is an inferior quality of turf. Occasionally the word is shortened to spatcha' *An Cho* (w. Mayo).

Spalpadh n. Burst (of running). Hence **spalther**: 'to dash forward in a wild, undirected

manner, taking large strides and practically falling headlong' O'K (Tyrone).

Spalpaire n. 'An active fellow' NB (w. Limerick).

Speach n. Also in forms **spack, sprack.** 'A kick, especially a kick from an animal' RBB (w. Waterford); H (n. Clare). 'I never heard spack or sprack used except to describe the short, sharp kick of a standing horse' By (s.e. Wexford).

Speallaire n. 'A mean person' NB (Limerick).

Spéic n. A speech. 'That was a great spéic he gave out of him' G (s. Kilkenny); AOL (mid-Waterford); JM (w. Cork).

Speilg n. In form **spellig.** A steep crag. 'A pointed rock' JB (s. Armagh & n. Louth).

Spialán n. 'A rafter' MS (e. Limerick).

Spinc n. In form **spink.** The point of a jutting rock; a steep bank, a cliff. Peadar O'Donnell, *The Knife* 189: 'The fighting in Dublin is spreadin'. If that happens, people may as well jump out with the spinks' (Donegal); Patrick Gallagher, *My Story* 52: 'When we came near the fairies' home we heard a fiddle up in the spink playing the most beautiful music' (Donegal); JB (s. Armagh & n. Louth).

Sping n. A hereditary fault in a person's character. 'There's a sping of madness in all of them' RBB (s. Kilkenny).

Spiocaid n. 'An icicle hanging from the thatch' Mac C (Monaghan).

Spiochaid n. A very small fire. 'Three or four wet sods – that's the kind of a spiochaid they call a fire' JL (w. Cork).

Spior-spear phr. Also as **spir-spar.** Smithereens, fragments *CBD* (n. Kerry); DOH (e. Limerick); JL (w. Cork). 'To make spior spear of an argument is to make it appear of no consequence' DOC (Limerick); George Fitzmaurice, *The Pie-Dish*: 'Houl your tongue, you fooleen, till I think of a good lie to whisper to the priest that'll make spir-spar of all the old man's raging' (Kerry).

Spiútar n. 'Entertainment' KB (e. Limerick); 'We had great spiútar, with drink and music and all sorts of divilment at the wakes long ago' JL (w. Cork).

Splanc n. Also in form **splunk**. A spark, flash. 'He hasn't a splanc of sense' JC (w. Cork); AOL (mid-Waterford); JJH (W. Waterford); 'Sparks in a forge are called splunks' H (n. Donegal).

Spleách adv. Dependant, subservient. 'I'm not spleách to you' CBE 98 (Kilkenny).

Spleodar n. Cheerfulness, vivacity. 'There's great spleodar in him, if he's in a wheelchair itself' JL (w. Cork).

Splinc n. In form **splink**. 1. A gleam, glimmer. Eric Cross, *The Tailor and Ansty* 163: '"England!", snorts the Tailor... "They start off without a splink of sense. They sell honey in order to buy sweets..."' (w. Cork). 2. 'The pinnacle of a rock' JL (w. Cork).

Spliúchán n. As **spleuchan, spleucan**. 1. A pouch, purse. 'Thon fellow is as tight as a minister's spleuchan' G (n.w. Donegal). Robert Burns, *Dr Hornibrook:* 'Deil mak his king's hood in a spleuchan.' 2. 'A spleucan is a blister' Con (Louth).

Spochaireacht n. (Act of) teasing, annoying. 'Stop your old spochaireacht' CBD (n. Kerry).

Spóilín n. Also as **spailin, spoileen**. 1. 'Meat killed, cooked and sold at a fair or gathering' Tr (Donegal); Seumus Mac-Manus, *A Lad of the O'Friels* 117: 'He observed the spailin tents, where potatoes and fish and mutton were boiled, and served up to hasty, hungry customers' (Donegal). 2. As **spoileen**. EASI 332: 'A coarse kind of soap made out of scraps of inferior grease and meat, often sold cheap at fairs and markets' (Derry and Tyrone).

Spóirseach n. *al.* **spóirteach**. A roaring fire. 'A spóirseach of a fire is always a good sign of a generous house' MJD (w. Cork); CBE 266 (mid-Tipperary); 'He put down a spóirteach of a fire' H (n. Clare).

Spothán n. 'A swelling under the neck of a sheep' CBE 34 S (Galway).

Sprais n. 'A sudden heavy shower' G (n.w. Donegal).

Spraoi n. In form **spree**. 1. Fun, sport. Somerville and Ross, *Holy Island* 110: 'That the wreck was regarded as a spree of the largest kind was sufficiently obvious' (w. Cork). 2. A prolonged drinking bout. Eric Cross, *The Tailor and Ansty* 96: '"... and there were times when he would drive the devil of a spree"' (w. Cork). 3. 'House-parties before dance-halls came in were called sprees' MC (e. Mayo).

Spreabhais n. 1. The area of the nose and mouth. 'He hit him a belt across the spreabhais' G (s. Kilkenny). 2. A sulky expression. 'Look at the spreabhais on him, just because he didn't get his own way' PD (s. Carlow).

Spréach n. Also as **spreeough**. Fire, spirit. 'There's no spréach in him' IG (Kilkenny). 'Spirit, dash ... an untranslatable word which Lord French should have used about the Irish regiments instead of "élan"' GC (Laois, n. Kilkenny).

Spreachall n. A sprinkling. 'I like a spreachall of salt on my porridge' MJD (w. Cork); 'We'll have a spreachall of rain, I'd say' JL (w. Cork).

Spreas n. A worthless person. 'He reared a good-for-nothing spreas' JL (w. Cork); RBB (w. Waterford).

Spreota n. 1. 'A log of firewood' JC (w. Cork). 2. Figuratively, 'a lazy lump of a man' JL (w. Cork).

Sprinlíní n. pl. In form **spreinleens**. 'We'll have spreinleens flying now when she gets home and finds that he's still in the pub' RBB (s. Kilkenny); PD (s. Carlow).

Sprioc n. 'Energy, life. "He has great sprioc in him, for an old man"' MC (e. Mayo).

Spríos n. Also as **sprees**. 1. A frown or grimace. 'I knew by the sprees of her that she had found me out' BASJ (Cavan); FF

(Monaghan). 2. Red-hot embers MS (e. Limerick); Con (Meath); *CBE* 266 (mid-Tipperary).

Spriosán n. Also in form **sprissaun**. Diminutive as **sprissawneen**. A worthless person. 'He's a good-for-nothing spriosán' RBB (Waterford); Michael Banim, *Crohoor of the Billhook* 1, 88: '"You're just a set of sprissauns", he said.' Glossed by Banim as 'silly fellows'. (Kilkenny); Gerald Griffin, *The Collegians* 87: 'The little sprissawneen' (Limerick).

Sprochall n. The gills of a cock. As **spruggil, spruggilla** in *EASI* 332 (Monaghan). See *preiceall*. [< Latin *spiraculum*]

Sprocht n. In form **spruck**. Dejection, great sorrow. 'The oul' spruck hits him at times' V (e. Wicklow).

Sprúilleog n. 'A scrap of anything' G (n.w. Donegal).

Sprus n. Smithereens. ' He made sprus of the hurl' Ham (e. Clare).

Spuaic n. Annoyance, vexation. 'It don't take much to put a spuaic on him' G (s. Kilkenny).

Sráid n. In translated form **street**. 1. Patrick MacGill, *Glenmornan* 129: 'A street, a farm-yard' (Donegal); 'The yard immediately outside a house' G (n.w. Donegal). 2. A boreen leading to a house' PJG (Donegal; Gen. Ulster).

Sráideog n. 'A shakedown' MG (n.w. Donegal).

Sráidí n. As **straddy**. *EASI* 336: 'A street-walker, an idle person always sauntering along the streets'.

Sram n. Also as **shram, shraum**. (Of eyes) rheumy matter. James Joyce, *Ulysses* 245: '... he wiped away the heavy shraums that clogged his eyes'; 'Wake up. Take the shrams out of your eyes' OCn. (Laois). Hence **sromach**, as **shromach**, bleary-eyed, in Patk. Kennedy, *Legends of Mount Leinster* 164. Glossed wrongly by Kennedy as 'unwashed' (Wexford). Hence **sram-**

achán, as **sramachaun** 'A red-eyed person' *Pe* (Wexford); 'A sleepy, miserable man' H (n. Clare).

Srán In form **srawn**. A rush, drive. 'He made a srawn at me' Mac C (Monaghan); JB (s Armagh).

Srath n. Also in form **strath** 1. 'A moor along a river or lake' McK (Leitrim). 2. 'A valley through which a stream flows' PJG (mid-Donegal). 3. "Meadows by a river' G (n.w. Donegal); Seumus MacManus, *Bold Blades of Donegal* 25: They'll spoil forever that sweet bit of a strath'.

Srathán n. 'A cake of oaten bread' *IG* (Cavan).

Srathar n. As **straar, sthraar**. A horse's straddle. *EASI* 336: 'The rough straddle which supports the back of a horse's harness, coming between the house's back and the band: straar or sthraar' (Derry). Sometimes **srathar fhada**, long straddle' *Sguab* (Cork).

Srón n. The nose. 'Match him better to keep his srón out of other people's business' PC (n. Clare); *CBE* 34 S (Galway).

Srúill n. As **shrule**. A stream. Hence **to shrule**: 'to rinse an article of clothing by pulling it backwards and forwards in a stream' *EASI* 322 (Carlow).

Sruthán n. As **strahane, strahaun, struhane** in *EASI* 336. (Munster). A stream.

Stáca an mhargaidh n. phr. Literally, stack of the market. As **staukan-vorraga**: *EASI* 335: 'Applied to a big, awkward fellow always visiting when he's not wanted, and always in the way' (s. Tipperary). Originally 'a small rick of turf in a market from which portions were continually sold away and as continually replaced: so that the stáca always stood in the people's way' ibid.

Stácaire n. 'A clumsy person' *IG* (Cavan).

Stácán n. Also as **stackan, stackan**. 1. Any large object standing in the ground, e.g. a stick or a stone. As stackan: 'the stump of a tree remaining after the tree itself has been cut or blown down' Simmons (Armagh). 2. Figuratively, a stupid, heedless person. Peadar O'Donnell, *Islanders* 155: 'A young girl that has no nature in her for a man's Sunday trousers is only a stacan.'

Stad interj. Stop. In phrase **stad anois**, as **stadh anish**, stop now, in Wm. Carleton, *Phil Purcel, the Pig-Driver* 1, 419 (Tyrone).

Stagalán n. 'A tall person who is not very strong' *CBD* (n. Kerry).

Stagún n. Also as **staigín, stag**. 1. Old gelding, old nag. 'That oul stagún of his should be sent to the knackers' AOL (mid-Waterford); 'A staigín is a castrated bull; a badly-made animal' NB (w. Limerick). 3. A stubborn person or animal. 'He's a conrairy stagún. You could neither lead nor drive him' By (s.e. Wexford). 4. Hence **staggened**. 'A stag is a potato that has been ruined by frost or decay. Such a potato is said to be staggened' O'K (Tyrone).

Staic n. 1. 'The handle of a spade' FF (Monaghan). 2. 'A short, thick-set person' MF (Westmeath). 3. A heartless woman *IG* (Cavan). 4. A sulk. 'Someone, even an adult, is passed over for a privilege or a gift and as a result he or she sits in a staic. A staic is usually accompanied by a belligerent silence; and the silence might be broken by a harmless-looking question: "Are you staicing?"' *An Cho* (w. Mayo). 5. 'An assumed bend or set in the neck' *IG* (Monaghan); Mac C (Monaghan).

Staidhce n. 'A lazy person' *CBE* 34 S (Galway).

Staig n. 'A worthless creature; a woman of low character' DOC (Limerick). In diminutive form **staggeen**. Gerald Griffin, *The Collegians* 44: '... a parcel of old staggeens' (Limerick); Somerville and Ross, *Lisheen Races, Second-hand* 78: 'Is it that little staggeen from the mountains? Sure, she's somethin' about the wan age with meself' (w. Cork).

Stail n. Also in form **shtal**. 1. Stallion. 2. Used to describe a likeable fellow who has made a fool of himself. Eric Cross, *The Tailor and Ansty* 102: ' Hould your blather, you ould shtal'. The Tailor would not have said *shtal*, however, but stail. Perhaps Cross meant to write *sthal*. 'He was showing off to the girl, and he slipped and fell into the river, the stail' JPL (w. Cork); PC (n. Clare); RBB (s. Kilkenny).

Stailc n. A stubborn trait; a fit of stubborness. 'There's a stailc in that horse ... He took a stailc at the fence and refused twice' MS (e. Limerick); H (n. Clare); NB (w. Limerick); *CBD* (n. Kerry); PB (s. Tipperary).

Stailceach adj. Stubborn. 'Is there anything worse than a stailceach horse?' PB (Tipperary).

Stáir n. 'A fit of anger or passion' *IG* (Meath); Con (Meath); MF (Westmeath).

Stait interj. 'A call to pigs' JPL (w. Cork).

Stalcaithe adj. As **stolky**. Stodgy. 'With all the rain we've had, I have a very stolky garden' *CBE* 266 (mid-Tipperary).

Stán n. 'Noise' NB (w. Limerick); 'He made stán over the milk being spilled' *CBD* (n. Kerry); *Sguab* (w. Cork).

Stang n. 'A small field of about one acre' *IG* (Meath). [Cf. *Stang:* A square perch of land' *Dinn.* Cf. German *stange*, Welsh *ystang, ystanc.*]

Stangaire n. 1. 'A high rock' *CBE* 104 (Leitrim). 2. 'A sulky horse or a sulky woman' JL (w. Cork).

Staoinse n. 'A stubborn person' NB (w. Limerick).

Staragán n. Obstacle, hindrance. 'The wedding was fixed but there was some staragán to put a stop to it' *CBD* (n. Kerry).

Stárr n. Fit, frenzy. 'You would not know what stárr he's take' MF (Westmeath).

Starrachán n. 'A person with projecting teeth' *IG* (Kilkenny).

Starrfhiacail n. In form **sturrah**. A prominent tooth. "I have a sturrah that must be drawn' *CBE* 266 (mid-Tipperary) See *stearagal*.

Steaghpar n. 'A horse so tall that you could damn near drive a car under him, or a lanky woman without shape or make. No good for working, either of them' JL (w. Cork).

Steaimpí n. Potato cake. Also in forms **stampy, stampey**. Eric Cross, *The Tailor and Ansty* 42: 'They used to make a kind of bread with potatoes called "Stampy". They would grate the potatoes on a tin grater, and then squeeze them into a tub of water. From the water they would get the starch for the clothes. There was no such thing as a bastable in those days. The "Stampy" was made on a bread-tree, which was a kind of sloping board before the fire to hold the bread, as you would make toast nowadays. "Stampy" was usually only made for Christmas or November Night, unless you had a good supply of potatoes, when you might make it once a week' (w. Cork); George Fitzmaurice, *The King of the Barna Men*: 'A strange thing occurred to myself a Friday night through taking my share of the stampey for supper' (Kerry).

Steall n., v. Also in form **stawl**. 1. Splash, gush, flow of liquid (Gen.). 2. To splash, spout, pour. 'Steall some water into that whiskey' JL (w. Cork); 'I must go out for a steall': to relieve myself' JM (w. Cork); Peadar O'Donnell, *Adrigoole* 126: 'Ye'll have another steall of tay' (Donegal); Patrick Gallagher, *My Story* 87: 'Madge would not let me go until I went over to the house and had a stawl of tea' (Donegal).

Stéamar n. 'A vain, boastful woman' JL (w. Cork).

Steancán n. A song, or verse of a song. 'I'll give ye a steancán about a murder that was committed here long ago' MS (e. Limerick); PC (n. Clare).

Stearagal n. 1. 'A tall, lanky person' NB (w. Limerick). 2. 'A big, long tooth' ibid. Variant of *starrfhiacail*.

Stéig n. A bleak, barren place. 'A German gave ten thousand for a stéig that wouldn't feed a snipe' JL (w. Cork).

Stéigeachaí n. pl. 'A word for the entrails of an animal. Ten years ago I heard an old man in the parish recall: "The old woman told him to drink up the tea and it will warm your stéigeachaí. They all thought she used a bad word; it was a good Irish word she used"' *An Cho* (w. Mayo).

Steobhaí n. As **stowie**. 'An idle person; a time-waster' JB (s. Armagh & n. Louth).

Steotar n. Rock candy. 'My mother would give out to my father for buying us steotar when he went to town' RBB (s. Kilkenny); PB (s. Tipperary).

Stiall n. Also in form **skjaul**. 1. A piece, portion. 'He gave me a fine stiall of bacon to take home with me' MS (e. Limerick); PB (s. Tipperary); *CBD* (n. Kerry); *IG* (Kilkenny); 'The sceachs tore a skjaul out of my coat' MW (s. Wexford). 2. A stroke, a lash. 'A few stialls of an ash plant across the ass would soon quieten the muggers and the hooligans' JL (w. Cork).

Stiúg n. A gasp. *al.* **stiúc**. Also as **stugue**. 'He was in stiúcs with the laughing' MF (Westmeath). Also as **stugue** in Patk. Kennedy, *Legendary Fictions of the Irish Celts* 170: 'I fell down in a stugue, and don't know how long I was in it' (Wexford). Hence **stuking**, 'gasping' H (n. Donegal).

Stiúir n. 1. An aggressive attitude. 'He had a dangerous stiúir on him towards me' MS (e. Limerick). 2. Tiller. In form **steer**. Somerville and Ross, *The Boat's Share* 237: 'Would you kindly explain what you mean by the steer of the boat? ... Sure 'tis the shtick, like, that they pulls here and there to go in their choice place'.

Stiúsaí n. 'A lazy woman' *CBD* (n. Kerry).

Stócach n. Also in forms **stoka, stockagh**. 1. 'A youth, a young man' MG (n.w. Donegal); John Boyce, *Shandy Maguire* 217: 'Brine's ouldest stockagh (note: boy) got sick' (Donegal). 2. 'An idle fellow who lives on the industry of others' H (n. Donegal); 'A young, lazy, good-for-nothing class of a lad' NB (w. Limerick); Dermot O'Byrne, *Children of the Hills* 49: 'And if this young fella is but a poor unmannerly drunken show of a stocach itself ...' (Donegal).

Stocaire n. 'An uninvited guest at a wedding, a gatecrasher, a scrounger' PJG (mid-Donegal); *IG* (Meath). Hence **stuchern**. 'A dog that sits watching a person at meals in expectation of getting food' Tr (Donegal).

Stóilín n. In form **stoleen**. 'An addition to a story. "Don't be puttin' a stoleen to it for a story"' *CBE* 266 (mid-Tipperary).

Stóinse n. A pillar. Figuratively, 'A strong, robust man' PB (s. Tipperary).

Stóinsithe adj. 'Tough, stubborn, unyielding' NB (w. Limerick)

Stoith v. In form **shtuck**. 'Pull up, uproot. "Shtuck them weeds"' *CBE* 266 (mid-Tipperary).

Stolla n. 'A high rock' JJH (w. Waterford).

Stollabhán n. 'A very old cow' NB (w. Limerick).

Stollach n. 'A big head of unruly hair' H (n. Clare).

Stollaire n. 1. 'A bad-tempered, stubborn, unreasonable person' RBB (s. Kilkenny); G (n.w. Donegal). 2. 'A big cow' NB (w. Limerick).

Stómaire n. 'An idle lump of a fellow' *IG* (Cavan).

Stopadán n. 'A short straw, stubble' *CBD* (n. Kerry); NB (w. Limerick).

Stórach n. In form **storeuck**. 'Treasured one. "Come here to me, storeuck"' *CBE* 266 (mid-Tipperary). See *a stór*.

Storc n. 1. 'A young bullock' H (n. Clare). 2. As **sturk, stirk, sterk**. *EASI* 338: 'Often applied to a stout, low-sized girl or boy.' 3. 'An unyielding person. It is very often someone who has possession of a needed object, a piece of land, a box of crayons — and will not budge. Such a person is never graceful in refusing: he just sits there (get the phrase right!) of a storc' *An Cho* (w. Mayo). 4. 'Applied to the corpse of one who dies in an upright posture' *Dinn*; James Joyce, *Finnegans Wake* 17: '... from sturk to finnic...'

Storcán n. 'A small, fat pig' H (n. Clare).

Stothall n. 'An unkempt head of hair' MC (w. Clare).

Strabh n. 'A little milk or water. "He got a strabh of milk from the cow"' *CBD* (n. Kerry).

Stracadh vb. n. 'Dragging, hauling; doing as best one can. 'How are you?' 'Musha, ag stracadh' NB (w. Limerick).

Strácáil vb n. Surviving, struggling., doing one's best in the circumstances. 'How is life?' 'Strácáil, boy, as usual' MJD (w. Cork). Hence **strácáling** JC (w. Cork) *CBD* (n. Kerry).

Stracaire n. Also as **strockara**. 'A strong, loose-limbed person' MS (e. Limerick). *EASI* 337: 'a very hard-working man' (Munster).

Strácálaí n. 1. 'A hard worker' JC (w. Cork); RBB (w. Waterford). 2. 'A drudge. An untidy worker who is usually pulling the devil by the tail' H (n. Clare).

Strachaille n. 1. 'An untidy person, a slut' PC (n. Clare). 2. 'An awkward person' *CBE* 34 S (Galway).

Stradhpán n. 'The afterbirth of a cow, mare, etc' *IG* (Kilkenny).

Straeire n. A rover. 'You wouldn't find him here at weekends at all. He's a bit of a straeire, like all young fellows' G (s. Kilkenny); RBB (w. Waterford).

Straibhéis n. Extravagance. 'How could they be well-to-do with her straibhéis?' S (n.w. Donegal).

Stráic n. 'A long, lanky person' *CBE* 34 S (s. Galway). diminutive **stráiceán**: 'A tall thin person' MW (s. Wexford).

Stráicín n. In form **strawkeen**. 'A bandage' *CBE* 266 (mid-Tipperary).

Straimeal n. In form **stramul**. 'A person who has the clothes hanging from him or her. An untidy person. "She was going around in an old stramul"' *CBE* 266 (mid-Tipperary). [Cf. *straiméad, straiméid,* tattered, worthless thing: *ODON.*]

Straimpín n. 'A fetter' *CBE* 104 (Leitrim). 'A goat's fetter' PLH (n. Roscommon).

Strainseach n. As **stransha**: 'A tall, thin person' JB (s. Armagh & n. Louth.);

Straip n. In form **strap**. 1. A whore. 2. An unruly woman. Anon., *Purgatorium Hibernicum*: "Amongst this traine, who (thinke you) espied he/ But his old mistresse, madam Dydy?-/ That pin'd to death, the fawneing strapp!/ Some say for love, some of a clapp'; Samuel Lover, *Handy Andy* 19: '"You infernal old strap!", shouted he, as he clutched a handful of bottles on the tables near him, and flung them at the nurse'. James Joyce, *Ulysses* 692: '... you be damned you lying strap...' Tom Murphy, *Bailegangaire* 23: 'Pat went back to his strap of a widdy. An' was dead in six months.'

Straipleach n. 'An untidy woman' JL (w. Cork).

Strampálaí n. 'A big awkward man who couldn't get out of his own way' JPL (w. Cork).

Strangalán n. 'A tall, weak person' NB (w. Limerick).

Straoil n., v. In form **streel**. 1. A slovenly woman, a slattern. James Joyce, *Ulysses* 358: '...and she did look a streel tugging the two kids along with the flimsy blouse she bought only a fortnight before like a rag on her back ...' (Gen.). Hence diminutives **straoilín** FM (s. Wexford); **straoileamán** G (n.w. Donegal); **straoileog** RBB (s. Kilkenny). 2. To go about aimlessly. W. H. Floredice, *Memories of a Month among the Mere Irish* 124: 'Sthreeling right through Drumnakilleugh' (Ulster); J. M. Synge, *The Playboy of the Western World* 106: 'An ugly young streeler with a murderous gob on him'. 3. To drag, trail one's clothes (Gen.) 4. A string (of beads etc.). A connected series (of words etc.). J. M. Synge, *The Playboy of the Western World* 87: 'If you weren't destroyed travelling, you'd have as

much talk and streeleen as Owen Roe O'Sullivan or the poets of the Dingle Bay ...'

Straoileog n. A lope, stride. 'Straoileog is what we have in Tipperary for a truslóg' (q.v.) PB (s. Tipperary).

Straois n. A broad grin. 'I gave him an answer that knocked the straois off his face' JC (w. Cork); MF (Westmeath); PLH (n. Roscommon).

Strapaire n. As **strapper**. 'A strapping young fellow' PC (n. Clare); G (n.w. Donegal).

Strapalach adj. 'Long corn, knocked and tangled. "It is very strapalach looking"' NB (w. Limerick); *CBD* (n. Kerry).

Streabhóg n. Also as **stravogue**. 'A thin, miserable looking person or animal' JL (w. Cork); 'An old, gaunt cow' *CBE* 266 (mid-Tipperary).

Streachailt n. Tearing, dragging, wrestling. Hence **strackle**. 'He **strackled** him to the ground and the referee gave a free the other way' TB (Cavan); Mac C (Monaghan).

Streachla n. As **strackla**: 'A young person who has grown up quickly' JB (n. Louth).

Streancán n. Also as **strounkawn**. 1. 'A tune played on a fiddle' JL (w. Cork). 2. 'A splash of liquid. "Throw a strounkawn of milk to the calf."' *CBE* 266 (mid-Tipperary).

Streill n. 1. A leer. 'A pity somebody wouldn't knock that streill off the face of that smart man' JPL (w. Cork). 2. A grimace of disappointment. 'The grimace that a child works up when he is told to be off to bed before the card-playing begins. He has done his physical utmost to cry but the tears won't come. So he splits the difference and settles for a streill' *An Cho* (w. Mayo). 3. 'A silly expression on the face' MC (e. Mayo).

Striapach n. As **strapach, sthreepa**. A whore. Dermot O'Byrne, *Children of the Hills* 53: 'To have taken up with a strapach salach the like of thon' (Donegal). Wm.

Carleton, *Fardorougha the Miser* 407: '... ha! anhien na sthreepa'. Glossed by Carleton as 'you daughter of a prostitute' (Tyrone). As genetive singular, **sthreepeea**. Michael Banim, *Crohoor of the Billhook* 1, 21: 'a vich-na-sthreepeea', *recte* 'a mhic na stríopaí': son of a whore. Glossed by Banim as 'son of a jade' (Kilkenny).

Striog n., v. 1. 'A droplet' Con (Meath). 2. 'To milk dry' MF (Westmeath). 'I must go out and striog the cow' McK (Leitrim).

Strioplín n. 'A person whose clothes are hanging limp, being wet' McK (Leitrim).

Stró n. Also as **strow**. 1. 'Boasting, pride in doing well. "The old man made great stró out of his sons when they won the match"' MC (e. Mayo). 2. 'Delay. "Who put the strow on you to-night?"' *CBE* 266 (mid-Tipperary).

Stróille n. In form **strollya**. 'A lazy, aimless person' J (s. e. Wexford). Diminutive, **stróilleán**, in form **strollyawn**. 'A person who dallies when running an errand' D (s. e. Wexford). Hence **strollyawnin**, dallying' D (s. e. Wexford).

Stróinse n. In forms **stroansha, stronsha, stronshuch, stronesha**. 'A lazy, useless stróinse of a girl' JL (w. Cork). 'A big stroansh of a girl' MP (mid-Tipperary). *EASI* 337: 'A big, idle, lazy stroansha of a girl, always gadding about'; Patk. Kennedy, *Legendary Fictions of the Irish Celts* 50: 'A stronshuch of a tailor came in.' Glossed as 'idler'. 'A lazy stronsha of a girl' JB (s. Armagh & n. Louth); 'A stronesha is an unreliable, clumsy girl or woman; sometimes said playfully of a little girl' LB (s.w. Dublin).

Stróire n. 'A wanderer, rover' RBB (w. Waterford); MJD (w. Cork).

Strolúsach adj. Rude, ill-mannered. 'A lot of the young ones going nowadays are strolúsach bitches, and that's a fact' JL (w. Cork); PB (s. Tipperary).

Stropais n. 1. 'A big, agreeable, well-disposed person. "There's no harm in him; the poor oul' stropais"' RBB (s. Kilkenny); PB (s.

Tipperary). 2. 'A poor, ragged woman' *IG* (Kilkenny).

Strus n. 1. Means, wealth. 'I haven't much strus' DOH (e. Limerick); JS (e. Kerry); JL (w. Cork). 2. Stress, strain. 'He puts fierce strus on himself trying to play the politician' JL (w. Cork).

Stua n. In form **stugue**. An arc, arch, bow, loop. Patk. Kennedy, *The Banks of the Boro* 337: 'He began to think that his inside would be all gone, and that he'd fall in a stugue on one of the big diamond-shaped flags of the floor'; ibid., *Evenings in the Duffrey* 353: 'to beg some good Christian to give him a drink of could wather, or he'd stugue up'; 'He made a stugue of him with the handle of the hurl' MH (s. Wexford).

Stuacach adj. Also in form **stubbach**. 'Stuacach is applied to one who goes into a huff easily' H (n. Clare); 'Stubbach, sulky, stubborn' *Pe* (Wexford).

Stuacán n. 'A stupid fellow' MJD (w. Cork); JS (e. Kerry); PC (n. Clare).

Stuaic n. Also as **sthuck**. 'A sthuck is a fit of sulking, a huff' PC (n. Clare); 'Whatever stuaic came on him, he just walked out of the meadow and went home' JC (w. Cork); PB (s. Tipperary); 'Whatever sthuck came over him ...' OC (Monaghan).

Stuc n. 'A low-sized, sturdy girl' MF (Westmeath).

Stupaire n. In form **stubishe**. A lethargic person. 'A person who is always late for work' *CBE* 98 (Kilkenny).

Stúrdam n. Impudence. 'He has too much stúrdam, that child' LOS (w. Clare). [Cf. *stúraí:* 'an impudent person' *Dinn.*]

Suaidín n. In form **swedgeen**. 'A mixture of raw oatmeal, sugar and milk' MC (e. Mayo).

Suaite adj. Also in form **suthin**. Agitated, disturbed. 'She'll foal to-night. She's very suaite in herself' JL (w. Cork); 'The goat was suthin, that is, grunting and behaving strangely' Mas (s. Tipperary).

Suarach adj. 'Small and miserable' H (n. Clare); 'That's suarach enough – said of poor grass' *CBE* 98 (Kilkenny).

Suarachán n. 'A small, miserable person' H (n. Clare).

Suasán n. 1. 'A heap of oats in the barn for flailing' *CBE* 34 S (Galway). 2. 'An untidy class of a woman, a kind of a straoil' JL (w. Cork).

Súdóg n. 'A soda cake' NB (w. Limerick).

Súgach adj. Merry with drink. Also in forms **suguch, soogah.** Michael Banim, *Crohoor of the Billhook* 1, 20: 'He became suguch; in Scotch fou; Anglice, approaching to intoxication ...' (Kilkenny); Wm. Carleton, *Ned M'Keown* 1, 4: 'soogah'. Glossed by Carleton as 'jolly' (Tyrone); 'He wasn't out of order in any way, just súgach' JM (w. Cork); H (n. Clare); AOL (mid-Waterford).

Súgán n. Also in forms **sukaun, suggaun, soogawn, sougawn, suggain, suggun, soogun.** 1. Straw rope. 'Irish recruits who did not know left foot from right in drilling are said to have been taught by tying a straw rope to the right foot, and a withy (gad) to the left, with the jingle, 'sukaun to gad, sukaun to gad, now you've got it, keep it my lad' H (n. Donegal); Eric Cross, *The Tailor and Ansty* 45: 'There was a dancing master in my time, by the name of Moriarty, who had an awful block of a fellow to teach. It was failing Moriarty altogether to teach him how to batter, so begod, he got a gad and put it on his left leg, and a sugan (hay rope) on the right, and he caught the ends of them in his two hands, and while the music was playing Moriarty sang this song. Rise upon sugan, Rise upon gad, Shuffle, me lad, Both Sugan and Gad' (w. Cork); Flann O'Brien, *At Swim-Two-Birds* 15: 'The knees and calves to him, swealed and swathed with soogawns.' 2. Straw collar. Wm. Carleton, *The Hedge School* 1, 320 (footnote): 'The suggaun was a collar of straw which was put around the necks of the dunces, who were then placed at the door, that their disgrace might be as public as possible' (Tyrone). 3. Straw saddle. Jonathan Swift, *A Dialogue in Hybernian Stile*: 'I have seen him often

riding on a sougawn.' 4. Straw garters. Anon., *Purgatorium Hibernicum*: ' But when he drew more near her quarters And knew her by her suggain garters.' 5. 'A lazy old person' *CBE* 34 S (Galway). 6. In compound **súgán chair** – 'a chair whose seat and back are made from súgáns' G. (s. Kilkenny); (Gen.); 'As 'soogun' and 'suggun' *An Cho* (w. Mayo).

Súghín n. As **sugeen.** *EASI* 338: 'Water in which oatmeal has ben steeped; often drunk by workmen on a hot day in place of plain water' (Roscommon).

Súil n. An eye. 'A hole in a ditch to let water through.' 'The pheasant ran out the súil' NB (w. Limerick).

Súileoga n. In form **soologues.** 'The globules on soup' OC (Monaghan). Also as **súilíní** MS (e. Limerick).

Suim n. Interest. As **seem, syme.** 'I put no seem in him at all' D (Kildare); H (n. Clare); JM (w. Cork); GC (Laois); 'I have no syme in soccer' AOL (s. Tipperary).

Suístín n. 'A seat made of plaited straw or rushes' JL (w. Cork); PD (s. Carlow).

Súite adv. As **sooteh.** 'Dried up, sapless. "He's gone very sooteh-looking"' *CBE* 266 (mid-Tipperary).

Súlach n. Also as **sooley.** Juice. 'More súlach, anyone?' JC (w. Cork); RBB (w. Waterford); 'You'd need plenty of sooley on the dry turkey meat' MW (s. Wexford); G (s. Kilkenny).

Sumachán n. 1. 'An easy-going, dilatory person' MF (Westmeath). 2. 'A bold boy' PB (s. Tipperary).

Súmadh vb. n. In form **soomin'.** Sucking. 'The pigs are only soomin' at their mess' *CBE* 266 (mid-Tipperary). See *súmáil.*

Súmáil vb. n. In form **súmáling.** 'Messing up one's food' SOM (w. Cork). See *súmadh* above.

Súmaire n. In form **soomerah.** 1. 'A parasite, scrounger, sponger' MS (e. Limerick).

2. 'A slow-moving, silent person' DOC (Limerick). 3. 'A place in a bog where one could be sucked under' Con (Meath). 4. The leech. 'That dike is full of soomerahs' *CBE* 266 (mid-Tipperary).

Sursaing n. 1. A surcingle. 'The sursaing broke and Jer Glas hit the road' JL (w. Cork). 2. 'A thick-set woman who tends to be clumsy' MJD (w. Cork).

Súsa n. 'A bed covering, or the like' JC (w. Cork); RBB (w. Waterford); Michael Banim, *Crohoor of the Billhook* 1, 7: 'the ancient ditty of Colloch-a-thusa ...'; recte *Cailleach an tSúsa*. Glossed, correctly, as 'the old hag of the blanket'.

Sutach n. In form **suttock**. 'A bold, bad-mannered child' *CBE* 266 (mid-Tipperary); 'A beefy young boy' H (n. Clare); 'A calf who is difficult to keep control of while feeding him' DOC (Limerick); 'A bold, insolent boy who always wants his own way' DOC (Limerick); 'A sulky young one' Mas (mid-Tipperary).

Súth n. *al.* **suth**. 'In expression **súth on you**, i.e. shame on you!' MF (Westmeath); 'Expresses disgust or disapproval. This is intensified in the phrases **suth an' suth salach!**, and **suth on you!** PLH (n. Roscommon).

Tá go breá phr. It is fine, excellent. As **tha go bragh** in Gerald Griffin, *The Collegians* 159 (Limerick).

Tá sé n., phr. Literally, it is. **1.** An Irish speaker. 'Your man is a tá sé' JV (Wicklow). Specifically, a member of the Irish- speaking First Battalion, Western Command, based in Galway. Plural, **tá sés.** 'Them tá sés would put ire on you' W (Wicklow). **2.** 'A sweetheart' GC (Laois). **3.** In phrase 'working like tá sé,' that is, very quickly NB (w. Limerick).

Tabhair dom phr. In form **thurm.** Give me. Wm. Carleton, *Tubber Derg* 2, 403: 'Gutsho, alanna ... thurm pogue', recte, 'gabh anseo a leanbh, tabhair dom póg' (Come here, child, give me a kiss).

Tabhaireog n. 'A little gift' Mac C (Monaghan).

Tabhairt amach phr. In form **toust amock.** Literally, a giving out; a scolding. 'The wife gave him some toust amock when he came drunk the other night' S (s. Wexford)

Taca n. A friend in need. 'He's a poor taca' CBD (n. Kerry).

Tachrán n. In form **thockran.** 'An orphan' TB (Cavan). As **theran.** 'A school-going youngster' Mac C (Monaghan).

Tadhg a' dá thaobh phr. Literally, Tadhg of the two sides. 'A two-faced person' H (n. Clare); JM (w. Cork).

Tadhg an Gheimhridh n. phr. Literally, Tadhg of the Winter. 'Meat left on rafters and then taken down for a cure. An old woman gave it as a sort of poultice to my sister, who had a boil on her nose near her eye. My sister remembers being afraid of losing her eye! Joe Daly (a distinguished collector for the Irish Folklore Commission) said to me that this cure survived only in Tipperary' MP (mid Tipperary).

Tadhg n. In form **Teague.** A male Christian name. A generic name for an Irishman. John Durant Breval, *The Play is the Plot*: 'Carbine: Thou hast the brogue then a little sure. Jeremy: As well as any Teague of them all Sir.'

Taibhse n. In form **thivish.** *EASI* 341: 'A ghost, spectre'.

Taidhgín n. In form **tiegeen.** 'Used in speaking of little bits of hay left scattered over a meadow. "Don't leave any tiegeens after you"' *CBE* 266 (mid-Tipperary).

Táille n. Fee, charge. In form **tally,** as in **tally-woman,** a kept woman. M.J. Mulloy, *The King of Friday's Men* 20: 'Master Hubert ... built it for his tally-woman ... when his wife was still living.'

Táilleog n. In form **thauloge. 1.** 'A chimney shelf' *Pe* (Wexford). **2.** *EASI* 340: 'A boarded-off square enclosure at one end of the kitchen fireplace of a farmhouse, where candlesticks, brushes, wet boots etc. are kept' (Carlow); PON (n. Dublin).

Tailseog n. 'The earwig' *CBE* 98 (Kilkenny). See *gailseach.*

Tairis interj. In form **herish.** 'Stop!; be quiet! Said coaxingly at milking-time to a fidgety cow' MF (Westmeath).

Taisce n. 'A dowry' MF (Westmeath). See *a thaisce.*

Taise n. In form **thigha.** A spectre. Michael Banim, *Crohoor of the Billhook* 1, 74: 'standin' close by you there was a thigha, fresh cum out o' the ground, fur the windin' sheet had the clay all over it'; ibid. 79: 'An' didn't the thigha give you ne'er a sthuck, or bate you, at-all-at-all?' Glossed by Banim as 'ghost' (Kilkenny).

Taithin n. 'A disappointed or wry face. "If you saw the taithin that was on the child who was overlooked in the division of the sweets"' S Ua G (s. Tipperary).

Táláid n. In form **thallidge**. 'A hay-loft' Mac C (Monaghan); Con (Louth); 'The half-loft in the old-time kitchens' McK (Leitrim).

Talamh íochtair n. Literally, low ground. '"He had his father's old coat that was down to talamh íochtair on him." Or by way of a compliment, "The dance frock suits her down to talamh íochtair"' *An Cho* (w. Mayo).

Talann n. Impulsive spirit. Peadar O'Donnell, *The Knife* 215: 'And she's a woman there's a bad talann in.'

Talpachán n. 'A fine, big, strong child of between five and twelve years old' DOC (Limerick).

Talpán n. 'Corn whose growth has been stunted, by drought or poor soil conditions' Fin (Mayo).

Tamáilseach adv., adj. In form **tomaulshock**. Poorly, sickly. 'The poor thing is only tomawlshuk'; 'a tomawlshuk old horse' D (s. e. Wexford).

Tamáilte adj. 1. 'Half-baked (bread); heavy, sticky' H (n. Clare).

Tamall n. A while. 'Will you stand in the goal for a tamall?' *CBD* (n. Kerry).

Támh n. 'An idler' *Dinn* (Monaghan).

Támhaí n. 'An unlikable woman' Mac C (Monaghan).

Támhán n. 'A cat-nap, a snooze' S (n.w. Donegal).

Tánaiste n. 1. Deputy Prime Minister. Modern usage. 2. As **tanist**. James Joyce, *Ulysses* 49: 'Lover, for her love he prowled with colonel Richard Burke, tanist of his

sept, under the walls of Clerkenwell and, crouching, saw a flame of vengeance hurl them upwards in the fog.'

Taobh n. Literally, side. A patch. 'Put a taobh on my shoe' H (n. Clare).

Taobh thíos phr. In translated form **belowside**. M.J. Mulloy, *The King Of Friday's Men* 68: 'The men are belowside.'

Taobhán n. Also in forms **thayvaun, theevaun**. 1. 'A patch on a the upper of a shoe' MS (e. Limerick). 2. *EASI* 340: 'The short beam of the rood crossing from one rafter to the opposite one' (Munster). See *taoibhín*.

Taobhfhód n. 'Lateral sod in a potato ridge' *CBD* (n. Kerry); JL (w. Cork); DOH (e. Limerick); 'Famous Jack Enright, full back, was as solid as a wall,/ Turning taobhfhóds along the field as kicked out the ball' PF (w. Limerick).

Taodach adj. 'Ill-tempered, quarrelsome' MF (Westmeath).

Taoibhín n. In form **theeveen**. 'A side-patch on a shoe. "Get a bit of theeveen leather for me"' OCn (Laois). See *taobhán*.

Taoiseach n. Prime Minister. Modern usage.

Taom n. Also as **teem**. A fit of anger, sickness, etc. 'He's a dangerous hurler; a taom can come on him for no reason at all' Smy (n. Clare); MS (e. Limerick); 'He took a teem of sickness' *BASJ* Cavan.

Taom v. As **teem**. *EASI* 339: 'To strain off or pour off water or any liquid. To teem potatoes is to pour the water off them when they are boiled. Hence **teeming** rain'; Jonathan Swift, *Directions to Servants*: 'Teem out ... the ale into the tankard.'

Taoscán n. Also as **taiscaun**. A small measure of drink. 'He gave me a taoscán of whiskey before I left' MS (e. Limerick); JM (w. Cork); PB (s. Tipperary); Flann O'Brien, *The Dalkey Archive*, 13: 'This is the best whiskey to be had in Ireland ... I know you won't refuse a taiscaun.'

Táth n. A tuft, bunch. 1. As **tat**. *EASI* 339: 'A tangled or matted wad or mass of hair on a girl or on an animal. "Come here till I comb the tats out of your hair"' (Ulster). 2. Diminutive, **táithín**, as **tawheen**. 'A fistful of rushes to fill a hole in a stack etc.' NB (w. Limerick). 3. 'Tawheen is what us girls called pubic hair, when we were young, in old God's time' J (s. e. Wexford).

Táthaím tú n. 'A rough children's schoolyard game. Two strong lads would catch a weaker lad by the arm and leg and bang his backside against that of a fourth lad' FM (s. Wexford).

Táthfhéileann n. Woodbine, honeysuckle. 'As tough as táthfhéileann' DOH (e. Limerick); MJD (w. Cork); PC (n. Clare).

Teach na mbó phr. In form **tamboo**. Literally, house of the cows. 'A contemptuous term for a house; a shebeen' PON (n. Dublin).

Teacht fé comp. n. Literally, coming under. 'Damp rising from the foundations of a house' MC (w. Clare).

Teachta Dála comp. n. Deputy of the Dáil (q.v.) Often abbreviated to T. D. As **t. d.** in James Joyce, *Finnegans Wake* 317.

Teangamhálaí n. In form **thongavawly**. 1. 'An interferer. "That old thongavawly should mind his own business"' *CBE* 266 (mid-Tipperary). 2. 'An unlucky or bad person to meet. "She married a right thongavawly"' ibid. 3. 'A person from whom it is difficult to get away' MS (e. Limerick).

Teann adj. Firm, tightly held. Seumus MacManus, *Bold Blades of Donegal* 298: 'A pair of divil's imps that are as teann in Hell as if they were born and bred here.'

Teannadh vb. n. Drawing up, coming near. In translated form in M. J. Mulloy, *The Wood of the Whispering* 136: 'To morrow night I'll draw to ye.'

Teanntobac n. 1. 'A good beating' *CBD* (n. Kerry). 2. Trouble, annoyance. 'He got teanntobac from it (a broken-down car etc.)' *CBD* (n. Kerry).

Teasaí adj. Hot-tempered. 'He's as teasaí as a young bull in spring' JL (w. Cork).

Teaspach n. Also **taspy**, **tasby**. Animal spirits, exuberance. 'Mind youself on that fellow to-night, girleen. There's the divil of a teaspach on him lately' JL (w. Cork); George Fitzmaurice, *The Pie-Dish*: '... it's tasby itself that's in me, Eugene' (Kerry); 'That work will knock the taspy out of him' AG (s. Tipperary).

Teipiúil adj. Risky, liable to fail. 'Farming is a teipiúil business' NB (w. Limerick).

Teo adj. In compound **teo-boy**. 'A high spirited, mischievous boy, given perhaps to acts which other people would call "unmannerly"' Tr (Donegal); Seumus MacManus, *Bold Blades of Donegal* 259: 'And if, his stern father said, any kind of work atween Heaven and Hell is fit to drive the divilty out of that teo-boy I give me 'davy the turf bog 'll do the trick'; Mac Manus, *A Lad of the O'Friels* 185: 'It was small wondher her own son was comin up the teo-boy he was, when that was the way she thraited wan who come in with a civil complaint again' him' (Donegal). [Cf. *teolaidh*, a thief *Dinn*]

Th'anam 'on diabhal! interj. Literally, your soul to the devil! In forms **honamaundhiaoul**, **thonomonduoul**. Michael Banim, *Crohoor of the Billhook* 1, 330: ' ... a thundering Irish curse, thonomonduoul' (Kilkenny); Somerville and Ross, *Occasional Licenses* 155: 'Honamaundhiaoul; she'll run off like an eel' (w. Cork); MS (e. Limerick); PC (n. Clare); JL (w. Cork).

Tiarna n. Lord. **A thiarna**, voc., interj., in form **hierna**. John Boyce, *Shandy Maguire* 178: 'Oh, hierna, it's the sodgers' (Donegal).

Tiarpa n. 'Any big load for a person to carry. Also a big backside. You'd say: that Judy have a big tiarpa of an ass on her' JL (w. Cork).

Timireacht n. In form **timerish**. Act of running errands, chores, household tasks.

Seumus MacManus, *Pearson's Magazine*, May 1900: 'To this an' that little timmerish that has to be done about a house after dark' (Donegal).

Tiolar n. In form **chuller**. 'A second, or double chin' OC (Monaghan).

Tiomáint n. Bustle, rush, haste. 'Such tiomáint over such a small thing' BMacM (Kerry).

Tír na nÓg n. Literally, Land of Youth. The land to which Niamh Cinn Óir brought Oisín in the Fenian story. James Joyce, *Ulysses* 195: 'East of the sun, west of the moon: Tir na n-og'. As **Tyre-nan-Og** in *Finnegans Wake* 91. As **Tir-na- n-Oge** in Patk. Kennedy, *Legendary Fictions of the Irish Celts* 45 (Wexford).

Tíriúil adj. 1. 'Affable, sociable' RBB (Waterford). 2. Confident. 'How tíriúil he walked in looking for a loan, taking it for granted' H (n. Clare).

Titimeas n. Epilepsy. NB (w. Limerick); CBD (n. Kerry).

Tiuc interj. 'Call to hens. Sometimes **tiucaí**' MF (Westmeath, Gen.).

Tlú n. Tongs. 'Give me the tlú' Ham (e. Clare); PB (s. Tipperary).

Tnúthán n. Longing. 'There is a great tnúthán on the cow – she is anxious to get her feed.' 'I have no great tnúthán to see him' H (n. Clare).

Tobán n. A tub. 'He must have drunk a tobán of buttermilk' MW (Wexford).

Tóch n. The rooting of pigs. Hence **tóchin**' 'The pigs have the field destroyed with their tóchin'' RBB (s. Kilkenny).

Tochamas n. 'A fit of bad temper' MS (e. Limerick).

Tóchar n. 1. 'A causeway' JM (w. Cork). 2. 'A path' McK (Leitrim). 3. 'A cluster or crowd of gulls or other sea-fowl when fishing at a school of fry' H (n. Donegal).

Tochas n. Also as **thuckas**. Itch, mange. In expletive **tochas ar do ghabhal**: the itch on your groin! JL (w. Cork). In phrase, 'He caught thuckas: he got a reprimand or a beating' CBE 266 (mid-Tipperary).

Tocht n. Deep emotion. 'I couldn't speak with the tocht that came over me' JL (w. Cork); MS (e. Limerick).

Tochtán n. Hoarseness *IG* (Kilkenny); 'There's a tochtán on you' PD (Carlow).

Tógálach adj. Cross, peevish. 'He gets fierce tógálach after a few drinks' NB (w. Limerick).

Togham n. 'A fit of weakness' JL (w. Cork). 'Some togham came on her in the chapel and she had to be carried out' MJD (w. Cork). See *taom*.

Toice n. Also as **tecka, thwacka, thecka, hecka**. Diminutives, **toicín**, as **thuckeen**. 'A girl a wench' PB (s. Tipperary); JL (w. Cork); 'Used both affectionately and contemptuously. Tecka is used ironically around Thurles, Co. Tipperary, to describe mutton dressed up as lamb' G (mid-Tipperary); 'Thecka and hecka are uncomplimentary terms for a woman' TOM (s. Tipperary); James Joyce, *Finnegans Wake* 434: 'thwacka'; 'Toicín is a word for a girl who is full of herself' J (Wexford); Patk. Kennedy, *Legendary Fictions of the Irish Celts* 158: '... when I was a thuckeen about fifteen years of age'. Glossed as 'young girl' (Wexford).

Tóim tuime n. 'Noise as of distant thunder (a sign of rain); e.g. "we'll soon have rain, there is the tóim tuime"' MF (Westmeath).

Tóin n. Backside, bottom. 1. 'Used through a sense of delicacy instead of the more vulgar English equivalent' H (n. Clare); JL (w. Cork). 2. 'Low-lying land' MC (e. Mayo). Diminutive, **tóineog**. 'The bottom of a pardóg, or pannier' MC (e. Mayo).

Tóin bhán n. Literally, white bottom. 'A hare's tail' CBE 104 (Leitrim).

Tóin le gaoith n. phr. Literally, backside to the wind. 'A dour fellow who keeps to himself' DOH (e. Limerick).

Tóin throm n. Literally, heavy bottom. 'So, a person who has offended by breaking something he sat awkwardly on; or simply a lazy person. "Get up, tóin trom!"' *An Cho* (w. Mayo).

Tóir n. Also as **tór**. 1. A search, pursuit. Peadar O'Donnell, *Storm* 80: 'There wasn't a decent man in the district but there was a tór after' (Donegal). 2. Bias against. 'He has a great tóir on John – he has a set on him' H (n. Clare); 'The Guards had a tóir on him' TOM (s. Tipperary). 3. 'A crowd, gang.' Local pronunciation, tór' MF (Westmeath). 4. Trouble. 'You're after drawing a nice tóir on yourself' MS (e. Limerick). 5. Desire for, interest in. 'I wouldn't have any great tóir on that horse' H (n. Clare).

Tóirpín n. Orpine, houseleek. 'Grown on thatch in the belief that it keeps the house from being burned' MS (e. Limerick).

Toirtéis n. Haughtiness, self-importance. 'God knows where he got the toirtéis. Him that was reared in a bothán at the side of the road' JL (w. Cork).

Toirtín n. As **turteen** 'A thick pancake. Applied to a thick-set man' Mac C (Monaghan); TB (Cavan); *CBE* 104 (Leitrim).

Tóiteán n. As **towkjaan**. Fire, conflagration. 1. 'Burned meat. "You couldn't offer that towkjaan to anyone"' D (s. e. Wexford). 2. 'A burned state, that is, sore, or in pain. "I'm in a towkjaan with the rheumatism"' D (s. e. Wexford).

Tóiteog n. 'A person who is too fond of sitting around the fire instead of going out working' MJD (w. Cork).

Tóla n. Abundance. 'A sum of money laid by in reserve, a stocking of gold' H (n. Donegal).

Tollamhóire n. Bumptiousness. 'For a toice from the middle of a bog, she have more tollamhóire than the queen of England' JL (w. Cork).

Tolpachán n. A small, stocky person or animal. 'Of a hurler – hard to shift. He's a strong tolpachán of a young fellow' G (s. Kilkenny).

Tom n. Diminutive, **tomán**. 'A bush' G (Donegal). See *tomóg*.

Tomhaisín n. 1. 'A small measure of drink' MC (w. Clare) 2. 'A cornet-shaped container, made of paper, used to hold sweets, etc' MS (e. Limerick).

Tomóg n. In form **tummock**. 'A small mound or heather tuft in a broken moor' H (n. Donegal). See *tom*.

Tor n. 1. 'A tuft of grass' C (Limerick) 2. 'A bush' MJD (w. Cork); F (Limerick) 3. 'A head of cabbage' G (s. Kilkenny).

Toradh n. In form **tor**. Esteem, regard. 'He has no tor on it' MS (Limerick); 5. 'Heed or satisfaction: "He gave me no tor"' DOH (e. Limerick).

Tóraí n. In form **tory**. 1. Bandit, outlaw. 2. A term of dislike or contempt. 'They (terrorists) should all be hanged, them bloody torys' G (n.w. Donegal). Also 'a playful term of abuse, especially to children. "A wee tory", used of a lively, mischievous child' H (n. Donegal); McK (Leitrim). 3. Used endearingly. 'And I hugg thee, sweete Tory, for it' in Anon., *The Welsh Embassador*; 'He's a right wee tory' MG (n.w. Donegal). 4. In compound **tory-whistle**. 'A mountainy man near Killybegs presented me with a tory-whistle. Made of hard wood, it had a very loud note, and was rudely adorned with scratches. He said it was not an old one, but of the same sort that used to be used to call boys for a row' H (n. Donegal); 'A policeman's whistle' Tr (Donegal). See *tóir*.

Tóralach adj. *al.* **tórsalach** Tidy, smart. 'She's a nice tórsalach girl' NB (w. Limerick)

Torán n. As **traan**. Wireworm. 'Traan water is blessed and distributed by the Augustinians, and sprinkled on the fields by the farmers in Forth and Bargy to rid the corn of traans' D (s. e. Wexford).

Torathar n. 'A big, fat, lazy person' NB (w. Limerick); *CBD* (n. Kerry)

Torc sa chró phr. Literally, a wild boar in the pig-sty. Great confusion; things tossed about and heaped on each other in confusion' *IG* (Kilkenny).

Tormas n. (Act of) grumbling, carping, especially over food. 'Give over your tormas and eat your dinner' MS (e. Limerick). Hence, 'the calf is tormas, that is, he refuses to drink' NB (w. Limerick); 'She had a tormas against eggs' *CBD* (n. Kerry); 'What the divil tormas is on you? Eat your dinner' JL (w. Cork).

Torpóg n. A plump woman. 'The Arabs are right about women. Like myself they like fine big turpógs, good for working' JL (w. Cork).

Tortóg n. 1. 'A small hillock. Properly speaking it is one of those jagged elevations which are so common in undrained moorland and which are such an obstruction to turf-saving operations' *An Cho* (w. Mayo); JL (w. Cork); *CBD* (n. Kerry); PB (s. Tipperary); *CBE* 34 S (Galway). 2. 'By a delightful piece of symbolism the term is freely applied to a child who "should be seen and not heard"' *An Cho* (w. Mayo) 3. 'A little dumpy woman. "For a small turtóg, she has the divil's own fire in her"' JL (w. Cork).

Tothardú n. 1. 'A left-handed person' Ju (Sligo). 2. An awkward person. 'Leave it! I'll finish the job myself, you tothardú!' ibid.

Traid n. A great amount. 'A traid of turnips, onions, even a traid of children' *An Cho* (w. Mayo).

Tráill n. Slave, wretched person. Hence trawly. 'She's a trawly girl, a trollop' Mac C (Monaghan).

Traisleach n. 'An tidy heap. Note the idiom "of a traisleach": "She carried a basket of eggs across the icy yard, but just as she came to the door she fell of a traisleach." "He got all his exams with honours until his final year but what did he do then but fall of a traisleach"' *An Cho* (w. Mayo)

Tráithnín n. Also in forms **traneen, thraneen**. A straw, and so, anything worthless. 'He's not worth a tráithnín' McK (Leitrim); PB (s. Kilkenny); Michael Banim, *Crohoor of the Billhook* 1, 273: '... no more hurt nor if I struck him wid a thrawneen ...' (Kilkenny); John Boyce, *Shandy Maguire* 47: 'I can't say but he done middlin' at the scriptur, sich as he had, that's ye know in quotin' what he didn't understan' a traneen about' (Donegal); Wm. Carleton, *Neal Malone* 2, 416: 'I don't care a traneen ...' (Tyrone); Mrs S. C. Hall, *Irish Life and Character 53:* 'Nobody breathin' can say ... ye owe me the value of a thraneen' (s. Leinster); J. M. Synge, *The Playboy of the Western World* 103: 'I wouldn't give a thraneen for a lad hadn't a mighty spirit in him and a gamey heart'.

Tráithnín mí n. 'An inferior grass, in English, weasel-tail' MF (Westmeath).

Tráithnín trosach n. As **trawneen trisech** 'Hoar frost on grass' MF (Westmeath).

Trálach n. *al.* **tálach**. Also as **tráileach, thraulagh, thaulagh**. 1. 'A soreness of the forearm, or wrist, due to heavy work' OCn (Laois); MF (Westmeath); 'Weakness of the wrist' MS (e. Limerick); H (n. Clare); 'Haymaking, if a person wasn't used to it, would give you tráleach' PB (s. Tipperary); *EASI* 341: 'Thraulagh, thaulagh: a soreness or painin the wrist of a reaper, caused by work' (Connaght). See **fulach**. 2. 'An eelskin bandage, often used as a cure' LB (s.w. Dublin).

Tranglam n. 'Confusion, disorder' *Sguab* (Cork); 'We're in some tranglam now' JL (w. Cork); *CBD* (n. Kerry).

Traochadh n. In form **trake**. Weariness, exhaustion. 'Children who became ill were often said to have caught some auld trake; or again you might hear that there was some auld trake going around' Cor (Cavan).

Traochta pp. Weary, exhausted. 'I'm traochta from you all' PB (s. Tipperary).

Tráth mo dhóthain phr. Literally, enough (of my time). Hence **trawmagone:** 'A trawmagone idiot, a helpless and guileless person' PON (n. Dublin).

Tráthúil adv. Timely. 'Tráthúil enough' PB (s. Tipperary). Used sarcastically: 'How tráthúil' H (n. Clare).

Treachlais n. Disorder. 'You have the house in treachlais' S (n.w. Donegal).

Treasal n. 'The threshold stone' *CBE* 98 (Kilkenny).

Treighdín n. The constellation Pleiades. 'When the Treighdín is in the skies – a sign of winter' LOS (w. Clare).

Treighid n. Also as **tried.** 'A fit of sickness' Mac C (Monaghan); 'Sickness, specifically colic. 'It's hard to cure the tried ina horse, no matter what they say' FF (Cavan).

Treise chugat interj. In translated form as **more power to you** in James Joyce, *Finnegans Wake* 140.

Trillín n. 'A lifeless or sickly person or animal. The word implies disappointment, as, for instance, when used of a young wife who is unable to attend to the house duties' *An Cho* (w. Mayo).

Trína chéile phr. Also as **treenahayla.** In translated form **through-other.** 1. Un-kempt, without order or neatness. 'It's a very through-other house since his wife died' O'K (Tyrone). 2. Agitated, flustered. William Carleton, *The Station* 1, 160: '... dhrop your joking ... and not be putting us through other' (Tyrone); 'He put me all through other with his questions and his big loud voice' O'K (Tyrone). 3. In phrase **through myself:** confused O'K (Tyrone). 4. Distress: 'They never got over that terrible trína chéile when the son was drowned' RBB (s. Kilkenny). 5. Mixed up. 'Your sheep and mine are treenahayla' LB (s. w. Dublin).

Trioc n. 'Pieces of furniture. "There's not much trioc in her house"' S (n.w. Donegal).

Triomach tramach phr. In a state of disarray. 'The house is triomach tramach' LOS (w. Clare).

Triopall n. 1. A tuft. 'I fell over a triopall of rushes' *CBD* (n. Kerry). 2. 'A cluster, bunch' *Sguab* (w. Cork).

Triopallach adj. Neat, tidy. 'A triopallach young girl' *CBD* (n. Kerry); *GC* (Laois); NB (w. Limerick).

Triuch n. Also as **treik, tiuch.** 1. Whooping cough. 'I often saw it: an old woman rubbing a mixture of poitín and holy water on a child's chest to beat the triuch' JL (w. Cork); 'He took the treik that is going' *BASJ* (Cavan, Leitrim). 2. 'The 'flu. Any "cold" epidemic that is going. If a person sneezes twice he is often greeted with "Have you the triuch?" Also called tiuch' *An Cho* (w. Mayo).

Triuch n. In form **truff.** 1. A trump in cards. Patrick MacGill, *Black Bonar* 64: 'What's truff?' (Donegal). 2. In phrase: **to put one to one's truff,** 'to make him look sharp to escape; used much as to put him to his trump card. "I put him to his truff"' H (n. Donegal).

Troisneach n. Noise, commotion. 'We heard the troisneach in the street outside' PJG (mid-Donegal).

Troitheán n. As **trihawn.** 'A stirrup; the pedal of a bicycle' S Ua G (s. Tipperary).

Troithín n. Also as **triathian.** 1. 'Troithín: soleless stocking worn without shoes: An old saying, " an old bróg will get an old troithín any day." (Said when an elderly couple marry.)' MF (Westmeath); PB (s. Tipperary); Lady Morgan, *The Wild Irish Girl* 69: 'A pair of yarn hose which scarcely reached mid-leg, left ancle and foot naked. They are called triathians.' 2. 'Troithín: Wooden stock of sleán (q.v.) on which foot rests' MF (Westmeath); 'The step of a spade' *GC* (Laois, n. Kilkenny). 3. 'A primitive light shoe or sandal' PLH (n. Roscommon).

Tromán n. 1. 'A weight, such as a swelling hanging down' *Pe* (Wexford). 2. Also in form **thrummin.** 'Elder or bore-tree.' (*sambucus nigra*): H (n. Donegal).

Tromluí n. 'A nightmare': H (n. Clare); *IG* (Kilkenny); *CBD* (n. Kerry).

Trompallán n. 'The dung beetle' *geotrupes*: RBB (w. Waterford).

Troscán n. Also as **trisgan** 1. 'Household furniture is called trisgan' *BASJ* (Cavan, Leitrim). 2. 'Troscán means a load' *CBE* 34 S (Galway).

Trostar n. 'Noise, commotion' H (n. Clare). 'Noise, such as that made by a careless housewife banging kitchen utensils; unnecessary domestic noises' MC (w. Clare).

Trotha n. 'A heavy, lazy heap of a person' NB (w. Limerick). 'If he had nothing else to fall over, that damn trotha would fall over himself' R (n. Clare).

Trua Mhuire phr. Literally, the pity of Mary. In phrase 'I'm the trua Mhuire by ye': I'm to be pitied because of you JL (w. Cork); H (n. Clare); R (s. Galway).

Truamhéil n. 1. Compassion, pity. 'You couldn't but have truamhéil for the poor devil' JPL (w. Cork). 2. Object of pity, compassion. 'Isn't he the truamhéil' H (n. Clare).

Trucaill n. A cart JL (w. Cork); RBB (w. Waterford).

Truip n. Also in form **trip**. Noise. Peadar O'Donnell, *On the Edge of the Stream* 248: 'There's somebody outside ... there's trip outside and thon's the bull awake' (Donegal).

Truslóg n. As **thrisloge** in *EASI* 342: 'A long loping stride; a hop' (Munster). See *straoileog*.

Tuaiplis n. Also as **tooplaish, tooplish, tuplish**. A blunder, a false move. 'He made a terrible tuaiplis when he sold his fine farm to go into the undertaking business' Ham (e. Clare); George Fitzmaurice, *The Pie-Dish* (Kerry): 'would the case have been any different now if she didn't go making all that tooplaish the time he got the weakness?'; 'I made a terrible tooplish, I'm afraid' AG (s. Tipperary); 'He done tuplish – he made a right mess of it' PD (s. Carlow).

Tuairgín n. 1. 'A wattle for mashing potatoes' Ham (e. Clare); *CBE* 98

(Kilkenny); GC (Laois). 2. Figuratively, a sturdy boy. '"He's a great little thoorgeen", a grandmother said of her sturdy wee grandson' *GC* (Laois).

Tuairim n. In form **toorim**. Opinion, estimate, guess. 'I haven't a toorim where she comes from' J (s.e. Wexford).

Tuairt n. A thud; a crash. 'I heard the tuairt when he fell out of the bed' JL (w. Cork); H (n. Clare); RBB (w. Waterford).

Tuapalach adj. 1. 'Awkward' NB (w. Limerick). 2. 'Stubborn' ibid.

Tuathalaí n. 'An awkward person' NB (w. Limerick).

Tubaiste n. As **tubbasta**. Calamity, disaster. 'Ironically, 'an unexpected local event giving rise to some celebration in the community, such as weddings, christenings etc.' JB (s. Armagh & n. Louth).

Tucálaí n. A fumbler. Hence **tucáling**. 'What tucáling have you?' MP (mid-Tipperary). [*tucáil*: act of tucking or fulling cloth *Dinn*]

Tufóg n. Puff, fart JL (w. Cork); RBB (w. Waterford); H (n. Clare). *al.* **tufaí** NB (w. Limerick).

Tuig v. As **twig**. Understand. 'I didn't twig what was going on until it was too late' AG (s. Tipperary).

Tuigeann tú sin? inter. phr. Do you understand that? In Wm. Carleton, *The Poor Scholar* 2, 281, as **thig in thu shinn?** As **thighun thu shin** in Carleton, *The Priest's Funeral* 77 (Tyrone).

Tuigim v. I understand. As **thigum** in Wm. Carleton, *The Poor Scholar* 2, 280 (Tyrone) 'Tuigim, faith' MS (e. Limerick). The phrase **tuigim é**, I understand it, as **tuggemi** in Richard Head, *Hic et Ubique*.

Tuigíos n. 'Sally rods, used in making baskets for carrying turf. "We went cutting tuigíos by the river"' JL (w. Cork). [< English *twigs* ?]

Tuilleadh n. In form **tilly**. Addition, more. 'A little bit extra thrown in for good measure; something over and above. A shopkeeper might, when weighing sweets or nuts, include a few extra as a tilly' O'K (Tyrone); James Joyce, *Ulysses* 20: 'She poured again a measureful and a tilly.'

Túirne n. 'A spinning wheel' GC (Galway); MC (e. Mayo). [Cf. Latin *tornus*: capstan or winding apparatus.]

Túirne Mháire n. 'A good trouncing. "She gave the children túirne Mháire when they arrived late"' MC (e. Mayo). [*lit.* Mary's spinning wheel. The title of a western children's song.]

Tuísteog n. 'A footstool made from plaited straw' *An Cho* (w. Mayo).

Tulach n. In form **tully**. A hillock. Seumus MacManus, *A Lad of the O'Friels* 74: 'And they (fairies) laughin' like murder from the top of the tully above the house'; ibid. 80: 'He went out up the tully and sat down' (Donegal).

Tulán n. 'A high, dry area ina bog. "That rick of turf is dry because I built it on a tulán"' H (n. Clare).

Tulcaer n. As **thullcare**. 'The gathering of eggs from farmers at Easter' PON (n. Dublin). See *clúideog*.

Tulcais n. *al.* **fulcais**. Also in form **tulkish**. 'A tulkish is a soft, fat person' *CBE* 266 (mid-Tipperary); 'A tulcais is a big, clumsy person. Fulcais sometimes heard' TOM (s. Tipperary).

Tur tar phr. Without condiment. 'I eat the bread tur tar: without butter etc.' PD (Carlow); *IG* (Kilkenny).

Turas n. 1. A journey. Patrick Gallagher, *My Story* 260: 'I got it into my head that I would go back to Scotland and round around through some of the places where I worked long ago ... They put a car at my disposal so that I might make my turas' (Donegal). 2. 'A pilgrimage to a holy well or ancient church' MG (n.w. Donegal); MJD (w. Cork).

Tús n. 'A free toss as practice before the start of a game of handball. A local use, now forgotten perhaps, had to do with the game of pitch and toss. When a newcomer joined the circle he was allowed a practice throw. "Give him a tús"' *An Cho* (w. Mayo).

Tútach adj. Also in form **toothagh**. 1. Awkward, clumsy. 'He's a toothagh class of a workman' FF (Monaghan). 2. 'Loutish, uncouth' PC (n. Clare); MC (e. Mayo).

U

Uachtarán n. The President.

Uailleán n. *al.* uallán. In form holyawn. 'A scatterbrained person, and not very fond of work, either' J (s.e. Wexford). Used when addressing a naughty child. Patk. Kennedy, *The View from Mount Leinster:* 'and no young holyawns to trouble me any more' (Wexford); 'That child is the greatest little holyawn in the parish' J (s.e. Wexford).

Uallach adj. 'Scatterbrained. "She's more uallach than stupid"' PJG (mid-Donegal).

Údarásach adj. Cheeky, presumptious, masterful NB (w. Limerick); *CBD* (n. Kerry).

Uisce beatha n. Literally, water of life. Whiskey. In forms usquebagh in Ben Jonson, *The Irish Masque*; usque bah in Anon., *The Welsh Embassador*; usquebah in Anon., *Bog Witticisms* and in Anon., *The Irish Hudibras*; usquebaugh in John Durant Breval, *The Play is the Plot* and in A. Hume, *Irish Dialects* (Antrim); usquebuidh in Patk. Kennedy, *Evenings in the Duffrey* 285 (Wexford); iska-behagh, Wm. Carleton, *Ned M'Keown* 1, 17 (Tyrone).

Uisce faoi thalamh Literally, water under ground. Conspiracy. 'There's some uisce faoi thalamh going on' JL (w. Cork); *CBD* (n. Kerry); DOH (e. Limerick).

Útamáil n. Fumbling. 'What útamáil have you? It's a simple job' H (n. Clare); RBB (s. Kilkenny); *An Cho* (w. Mayo). Hence útamáiling. 'He's utamáiling with the engine for the past hour, and no sign of him starting it' H (n. Clare).

Útamálaí n. A fumbler, bungler. 'Don't let him service your car. He's the biggest útamálaí God ever put life into' RBB (s. Kilkenny); MS (e. Limerick); H (n. Clare); PB (s. Tipperary); *Sguab* (Cork).

Bibliography

Allingham, William. *Poems*, London,1912.

An Choineall, Journal of Louisburgh Parish,1961-1983. Collector, Rev. Leo Morahan. Herein *An Cho*

Anon. *Sir John Oldcastle*, 1599/1600.

———. *Captain Thomas Stukeley*, 1596/1605.

———. *Lays and Legends of the North of Ireland*, London,1884.

———. *Purgatorium Hibernicum*, 1670/1675.

———. *Sir John Oldcastle*, 1599/1600.

———. *The Irish Hudibras*, 1689.

———. *The Irishman's Prayers*, 1689.

———. *The Pretender's Exercise*, c.1727.

———. *The Welsh Embassador*,1623.

———. *A Dialogue Between Teague and Dermot*, 1713.

Bailey, Nathan. *An Universal Etymological Dictionary*, London,1755.

Ballyguiltenane Rural Journal, 1995. Contributor, Kathleen Breathnach. Herein, KB (e. Limerick).

Ballymena Observer. ed. W.J. Knowles, 1892.

Bandon Historical Journal 1, 1984. Collector, Bruno O'Donoghue. Herein *BHJ*.

Banim, John. *John Doe*, London, 1825; *Peter of the Castle*, London, 1826; (with M. Banim) *The Fetches*, London,1825.

Banim, John and Michael. *Tales of the O'Hara Family*, Dublin, 1865.

Banim, Michael. *Crohoor of the Billhook*; *The Croppy*, London, 1828.

Barlow, Jane. *Irish Idylls*, New York, 1892.

———. *Strangers at Lisconnel*, New York, 1895.

———. *Bogland Studies*, New York, 1892.

———. *Kerrigan's Quality*, New York, 1894.

Barrington, Jonah. *Personal Sketches of His Own Times*, London, 1827-32.

Béaloideas xvii, 1947. Collector, Paddy O'Neill. Herein PON (n. Co. Dublin).

Beaumont and Fletcher. *The Coxcomb*, in *The Dramatic Works of Beaumont and Fletcher*, ed. A.H. Bullen, London, 1904-12.

Black, Wm. *Folk Medicine*, London, 1883.

Blount's Law Dictionary, 1681.

Boyce, John. *Shandy Maguire*, London, 1840.

———. *Mary Lee, or The Yank in Ireland*, London, 1864.

Breatnach, R.B. *Seana Chaint na nDéise* 2, Dublin, 1961.

Breifny Antiquarian Society's Journal, 1929-32. Collector, Peter Martin. Herein. *BASJ*.

Breval, John Durant. *The Play Is the Plot*, 1718.

Brittaine, George. *Irishmen and Irishwomen*, London, 1879.

Brooke, A.S. *The Story of Parson Annaly*, London, 1870.

Burns, Robert. *The Complete Works of Robert Burns*, Ayr, 1990.

Carleton, William. *Traits and Stories of the Irish Peasantry*, London, 2 vols., 1843; and 1844;

——. *The Priest's Funeral, The Illicit Distiller, Lachlin Murray, The Brothers, The Dream of a Broken Heart* from *Tales of Ireland*, Dublin and London, 1834;

——. *Fardorougha the Miser*, Philadelphia, 1840.

——. *Sir Turlough, or The Churchyard Bride* from *Characteristic Sketches of Ireland and the Irish*, Dublin and London, 1840.

——. *Val M'Clutchy, the Irish Agent*, Dublin, London and Edinburgh, 1845.

Century Magazine, Feb 1990.

Clogher Record v 1936. Contributor, Canon M. Mac Carville. Herein, Mac C.

Cnósach Focal ó Bhaile Bhúirne. Edited by Brian Ó Cuív, Dublin 1947.

Colfer, B. *The Promontory of Hook*, Wexford, 1978. Herein *BC*.

Corkery, Daniel. *The Threshhold of Quiet*, Dublin, 1917.

County Louth Archaeological Journal xiv 1957-60. Collector, Margaret Conway. Herein *CON*.

Croker, Thomas Crofton. *Popular Songs of Ireland*, London, 1860.

——. *Fairy Legends and Traditions of South Ireland*, London, 1862.

Cross, Eric. *The Tailor and Ansty*, London, 1964.

Danaher, Kevin. *The Year in Ireland*, Dublin, 1972.

Decker, Thomas. *The Honest Whore*, 2, 1605/1630.

Deeney, D. *Peasant Lore from Gaelic Ireland*, Dublin,1 900.

de Vere, Aubrey. *Collected Works*, New York, 1884.

Dictionary of the Irish Language, Royal Irish Academy, Compact edition, Dublin, 1990. Herein *RIA Dictionary*.

Dinneen, P.S. *Irish English Dictionary*, Dublin 1827. Herein *Dinn*.

Dunton, John. *Report of a Sermon*, 1698, quoted in Alan Bliss, *Spoken English in Ireland, 1600-1740*, Dublin 1979.

English Dialect Dictionary. Edited by Joseph Wright, Oxford, 1905. Herein *EDD*.

Edgeworth, Maria. *Castle Rackrent*, London, 1832.

—— with R. Edgeworth, *An Essay on Irish Bulls*, London, 1830.

Éigse. A Journal of Irish Studies v 1945-47. Collector, Eamonn Mhac an Fhailigh in Empor, north of Mullingar; herein MF (Westmeath). In v, vi and vii, words from Limerick: collector, Nioclás Breatnach; herein NB (w. Limerick). In v, words from Durrow: collector, Donnchadh Ó Conchubhair; herein DOC (Offaly). Also in v: words from Wexford: collector, Riobárd A. Ó Scannláin; herein, OS (s. Wexford).

Farquhar, George. *The Twin Rivals*, 1702/1703.

Fitzmaurice, George. *The Plays of George Fitzmaurice*, Dublin, 1969.

Floredice, W.H. (W. Hart). *Memories of a Month among the 'Mere' Irish*, London, 1881.

———. *Derryreel*, London, 1889.

Folk Lore Record . Various dates, 19th century.

French, Percy. *Songs*, London, n.d.

Friel, Brian. *Translations*, London, 1981.

Gaelic Churchman, 1922-27. Collector, K.E. Young. Herein *GC*.

Gaelic Journal, 1900, 1901, 1902. Entries for Competition no. 3 in the Leinster Feis. Herein *IG*.

Gallagher, Patrick. *My Story* , Dungloe, 1979.

Griffin, Gerald. *The Collegians*, London, 1896.

Gwynn, Stephen, *The Glade in the Forest*, London, n.d.

Hall, Mrs S.C. *Tales of Irish Life and Character*, London, 1909.

———. and S.C. Hall, *Ireland, Its Scenery and Character*, 3 vols., London 1841-43.

———. *The Maid of Bannow*, London, 1876 .

Harkin, Michael ('Maghtochair'). *Inisowen, Its History, Conditions and Antiquities*, 1867.

Hart, H.C. *Notes on Ulster Dialect, chiefly Donegal.* Philological Society, London, 1900.

Head, Richard, *Hic et Ubique*, 1663.

Heaney, Seamus. *Wintering Out*, London, 1977.

———. *Death of a Naturalist*, London, 1966.

Heart of Breifne, vol. 2, no. 2. Collector, Pádraig Ó Corbaidh. Herein POC.

Henry, P.L., *An Anglo-Irish Dialect of North Roscommon*, Dublin, 1957. Herein PLH (n. Roscommon).

Hume, A. *Origin and Characteristics in the People of Down and Antrim*, Belfast, 1874.

———. 'Remarks on the Irish Dialect of the English Language', in *Transactions of the Historical Society of Lancashire and Cheshire* xxx, Liverpool, 1878.

Hunt, B. *Folk Tales of Breffny*, London, 1912.

Jonson, Ben. *The Irish Masque*, 1613/1616.

Journal of the Cork Historical and Archaeological Society xlix 1944. Contributor, D. Ó hEalaithe. Herein, *JCHAS*.

Journal of the County Louth Archaeological and Historical Society, vol. xix, no. 4, 1980. Collector, Etienne Rynne. Herein, ER

Journal of the Kildare Archaeological Society vi 1909, 1910.

Joyce, James. *Dubliners*, New York 1969.

———. *Ulysses*, New York, 1961.

———. *Finnegans Wake*, New York, 1959.

———. *A Portrait of the Artist as a Young Man*, New York, 1964.

Joyce, P.W. *English As We Speak It In Ireland*, London, 1910; Dublin, 1988. Herein *EASI*.

Kelly, J. *Collected Proverbs*, Edinburgh, 1751.

Kennedy, Patrick. *Legendary Fictions of the Irish Celts*, London, 1866.

——. *The Fireside Stories of Ireland*, Dublin 1870.

——. *The Banks of the Boro*, London, 1867.

——. *Evenings in the Duffrey*, Dublin, 1869.

——. *Legends of Mount Leinster*, Dublin, 1855, under pseudonym, 'Harry Whitney, philomath.'

Kickham, Charles J. *Knocknagow*, Dublin, n.d.

Lawless, Emily. *Grania*, London, 1892.

Lever, Charles James. *The Confessions of Harry Lorrequer*, London, 1839.

——. *Charles O'Malley*, London, 1841.

——. *The Martins of Cro' Martin*, London, 1856.

——. *Davenport Dunn*, London, 1859.

Little, George. *Malachy Horan Remembers*, Dublin, 1943.

Lover, Samuel. *Legends and Stories of Ireland*, 1848.

——. *Paddy at Sea*, London, 1845.

——. *Rory O'More*, 1837.

——. *Handy Andy*,1842.

——. *Molly Carew*, 1846.

M'Parlan, J. *Statistical Survey of the County of Donegal*, London, 1801.

MacGill, Patrick. *The Rat Pit*, London, 1915.

——. *Glenmornan*, London, 1919.

——. *Maureen*, London,1920.

Macken, Walter. *Mungo's Mansion,* Dublin, 1946.

MacManus, Seumas. *Bold Blades of Donegal*, London, 1937.

——. *In Chimney Corners*, New York, 1899.

——. *A Lad of the O'Friels*, London, 1897.

——. *The Bend of the Road*, London, 1898.

——. *The Leadin' Road to Donegal and Other Stories*, London, 1895.

Marshall, Rev. Wm. *Ballads and Verses from Tyrone*, Dublin, 1929.

Michelburne, John. *Ireland Preserved*, 1705.

Molloy, M.J. *The King of Friday's Men*.

——. *The Paddy Pedlar; The Wood of the Whispering*, Delaware, 1975.

Morgan, Lady. *The Wild Irish Girl*, London, 1806.

Murphy, Tom (Galway): *Bailegangaire*, 1990.

Notes and Queries. various dates. Herein *N&Q*

North Munster Antiquarian Journal xvii 1975. Collector, Patrick Henchy; herein H (Clare). Also xi, 1968: collector, Monsignor Michael Hamilton; herein Ham (Clare). Also xxix 1987: collector, Patrick Lysaght; herein, Lys (n. Kerry).

Ó hAnnracháin, Stiofán, *Caint an Bhaile Dhuibh*, Dublin 1964. Herein *CBD*.

Ó Dónaill, Niall, *Foclóir Gaeilge Béarla*, Dublin 1977. Herein *ODON*.

O hAirt, Diarmaid: *Díolaim Dheiseach*, Dublin, 1988.

O'Brien, Flann: *At-Swim-Two-Birds*, London, 1967.

——. *The Dalkey Archive*, London, 1976.

O'Byrne, Dermot (Sir Arnold Bax): *Children of the Hills*, 1915.

O'Casey, Seán. *Cock-a-doodle-Dandy*, London, 1949.

O'Curry, Eugene. *Manners and Customs of the Ancient Irish*, London and Dublin 1873.

O'Donnell, Peadar. *Adrigoole*, 1929.

——. *The Knife*, 1930.

——. *Islanders*, London, 1928.

——. *Storm*, 1925.

O'Flanagan, T. ('Samoath). *Ned m' Cool and His Foster Brother*, London, 1871.

O'Reilly, Edward. *Irish-English Dictionary*, 1877.

Paddiana, London, 1842.

Patterson, W.H. *A Glossary of Words in Use in the Counties of Antrim and Down*, 1880.

People, The. Wordlists from Co. Wexford. Various dates in the 1950s.

Poole, Jacob. *Poole's Glossary with Some Pieces of Verse, of the Old Dialect of the English Colony in the Baronies of Forth and Bargy, County of Wexford.* Edited by T.P. Dolan and Diarmaid Ó Muirithe, Wexford, 1979; new edition, Dublin, 1996.

Quiggin, E.C. *A Dialect of Donegal*, London, 1906.

Ríocht na Midhe, 1960-61. Collector, Margaret Conway. Herein Con.

Revue Celtique, xliv.

Robinson, Lennox. *The White-headed Boy*, Dublin, 1920.

Sguab, 1923-26. Collector, Seán Ua Síothcháin. Herein *Sguab* (w. Cork).

Shakespeare, William: *Twelfth Night; Cymbeline.*

Shamrock Magazine. For P.J. MacCall, *Fenian Night's Entertainment*, 1894.

Sheridan, Thomas. *The Brave Irishman*, 1740/1754.

Simmons, D.A. *A List of Peculiar Words and Phrases formerly in common use in the County Armagh, together with expressions at one time current in south Donegal.* Dublin, 1890 (reprinted from the *Educational Gazette*).

Somerville, E. and Ross, M. All stories quoted are from *Some Experiences of an Irish R.M.*, London, 1956.

Spenser, Edmund. *A View of the State of Ireland*, London, 1887.

Stanihurst, Richard, *Chronicles*, 1577.

Stephens, James. *The Crock of Gold*, London, 1973.

Stoker, Bram. *The Snake's Pass*, London, 1891.

Swift, Jonathan. *A Dialogue in Hibernian Stile*, 1735.

——. *A Modest Proposal*, 1765-67.

——. *Directions to Servants*, 1745.

Synge, J.M. *Plays, Poems and Prose*, London, 1977.

Threlkeld, W. *Essays*, London, 1878.

Tennyson, Lord Alfred. *Complete Works*, London, 1894.

Traynor, Michael, *The English Dialect of Donegal*, Dublin, 1953. Herein Tr.
Ulster Folk Life, vol. 32, 1986: Contributor, J. Bradley. Herein, JB (Armagh,
    Louth).
Ulster Journal of Archaeology, series i, vol. i. Herein *UJA*.
Yeats, W.B. *Fairy and Folk Tales of the Irish Peasantry*, London 1888
——. *The Countess Cathleen*, in *Plays*, London,1924.

Index

glaff 111
glaffer 111
glagaire 111-112
glaicín 111
glaise 111
glak 110
glak shogh 110
glake 112
glam 111
glám 111
glámhán 111
glamaire 111
glamaisc 111
glámhánaí 111
glamóg 111
glamoge 111
glanadh amach 111
glantóir 111
glar 111
glár 111
glas gaoithe 111
glasair léana 111
glasán 111
glasgeehy 111
glashan 111
glassan 111
glassin 111
glaum 129
glé 111
gleabhac 111
gleacaí 111
gleadhrach 111
gleamaighdear 112
gleann 112
gleeks 112
gleic 112
gléic 112
gléireán 112
gleo 112
gleoisín 112
gleoite 112
gleoiteog 112
gleorán 112
glib 112
glic 112
glifin 112
glig 112
glig gleaig 112
gligeen 112
gligin 112
gligín 112
glincín 112
glinkeen 112
gliogaire 111-112
gliogar 112
gliomach 112
glisín 112
gliúcach 112
Glóire do Mhuire 112
glooracks 113
glórach 112
glorhia wurrah! 112
glothar 112
glow 112
glug 113

glugar 113
glugger 39 112
gluggerin' 112
gluher 112
glúiníneach 113
glun ta mee 27
glúnach 113
gluntho ma 27
glúracáin 113
gnúis 113
Go bhféacha Dia oraibh 113
Go bhfóire Dia orainn 113
Go bhfóire Dia ort 113
go deimhin 113, 172
go deine 113
go leor 113, 133
go mah a shin 102
Go mbeannaí Dia dhuit 113
Go raibh ádh ó Dhia orainn 113
go seolta 175
go socair 22 183
go vioch a Dieu uriv 113
gob 113, 151, 191
gobach 113
gobadán 113
gobán 113
gobóg 113
gobshell 113
gog 114
gogaí 114
gogaire 114
gogalach 114
goic 114
goidé deir sé 114
goidé mar tá tú 114
góilín 114
goirge 114
goirt 114
goirtín 114
góislín 114
goldar 114
goleen 102-103
gombeen 103-104
gombeen man 103-104
gommach 105
gommagh 105
gommologue 105
gommula 105
gon rahid 105
gonc 114
gondoutha 105
gongy 105
good people 80
googeen 117
gooleen 75
goon roo 105
gor 28, 114
gorán 114
gorb 114
gorban 114
gorbán 114
gorcoon 106
gorravogue 106
gort 114
gorta 114

gortach 96, 114
goson 106
gossan 106
gossoon 106
gosther 106
gosur 106
gotha 114
gothaí 114
gothaw 114
goul 102
goureen 102
gow 57, 102, 105
gowereen roe 102
gowlogue 102
gown gree 105
grá 54, 114-115
gra agra 21
grá Dé 115
gra machree 115
gra-ma-cree 115
grá mo chroí 115
graanbroo 116
graanshaghaun 115
grabach 115
grábach 115
grabaire 115
grabaireacht 115
grabhar móna 115
gradam 115
grádh 114
grafán 115
grag 115
grág 115
gragan 115
grágán 115
gragh 114-115
grah 114
grahin 115
graidhin 115
gráig 115
gráin 115
gráín 115
gráin dearg 115
gráinne 115
gráinneog 115
gráinseachán 115
graithin 115
graitseachán 115
gramaisc 115
grámhar 116
gramhas 116
gran 116
grán bruite 116
grán buí 116
grán tonóg 116
granbuidh 116
gránlach 116
gránna 116
grannycoreesk 69
gráscar 116
grass 86
grauver 116
graw 114-115
grawna 38, 116
greadadh 116, 163